Finland–India Business Opportunities

Ajeet N. Mathur

Finland–India Business Opportunities

Connecting the Swan and the Elephant

 Springer

Ajeet N. Mathur
Professor of Strategy and International Business
Business Policy and Economics
Indian Institute of Management Ahmedabad
Ahmedabad, India

ISBN 978-981-10-8018-0   ISBN 978-981-10-8019-7 (eBook)
https://doi.org/10.1007/978-981-10-8019-7

Library of Congress Control Number: 2019934802

© Springer Nature Singapore Pte Ltd. 2019
This work is subject to copyright. All rights are reserved by the Publisher, whether the whole or part of the material is concerned, specifically the rights of translation, reprinting, reuse of illustrations, recitation, broadcasting, reproduction on microfilms or in any other physical way, and transmission or information storage and retrieval, electronic adaptation, computer software, or by similar or dissimilar methodology now known or hereafter developed.
The use of general descriptive names, registered names, trademarks, service marks, etc. in this publication does not imply, even in the absence of a specific statement, that such names are exempt from the relevant protective laws and regulations and therefore free for general use.
The publisher, the authors and the editors are safe to assume that the advice and information in this book are believed to be true and accurate at the date of publication. Neither the publisher nor the authors or the editors give a warranty, expressed or implied, with respect to the material contained herein or for any errors or omissions that may have been made. The publisher remains neutral with regard to jurisdictional claims in published maps and institutional affiliations.

This Springer imprint is published by the registered company Springer Nature Singapore Pte Ltd.
The registered company address is: 152 Beach Road, #21-01/04 Gateway East, Singapore 189721, Singapore

Foreword

भारत का राजदूत
हेलसिंकी
Ambassador of India
Helsinki

29th June, 2017

Dear Readers,

During my sojourn as India's Ambassador to Finland in Helsinki, I have realised that there is lack of awareness about the enormous scope of business opportunities in India among Finnish companies and business opportunities in Finland among Indian businessmen. I am glad that Professor Ajeet Mathur of IIM Ahmedabad has authored this book to create one more bridge for anyone interested in participating in and benefitting from Finland-India Economic Relations. The author has worked in business, government and academia in India and abroad. He also has a long association with Finland and is able to bring to you an insider's perspective of both countries.

The distilled insights brought to you in this book have been researched over 20 years. Written in a conversational style with numerous illustrations from the world of practice, this book is a treasure trove of knowledge explaining the business opportunities, policies, cultures, institutions, country trajectories, and nuances pertaining to Finland and India that may help the readers in strategic analysis and planning at the corporate and at the business level.

This book is an important guide for those aspiring to identify opportunities in their areas of interest. It is likely to provide useful guidance in structuring collaborations and partnerships as well as help in achieving synergy to compete in world markets.

Prof. Ajeet Mathur has been in touch with me since my arrival in Helsinki in September, 2014. I also had the privilege of visiting him in IIM Ahmedabad in June, 2016. I have enjoyed my interactions with him during my tenure and benefitted from his vast experience.

(Ashok Kumar Sharma)

Mailing Address : Kulosaarentie 32, 00570 Helsinki (Finland)
Phone: 00 358 9 22899116; Fax: 00 358 9 6221208
E-Mail: amb.helsinki@mea.gov.in
Website: www.indianembassy.fi / Facebook Page: India in Finland

Preface

"Why is 'neem' toothpaste for brushing teeth not available in Finland? Why are adhesive rolls for brushing dirt and dust off clothes ('*teippiharja*', in Finnish) not found in India?" I used to be asked such questions in Finland. I had begun to wonder why Finland and India were not better connected. Then, by sheer chance, I literally bumped into Pentti Vartia on the front steps of the main building of the Helsinki School of Economics. Pentti headed the Research Institute of the Finnish Economy (ETLA) at the time. When we introduced ourselves and Pentti learnt that I was on leave from IIM in Finland, he offered that ETLA could sponsor the first-ever study of Finland–India Economic Relations. I thought to myself that a systematic study could identify many gaps. Were these to be made known, wouldn't entrepreneurs who become aware of the opportunities step in to earn profits and boost trade?

The ETLA study analysed mutual trade and investment potential but was limited to goods trade. An estimation of trade potential and attractiveness of trade-substituting foreign direct investment were made based on projected demand in the growth sectors. The potential entrepreneurial initiatives were listed and made publicly known by enabling the study to be freely downloadable from the University of Tampere and ETLA websites. An unintended consequence of this was that within a few years, Finnish exports of goods to India trebled while the exports of Indian goods to Finland grew modestly and the trade balance expanded in favour of Finland. An unintended consequence! This happened because Finnish entrepreneurs were more Internet savvy than their Indian counterparts and were accustomed to respecting and using results of university research. It was only after the Indian IT boom in the first decade of this millennium that the combined bilateral trade of goods and services became more balanced.

In recent years, considering both goods and services together, India has a small favourable balance of trade with Finland. Yet, despite proven feasibility for vast, mutually beneficial synergies, mutual investments have remained small and trade diversions via Germany, Sweden, UK and Russia have continued. This trade diversion partially accounts for the low level of direct economic contact between Finland and India at the enterprise level. Often, business firms of third countries are included as Finnish firms investing in India or Indian firms investing in Finland. This is indicative of how Finland–India business can be of interest to enterprises anywhere.

Bilateral internationalisation consistent with multilateral regimes can take different forms and paths for different sectors, especially in knowledge-intensive technology-driven arenas. For branded consumer durables and industrial intermediates, foreign direct investment can be a superior alternative to exporting for both countries. This points to the need for understanding the potential magnitude of mutual trade and investments and also the scope for collaborative leveraging for third-country markets, besides foreign direct investments from third-country jurisdictions.

The low level of mutual entrepreneurial interest between Finland and India and lack of effective exploration of identified synergies are intriguing. The potential that remains untapped is routinely attributed to institutional barriers by government and parastatal representatives. Yet, institutional barriers are precisely the ones that can be removed, dissolved, circumvented or renegotiated with new bridges and creative gateways.

These horizons of possibilities excited my curiosity. I have attempted to understand the phenomena around the Finland–India Economic Relations potential and the hurdles that stand in the way over the past twenty-five years. This book has been in the making a long time—a longer time than any of my previous books. There have been occasions to rejoice when I have been a witness to entrepreneurs—small and big who have been able to stay the course with courage and overcome difficulties and expand their capabilities to do business in the other country. Successful experiences by Finnish and Indian enterprises require understanding, comparing, distinguishing and perhaps even emulating. There is also the need to demystify why so many Finnish and Indian investments experience or anticipate hurdles and don't even reach the starting post. Also, why so many of those who do begin, tend to experience difficulties and give up was a mystery. I have watched with anticipation over small hesitant steps that business leaders, enterprises, institutions and governments in the two countries have taken towards each other. I have gasped in anguish when I have observed at close range, opportunities that were missed or lost, gains floundered, and when animosities and misunderstandings arose. I am both excited and nervous to be now sharing the results of my endeavours, findings and insights with you.

This is a first-of-its-kind book in many respects. The book introduces readers to business opportunities and to nuances of prospecting, structuring and organising for doing business in India and Finland. This has been done with two aims in mind. For a variety of reasons arising from policy changes in India and Finland in recent years and also European and international developments, the attractiveness of doing business in India and Finland has aroused fresh interest among individuals, enterprises and governments of India and Finland. And for another set of reasons that have to do with the visible hand of government initiatives and imperatives of business restructuring, new horizons have appeared from the perspective of expanding and actualising the potential by combining and synergising the resources and competitive advantages of India and Finland in mutual trade, investments and collaborations. This is of interest to business opportunity seekers and investors anywhere, not only those located in Finland or India.

This book introduces you to the enormous opportunities and large untapped potential in the two countries to be actualised by structuring trade, investments, partnerships and collaborations. You can be among the pioneers who are building the bridges and test them. The shift from 'Made in Finland' or 'Made in India' to 'Made by Finland', 'Made by India' and 'Made by Finland and India' is underway. Value is being created by people who have courage to collaborate. How that value gets apportioned between country jurisdictions depends on several factors that get clarified and reinforced when new platforms, new arenas and new horizons arise. One of the founding fathers of the European Union, Jean Monnet (of the cognac business family), had wisely remarked, "Nothing is possible without people. Nothing is lasting without institutions".

Finland and India are as different as chalk and cheese. Finland is a developed country, the sixth largest in Europe and the only Nordic member State of the EU that is in both the Eurozone and Schengen visa travel area. Finland defends EU's longest land border with Russia without NATO membership that speaks volumes for its commitment to neutrality, peace and diplomacy. The Trump-Putin summit meeting in July 2018 was hosted by Finland in Helsinki. Finland ranks among the top five countries in the world on indicators such as competitiveness, innovativeness, education quality, press freedom, transparency, happiness, and acceptability of its citizens abroad. But its economic growth rates have lately been modest, and its current account surpluses have shrunk stressing the basic foundations of community life in a welfare state. There are warning signals that it would not be possible to preserve a social paradise if it were to become an economic graveyard.

India, the world's largest democracy with one of the highest GDP growth rates in the world, is among the top investment destinations with abundant business opportunities in the context of development. But there are also leaks and creaks in governance, social architecture, the quality of civil society and environmental quality deficits besides moans and groans about poverty, corruption, nepotism and infrastructural deficits. It has become obvious that it is not easy to plant an economic orchard in a social desert where violence in its many forms and manifestations is yet to be expunged. The eminent economist, Joan Robinson, was the first to observe that, "anything you can say about India, the opposite is also true". This is also the land of *Ahimsa* (non-violence), and nowhere on the planet have so many people been taken out of poverty so rapidly under democratic conditions as in India after 190 years of colonial exploitation. The right to information, public interest litigation and an independent justice system have illumined many dark corners and continue to improve governance and social and economic justice. The paradoxes and contradictions make it difficult to characterise India.

People in Finland and India have much to learn from each other and about each other. The magnitude of the awareness gap is colossal. Each of these countries has an abundance of expertise and resources of the kind badly needed in the other country. The technology gap between Finland and India is relatively large and can itself be considered an opportunity for joint efforts. And the gap is not unidirectional. The socio-technical prowess of Finland as manifest in the way civic and community life, vocational education, sports, innovation engines, social support architecture, environmental quality, infrastructure, health care, public procurements, school education and higher education are organised alongside high-technology industry in mechanical engineering, shipbuilding, forestry and paper, speciality chemicals, telecommunication networks, medical technologies, district heating and road transport are of interest to India. India's advances in space technologies, biotechnology, nuclear energy, supercomputing, aircraft manufacturing, ships, submarines, offshore oil platforms, mining equipment, synthetic chemistry, water desalination and solar energy storage are of interest to Finland. India's publicly funded infrastructure projects in energy and urban infrastructure, over a hundred new smart cities being built, plan for new airports, ports and docks, and industrial growth engines requiring manufacturing technologies and expertise across a range of intermediate engineering goods present opportunities for Finnish enterprises of every kind and all shapes and sizes.

The thriving private capital market in India enables good ideas to be actioned without undue reliance on debt capital. India's, IT prowess is enabling platforms for distributed enterprising that have already begun to be used in Finland by icons such as Finnair, Holiday Club, Nokia, Normet, Orion, R-kioski, Sampo Rosenlew, Siemens and Trivitron, among others. India's management expertise and experience for large, complex projects alongside new techno-economic models and grass-roots innovations is valuable for Finland to develop capabilities. These can enable prospecting and structuring partnerships with Indian enterprises for business opportunities of similar kinds elsewhere in the developing world that would otherwise be considered too risky by Finnish enterprises.

There are developments in India in relevant areas such as taxation (for instance, the new General Sales Tax or GST which is India's equivalent of the European value-added tax or VAT) and company law (The Companies Act and the liquidation and restructuring procedures), where fundamental changes in India have been implemented in 2017–2018. In India, practically everyone is a foreigner outside his home state. Many Indians in professional circles have no roots anywhere and are part of a large floating population. Being a foreigner and not knowing the local language are not constraints in India because knowing English is quite enough for doing business. India is one of the few countries that provides all its laws in English, and there is equality to citizens and non-citizens practically in all matters except for a few issues such as ownership of agricultural land.

The lack of awareness about India in Finland and about Finland in India has come in the way of developing stronger business ties. The kind of news that seems to cross the Finland–India borders easily is of the scandalous kind. The Indian media regularly reports the drowning of people in Finnish lakes after getting drunk every mid-summer and Finns skinny-dipping in the holy Pushkar Lake. The Finnish media doesn't miss reporting when vigilante squads (such as the '*gaurakshaks*') terrorise people in the name of cow protection or when Dalits or women are mistreated on the grounds of caste or gender discrimination in India. Indian business firms and successive governments have tended to undervalue Finland with a picture in the mind that Finland is a small country of 5.6 million people and quite far away, instead of noticing and giving attention to its economic prowess. The geographical distance is not as huge as the cultural and institutional distance which can be bridged. This, despite the nation-wide presence in India of Finnish brands such as Wärtsilä and Kone that have been famous since the 1980s (before 'Nokia' appeared in 1994 and was considered a Japanese brand!) and the popularity of 'Angry Birds' merchandise even in villages. India's preoccupation with 'Make in India' has come in the way of encouraging potential 'Made by India' or 'Made by Finland and India' initiatives. Indian Railways experiences enormous delays and disruptions of its timetables every winter due to fog conditions, but decision-makers haven't yet adopted Finnish fog lights that would solve this problem straightaway.

Successive Finnish governments and Finnish business firms have undervalued India as a small market and poor country where Finnish products would not be able to command premium prices. Appearances can be deceptive. When direct flights started between Finland and India, Finnair was the first to discover that a flight ticket Delhi–Helsinki–Delhi can be (and is!) priced higher than Helsinki–Delhi–Helsinki for most of the year! The preoccupation with exports of goods by Finland led to the neglect of product-services linkages and trade-substituting investments. Finland's inward-looking perspective on innovations and venture capital for innovations such as in its 'slush-centric' event-dominated modality has also contributed to overlooking the fact that the world's largest registry of grass-root innovations is in India.

Visiting Finnish business delegations seldom invest in developing capabilities for doing business in India. Finnish parastatals that are supposed to help them have themselves been reluctant to invest in expertise development programmes for doing business in India. On the Indian side, the optimism of investors and bureaucrats is often insensitive to Finnish protocols. The low level of interest in Finland also keeps getting dampened because the Finnish authorities do not provide Finnish business laws and rules in English. Finnish authorities expect Indian investors to turn to Finnish lawyers or Finnish parastatal institutions. Large Indian firms have their own internal business development cells and experts who would want to understand the Finnish regulatory environment for themselves directly from the laws and rules and regulations were these to be available in English. But now changes are on the anvil, the Indo-Finnish Joint Commission has met after a long gap, and there is hope again on both sides. There is also a Finland–India parliamentary group that was formed, and this can be rejuvenated after parliamentary elections of both countries due in 2019 are completed.

India is often imprinted by the foreign media in the popular imagination as a huge slow-moving elephant with legacies and burdens of layers of history, civilisation, culture, society and spirituality. Indian mythology accords Ganesha with the elephant head the status of a sacred augury and remover of obstacles. The swan (*Cygnus cygnus*) is the national bird of Finland, and a powerful metaphor from the National Epic, the Kalevala, that inspired Sibelius to compose 'The Swan of Tuonela'. The Hanseatic League adopted the Hansa (Hansa means 'Swan' in

Sanskrit) as its logo. What can connect the swan to the elephant? India's goddess of knowing, Saraswati has the swan as her iconic companion. And the proverbial memory of an elephant in popular folklore comes to mind. Might knowing and remembering have a connection? According to Plato, knowing is a process of recollection, and he demonstrated this in his famous dialogue with Meno who was able to eventually acknowledge knowing that the square of the two sides of a right-angled triangle is equal to the square of its hypotenuse (the Pythagoras' theorem). May we similarly recollect all that we can know so that 'unthought knowns' reveal themselves?

Chapter 1 titled 'Finland and India: Unlikely Twins?' introduces the two countries, provides a historical perspective and compares and contrasts differences and needs to highlight that Finland and India have enormous synergies despite considerable differences on many dimensions. The constitutional logic of social and political construction and economic value creation in both countries is also discussed. The major actors in the business arena are identified together with an overview of what has so far been realised, what could not be achieved and why.

Chapter 2 titled 'Business Opportunities in India?' maps the universe of business opportunities in India using several different methodologies. The discussion from the analysis then focuses on how these may be approached together with the identification of prospects for technology transfers, trade, trade-substituting investments and product-services linkages. Modalities including modes of entry and mobilisation of resources and responses needed are also covered. Chapter 3 titled 'Business Opportunities in Finland?' presents a schema of business opportunities in Finland and how these may be approached keeping the European Union in view with the identification of prospects for trade, trade-substituting investments and product-services linkages. The advantages of Finland as a host country for foreign direct investments inwards are discussed. Finland as a gateway to the European Union is also considered. This is particularly relevant because in the uncertainties associated with Brexit in the UK, about 900 Indian enterprises in the UK could be scrambling to relocate.

Chapter 4 titled 'Managing Finland–India Cultural Differences' explores the cultural dimensions on which Finland and India differ and what this implies for negotiating boundaries of tasks, time, territory, technology, sentience and understanding. In order that dialogues of the deaf are avoided, negotiating strategies, tactics, styles, gambits, pitfalls and traps typically used by Finns and Indians are explained with examples from actual business situations of success cases and failures. Cultural differences between Finland and India are not going to vanish, and the cultural differences need managing.

Chapter 5 titled 'Managing Institutional Differences in Finland–India Business' introduces the important institutions in both countries. This chapter also explains how the Finnish Code Law-based justice system and India's common law-based justice system differ from each other. This has important implications for designing collaborations, drafting contracts and enforcing obligations. Very different kinds of attention are required when prosecuting or defending court actions in Finland and India. This chapter also covers how Finland's welfare state systems and India's absence of state intervention except for the very poor affect the structuring of investments and financial commitments. There is also a discussion of differences in labour markets, capital markets, community laws and bankruptcy procedures. Some actual success and failure cases in Finland and in India are discussed.

Chapter 6 titled 'Bridges for Finland–India Business' introduces the four main gateways: B2C (Business to Consumers), B2B (Business to Business), B2G (Business to Government) and G2G (Government to Government). Here, the gamut of mutually supporting initiatives and the differences in the value-creation logic between businesses that are industrial or infrastructural in character and those that are consumer-oriented are discussed with examples. The modalities for structuring Finland–India business are asymmetric because of the differences in size, degree of competition, nature of contracts, trust in public–private partnerships and the Finnish practice of statal and parastatal involvement to support Finnish private businesses abroad.

Finnish firms have difficulty understanding the complex centre-state duality in governance that affects industrial projects in India. Chapter 7 titled 'Organising for Business in India: Systems, Structures and Processes' introduces characteristics and idiosyncrasies of India's constitutional, legal, political, economic and social systems, organisation structures and typical Indian management processes that can be experienced by foreigners as exasperating.

Chapter 8 titled 'Organising for Business in Finland: Systems, Structures and Processes' discusses typical problems that are faced when organising to do business in or with Finnish partners by drawing attention to how the trine of national, regional, local authorities affects business initiatives in Finland. The logic of the Nordic business model is introduced and what it implies for legal, political, economic and social systems, organisation structures. Finnish management and control processes that require detailed planning to be credible are also discussed.

Chapter 9 titled 'Future Trajectories of Finland and India' charts out the future traverse for both countries and how this would bring new opportunities, new risks and also new enabling social and political innovations. The world is at the cusp of entering the third decade of the twenty-first century with considerable residues and flashpoints. Finland and India both have their residues as well as notable transitions impacting their traverses. In Finland, the demographic transition is associated with skills shortages alongside endemic unemployment. Employment-intensive knowledge services require to be leveraged for commercial uses beyond Finland. In India, the demographic dividend period would be ending except in some eastern and north-eastern states. Services internationalisation would hold the key to new forms of international product-service linkages. Far-reaching political, economic, social and institutional changes are likely to characterise more open international economic relations. But there would be a need for more active bilateral and plurilateral initiatives because multilateral institutions such as WTO and OECD are showing signs of becoming sclerotic.

The final Chapter 10 titled 'Conclusions' proposes a new institutionality for Finland–India business to provide a platform for bringing together businesses, governments and academia in the two countries: Finland and India. Anticipations and preparedness for surprises in a dynamic environment require access to timely and relevant information as well as ready bridges where people from both sides can connect and provide support to emerging initiatives, test new ideas, share knowledge and experiences and mobilise responses in an effective cost-efficient way.

The list of references at the end of each chapter is for those readers who may want to access more information in greater detail. In addition to references, there are also glossaries of Finnish and Indian words that are commonly assumed to be known within the countries. An index is also provided to cross-refer different aspects quickly. In both Finland and India, change is the only constant. Economic, social and political conditions can change, and such changes can affect businesses. A useful caveat from my side would be that facts should be verified afresh when committing resources or making investments for Finland–India business because nothing can be carved in stone for all times. Care has been taken to update facts, statistics and the analysis until 1 February 2019. Yet, if you come across any error or omission, this can be corrected in future editions and reprints, and I would gratefully appreciate it if you would send me an email to anmathur@iima.ac.in.

The year 2017 marked the 100th anniversary of Finnish independence and the 70th year of Indian independence. Over the next thirty years by the time, India celebrates its centenary year and Finland traverses another thirty years, much would have changed in the world. One such transformation to be wished is the twinning of these two seemingly 'unlikely' partner countries that actually share many common interests, values and aspirations. The choice between sleepwalking into the future in a mode of procrastination or traversing along a dynamic trajectory involving active steps by learning from doing and doing by learning is not an easy one. I hope this book will be a resource for companies of all sizes and business leaders, managers, entrepreneurs, professional service practitioners and policy-makers in understanding India and Finland and the business potential that these two countries offer singly and through their synergies. I have tried in this book to candidly bring to your attention the realms of the possible, to hold the fragrance of roses right under your nose without concealing the thorns, warts and all. If you can identify your own business opportunities in India and/or Finland in your preferred arenas of endeavour, and are able to understand and appreciate possibilities and this kindles the curiosity to go further with courage and sensitivity, this book would have served its purpose.

Ahmedabad, India Ajeet N. Mathur
February 2019

Acknowledgements

This book has its genesis in my serendipitous, unplanned, unforeseen contact with Finland since 1993. There are institutions to acknowledge without whom my life in academia, researching, writing and straddling two countries while doing so would have been impossible. The Research and Publications Wing of IIM Ahmedabad in India and Liikesivistysrahasto in Finland supported the research for this book with financial grants. I was also supported by the Research and Publications Wing of IIM Ahmedabad with a grant that funded research assistance required in the concluding stages of this work. I thank the Helsinki School of Economics, Aalto University, University of Turku and University of Tampere where I was employed at different times for supporting this work over its long gestation period. In India, the Indian Council for Research on International Economic Relations (ICRIER) generously permitted me long spells of leave for this work during the period I held the IFCI Chair Professorship with ICRIER in New Delhi.

Three sets of persons were pivotal to the making of this book over a long period of time: the ones whose knowledge and experience of Finland and/or India informed me, the ones who helped me with the writing, making suggestions, critically commenting on drafts of the chapters at various stages, checking the text and editing, and the ones who generously gave their time for personal meetings to express their views, hopes and insights and enabled me clarify facts. As a work in progress, this book benefitted from suggestions of so many friends, colleagues and external collaborators that I cannot list them all. However, I wish to especially thank Risto Nuolimaa, Seppo Penttila, Petri Laine, Teemu Torvelainen, Partho Datta and Paranjoy Guha Thakurta for commenting on different parts of the text.

My research associate, Ravish Rana, spent many long hours in the Vikram Sarabhai Library at IIM Ahmedabad collecting data from trade databases and assisting me in conducting the technical analysis of trade data using mathematical models to identify the revealed comparative advantage for all tradeable items in the export and import lists of Finland and India. I thank Ravish for his enthusiasm and hard work that has enabled all available data to be analysed, and the essence of it has been placed in the Annexures. I am grateful to Ankur Sumesra for cheerfully helping me organise the tables and figures.

My wife and other family members in Finland and India have suffered the brunt of my enthusiasm and commitment to this work. But they always found ways to make time and space for my work and to contribute to it while reminding me that there is life besides this work. My thanks to them are boundless.

No author could be more fortunate than to be in the capable hands of the editors at Springer. I thank Sagarika Ghosh and Nupoor Singh for their meticulous attention to detail, thoughtfulness and care that enabled give shape to this work towards its final form. I am grateful to the Springer Production team of Parimel Azhagan T., Jennifer Sweety Johnson and Ashok Kumar for the care, precision and enthusiasm with which this book was produced.

Ajeet N. Mathur

"Due to his long and rich experience of working with Finnish and Indian companies and passionate research at IIM Ahmedabad in India, Aalto University, Helsinki and University of Tampere in Finland, Professor Mathur has a very deep knowledge of how to do business in both countries. I think that every company leader who considers starting Finnish-Indian business should read this new book. This valuable new book will help companies entering new markets to flourish by building robust sustainable business relations."
— Päivi Leiwo, Chairperson Oilon Oy, *Lahti, Finland*

"This book is a treasure trove of knowledge explaining the business opportunities, policies, cultures, institutions, country trajectories and nuances pertaining to Finland and India. The author has worked in business, government and academia in India and abroad. He has also had a long association with Finland and is able to bring you an insider's perspective of both countries."
—Ashok Sharma, Ambassador of India

"The author's deep insider experience in the two countries enables him to make very sharp observations on both sides. This book will definitely help in understanding the cultural differences and in making all interactions and communications smoother. It is also very interesting and helpful to read about the differences in legal structures and where these differences originate from."
—Iiro Rossi, Managing Director, *Holiday Club Resorts, Helsinki*

"This book is a delightful and important guide for those who want to do business between Finland and India. It brings you the numerous business opportunities which wait to be availed, and highlights the deep understanding of the author of the culture and institutional environment of both countries. Read this book, learn and be surprised!"
—Niina Nummela, Vice Dean, Professor of International Business, *Turku School of Economics, University of Turku, Finland*

"This book is a reflection of Ajeet's penchant for deep research on a topic and ability to structure and articulate content. This will be extremely helpful to both academia and practitioners who want to develop Indo-Finnish business relations specifically and international business in general. Sonata is currently engaged with business in Finland."
—Srikar Reddy, Managing Director, *Sonata Software Limited, Bangalore*

Contents

1	**Finland and India: Unlikely Twins?**	1
	Introduction	1
	Business Opportunities in Expanding Frontiers	4
	Challenges in New Horizons and Transforming Arenas	5
	Barriers and Gateways	8
	When the Twain Meet	10
	Economic Development of Finland and India	10
	Finland: Nature and Climate	13
	Demography, History and Governance Trajectory of Finland	14
	Post-war Finland, Cold War Politics and European Integration	16
	Finland's Political System and Outlook	17
	The Political Spectrum with Shades of Differences	18
	Economic Policy and Outlook	20
	International Orientation of Finnish Firms	22
	India: Discovery or Invention?	24
	International Orientation of Indian Firms	28
	Invisibles in India's Balance of Payments	29
	Home and Host Government Intervention in India and Finland	31
	India and Climate Change	34
	The Indian Economy's Trajectory	35
	Compost Heap of Indian Politics	37
	Industry–Academia–Government Partnerships	41
	References	42
2	**Business Opportunities in India**	45
	Introduction	45
	Finland's Exports to the World and India	46
	Finland–India Trade	58
	Potential Finnish Exports to India by Specific Items	59
	New Opportunities for Finland–India Trade	61

	Finnish Priorities: Too Few or Too Many?.	64
	Opportunities Financed by Government Outlays and Multilateral Assistance	66
	Water Pollution	68
	Air Pollution	68
	Make in India.	69
	Make in India but Made by Finland and India	69
	Roads Infrastructure	70
	New Airports	70
	Shipping	71
	Telecom.	72
	Oil and Gas Projects	72
	References	73
3	**Business Opportunities in Finland**	75
	Introduction	75
	Indian Export Potential to Finland	77
	Primary Products Neglected in Indian Exports to Finland.	85
	Potential Unconventional Indian Exports to Finland	86
	Potential for Trade-Substituting Investments	89
	Finnish Industrial Structure	90
	Challenges for Indian Firms	90
	Indian Priorities: Lethargy or Red Tape?	91
	Made by India and Finland or Made in Finland/Made in India?.	93
	New Opportunities for India-Finland Trade	94
	References	96
4	**Managing Finland–India Cultural Differences**	99
	Introduction	99
	Language	100
	Religion	102
	Time	105
	Sentient Boundaries and Authority Relations	109
	Task Boundaries.	113
	Space Boundaries	115
	Special Characteristics of Finnish and Indian Cultures	116
	Social and Cultural Barriers.	120
	References	121
5	**Managing Institutional Differences in Finland–India Business**	123
	Introduction	123
	Enterprise Formation.	124
	Taxation.	127

	International Taxation in Finland and India	129
	Employment Contracts	131
	Management Style and Practices	133
	Support to Finnish Enterprises for International Business	133
	Business–Government Interface	134
	Legal Systems, Transparency and Disclosure	135
	Business Practices and Commercial Laws	137
	Investment Incentives and Disincentives	139
	Exit Policies	139
	References	140
6	**Bridges for Finland–India Business**	**141**
	Introduction	141
	Four Important Questions	142
	The Paradox of Competitiveness and Collaborations	143
	Foreign Business Investments by Indian Firms	144
	B2B and B2C Bridges from India to Finland	145
	B2B and B2C Bridges from Finland to India	147
	What Has Been Done and Further Research Envisaged	151
	Government to Government Business (G2G)	153
	Cleantech, Water and Waste Management	157
	Science, Technology and Innovations	158
	Education and Skill Development	159
	Information Technology and Telecommunications	160
	Transportation: Roads, Railways, Aviation and Shipping	160
	Cooperation in Textiles Sector	161
	Tourism Cooperation	161
	Non-Tariff Barriers and Protection of Bilateral Investments	162
	Trade Promotion Measures	162
	G2G and B2B Joint Efforts	164
	References	166
7	**Organising for Business in India**	**167**
	Introduction	167
	Orientation of Finnish Firms	169
	India's Governance Frame	170
	Establishing a Business in India	172
	Entry Criteria and Preferred Forms	175
	Positioning Talent	177
	Financing a Business in India	177
	Intellectual Property Rights (IPR)	178
	Competition Policy in India	179
	Environment Protection Law	179
	Taxation	179

	Special Features of the Indian Market	180
	References	182
8	**Organising for Business in Finland**	183
	Introduction	183
	Paradox of Continuity and Change	184
	Practicalities of Organising for Business in Finland	185
	Language	185
	Credibility	185
	Taxation	186
	Banking and Insurance	186
	Community Relations	187
	The Business Ecosystem in Finland	187
	Finnish Business Corporations: Genesis and Trajectory	190
	The Nokia Phenomenon	191
	The Rise and Fall of Nokia and the new Nokia	192
	The Growth of Finnish Firms Beyond the Forest Sector	193
	Media and Multimedia	194
	Investment Thinking of Indian Industry	195
	Indian Investments in Finland	195
	References	197
9	**Future Trajectories of Finland and India**	199
	Introduction	199
	India's Challenges	200
	Four Critical Questions	201
	Economic Growth Models	202
	Paradox of Competitiveness and Collaborations	202
	Downsizing Trends in Finland	204
	Future Studies	205
	Team Finland	206
	Finnish Plans	210
	Policy Gaps	214
	Future of India	214
	References	215
10	**Conclusions: After the End and with New Beginnings**	217
	Introduction	217
	Need for a New Finland–India Institutional Bridge	218
	Why Development Cooperation Would not Work as a Bridge	221

Annexure I: Finnish RCA-Led Exports to the World Importable
              by India 223
Annexure II: High-Value Items Exportable from Finland to India..... 227
Annexure III: Indian Imports from EU that Finland Exports
              Worldwide... 229
Annexure IV: High-Value Indian Imports from EU that Finland
              Exports to India 233
Annexure V: High-Value RCA-Led Indian Exports to the World
              Importable by Finland 235
Annexure VI: High-Value RCA-Led Indian Exports to EU importable
              by Finland 239
Annexure VII: Top Ten Indian High-Value Exports to Finland
              According to CMIE Data 241
Annexure VIII: High-Value Indian Exports to European Union
              importable from India by Finland 243
Annexure IX: Finland's 500 biggest companies
              (The Talouselämä 500) 245
Annexure X: India's 500 biggest companies (The ET-500) 279
Glossaries.. 315
Index 333

About the Author

Dr. Ajeet N. Mathur is a professor of Strategy and International Business, concurrently affiliated to the Business Policy and Economics Areas at the Indian Institute of Management Ahmedabad. He received his doctoral degree from the Indian Institute of Science, Bangalore. He is the Faculty Chair of the IIMA Programme on 'Family Businesses: organisation, strategies, internationalisation and succession' and the IIMA programme on 'International Business'. His interests are at the crossroads of economics, human behaviour in groups, law, strategic management of organisational knowledge and international business. These are reflected in his multi-disciplinary and inter-disciplinary work with corporations and as an expert in change management, institutional design and missing markets with the ILO, WHO, Asian Development Bank, Competition Commission of India and the European Commission. His research particularly focuses on pervasive uncertainty and systemic risks; how motives and powerbases combine in group relations and the unconscious dynamics of large groups; bridging strategy with organization development; the dynamic co-evolution of capabilities; politics of disharmony in the management of gender differences; why missing markets remain; market barriers; the management of institutional diversity in cross-border value chains and the behavioural foundations of economics.

Before joining IIM Ahmedabad, he served as the Founding Professor of International Business, University of Tampere, Finland, EU-TEMPUS Professor of European Integration and Internationalization, as IFCI Chair Professor, Indian Council of Research on International Economic Relations, and as a tenured professor at IIM Calcutta for ten years. He has been a Senior Fulbright Fellow and a Friedrich Ebert Stiftung Scholar. He was nominated as India's National Expert on managerial productivity with APO Tokyo. He has served a term as the Director and CEO of the Institute of Applied Manpower Research with the rank of Secretary in the Government of India. He has been the Chairperson, Centre for Gender Equity, Diversity and Inclusivity at IIM Ahmedabad, a member of the Board, School of Interdisciplinary Studies, Indira Gandhi National Open University and served as a Director on boards of various Corporates in India and Europe. He is a member of the Governing Board of the Global Foundation for Integrating Spirituality and Organisational Leadership. In his early career he worked in positions of managerial responsibility in industry for more than a decade. He has held visiting academic appointments at K.U. Leuven, Belgium, University of Edinburgh, Cornell University, University of California at Berkeley, University of Bielefeld, Germany, Helsinki School of Economics, Aalto University, Turku School of Economics, Royal University of Bhutan, and Fresenius University, Cologne. His publications include 29 books and over 150 papers in scientific journals and anthologies. He is one of the authors of the International Encyclopedia of Laws. He is a recipient of several national and international awards. He is an Affiliate Life Member of the Indian Psychoanalytic Society, a Fellow of the Sumedhas Academy, a 'Yoga Shikshak' and 'Karma Sannyasin' of the Bihar School of Yoga, a Founding Member of Harmoninen Laulu Yhdistys Ry and an invitee to the Finnish Chapter of the 'Club of Rome.'

Abbreviations

AADHAAR	The universal identity card in India which is linked to a biometric database
AAY	Antyodaya Anna Yojana
ALV	Arvonlisävero (Value Added Tax in Finland)
AY	Assessment Year (the year in which a tax assessment is done for the previous financial year)
BE	Budget Estimates
BPL	Below Poverty Line
BRICS	Brazil, Russia, India, China and South Africa
CAD	Current Account Deficit
CCI	Competition Commission of India
CGST	Central Goods and Services Tax
CIC	Currency in circulation
CII	Confederation of Indian Industry
CIRP	Corporate insolvency resolution process
CPI	Consumer Price Index
CPI (IW)	Consumer Price Index (industrial workers)
CSIR	Council for Scientific and Industrial Research (in India)
DALYs	Disability-adjusted life years
DBT	Direct benefit transfer
DDA	Doha Development Agenda or Delhi Development Authority (depending on context)
DGCI&S	Directorate General of Commercial Intelligence and Statistics
DGFT	Directorate General of Foreign Trade
DIPAM	Department of Investment and Public Asset Management
DIPP	Department of Industrial Policy and Promotion
DISCOMS	Distribution companies
DSIR	Department of Scientific and Industrial Research
DTA	Domestic tariff area
EFTA	European Free Trade Area

EK	Elinkeinoelämän Keskusliitto (Confederation of Finnish Industries)
EMU	Economic and Monetary Union (in European Union Eurozone)
FCI	Food Corporation of India
FDI	Foreign Direct Investment
FEMA	Foreign Exchange Management Act
FICCI	Federation of Indian Chamber of Commerce and Industry
FII	Foreign Institutional Investor
FIPB	Foreign Investment Promotion Board
FY	India's Financial year (1 April to 31 March)
GCC	Gulf Cooperation Council
GCF	Gross Capital Formation
GDP	Gross Domestic Product
GFCF	Gross-fixed capital formation
GNI	Gross National Income
GPI	Gender Parity Index
GSDP	Gross State Domestic Product
GST	Goods and Services Tax
GVA	Gross value added
GW	Gigawatt
HFCs	Housing finance companies
HYVs	High-yielding varieties
IBC	Insolvency and bankruptcy code
ICAR	Indian Council of Agricultural Research
ICT	Information and Communication Technologies
IIMA	Indian Institute of Management Ahmedabad
IMF	International Monetary Fund
IPO	Indian Patent Office or Initial Public Offering (of shares) - depending on context
IRS	Indian remote sensing
JAM	Jan Dhan-Aadhaar-Mobile
KELA	Kansanläakelaitos (The Social Insurance Institution of Finland)
LIC	Life Insurance Corporation of India
LPG	Liquefied petroleum gas
MoEFCC	Ministry of Environment, Forest and Climate Change
MSME	Micro, Small and Medium Enterprises
MSP	Minimum support price
NABARD	National Bank for Agriculture and Rural Development
NASSCOM	National Association of Software and Services Companies
NBFC	Non-banking financial company
NCLT	National Company Law Tribunal
NCT	National capital territory
NCW	National Commission for Women
NGO	Non-Government Organisation
NHB	National Housing Bank
NHDP	National Highways Development Project

NPAs	Non-performing assets
NRI	Non-Resident Indian
NSDC	National Skill Development Council
NSSO	National Sample Survey Office
OBC	Other Backward Classes
OCI	Overseas Citizen of India
PAN	Permanent Account Number (number required by taxpayers who file income tax returns in India)
PDS	Public distribution system
PE	Private equity
PMAY	Pradhan Mantri Awas Yojana (Prime Minister's Housing Scheme)
PMFBY	Pradhan Mantri Fasal Bima Yojana (Prime Minister's Crop Insurance Scheme)
PMKSY	Pradhan Mantri Krishi Sinchayee Yojana (Prime Minister's Agricultural Irrigation Scheme)
PMMVY	Pradhan Mantri Matru Vandana Yojana for eligible pregnant women and lactating mothers
PMUY	Pradhan Mantri Ujjwala Yojana to provide cooking gas to below poverty line households
PoS	Point of sale
PPI	Producer Price Index
PRIs	Panchayati Raj Institutions
PRH	Patentti ja rekisterihallitus (Finnish Registration Office for Company Matters and Intellectual Property Registrations)
PSBs	Public sector banks
PSE	Public sector enterprise
PVB	Private sector bank
QFI	Qualified Foreign Investor
RBI	Reserve Bank of India
RE	Revised Estimates
RGI	Registrar General of India
RMSA	Rashtriya Madhyamik Shiksha Abhiyan
RoA	Return on Assets
RoE	Return on Equity
RRBs	Regional rural banks
RRR	Reverse Repo Rate
RTE	Right to education
SBM(G)	Swachh Bharat Mission (Gramin)
SC	Scheduled Caste or Supreme Court (depending on context)
SCB	Scheduled Commercial Bank
SEBI	Securities and Exchange Board of India
SEIS	Services Exports from India Scheme
SHG	Self-Help Group
SLR	Statutory liquidity ratio
SSA	Sarva Shiksha Abhiyan

ST	Scheduled Tribe
TAN	Tax deduction account number
TB	Treasury bill
TPDS	Targeted public distribution system
TRAI	Telecom Regulatory Authority of India
TRIPS	The WTO Agreement on Trade Related Aspects of Intellectual Property Rights
UDAN	Ude Desh Ka Aam Nagrik (acronym for scheme of subsidised air travel on short-haul destinations for the average person)
UDAY	Ujjwal DISCOM Assurance Yojana
ULBs	Urban Local Bodies
UN	United Nations
UTI	Unit Trust of India
UTs	Union Territories
VGF	Viability gap funding
WPI	Wholesale Price Index
WTO	World Trade Organisation

Chapter 1
Finland and India: Unlikely Twins?

> *The inevitable never happens. It's the unexpected always.*
> John Maynard Keynes
>
> *Dream, Dream, Dream*
> *Dreams transform into thoughts*
> *And thoughts result in action.*
> APJ Abdul Kalam

Abstract This introductory chapter introduces the two countries, Finland and India, to the reader to familiarise the context in which business opportunities and challenges are prospected in the rest of the book. There is a discussion on the differences in endowments, societal trajectories, economic systems, industrial structures and needs and what Finland and India can provide each other. The logic of policies and value creation in both countries are discussed. The political actors are introduced, and the dimensions to be explored more deeply in later chapters are identified institutionally together with an overview of bilateral collaboration and the enormous scope for building more connections.

Introduction

It is understandable that the idea of twinning Finland and India for synergies in economic relations could surprise many and evoke a gasp of disbelief. Finland and India present a stark contrast on many dimensions: in population size, demographic structure, economic and social development, per capita consumption, infrastructure, natural resource endowments such as forest cover, water availability, clean air, national priorities and policies, production of goods and services, structure of markets, institutional architecture that governs capital markets, money markets, labour markets, product markets, organisation of industry, science and technology development and innovation diffusion. Paradoxically, such differences, and many more, are fertile ground for the design of synergies based on complementarities and the creation of new value chains for cross-border collaborations as scoped in previously published studies (Mathur 1998, 2007, 2008a, b; Mattila 2008; Mathur and Mattila 2009).

Table 1.1 Comparison of India and Finland's key indicators

	Finland	India
Population 2018 (millions)	5.6	1,356
Area (km^2)	338,440	3,287,263
Gross domestic product 2017 (GDP)	€215.62 billion	€3,170.63 billion
GDP per capita 2017	€38,503	€2,338
GDP per capita PPP	€12,834	€6,671
GDP growth rate, three-year average	2.2%	7.3%
Fiscal deficit as % of GDP 2017	1.8%	3.2%
Merchandise exports in billion euros 2016	52	237
Merchandise imports in billion euros 2016	55	329
Trade-to-GDP ratio	49.6%	15.7%
Surplus from BOP invisibles (services) in billion euros	−2,669	90
Change in FDI annual flow (inwards)	−3%	+8%
Change in FDI annual flow (outwards)	−0.9%	+10%
Annual R&D expenditure 2017 in billion euros (and as percentage of GDP in parenthesis)	6 (2.7% of GDP)	15 (0.7% of GDP)
Average annual growth in gross capital formation	8.7%	26%
Foreign exchange balance (FOREX) in billion euros	15.3	355
Import cover of FOREX in 2018	3.3 months	12 months
External debt in billion euros	678	425

Source This table has been compiled by the author from the official statistics of the governments of India and Finland available in the public domain from India's Central Statistical Organisation and Finland's Tilastokeskus, respectively. Economic data have been converted to common denominations for comparability using currency rates, international benchmarks and standards adopted by IMF and World Bank. For commensurability, data of Finland's fiscal year (January–December) and India's fiscal year (April–March) have been adjusted

The contrast between India and Finland can be viewed from the key indicators listed in Table 1.1.

India is an ancient civilisation but a young country with a remarkable diversity. India has been independent as a democracy in its present form since 1947. In 2018, India was the world's fastest growing major economy and the sixth largest economy in the world. In purchasing power parity (PPP) terms, it was third largest country after China and USA. The size of the Indian economy in PPP terms is more than Japan and Germany put together. In PPP terms, India's GDP is thrice the size of UK as well as France, double the size of the Russian Federation, four times the size of Korea and five times the size of Spain. With a population of 1.32 billion and extreme social and economic disparities, India adopts policies that aim to sustain high growth under conditions of economic dualism with unmet development needs for about a quarter of its population below the poverty line. In international business, India aims at a healthy trade balance, trade diversification and a modestly increasing trade-to-GDP proportion which is less than Finland.

Finland is a democratic republic that celebrated 100 years of its independence in 2017 and is quite homogenous. It is the only Nordic country of the European Union to be part of the Eurozone and the Schengen travel area. In land area, Finland is Europe's sixth largest country and has the European Union's longest land border and a population of about 5.6 million people. Finland is the only country in the world to settle a population of this size above 60° north latitude. As a small open economy, Finland pursues export-oriented economic policies to maintain a high trade-to-gross domestic product (GDP) ratio, aims at preserving an egalitarian society and strives for guaranteed minimum consumption standards with high gender equity and a high labour participation rate.

In terms of the Global Competitiveness Index estimated periodically by the World Economic Forum, Finland was ranked the highest among all countries in the year 2004. In 2018, Finland was in the 10th position and India ranked 39th in competitiveness. But nobody is able to explain why the competitive economy of Finland has not attracted significant flows of foreign direct investment. In Asia, India was the highest recipient of foreign direct investment flows in 2018. In world rankings of ease of doing business, India improved its position from 142 in 2014 to 77 in 2018 (World Bank 2018) and in 2019 was expected to be in the top 50 countries and continuing to rise. During the period 2014–2018, India received $239 billion in foreign direct investments into the country according to the Finance Minister's budget speech in Parliament on 1 February 2019.

At a time when several Finnish brand names such as Kone, Nokia, Wärtsila, Fiskars, Angry Birds and Clash of Clans are widely known in India and Indian business houses such as Tata, ITC, Wipro, Mahindra, Havells, Trivitron and Sonata are actively involved with doing business in Finland, it seems distant history that trade, investments and technology collaborations between Finland and India stagnated at a low level in value and volumes during the period 1947–97. A serious problem was lack of awareness of the potential scale and scope of mutual engagement for two reasons. Due to its small population, Finland did not appear an attractive market to Indian firms for their traditional exports, and this mindset also obscured awareness in India of the technology prowess of Finnish firms. There was also the reluctance of Indian business leaders and entrepreneurs to prospect business outside English-speaking areas.

Another reason was inadequate international business acumen among small- and medium-sized Finnish technology firms. India was regarded as a developing country with unknowable risks and uncertainties with vast differences in business styles and institutions from Finland. To Finnish firms unfamiliar with India, the entry costs for prospecting business in India appeared prohibitive. The mutual business possibilities were underestimated, with preference for 'ready-made markets'. For doing business abroad, Finns looked to Russia, the Baltics, Germany, other Nordic countries and the UK. Indian businesses preferred to prospect first in the unsaturated domestic market, and then in the Middle East, Southeast Asia and Africa which were considered attractive markets with low-hanging fruit.

This did not deter large Finnish firms in the paper machinery industry, power generating sets, earthmoving equipment and the engineering industry to service customers in India. Also, it did not stop Indian tea, spices, textiles, garments, chemicals and pharmaceuticals, gems and jewellery from reaching Finland. But the economic contact failed to grow or diversify for a long time. Finland–India business was mainly intermediated by British, German, Russian and Swedish firms. This also caused trade diversion in which Indian goods were delivered in Finland at Finnish prices, but a large part of the profits were pocketed elsewhere than in Finland or India.

Business Opportunities in Expanding Frontiers

The gap between the true potential and the actual situation came to light from the ETLA (Research Institute of the Finnish Economy) study on Finland–India Trade and Investment in 1998 (Mathur, ETLA 1998). An interesting feature of this study was its dissemination with lists of profitably exportable products from Finland to India and India to Finland at a disaggregated level right down to the four-digit and six-digit SITC item codes. The entire study was made freely available on the World Wide Web through the ETLA website and through the University of Tampere's School of Business website http://www.uta.fi/kati. This enabled the more net-savvy Finnish SMEs to expand trade at a faster pace than their Indian counterparts. During the period 1999–2011, Finland's exports to India more than trebled while India's exports to Finland doubled, opening up new possibilities of trade-substituting investments.

How, at what cost and with what pace firms access missing markets can make a tremendous difference to economic engagement. When a critical minimum threshold is crossed, prospects of cultural, social and political ties also open up in new ways. For instance, despite dozens of bilateral meetings, France and India were finding it difficult to establish a strategic partnership because the mutual economic engagement was miniscule until 2002. Only after a study on prospects of missing markets in Indo-French Economic Relations was published (Mathur 2002), the level of bilateral trade and investment multiplied and made that possible within a decade. The same kind of expansion is on the anvil between India and South Africa, India and Norway, and India and Israel. So why not between India and Finland?

The Finland–India Economic Relations research project was deepened in 2005 to include services after the IT boom in India. The entire spectrum of potential trade and trade-substituting investments between Finland and India was analysed in a new study (Mathur 2007). Many more business opportunities were identified. Some of these have since been actioned, but many remain underexploited. When cross-border flows of incomes in the form of wages, profits, interests and rents exceed private and public costs for production and delivery, trade-substituting investments and technology collaborations become an attractive proposition. 'Made in India' or 'Made in Finland' is then less relevant than 'Made by India' or 'Made by Finland' and even 'Made by Finland and India'.

Challenges in New Horizons and Transforming Arenas

The post-1995 World Trade Organization (WTO) regimes in General Agreement on Trade in Services (GATS) and Trade Related Intellectual Property Rights (TRIPS) became fully operational in 2006 after the transition period. This allayed apprehensions over intellectual property rights protection in both countries, Finland and India, and augurs well for knowledge-intensive businesses. The burgeoning trade in world services has enabled new cross-border product-service linkages spawning innovative forms of international business structuring. These are very early days for Finland and India to be joining hands for new horizons.

Services constitute two-thirds of the Finnish economy and more than half of the Indian economy. This points to the need to deepen and widen the delivery of services abroad to leverage high-technology investments. But there is inertia over this. The reliance in Finland on EU mechanisms for facilitating GATS is misplaced because only electronic cross-border supply (Mode 1) is under the exclusive competence of the EU under the Maastricht Treaty. This has been confirmed by a judgement of the European Court of Justice. The three other service delivery modes, consumption abroad (Mode 2), foreign commercial presence (Mode 3) and Movement of Natural Persons (Mode 4), require bilateral prospecting between Finland and non-EU members like India and cannot be determined under the exclusive competence of the EU.[1] For this reason alone, and also because of other reasons that have to do with factor market rigidities (including labour markets), asymmetric country effects within the EU are the norm because how member states would relate on these modes with non-member states is governed by the principle of subsidiarity. EU's principle of subsidiarity requires Modes 2, 3 and 4 to be prospected bilaterally between member states and non-member states, requiring actions by firms and policy-makers in national and sub-national spaces to link with distant cross-border locales for product-service linkages in international business. It is only in countries with bureaucrats who would not want to expend efforts to take initiatives that a false notion prevails that a member state is dependent on what EU arranges with non-member states. From the perspective of Finland, Mode 2 and Mode 3 are both attractive options for business with India. From the perspective of India, Mode 4 has traditionally been constrained due to high barriers of entry for independent services. Promoting Mode 3 that supports dependent services is a better way of getting around that, and it can be a fast, inexpensive and elegant solution in the Finland–India context.

Service sectors like education and health care which were traditionally domestic sectors are among the fastest expanding international business arenas undergoing rapid transformation worldwide. There are technologies involved in such sectors for

---

[1]For the same reasons, the High Level Trade Group (HLTG) mandated by the India-EU summit in New Delhi on 7.9.2005 to launch negotiations for a comprehensive trade and investment agreement that could presumably also cover GATS services has not produced anything implementable, to date, and remains an empty show of appearances that someday something will be worked out.

the development of procedures, knowledge creation, distribution and transfer. The scope for scholars and scientists to gain experience of the other countries could accelerate collaborations to the advantage of both countries. The formidable barriers in the form of the absence of reciprocal treatment of professional qualifications, accreditations, recognition of vocations require revisiting for transforming perspectives about human capital demand and supply. India and France have worked out double degree programmes with premier internationally ranked institutions where students from either country can study in two universities, one in France and one in India dividing time between them. In the very first top-tier exchange collaboration between a Finnish institution (Helsinki School of Economics) and the Indian Institutes of Management Ahmedabad, Bangalore and Calcutta, the first eight students who visited India did not return to Finland to seek employment because they were launched into international careers in India, Germany and USA.

India was the eighth largest exporter of commercial services (IT, travel and tourism being prominent) in the world in 2016 (WTO 2017). India's share of the world market in commercial services is about 4%, which is double the share of India's merchandise exports in the world. In 2016, foreign tourist arrivals (FTAs) were 8.8 million and foreign exchange earnings (FEEs) from tourism grew at 8.8% to US$22.9 billion. There has also been growth in outbound tourism, and departures of Indian nationals from India, estimated at about 22 million annually, are growing at the rate of 7.3%. This is more than double the foreign tourist arrivals in India.[2]

According to NASSCOM data cited in the Economic Survey 2017–18, India's information technology-business process management (IT-BPM) industry grew by 8.1% in 2016–17 to US$139.9 billion (excluding e-commerce and hardware). IT-BPM exports grew by 7.6% to US$116.1 billion in 2016–17. E-commerce market is estimated at US$33 billion, with a 19.1% growth in 2016–17. India-based R&D service firms which account for almost 22% of the global market grew by 12.7%. Foreign exchange earnings of India from export of satellite launch services have also increased noticeably in recent years. Water on the moon was first confirmed by India's Chandrayaan, and more and more countries are now sending payloads into space using Indian satellites. In 2018, Finland collaborated with Indian Space Research Organisation (ISRO) for a Finnish satellite to be launched into space on an ISRO Mission.

There have been numerous new initiatives in different segments of the service sector in India. These include payments and accounting digitisation, e-visas, infrastructure status monitoring, logistics, start-up India programme, National Skills Qualification Framework and schemes for the housing sector. These have given much boost to the service sector. Sub-sectors like tourism, aviation and telecom continue to grow at double-digit rates. Airlines facing shortage of pilots have recruited several hundred foreign pilots, and the tourism infrastructure growth is

---

[2]http://mofapp.nic.in:8080/economicsurvey/pdf/001-027_Chapter_01_Economic_Survey_2017-18.pdf.

unabated. The telecom arena has many players—Indian and foreign, with high density of mobile phone penetration where growth is far from saturated.

Indians can learn much from how well Finland has organised its civic systems in health care and education. To mention just one example, even the National Capital Region of Delhi does not have a system of pooling blood plasma for research although the University of Delhi and other scientific institutions have equipment as well as trained human resource at postdoctoral level. In contrast, Finland has a nationwide system of pooling blood plasma and can afford the equipment but has paucity of postdoctoral level talent for blood plasma research. This is a clear case that challenges the conventional prejudices of unlikely twinning between Finland and India. When attention of BioCity Turku was drawn to this, they quickly developed a collaboration.

About 55% of India's gross value added (GVA) in 2018 was contributed by the service sector. This is expected to grow further to contribute almost 72.5% of annual GVA growth in the coming years. While the growth of the service sector in 2017–18 was 8.3%, the growth in service exports and net services was robust at 16.2% and 14.6%, respectively.

Service delivery from India to Finland is growing rapidly in IT and biotechnology. For example, Finnair's back office work is handled by the IT division of a multinational firm that is headquartered in Kolkata. R-kioski's management information system including sales, accounting, inventory control, operational logistics at its outlets and stock reordering is managed by an Indian IT firm from Bengaluru. Indian scientists and technologists are involved with biocity projects in Finland such as BioCity Turku. There is much more scope for technology collaborations in science and technology in a number of fields. This is evidenced by the recent bilateral agreements involving the Department of Biotechnology and the Department of Science and Technology in India with their Finnish counterparts. More such agreements have since been made involving collaborations in energy and environment, road building and transportation. Finland's cleantech cluster specialises in environmental know-how and focuses on air pollution control, vehicular pollution control, solid waste management and renewable energy solutions. India's National Action Plan on Climate Change covers many aspects of mutual interest to India and Finland. The most promising avenues of India–Finland collaborations have arisen in knowledge-intensive services and product-service bundling solutions for third-country markets where India's advantage in service delivery and Finnish technology's cutting-edge product designs combine for delivering high value to customers.

The officially declared sectors of Finnish interest in India are telecom, electronics, IT-enabled services, offshoring and outsourcing, food processing, medical instruments, environmental technologies, carbon credits, forestry products and technologies, paper machinery, construction and project goods. India is providing technology support to Finland in biotechnology, biopharmaceuticals, health research, earth sciences, nanoscience/nanotechnology, aerospace engineering, nuclear power machinery, photonics and synchrotron science. The expanding frontiers of cooperation and the new horizons are as exciting as the transformations in arenas of existing cooperation which include telecom, paper machinery, mining machinery, construction and project goods for the infrastructure projects.

Many EU countries including Finland face the twin burden of demographic shock (with skills shortages) and economic slowdown that stresses sub-national fiscal transfer mechanisms and makes returns from commercial investments in high technology uncertain in a high cost and demand-constrained scenario. The buoyant demand in India for competitively produced goods and knowledge-intensive services is unabated, and foreign direct investment inflows exceed portfolio fund flows. Yet, despite high and sustained GDP growth, India's growth trajectory is constrained by inadequacy of infrastructure (roads, railways, ports, airports, energy), poorly resourced local governance for public goods and the commons, skills shortages in new technologies, lack of science and technology diffusion on a nationwide scale, and social and economic distress for large numbers of people in its population who lack access to safe drinking water, affordable quality health care (especially childcare and maternity care), affordable quality education, especially vocational education, and housing.

India has just about 2.4% of the planet's land area, 4% of freshwater resources and 1% of the world's forests, although 18% of the world's population lives here and 70% of the population is under 40 years of age. There is an enormous need for productive investments using proven new technologies in this supply-constrained scenario. Israel has been quicker than Finland in bringing its solutions. Finnish technology solutions, many of which are superior and less costly, have enormous scope to be used in India.

There are many arenas with business potential financed by public outlays and public–private partnerships, besides the obvious pull from demand of a vibrant industrial sector serving business to business (B2B) and business to consumer (B2C) with a range of products and services. There are both an acute need and considerable scope to optimise resources. Some of the most exciting possibilities concern expanding of the use of marine resources along India's long coastline. Finland's neighbour, Norway, is prospecting these opportunities in India.

Barriers and Gateways

The development and diffusion of Finnish technology in Finland is well supported by Finnish institutions such as Tekes (Finnish Funding Agency for Technology and Innovation), SITRA (the Finnish Innovation Fund), VTT (Technical Research Centre of Finland), TEM (Ministry of Employment and the Economy) and Finpro (Global Expert Network established for Finnish companies). This has reinforced confidence and pride but also created a norm among Finnish firms of 'bowling alone' or limiting their activities to Finnish clusters, and competing abroad mainly through Finnish institutions, seeking cooperation through intergovernmental pathways or momentum from the tailwind of some large Finnish firm rather than direct explorations or negotiated collaboration with foreign business firms.

According to Finland's Minister for Foreign Trade and Development Anne-Mari Virolainen, who led the Finnish business delegation to India during November–December 2018, new areas of Finnish interest in India were artificial intelligence applications, digital education, digital solutions besides ICT cooperation and sales of Finnish pulp and paper and heavy machinery (according to the Indian Express, 9 December 2018, Sunny Verma's interview with the Minister). In the same interview, Minister Virolainen was reported to have stated that Finland was not taking new initiatives in India because it was waiting for an EU-India deal to fructify. India's biennial mega event for international business investors and collaborations 'Vibrant Gujarat' was in its ninth edition in January 2019. Denmark and Norway were among partner countries at the event. Sweden was represented by its business enterprises and government representatives. Finland was conspicuous by its absence. The Finnish event around innovations, start-ups and venture financing, Slush, that has been held annually in November has also hardly drawn any interest from India.

The commercialisation of technologies and travelling the last mile to seed a technology innovation abroad in the form of investments for harvesting returns from it needs investment in management capabilities (in both small and large firms). There is a need for development of various forms of international business (such as licensing, franchising, strategic alliances, joint ventures, 51% owned subsidiaries) and not merely exporting or 100% subsidiaries in SEZs. Indian firms are surprised, even impressed by the degree of cohesiveness and trust between Finnish businesses and the Finnish government and parastatal institutions. But they are also daunted by the slow pace of decision-making, hesitations and reluctance of Finnish firms to invest in building new managerial capabilities for doing business in India and take risks without government subventions and guarantees.

Finnish firms find it strange that there are not corresponding institutions in India to the ones that exist in Finland. Indian and Finnish firms structuring a collaboration for the first time would both need to recognise that their decision-making logic is unlikely to be symmetric. In a Finnish doctoral dissertation (Mattila 2008), the processes of building Finland–India collaborations were studied using action research methods. The study concluded that productive and harmonious collaborations among Finns and Indians required making efforts and investing in time for understanding cultural and institutional differences and respect for differences in business norms, values, beliefs and attitudes. Pressures that have arisen from climate change, deforestation, urbanisation, transportation deficits, mining, irrigation needs of agriculture represent opportunities, but some of them come bundled with deteriorating law and order situation in certain parts of India which makes it important to choose project locations carefully.

When the Twain Meet

According to the Economic Survey of India 2017–18, the prosperity of Indian States is correlated with their international and interstate trade. States that export more internationally, and trade more with other states, tend to be more prosperous. And the correlation is stronger with international trade. It is also remarkable that India's export structure is substantially more broad-based and egalitarian than in other countries with the top one per cent of Indian firms accounting for only 38% of exports, whereas in all other countries, including Finland, they account for a substantially greater share.

In 2017, there were about 30 Indian companies (excluding shops and eateries registered as companies) with offices in Finland and approximately 90 Finnish firms with offices in India. Excluding exporters, there were about 400 firms that had contracts or collaborations spanning the two countries. There also exist cooperation agreements between Finnfund and Exim Bank, between FICCI and the Confederation of Finnish Industries (Elinkeinoelämän Keskusliitto or EK for short) and, as already mentioned earlier, between IIM Ahmedabad (India's top-ranked management institute which is more than a business school) and the Helsinki School of Economics, now part of Aalto University as its business school. There are also arrangements Finnish institutions have made with NGOs in Rajasthan and Haryana. Finnish educational institutions have connections with a few private Indian universities in Haryana and Maharashtra to send university students for some experience of India.

Economic Development of Finland and India

Research studies extrapolating trends in international trade based on existing patterns obscure choices not exercised or not visualised. Each country evolves its pattern of trade from historical circumstances shaped by decisions of a unique set of actors that define the prospective and favoured international arena for its investments and trade in goods and services. A closer look at the decision-makers in Finland and India reveals that the number of such decision-makers has been small in both countries. Both countries are outstanding examples of state-supported investments in technologies, industrialisation and trade where investment and trade flows occurred along paths of least effort.

The growth path taken by Finland after World War II, on the back of war reparations that it paid fully, eventually led to a tenfold real GDP increase over five decades. This was associated with sectoral shares rising to 30% of GDP in manufacturing and to over 65% in services. Manufacturing industries of Finland were the engine of growth when industrial production grew 50% faster than aggregate output until the end of the 1980s. After recovery from the great recession of the 1990s, Finland's growth has mainly been in the new economy industries, especially telecom, energy and environment, away from the traditional smokestack industries in forestry (paper and paperboard), and engineering of metals. Since the domestic market was limited in size, expansion of the production possibility frontiers required Finland to depend on demand from abroad to the extent that export demand as the constraint became a permanent feature in its growth model.

In India, there is a supply-constrained scenario, where manufacturing industries are growing at a rapid pace in every industrial activity. This assures high profitability in a large and growing domestic market. The prospects of trade in manufactured products are also bright. Less than 5% of Indian manufacturing output is presently targeted to export markets, but about 75% of India's exports in volume and value are manufactured goods. At Indian price points, Finnish goods made in India for developing country markets can open new avenues in other markets too. American firms such as GE have changed their approach to developing country markets after realising that their product development can be revolutionised in India in ways that even home markets benefit when costs are brought down to serve segments that were previously unserved or underserved.

India and Finland differ in their economic model of growth. In India, the development and industrialisation process are being telescoped. In pursuing self-reliance to the point of mistaking self-reliance with self-sufficiency, industrialisation of the Indian economy has covered a wide range of industry with a presence in every sector. When the new economic policies were adopted in 1991 with significant departures from protectionism, every sector underwent restructuring. Yet, India did not abandon public planning for development of infrastructure, energy, transportation, telecom and urbanisation. Significant public outlays from national finances are annually allocated for investments in these sectors. These outlays translate into demand for project goods and investment opportunities. Since 1991, these opportunities are open to the domestic and foreign private sector.

India's Planning Commission was abolished in 2014 and replaced by the '*NITI Aayog*' (the acronym 'NITI' translates as 'policy' and stands for 'National Institution for Transforming India). The Government of India, through its ministries, continues to finance a large public outlay to promote priorities in urban and rural infrastructure, housing construction, education, health care, sanitation, transport and communications infrastructure, energy, water management, roads, railways, ports, airports and defence. Major reforms were undertaken in India during 2017. The Goods and Services Tax (GST) was launched to replace state sales taxes in July 2017. The festering twin balance sheet (TBS) problem was solved by sending the major stressed companies for resolution under the new Indian Insolvency and Bankruptcy Code. A major recapitalisation package to strengthen the public sector banks that were weighed under by stressed assets has also been implemented.

In Finland, policy-makers, firms and researchers visualise Finnish models of industrial structures and markets as vertical clusters with orchestrated linkage effects (that typically occur with a time lag). The priorities engineered through subsidies and incentives are brokered between the clusters with consultations through parastatal institutions, state-supported associations and financial institutions. In such a model, pioneering technologies can fail to be exploited timely in international markets because the wait for market signals or prioritisation is uncertain. For example, radio isotopical research was commercialised in Wallac in 1950, but X-ray apparatuses using the same technology developed only in the 1960s and the first X-ray apparatus to India was exported in 1997. Another example: investments in telecom technologies between 1950 and 1980 could be reaped only after bundling all the public investments and proprietary technologies of Televa and Salora and others into the flagship, Nokia in the 1980s. Also, a 1939 law was invoked that placed restrictions on Ericsson and Siemens in Finland and protected Nokia from international competition until 1994, giving it the breathing space (Ahonen 1995).

The initial success of products in international markets also inhibits waves of development that might follow if declining techno-commercial feasibilities are not noticed for raising alarm early enough. The success of Wärtsilä Diesel with small captive generators became their Achilles' heel when rising energy capacity, scale economies and declining energy costs per unit of investments in large public systems in developing economies made marketing of existing products difficult.

The experience of developed economies in post-industrial societies suggests that only the first phase in Michael Porter's model of transition from factor-driven to investment-driven to innovation-driven to wealth-driven (Porter 1991) accurately portrays transition to a post-industrial society. The overheating in the innovation and wealth phases (as in Finland of the 1980s) is cyclic rather than a one-time event. This is so because societies are transformed through a changed pattern of investments in knowledge where knowledge pushes the economy into another cycle of factor-driven investments and knowledge itself becomes a factor.

The experience of developing economies (for instance, China, Brazil, India) also shows up other interesting differences. It is not necessary for a whole economy to become wealth-driven before knowledge intensity investments redrive a new factor-driven phase. Porter had not considered these countries in his analysis. It is unclear from our state of knowledge whether this occurs because inefficient firms are crowded out or simply because knowledge investments and their diffusion become more ubiquitous and linkable thanks to telematics. Indeed, the persisting chronic unemployment in Europe is partly the result of an insufficient number of competitive firms. Such firms in the EU-28 are a drag for countries where knowledge investments do not correspond to private and social rates of return on these investments. Knowledge investments and size of accessible markets are closely related. The success of Finnish enterprises has been organised mainly on business-to-business deals in niche spectra of industrial products in forestry, metals, energy and techno-electronics. Another anomaly in Finland is the high degrees of concentration in consumer markets with few entrenched players and with hardly any incentive to develop international consumer brands. Nokia with its handsets, Marimekko with fashion clothing and accessories, Finncrisp bread and Finlandia Vodka are some of the exceptions. The small size of the economy generally resulted in proliferation of duopolies and oligopolies on one side and duopsonies and oligopsonies on the other. This has implications for organising for business in Finland.

The success of Indian firms, initially in insular and protected markets under the patronage of the licensing system, resulted in endemic shortages and black markets. This has changed. It is now based on access to a large and growing domestic consumer market and exports. There is fierce competition among brands. In the historically sheltered industrial product market in India, once it got opened to domestic and foreign competition in 1991, enterprise profitability corresponds to development and diffusion of technologies and competitive business models for identified segments of growth sectors. Further, growth involves investments across a wide range of industrial goods and intermediate inputs that sustain the consumer product manufacturing. However, limits to technology development and diffusion can translate into severe capital and capacity constraints, inhibiting pace of infrastructure development and leading to reduced economic growth and social progress. The enormity of the development agenda, the size of market and technology diffusion and development are all closely related.

Thus, resource bases and opportunity horizons in the two countries differ in stark contrast to the point of potential complementarity. For an understanding of the economic incentives propelling the actors in the Finnish and Indian economies, we review the salient features of their societies' state of their domestic economies and linkages to external dimensions.

Finland: Nature and Climate

Finland has common borders with Norway, Russia and Sweden and a long coastline along the Baltic Sea and the Gulf of Bothnia. More than two-thirds of the country is forested, with 168,000 lakes, with white nights and midnight sun in the summer and the prospect of seeing the Aurora Borealis (Northern Lights) in the dark winters. There are four clear seasons of climate: winter (from December to February), spring (from March to May), summer (from June to August) and autumn (from September to November). The precise duration of seasons varies from the Arctic North to the Baltic South part. Life and economic activity are organised differently by the seasons.

People joke that there are three kinds of temperatures in Finland: cold, freezing cold and biting cold. When it is plain cold, it is called summer and it is rather short. In 2017, it is said that summer was on a Thursday. In 2018, there were many warm days during July and August when summer temperatures rose and touched close to 30 °C on some days which was considered a heat wave. The very first sentence in my Finnish language book reads "Finland is a warm country and warmer than Alaska". The lowest winter temperature I have experienced in Finland was minus 52 °C at Kittilä. That is cold considering that the ambient temperature on Mars is a warmer minus 48 °C. The Finnish climate has instilled a sense of grit, resilience, tenacity, resourcefulness and an instinct for survival that is unparalleled. The Finns call this 'SISU', and it is a core value of the Finnish national identity.

Foreigners visiting Finland need not fear the cold because the indoors of all public places, offices, homes, hotels, restaurants, shopping centres, trains, buses, cars, taxis are heated. A North Indian winter when the temperature is sub-zero in some parts and in others between zero and five degrees Celsius from evenings to mornings feels colder without indoor heating.

Demography, History and Governance Trajectory of Finland

The population that is settled in what constitutes the present geographical boundaries of Finland arrived in waves mainly from the East and Southeast more than 5000 years ago. Samis were the original inhabitants that were pushed northwards to what is now called Lapland when more hordes arrived. Ethnically, the majority population in Finland is Finno-Ugric and 86% Finnish-speaking, sharing their Finno-Ugricness with Estonians and Hungarians. The Finno-Ugric people are said to have originally inhabited the region near the Ural Mountains, now in Russia, and some hordes may have arrived also from Central Europe. For about six hundred years until 1809, Finland was part of Sweden. Finland and Estonia were part of the same country, Sweden, from 1629 to 1710.

In 1809, after the Napoleonic Wars, Finland became an autonomous Grand Duchy of the Russian Empire until 1917. The Swedish Civil and Criminal Codes were adopted in Finland from 1734 and remained in force throughout the Russian period. The Russian rule did not interfere with Finnish religious traditions or the use of Finnish language because these provided a natural buffer zone barrier against the West. There was no customs duty for Finnish exports to Russia at this time. There was also no income tax in Finland until 1920, except during short periods of emergencies.

There was an estate-based parliamentary representation by the nobility, the clergy, the bourgeoise and peasants. The Bank of Finland, the education system and the press were among the first national institutions established during the Russian governed period. Initially, the Swedish-speaking elite were the dominant business owners in Finland. The linguistic cleavage remains to this day with two official languages, Finnish and Swedish, and with special status for the Sami language which is allowed to be used. Economic power was also vertically divided by this linguistic cleavage. Only for a brief period of Russification, Russian was added as an official language in Finland between 1899 and 1917.

The Finnish language owes its formalisation to the first liturgical translations of the New Testament by Mikael Agricola that brought with it the Lutheran influence. Although Finland is officially described as Evangelical Lutheran, other religions being practised include Greek Orthodox Christianity, Catholic Christianity, Jehovah's Witnesses, Laestadian Christianity, Free Church of Finland, Islam and Buddhism, among others.

The Finnish national identity coalesced around the national epic 'Kalevala'. This epic was compiled by Elias Lönnrot and published in 1835. There was a clamour for Finnish to be an official language alongside Swedish. A part of the Swedish-speaking elite decided to integrate themselves with the Finnish-speaking majority by launching, around 1880, a cultural, political and social initiative around nation-building which became known as the 'Fennoman movement'.

In 1862, the Swedish-speaking elite established the Union Bank of Finland (*Suomen Yhdyspankki* known by its abbreviation, SYP) to control and own a new financial institution for the interests of the Swedish-speaking elite. In 1889, the Finnish-speaking industrialists established their own bank, the National Bank of Finland (*Kansallis-Osake-Pankki*, known by its abbreviation, KOP). Two insurance companies, Suomi in 1890 and Pohjola in 1891, also got established. The economic cleavage between Swedish speakers and Finnish speakers became ossified over the tussle for influence over business activities in manufacturing and distribution, especially paper manufacturing. Repola Oy (financed by the National Bank of Finland, KOP) was the flagship company of the Finnish-speaking industrialists, and Kymmene Oy (financed by the Union Bank of Finland, SYP) became the hub and core of the Swedish-speaking elite. Both Repola (through UPM) and Kymmene were paper manufacturers. Their recent trajectory after they amalgamated is narrated later in Chap. 3 where the Finnish business ecosystem and business opportunities are discussed in more detail.

Nineteenth-century Finland was characterised by farming, trade and incipient industrialisation that created the first factory workers distinct from artisans. Finland was remarkably international in the late nineteenth and early twentieth century. Its four ports, Viipuri, Helsinki, Turku and Mariehamn, were hubs of maritime activity. Mariehamn was home to the world's largest fleet of sailing ships. Finlayson, the Scot, invested the Calcutta tea trade profits of James Finlay in Tampere in a cotton spinning mill. The Company James Finlay became Tata Finlay when the Indian business house Tata took a controlling stake, and it later changed its name to Tata Tea. After acquiring Tetley, it morphed into Tata Tetley and was renamed Tata Global Beverages. Meanwhile, Finlayson, considered the first modern factory in Finland (there had previously only been iron foundries since 1616), continues its legendary trajectory even though its most glorious days belong to the past.

Many iconic Finnish enterprises and brands have foreign origins. Johan Friedrich Hackman from Bremen, Germany, established Hackman (now part of Iittala Group owned by Fiskars) to make kitchenware. Karl Fazer, the son of a Swiss immigrant, established a confectionary business and chocolate factory in Finland. Wilhelm Gutzeit from Königsberg started a paper mill in Norway which his son Hans Gutzeit moved to Finland and which became Enso-Gutzeit, later renamed Enso Oyj after merging with Veitsiluoto (now Stora Enso after amalgamation with Stora). The Russian Nikolai Sinebrychoff from Polish-speaking Germany established a brewery associated with Koff and Karhu brands and also as a bottler for Coca-Cola beverages in Finland. This should inspire confidence that foreign investment from other parts of the world can be attracted to Finland.

Not to be left behind, the farmers' cooperative movement and the working class elites noticed the benefits of bloc formation and established their own organisations. The farmers' cooperative movement created the Forestry Confederation (*Metsäliitto-Yhtymä*) and the Cooperative Syndicate Bank (*Osuuspankki* known by its abbreviation, OP) with control over food and agriculture. The workers' movement also became influential in retailing and construction and established its own bank, SKOP. The tripolar power structure this created is explained in Chap. 5.

After the parliamentary elections of 1906 held under Russian rule (when for the first time in Europe, women voted), collective interest organisations were formed. During the Russian Revolution, the Red Army defeated the White Army (Tsarist) in Russia but the White Army defeated the Red Army in the Grand Duchy of Finland. With no Tsar left to rule the Grand Duchy, Finland became independent. It is said that Lenin who had used Tampere in Finland as a hideout during his days of exile and plotting was sympathetic to the Finnish predicament. Independence on 6th December 1917 brought about a republican form of government in Finland. Initially, the Finns tried to reinstate a monarchy by inviting a German Prince, the *Landgraf* of Hessen, Friedrich Karl to become the King in 1918, but he declined due to changes in the political climate of Europe with the collapse of empires after World War I. The German influence in Finland was always important because there was a tradition of Finns going to Germany for vocational education, professional education and higher studies in Germany and Finns tended to learn German as a third language. During the civil war in Finland after independence, the German Imperial Forces helped the White Army to fight the reds.

In the build-up to World War II, Finland got sandwiched between the Russian demand for access to Finnish territory for defensive fortifications by the Soviet Union against the expected invasion by Germany and German plans for occupation of parts of Scandinavia. For Finland, there were three phases in World War II. In the first phase 1939–40, the Soviet Union attacked Finland after Finland's refusal to allow Soviet military bases as defence fortifications on Finnish territory in what is remembered as the 'Winter War'. In the second phase, there was a 'Continuation War' with Soviet Union (1942–44) in which Finland allied with Germany to fight the Soviet Army. In the third phase (1944–45), Finland accepted peace terms from the Soviet Union that required it to forcibly expel German forces from Finnish territory in the North of Finland in what is referred as the 'Lapland War'.

Post-war Finland, Cold War Politics and European Integration

The basis of the new Foreign Policy of Finland after World War II was the Treaty of Paris, 1947, under terms of which a final peace conference was to be convened. This never took place. Finland paid its war reparations fully under the Paris Peace

Treaty. Finland's Treaty of Friendship, Co-operation and Mutual Assistance with Russia signed in 1948 was revised in 1992 when its military provisions were removed. Finland joined the International Monetary Fund in 1948, GATT in 1950 and the Nordic Council in 1956. In 1956, Finland also joined the UN and was admitted to the OECD in 1969.

As a neutral country, Finland hosted the 1975 Conference on Security and Cooperation in Europe (CSCE). Finland joined the European Free Trade Agreement (EFTA) in 1986 as part of the group of countries (Austria, Norway, Sweden, Iceland and Switzerland) that had opposed the customs union in 1957. By this time, UK (also an EFTA member) had already defected to join the European Customs Union. Finland joined the Council of Europe in 1989 but did not initially sign up to all of its conventions. In 1992, Finland applied for membership of the European Union and after a national referendum in 1994 approved the joining, Finland became a member of the EU from 1.1.1995. When the Economic and Monetary Union introduced the Euro, Finland became a member of the Eurozone and adopted the Euro giving up its national currency, the Finnish Markka.

Finland's Political System and Outlook

Elections to the unicameral Parliament are held with predictable regularity, precisely on the third Sunday in April every four years. Every Finnish citizen who is at least 18 years old on election day is eligible to vote in parliamentary elections. At the time of writing, the next parliamentary elections are to be held on Sunday, 14 April 2019. Ten political parties are currently represented in Parliament.

Coalition government is the norm in Finland, with no party winning more than about one-quarter of the vote in recent elections. Theoretically, any of the ten parties could get involved for participating in a coalition government. Negotiating with numbers to form a government happens after the election results are announced. Coalitions have formed despite differences in stances on the political, economic and social issues. The four big parties, any of which could be part of a coalition after the next election, are the Centre Party (Keskusta), the National Coalition Party (Conservatives or Kokoomus), Social Democratic Party (SDP or Demarit) and True Finns or Finns Party (Perussuomalaiset or PS). Besides perennial domestic issues such as unemployment, social security, tax reform, support for local communities, contraction in public services including health care, and rising prices of essential goods and services, the policy on migrants and refugees, national security and relations with Russia occupy centre stage in the debates.

The political party representation following the last three general elections shown below provides a glimpse of the shifting sands in the political spectrum (Table 1.2).

Table 1.2 Political party representation in Finnish Parliament

	No. of seats		
	2007	2011	2018
National Coalition Party (Conservatives or Kokoomus)	50	44	38
Social Democratic Party (SDP)	45	42	35
Finns Party (PS)	5	39	17
Centre Party (KESK)	51	35	49
Left Alliance (VAS)	17	14	12
Green Party (VIHR)	15	10	15
Swedish People's Party (RKP)	9	9	10
Christian Democrats (KD)	7	6	5
Others (includes 18 of Blue Reform)	1	1	19
Total	200	200	200

Source Parliament of Finland

The Political Spectrum with Shades of Differences

Finland's political spectrum can be studied by giving attention to the public posturing by various parties on their own websites. The Social Democratic Party (SDP) with its catchy slogan '*We want everyone aboard*' proclaims that its values do not stop at boundaries of language, nationality or background and claims to be committed to making Finland a fairer, more compassionate and more respectful society. While SDP draws its supporters from a wide cross section of society, industrial workers have been a prominent constituency of support.

The National Coalition Party or Conservatives (Kokoomus) is one of the oldest political parties in Finland and draws much of its support from business leaders and entrepreneurs. The Kokoomus identifies itself as a liberal and conservative party supporting free trade and a free market economy. It has also been active in national security discussions.

The Centre Party of Finland (Keskusta), according to its declared intents in Finnish on its own website, has proclaimed that it stands for a society with 'happy, healthy homes and narrowing welfare gaps' and that it wants to "make Finland a pioneer in creativity and competence, reduce bureaucratic burden and introduce a new political culture of bold experiments to secure the foundations of well-being". It claims to be committed to getting Finland back on the path of sustainable growth by encouraging work and entrepreneurship and putting an end to living in debt. Keskusta promises growth in bioeconomy and digitisation, 200,000 new jobs, balanced municipal services, commitment to continued non-alignment, social and healthcare reform and care for the elderly, among other things.

The most enigmatic among the major political parties of Finland is the Finns Party (Perussuomalaiset or PS, for short) which has been gaining vote shares in national and municipal elections in the previous two decades except for a small dip of a percentage point in the 2015 national parliamentary elections which reduced its seats' tally from 39 to 38 and its number of seats reduced to 17 after SINISET splintered away from it. PS claims to be a revived version of the National Rural Party that was disbanded in the 1990s. According to its own website (www.perussuomalaiset.org), the credo of the Finns Party and its policies are focused "on the work ethic, entrepreneurship and a balanced social welfare system linked to Christian values". The party resists being classified into any traditional left–right taxonomy. PS is staunchly nationalist and appeals to patriotic nationalism to defend the economically disadvantaged with its slogan 'justice for all' and emphasis on productivity and its anti-corruption stance.

The Finns Party is the leading EU-sceptic party in Finland and believes that the EU meddles more than it should into citizens' everyday affairs and is creating excessive central governance in Brussels. This party propagates the notion that EU membership costs for Finland are excessive and the computation process for Finnish contributions needs reassessment and adjustment. The party wants Finland to renegotiate its EU membership, transfer more power back to Finland from Brussels, reduce the power of the EU Commission and diminish common responsibility in economic affairs. The party is opposed to distributing existing bank debt across Europe and is against the idea that EU public finances are used to rescue financial disasters of investment bankers.

The new Blue Reform Party (Sininen tulevaisuus or SINISET for short) is a splinter group that broke away from the Finns Party after the 2015 general elections. It identifies itself as the movement for tax revolt of the middle classes which certainly has an appeal in a country where individual workers are taxed at a higher rate than businesses. It promises labour market reforms and tax reforms and appeals to small business owners and self-employed with its commitment to closing tax loopholes to prevent Finland's wealth to drift to tax havens. SINISET asserts security as a fundamental right, commits itself to combating social exclusion, supports army conscription and values strength and trust in the civil service with attention to Nordic cooperation and Finland's place in the EU.

The Green Party (VIHR), formed in 1987, won 15 parliament seats in the general elections of 2015. VIHR was the first European Green Party to be part of a state-level coalition cabinet in 1995. It stands for choice, fairness and climate responsibility. At the local level, Greens are strong in the big cities. In the national capital, Helsinki, the Greens are the second largest party with 23.5% of the vote. In some other towns and cities, the Greens are the third largest party.

The Left Alliance (VAS) is the fifth biggest political group in the Finnish Parliament. The Left Alliance has positioned itself as a labour party committed to rooting out the grey economy. VAS is committed to public provisioning for good-quality education, health care and a culture of caring. It promises a society with progressive taxes, decent wages, good working conditions and basic security to workers, small entrepreneurs and the self-employed, to people in fixed term as well as in regular work contracts. It wants to bring back property taxes and introduce new taxes on nuclear fuel and stock exchange transactions and is opposed to raising indirect taxes such as VAT or real estate duties.

The Swedish People's Party (RKP) represents the Swedish-speaking Finns and is one of the small parties representing an affluent but small linguistic group with its support base mainly in Southern Finland and areas adjacent to Sweden in the coast of Turku, Åland Islands and Finnish Ostrobothnia in the North-west of Finland.

The Christian Democratic Party is another small party that stands for Christian values of caring for families, children and their hobbies, the elderly and the dying through provisioning of municipal services such as day care, palliative services and support to small groups. It is committed to reforming Finland's system of facilitating economic livelihoods and social support, advocates more support for waste recycling, healthcare reform, maintaining healthy premises for living and working, support for health care, including mental health, drug de-addiction facilities, clean water and renewable energy.

Economic Policy and Outlook

Economic policy-making in Finland is going through an uncertain phase with very little agreement among the major political parties. PS and SDP would wish to insulate Finland from the world to avoid effects of globalisation, but in practice they have been unable to do so even when they were part of government coalitions.

Finland has grown steadily since mid-1993, the turning point of its deepest economic crisis of the twentieth century when output contracted by about 24%. Economic activity rebounded in 1997 and 1998 and was associated with expansion of retail trade and construction volumes. Finland became an EU member in January 1995. It became a member of the exchange rate mechanism (ERM) in October 1996. Finland achieved the required criteria for membership of the Economic and Monetary Union (EMU). Fiscal compression (involving FIM 22 billion of government expenditure cuts amounting to 4% of GDP) was successfully accomplished to reduce the deficit and the tax burden with a sum total of FIM 57 billion of permanent cuts by end-1999 (equivalent to 10% of the 1996 GDP). Most of these cuts were in education, health and social welfare putting to rest the debate on how to reconcile the welfare state with EU accession. Gross Domestic Investment during 1990–97 was negative with an annual average contraction of −5.7% corresponding to an average annual increase of 1.1% in GDP (both figures according to World Development Report 1998). The export of goods and services grew in the corresponding period by an annual average of 9.3%. Private consumption demand as a proportion of GDP remained at the same level in the 1990s as in the 1980s, i.e. at 53% of GDP. Trade in goods and services accounted for about 73% of Finnish GDP in 2017.

Although the net external debt has remained high in the region of 28% of GDP, the sterling export performance raised the external current account surplus to a record of 5.5% until the financial crisis in 2008. It remains unclear whether

Finland's public finances are prepared for the sizable demographic shock that it is undergoing, the risk of overheating, the required flexibility in fiscal policy and in the labour market to offset the loss of competitive devaluation as an instrument to promote exports after adopting the Euro in place of the markka. The exchange rate parity was fixed at €1 = FIM 5.94573 when Finland entered the exchange rate mechanism enroute to adopting the Euro as its new currency. Finland's industrial structure radically changed in the 1990s, and the previous two decades have witnessed cataclysmic transformations with large-scale redundancies. The development of high-tech firms, a process associated with the growth phase of the 1980s, intensified. Manufacturing capacity underwent considerable restructuring with growth in telecom, electronics, metals and chemicals and a shrinkage in paper and pulp, wood and wood-based industries.

Finland's export growth began to slow down in the second half of 1998. This was not because of the East Asian crisis. Asia did not account for a high proportion of Finnish exports, and Finnish exports to China and Hong Kong grew by over 60% in 1998, more than compensating for the combined losses from export slowdowns in trade with Malaysia, South Korea, the Philippines, Thailand and Indonesia. Finnish exports within the EU and to USA were adversely affected due to competitive pressures. Growth in techno-electrical industries remained buoyant in double-digit figures (29% in electronics and 50% in telecom), and housing construction activity in the Greater Helsinki area showed remarkable upturn with modest growth annualised at 3% in wood and paper and chemicals but GDP contribution of the aggregate of all other sectors was less than 1% in 1998. The size of the Finnish economy was estimated to be 216 billion Euros in 2017 in absolute terms and 173 billion Euros in PPP terms. About 60% of Finland's population (about 3 million) belongs to the economically active age group. The stock market capitalisation at 63 billion dollars is a trifle misleading because it also includes value of houses and other buildings as assets held by stock issue. There were 141 firms listed on the Helsinki Stock Exchange (fewer are actively traded) in September 2018. The preponderance of firms (listed and unlisted) partially reflects the enormous spread of 33% between the peak marginal individual tax rate (53%) and the corporate tax rate (20%).

Finland's challenges comprise stimulating the domestic economy, developing trade and designing profitable returns on foreign direct investment (FDI) to provide incentives against capital flight and out-migration of talent. The regional spread of economic growth is also linked to international specialisation with eight relevant urban infrastructure zones: Helsinki–Tampere, Southern coastal areas, Karelian development corridor (Salpausselkä zone) extending to the harbour in Hanko, Turku, Naantali, the Kokemäenjoki river valley linking the West coast harbours Pori and Rauma to industrial centres in central Finland by railroad networks, the Kymijoki river valley important for the forest industry, the Perämeri coastal zone (Raahe–Oulu–Kemi–Tornio), Central Finland and Merenkurkku linking Vaasa to Kokkola.

International Orientation of Finnish Firms

Finnish firms originally developed their international orientation historically from two sources, trade in wood along with paper and pulp products as commodities and from trade with Russia as a follow-through of the customs union in the Grand Duchy days and the war reparation period after 1955. The diffusion of German technology and Swedish and Swedish-speaking Finnish private investment was supplemented by state initiatives in mining and manufacturing and also in the development of technologies with the gradual emergence of indigenous Finnish entrepreneurship in the late nineteenth century.

The category of Finland's highest valued exports is machinery and transport equipment. Of this, 57% of the exports are to other EU countries and 60% of all Finnish imports are also sourced from within the EU, the comparative figure for India being 25%. Germany replaced Russia as Finland's largest trading partner in the 1990s with trade equally balanced between exports and imports. Germany remains Finland's largest trading partner in 2018 with Sweden second. The third and fourth places in Finnish imports belong to Russia and China but in exports USA is third and the Netherlands, fourth.

In Asia, the main direction of Finnish imports is China, Korea, Taiwan, India, Thailand, Indonesia and Singapore in that order. The important countries for Finnish exports to Asia listed by value of exports are China, India, Singapore, Thailand, Taiwan and Indonesia. Trade with China in terms of both exports (€2,680 million) and imports (€4,067 million) taken together is eight times larger than the Finnish trade with India (exports to India €521 million and imports from India €329 million). Chinese trade stresses Finland's balance of trade being unbalanced in favour of China, whereas Indian trade contributes to Finland a positive balance of trade which is offset by services where India is a net exporter to Finland. Were Finland to expand manufacturing in India and import services from India through joint ventures with Finnish participation, the negative gap in Finland's balance of payments (with China, and also worldwide) could be corrected quite swiftly.

Finnish internationalisation was initially associated with increased levels of outward foreign direct investment to all Nordic countries during the 1980s and the 1990s. In FDI inflows of Finland, it is UK, rather than Germany, which is the main source country for Finland, followed by Germany, Sweden and USA. Finnish outward FDI is mainly directed to Sweden, Switzerland, Germany and France. After considering outward FDI flows from Finland, Finnish firms, in the net, tend to export capital to Sweden and Germany most years. It is not clear whether the acquisition of Finnish equity abroad by conversion of debt to equity really involves any capital inflow at all. This doubt arises because inflows from the UK are associated with change of ownership of companies in Finland according to the Central Bank of Finland reports.

The forest cluster is traditionally regarded as the mainstay of Finnish prosperity. Commodity exports from this cluster used to account for 40% of total national exports, with Finland being the largest exporter of paper and paperboard in the world. Despite modest sales growth, Finland's share of the world market in paper and paperboard has shrunk. This is due to the creation of domestic capacity in other countries, and with Germany and England as competing locations in Europe for new capacity. Also, profitability of the industry is out of national control without the instrument of competitive devaluation because of Economic and Monetary Union (EMU). There are also more but smaller-sized orders outside EU, and the fibre shortage is in hardwood, which Finland imports from Russia. Volume leaders like UPM-Kymmene, Stora Enso and M-Real have all been dismantling capacity in Finland while creating new capacity elsewhere. There are fewer than 40 significant buyers in the whole of Europe for paper and paperboard machinery and fibre processing machinery. This points to the growing interest of firms like Ahlström and Valmet to link fresh investment abroad.

The metal manufacturers like SSAB (formerly, Rautaruukki), Ovako and Outokumpu having specialised in high-grade structurals have an incentive to invest in finishing lines (for construction structurals and automotives) closer to the customer too. Energy firms like IVO-Neste and ancillary units connected to them also find their markets saturated in the neighbourhood and must look further to where their technology investments and electrical manufacturing expertise are in demand. The core investments in Finland require to be supported by growing market access where economies are growing. This is also true of firms in environmental technologies whose growth has been linked to industries in forestry, energy, chemicals and metals and which now engineer solutions and systems closer to customers abroad. The higher logistics costs of transportation equipment firms further point to the need to locate their services and infrastructure closer to ports and mines in the world's growing areas.

There are no raw material advantages in Finland for the chemical industry. When linkage effects with forestry weaken, chemical firms also have an incentive to relocate. Kemira and Kiilto are exceptions having developed speciality pigments and chemicals and gained worldwide recognition. Kone and Partek in construction industry were early internationalisers in recognition of the cyclical nature of the industry. Energy policy will remain a priority because Finland imports oil. Two additional nuclear power stations are going to be built in addition to the four in use and one under construction. Mineral fuels, rare earths such as lithium, cobalt, tungsten, tar-based organic chemicals, plastics, articles made of wood and wood charcoal, iron and steel products, nuclear reactors and pressure vessels, electrical equipment and sound and acoustics machinery, cinematographic, optical and photographic products, are now the leading export items.

Another noticeable trend in Finland is consolidation of firms through hectic merger and acquisition activity in all of the identifiable clusters regarded as the pillars of the economy. Since the industrial and financial sectors have been closely linked, and for other reasons too, the financial sector is scrambling to consolidate and many banks and insurance companies have already done so. In pharmaceuticals, the introduction of the new patent regime has reduced the number of Finnish players from thirteen to two. Many of these consolidations involved firms in

Sweden, UK and USA, and it has been difficult to distinguish acquisitions from mergers. What has made the task of business researchers tricky is also the Finnish penchant for changing company names to new names and then changing some other group company's name to the old company's name. This makes it difficult to make inter-temporal comparisons of a company just by its old name or current name.

As the industrial profile of Finland changes with restructurings in the strong production and traded sectors as part of the consolidation trends in the EU, factor returns and production shares of Finnish firms relative to the EU-28 can provide clues to Finland's revealed comparative advantage. The Confederation of Finnish Industries (EK) continues to lobby for tax reforms, more internationalisation, support to small and medium enterprises, and increased labour market flexibility. The trade unions have become weak except for the unions of firemen, doctors, nurses, pilots and drivers in the transport sector. Since mid-2010, the European Central Bank (ECB) has taken small steps to move away from 'enhanced credit easing' but continues to make 'sterilised' purchases of Euro area government bonds and private sector assets in secondary markets in order to keep peripheral bond yields in check. There is opposition in Germany to any open-ended commitment, but central bank support in some form can nevertheless be expected to continue for as long as liquidity and solvency concerns about Euro area members persist.

India: Discovery or Invention?

India is an old confluence of cultural unity but a young country as a political unit unified within its present geographical boundaries only since 1947. At no previous juncture in history was India so unified. When we take a historical perspective and examine the greatest of empires, Emperor Ashoka's kingdom did not extend to all the Southern parts and at the height of Akbar's Rule, he did not have full control over the Deccan and the Eastern and North-eastern parts. Beginning with the loss of Bengal in 1757 to the East India Company, parts of India kept falling like dominoes until the British Crown took over governance directly in 1858 (India Office Records 1858).

The 190-year period of British colonisation from 1757 to 1947 has been considered as an era of darkness associated with de-industrialisation, forced cultivation of cash crops such as indigo, famines, export of slave labour to plantations in the Caribbean and unjust extraction of natural resources to be shipped abroad for the UK (Tharoor 2016). India is a case of late industrialisation because the hegemony of the three port economies of Bombay (now renamed Mumbai), Madras (now renamed Chennai) and Calcutta (now renamed Kolkata) over two centuries bypassed development in the rest of the country ruled by the British. The economy flourished mainly on trade with unjust enrichment and classical port-hinterland economics. Some of the larger princely States like Mysore, Hyderabad, Kashmir, Patiala, Indore, Gwalior, Baroda and Jaipur had their own native rulers who made peace with the British and undertook some development measures within their kingdoms.

Indian independence was marred by the bloodshed of the partition and the invasion of Kashmir soon after independence. The constitution was promulgated in 1950. The development agenda focused on infrastructure, national defence, education, food security, financial institutions and industrialisation with public sector investments in steel, railways, heavy machinery, aeronautics, machine tools, electronics and telecommunications. A blueprint for industrial planning called 'The Bombay Plan' had been made by a group of industrialists before independence. After independence, the Planning Commission was established and India embarked on a system of five-year plans in 1951. Planning was alongside the free market economy where capital was rationed and production of goods and services limited by licences in a bid to conserve scarce investible capital. During the first three decades after India became independent, the growth of the Indian economy was characterised by slow and steady average rate of about 4% per annum which the Economist Raj Krishna labelled as 'Hindu rate of growth'. The trauma of political invasion by a trading company, the East India Company, had reinforced an 'invader-in-the-mind' mentality that fuelled xenophobia. This period was marked by an anti-trade rhetoric of self-sufficiency and self-reliance that guided industrial, trade and investment policies until 1991. This accounts for the large protected domestic sector that was opened to competition of the rest of the world for the first time in the 1990s with economic reforms associated with facilitating liberalisation, privatisation and globalisation. In 1991, the industrial licensing system was abolished and foreign direct investment welcomed.

Since 1991, production, investment and trade have grown rapidly and relentlessly and confirmed the appropriateness of the policy change decision. Only a few domestic businesses collapsed confirming the competitive strength of the domestic industrial base. Growth of the Indian economy accelerated from 6% per annum during 1985–90 to 6.8% during the five-year period 1992–97 reaching a high of 7.5% per annum during the period 1994–95 to 1996–97. The drop to 5% annual growth in 1997–98 was mainly due to a bad year in agriculture (with −2% change over the previous year, including high drama over onion shortage, an important ingredient of Indian cuisine) and some slowdown in a few sectors of industry such as mining. India's 5% annual growth rate was among the highest growth rates in the world economy of those times. Since then, the GDP growth rate continued to be in the range 5.5–7.5% reaching a peak of 9% in 2006–07 before the global financial meltdown of 2008. The period after that witnessed a return to high GDP growth rates, and the current annual growth rate of 7.6% is the highest among all major economies of the world.

The years of democratic self-governance since independence brought about remarkable transformations. Poverty ratios have systematically and continuously declined, although the number of the poor remained the same due to population increases. During the period 1973–98, the poverty ratio declined from 55% to under 33%, an indicator of rising distributive shares in private consumption. On current trends, poverty ratios are estimated to reach near zero sometime between 2030 and

2040 depending on the growth rate. India's consumer base is highly diverse. About 587 million of its population belongs to the economically active age group of which about 40 million are considered involuntarily unemployed on the basis of registration.

A daily wage of about INR 400 per day (the average minimum wage equivalent to 5 Euros) in India corresponds to a basket of consumption of Euro 400 per month in Finland (approximately equal to the minimum income support for one person in Finland). India's price level (for equivalent quality) is generally lower for food and beverages and clothing and transportation but higher than Finland for industrial goods, consumer durables and housing. The differences in post-tax salary incomes in India are 100:1 between the highest paid and the least paid salary earners. In 2018, just under 350 million of India's 1.32 billion population consumed to the average European consumption standards. However, this figure is the same size as the EU market, although the effort required in preparing to access this market may appear a formidable complex endeavour to small overseas firms. Indicative of growth conditions in domestic consumer durables is the production of consumer electronics (production of mobile phones, television sets growing annually at 25%, watches and cameras by 20%, VCRs and washing machines by 8%), and the growth in education, health, construction, tourism and telematics is indicative of the expansion in services where private rates of return exceed those in manufacturing.

Spatially dispersed industrialisation has witnessed the growth of 35 major urban centres and thousands of industrial sites because the planning model spaced diffusion of technology and public investments across the country. State governments reinforce (through their elected legislatures) industrial policies concurrently with the central government as well as autonomously. Comprising a mix of public and private investment, the industrial structure reflects a production base that is large, growing and comprehensive. Competition policies and performance criteria reinforced after revoking the industrial licensing system in 1991 successfully limited losses of public enterprises whose profits in 1997 and 1998 exceed expectations. After weeding out sick public sector enterprises (PSEs), all except seven of these firms make profits under conditions of competition from the private sector. The nine best ones are colloquially referred to as '*navratnas*' (nine jewels). This is a different situation from countries where wholesale privatisation is regarded as the only solution to an ailing public sector. Public enterprises will continue in India (with revenue-raising equity divestments to reduce government participation to under 49%). No new investments are being made to promote public enterprises in any industry where private investment is adequate from a development and consumer perspective.

The high growth sectors are energy, transportation, infrastructure, chemicals, construction and machine-building. IT, food and beverages, chemicals, electronics, iron and steel, metal manufactures, textile manufacturing and handicrafts are the fastest growing export sectors. The stock market is a major source of funds for industrial capital through invited public subscription besides private equity, consortia equity, credit lines and term loans from banks and financial institutions. As many as 1,088,780 active companies were registered under the Companies Act which points to the likelihood that several of them could have potential interest in developing business relations outside India. There are 21 stock exchanges in India where companies can be listed for trading. Financial institutions (like Unit Trust of India (UTI), Industrial Development Bank of India, Industrial Finance Corporation of India) combine features of widely held mutual funds with merchant banking and as sources of venture capital. A speculative run on UTI in 1998 in the wake of the Asian crisis demonstrated the resilience of this institution when it absorbed a loss of INR 101.48 billion in the year ended June 1998, remained profitable and paid higher dividends to its investors.

In India, the commercial vehicle sector and the petrochemical sector are usually good indicators of industrial growth in times of uncertainty because of their linkage effects with other sectors. Both have registered sharp uptrend in production during 2010–18. Steel, cement, hotels and paper industries also indicate a distinct growth upsurge. The real estate market is buoyant, and the construction industry is booming. An export slowdown in 2018 occurred partly because of slowdown in the world economy and also because the accelerated growth rates in Indian trade and investment following euphoria over new policies are settling down. This reflects a more mature phase towards full capital account convertibility in future of a currency that has already been made convertible for trade and current account transactions.

The strain on public finances to sustain rural development and the capacity of the financial sector to keep pace with internationalisation remains unclear, though no Indian banking company has ever collapsed. The statutory capital adequacy ratio in India is 2% higher than the Basel international norm. No foreign debt obligation has ever been reneged requiring renegotiation. The expansion of trade and technology diffusion in a market-driven mode remains important as India balances the needs of its poor with the aspirations of the growing middle class and the imperatives of internationalisation.

Actions to liberalise the foreign direct investment (FDI) regime helped increase FDI inflows by 20%. Fiscal deficits, the current account deficits and inflation were all higher than before, reflecting in part higher international oil prices. Demonetisation did not succeed in extinguishing the stashes of black money that it targeted and over 99% of the currency was swapped with new notes. But it yielded considerable information to target better fiscal compliance in future. The tax base almost doubled between 2014 and 2018. Another irritant, the facilitating of 'exits' and asset restructuring had been one of India's intractable challenges, evoking the generalisation that India believed in perpetual reincarnation and metamorphoses of ailing enterprises moving from licensed socialism with limited entry to competitive markets without exit. The new time-bound insolvency resolution process is now in place to correct this.

India has two chronic macroeconomic vulnerabilities; India's fiscal and current accounts both tend to deteriorate when oil prices rise. This is also true in Finland. This mutual lament can be jointly addressed with new non-conventional energy projects in both countries by leveraging the technologies that each country has developed. Addressing the current account vulnerability requires raising the trajectory of export growth or increasing returns from foreign direct investment.

Finland no longer has the instrument of currency devaluation to boost exports because the Euro is governed by the European Central Bank and countries like Germany which have ambitious FDI programmes would not favour a weak Euro. In India, there is always the temptation to let the rupee depreciate in a bid to stimulate exports although that is myopic because it also makes imports, outward FDI and remitted factor earnings from India more expensive.

Internationally competitive manufacturing has been a goal of the Make in India programme, but the declining manufacturing export–GDP ratio and manufacturing trade balance indicate that Indian manufacturing lacks productivity and is import-dependent. Public auctions for spectrum, coal and infrastructure projects introduced some transparency, but they also came in for criticism because the shift from 'crony socialism to stigmatised capitalism' (as the Economic Survey 2017–18 puts it) continues to show up business houses close to politicians in power grabbing many new contracts. This produces incessant clamour for investigations to be undertaken for unearthing wrongdoings.

International Orientation of Indian Firms

Indian firms initially developed their international orientation from trading in primary commodities (cotton, jute, rice, minerals, gems and jewellery, spices, tea, rubber, etc.) and in manufactured textiles and chemicals, slowly diversifying into a range of manufactured goods. The main motive was the earning of foreign exchange to finance firm-specific imports under an exchange control regime. It was not unusual for a light engineering firm to be exporting tea or shrimps or bras as a side business. European and American multinationals, some of which (like Unilever, Colgate, Nestle, BAT) had a presence predating independence, were mainly in consumer products marketing supported by international brands and manufacturing. They thrived under the licensing system because equal treatment of incorporated entities also afforded them protection from competition. Engineering firms like Larsen & Toubro, Siemens, Andrew Yule represented foreign investments in industrial products and were also protected like their public sector competitors.

The direction of trade as well as its composition did not change much until the 1970s when the construction boom in the Middle East diversified into trade in construction equipment and services and the Indo-Soviet Treaty expanded trade under rupee-rouble arrangements. The software boom since the 1980s increased the proportion of service trade with the North American region. Business contact with Japan expanded after 1984 and led to expansion of electronics trade and trade in automobile ancillaries and engineering with Southeast Asia and East Asia. Bilateral initiatives increased EU-India trade in the direction of Germany and France which sought to challenge UK's special position with respect to historical ties and Germany became India's largest trading partner in the 1990s. The South Americas and Nordic Europe remained neglected, and India's large and growing sheltered domestic market provided no incentives to search for new export markets until 1991. The stock market expansion, first in the 1970s on the back of mandated Foreign Exchange Regulation Act (FERA) dilutions and in the 1980s with expansion of sectors like petrochemicals and a whole range of consumer durables called 'white goods', did not require firms to seek capital abroad. The first Eurobonds and global depository receipts (GDRs) were raised in 1992–93. Euro issues by Indian companies are miniscule. About 400 additional foreign companies from the EU register in India every year, and each is involved in an average of five collaborations.

The duty drawback facilities, tax exemptions, foreign trips and easier access to rationed foreign exchange weighed prominently among the motives for international business among Indian entrepreneurs. Asian cities like Bangkok, Singapore and Hong Kong and English-speaking East Africa were the mainstay of Indian traders. Trade with UK, Germany, France, the Netherlands, Sweden, USA was the province of large Indian firms (business houses like the Tatas and Birlas) and multinational subsidiaries and joint ventures. Among India's trading partners, the top five countries with which India has a negative bilateral trade balance are China, Switzerland, Saudi Arabia, Iraq and South Korea. The top five countries with which India has a surplus trade balance are USA, UAE, Bangladesh, Nepal and the UK.

India's highest trade deficit is with China. China's share in India's total trade deficit increased from 20.3% in 2012–13 to 47.1% in 2016–17, and it stood at 43.2% in 2017–18 (April–September). According to the Economic Survey 2017–18, India's major items of imports from China are telephone sets including mobiles, automatic data processing machines, diodes and other semiconductor devices, electronic devices, chemical fertilisers, etc. India's major items of exports to China are cotton yarn, copper and copper alloys, granite, aluminium ores, other fixed vegetable fats and oils, cyclic hydrocarbons, cotton, polymers and iron ore. In the case of Switzerland, the trade deficit is mainly due to import of gold. This deficit has fallen in the last two years. Moreover, a part of it is used in exports. In the case of Saudi Arabia and Iraq, the deficit is due to crude oil imports, while for South Korea it is due to import of electrical machinery and equipments and iron and steel[3] (Economic Survey 2017–2018 Chap. 6, 2018).

Invisibles in India's Balance of Payments

Information technology (IT) and IT-enabled services have opened up a huge market spawning a burgeoning skilled labour force. The contribution of earnings from invisibles in India's external account is an important balancing factor in India's trade. Net invisible earnings that were less than €3 billion until 1993–94 rose to

---

[3]http://mofapp.nic.in:8080/economicsurvey/pdf/080-098_Chapter_06_Economic_Survey_2017-18.pdf.

over €24 billion by the year end March 2005 and were estimated to be about €90 billion in 2017–18. IT services have driven this increase. Net invisibles have grown at an annual rate of 15% in dollar terms during 2000–2018. The annual growth rate of merchandise exports during the same period was about 9%.

Net invisibles surplus fell from US$118.1 billion in 2014–15 to US$107.9 billion in 2015–16 and US$97.1 billion in 2016–17. However, in the first half of 2017–18 there has been an increase in net invisibles surplus to US$52.5 billion from US$45.6 billion in the first half of 2016–17, with increase observed in both net services and net private transfers. Net service receipts increased by 14.6% on a year-to-year comparison with the first half of 2017–18, primarily on account of the rise in net earnings from travel and telecommunications, and computer-related information technology services. Net travel receipts more than doubled, as foreign tourist arrivals increased significantly during the first half of 2017–18. Notwithstanding uncertainties in the Indian IT industry from tougher visa policies in some countries, software exports recorded a growth of 2.3% in the first half of 2017–18 and the weaker rupee after August 2018 will actually boost profits of Indian IT companies. According to the official statistics of the Government of India, private transfer receipts, consisting chiefly of remittances by Indian diaspora working abroad, increased by 10% to US$33.5 billion in the first half of 2017–18 over the corresponding period of the previous year.

According to the World Bank (2017), India is one of the major recipients of cross-border remittances, followed by China, the Philippines and Mexico. However, the private transfers (gross) inflows to India declined by 6.1% in 2015–16 and 6.5% in 2016–17. This was due to constrained labour market conditions in the source countries, particularly Gulf Cooperation Council (GCC) countries, largely caused by the fall in international crude oil prices. Gross private transfer inflows fell to US$65.6 billion and US$61.3 billion in 2015–16 and 2016–17, respectively, from US$69.8 billion in 2014–15. According to the World Bank (2017), the number of Indian workers emigrating to Saudi Arabia (India's third largest remittance sender) dropped from 300,000 in 2015 to 160,000 in 2016, and to the United Arab Emirates (India's largest inward remittance contributor) from 220,000 in 2015 to 160,000 in 2016. Total Indian workers outflow also decreased from 780,000 in 2015 to 510,000 in 2016. Among the structural factors, tightening norms of permitting foreign workers in a post-Trump USA, labour market adjustments in Gulf Cooperation Council (GCC) countries and the surge in anti-immigration sentiments in many countries pose some downside risk. But this also means that there would be talent available to go to non-traditional destination countries such as Finland. In 2017, there were 6,595 Indians of all ages in Finland according to Statistics Finland.

The future of India's policies on investment liberalisation is predicated on the effects of foreign investment on domestic and export growth. Opponents of India's internationalisation (there still exist critics who desire self-reliance) point to the absence of systematic empirical support for the notion that a higher level of foreign ownership is associated with a higher ratio of export sales. An analysis of firm-level data from 1,000 firms listed on the Bombay Stock Exchange shows that foreign firms that invested at levels that gave them control performed better than other firms.

The new economic policies of 1991 increased the number of foreign collaborations and foreign trade when 51% foreign ownership as the general rule with automatic approval in 35 sectors and 100% foreign ownership in some sectors (e.g. for establishing asset management companies) were allowed. Between 1970 and 1990, the twenty-year period saw a mere 4,196 foreign collaborations, the corresponding figure during 1991–96 was 9,885 and during 1997–2018 it was 16,112. Foreign direct investment (FDI) inflows have been the largest in telecom, electrical machinery, energy and chemicals which account for just over half of the FDI inflows. Other sectors which have been considered attractive by foreign investors are oil exploration and refining, power generation, transport equipment, chemicals, basic metals, non-electrical machinery, packaged foods and beverages, textiles, construction and leather.

India's traditional trade with the EU suffered after Turkey joined the customs union of the EU. It suffered again in the aftermath of devaluations in East and Southeast Asia. China, Turkey and USA have larger shares of the EU's import market for textiles. In leather and leather goods, India remains the leader but faces competition from China, Brazil, Pakistan and USA. In gems and jewellery, Israel, Switzerland and Thailand have the same shares as India. In marine products, India's export share is smaller than Norway, Iceland, USA, Argentina and Thailand. In electronics, Singapore, Taiwan, Malaysia and South Korea have larger shares. The most unimpressive of Indian export sectors is chemicals where Indian industry is strong and where China's share of the EU market is four times India's. In carpets, Iran and Nepal have emerged as major competitors to India for the EU market.

Home and Host Government Intervention in India and Finland

Government policies at the national level remain important because much of what is depicted as globalisation is actually bilateral or plurilateral. In government-to-government (G2G) initiatives, the Finland–India Trade Agreement was first made in 1967 and the India–Finland Joint Commission constituted in 1974. There were ten meetings in 24 years, but not much was achieved. The governments identified forest-based industries, environmental industries, energy, ports, electronics and software, packaging, cold-chain systems for food processing, power generation and transmission including coal and biomass gasification-based power and mini-hydel power as areas of potential collaboration. According to the Indian government statistics, Finnish investment in India during 1991–96 was INR 385 million but very few of the 57 'ventures' in which it is claimed to have been made could be found and it is possible that this number was a count largely of representative offices and defunct entities.

There are agreements on double-taxation avoidance, promotion and protection of investments, a cultural agreement, an agreement on hand-woven cotton fabrics, an MOU on textiles, an agreement in science and technology cooperation and others in road transport, power and biotechnology. The Department of Science and Technology and the Department of Biotechnology of the Government of India are part of an agreement on researcher mobility. However, for the most part, these agreements have only touched the tip of the iceberg and much more can be done for symbolic connections to become real bridges and networks of value to their constituents by taking bigger leaps.

Following the air service agreement in 1995, a direct flight between Finland and India was introduced by Finnair in 2006 after eleven years. Air India has not asked for a corresponding slot till date. Delhi and Helsinki are now connected by a direct flight of Finnair but the Mumbai–Helsinki flight was discontinued after a short period. Finnair announced a new Goa–Helsinki direct flight in 2017. Most of the passengers on the Finnair flights are transit passengers proceeding to other destinations than Finland, a testimony to the continuing low volume of direct traffic between the two countries. This reflects on the need for processes and scope of outcomes that could raise the level of engagement and economic contact between Finland and India. The picture portrayed by SITRA Report 56 by Grundström and Lahti (2005) that flights to India were crowded with Finnish civil servants and businessmen is far from reality. Finnair flights have been mainly transporting passengers transiting via Helsinki to or from other countries.

Since Finland is a member of the EU, EU-India relations require mention. When UK joined the EC in 1973, India did not acquire the 'associate' status like French and Belgian ex-colonies and was considered a major independent country like Brazil and China. India was the first Asian country to sign a cooperation agreement with the EC but when EC-ASEAN and the EC-Gulf Co-operation Council agreements were made, despite an exhortation from the European Parliament for an EC-SAARC agreement, nothing happened. EC preferred to develop an India policy rather than a policy for the entire South Asian region on grounds that SAARC was not a viable economic grouping and that the Union of India comprising States shared many characteristics and problems with a uniting Europe.

The most significant government policy changes in India occurred in 1991 when industrial licensing was abolished, public sector reservations were removed, tariffs were reduced, the capital market was opened to foreign investors and India became a member of the Multilateral Investment Guarantee Agency. The adoption of a long-term fiscal policy is accompanied by financial sector reforms and bilateral investment promotion agreements with 46 countries (which include other Nordic countries but not Finland) together with a package of investment incentives for foreign investors. India's package of incentives is unusual because it includes land subsidies, tax holidays, duty-free imports for exporting industries, zero tax on export earnings and equal treatment of foreign companies.

An important area of resource allocation predictability in Indian growth lies in the planning of public expenditure outlays for planned infrastructure development.

Opportunities for firms–domestic and foreign to provide the goods and services for which resources are allocated are transparently known from the host government's declared intentions supported by budgetary outlays, including but not limited to national public finances and multilateral agencies. This neutralises any adverse impact in the pro-cyclicality of the alternative, foreign portfolio investments.

India's declared intent to develop resources in agro-climatic zones should be of particular interest to Finland. The worldwide fibre shortage (especially hardwood fibres) is critical for the pulp and paper industry firms irrespective of where they manufacture. This can be solved with new commercial eco-friendly forest plantations in India in the sub-Himalayan regions which stretch from Himachal Pradesh through Uttar Pradesh, Uttarakhand, Bihar and West Bengal to the North-Eastern States of Arunachal Pradesh, Assam, Meghalaya, Manipur, Tripura and the Andaman and Nicobar Islands. Afforestation of Himachal Pradesh is a declared priority. Sweden's SWEDFOREST has already carried out pilot projects in five States and established the feasibility of commercial forestry without compromising on the environment protection aspects.

The planned outlay for telecommunication is another area. The investments allocated to construction of new urban areas and to railways, ports, airports, roads, environment, forestry and wasteland development, power generation, biomass production, development of islands translate into numerous business opportunities. The planning framework covers all States and Union territories. These opportunities are available to firms, small and large, although the capacity to reap best advantage rests with large companies that typically diversify their involvement geographically to many locations achieving scale economies in management costs as well. The asset growth of the twenty largest firms in India reflects this. For example, the engineering giant Larsen & Toubro increased its asset base, with the help of projects to six times its size every decade since the 1990s. Every large firm among the top 20 firms increased its asset base at least fourfold. The average profit-after-tax of industrial units ranged between 12.6% and 17.5% of capital employed.

Finland's export diversification to Asia occurred in the aftermath of a double devaluation, the sharp reduction in trade due to the collapse of the Soviet Union and the banking crisis, all during the period 1989–91. Hong Kong, Thailand and Singapore were the main target markets, partly because there was Finnish government support for these markets and because Finnish business people found it easier to visit and relate to Singapore, Bangkok and Hong Kong as cities. In the aftermath of the East Asian crisis, much of the trade in these export markets collapsed and there has been a shift in interest to locations like Shanghai, Hanoi and the Indian cities of Hyderabad, Pune, Bangalore, Chennai and towns like Surat and Rajkot in Gujarat, Cochin in Kerala, Visakhapatnam in Andhra Pradesh, Kansbahal in Orissa, Ranchi in Jharkhand, Kashipur in Uttarakhand and Baddi and Kasauli in Himachal Pradesh.

The identified areas of economic and industrial growth in the two countries offer considerable scope for synergies, but this synergy requires to be developed and facilitated. With changes in the role of government, industrial and commercial activity is increasingly left to private initiatives in both countries. Firms need to consolidate their techno-commercial feasibility analysis on new projects through structures of support they require to build based on greater awareness of how macroeconomics of demand and supply interactions in the two countries have micro-economic underpinnings related to these synergies.

For Indian firms to regard Finland as just another part of Europe would be a mistake just as it would also be wrong for Finnish firms to regard India as just another part of Asia or a homogenous territory. Nordic Europe can be distinguished from other parts of Europe on many dimensions and the five nordic countries (Denmark, Finland, Iceland, Norway and Sweden) have their own unifying features in common. In the Union of India, each of the 29 states much like the EU-28 has characteristics that distinguish them from one another, institutionally, culturally and economically. The motives and powerbases of host and home government with respect to industrial policies, FDI, markets and institutions need to be analysed for all the promising areas of identified synergy. To know what opportunities are feasible thus acquires more importance and could precede developing forms of business and the structuring of investments because pursuit of preconceived preferences may actually limit mutual trade and investment out of roadblocks and risk averseness. Indeed, we shall examine later in the book how perceptions differ in both countries from the reality of appropriate entry criteria.

EU firms have been the biggest investors in India. Home countries most strongly represented from the EU in order of magnitude of investment are UK, Germany, the Netherlands, France, Italy and Sweden. The liberalisation of the financial sector drew 23 foreign banks into India, of which 8 are from the EU. The privatisation of the insurance sector has also drawn European insurance firms to India. Over 75% of all the foreign investment went to Maharashtra, Telangana, Andhra Pradesh, West Bengal, Tamil Nadu, Delhi, Gujarat, Orissa and Karnataka. The pace of implementation was fastest in Andhra Pradesh, Gujarat, Madhya Pradesh, Tamil Nadu and Haryana and slowest in Karnataka.

The level of preparedness among Indian firms for doing business in and with European firms varies widely. The star trading houses and manufacturing enterprises have been content with modest volumes and participation in European fairs and exhibitions. Bilateral initiatives are strong in trade and investment links with Germany, France, UK and Sweden. According to the Economic Survey 2017–18, the five largest exporting States in India are Maharashtra, Gujarat, Haryana, Tamil Nadu and Karnataka and the five largest importing States are Maharashtra, Tamil Nadu, Uttar Pradesh, Karnataka and Gujarat. The states with the largest internal trade surpluses are Gujarat, Haryana, Maharashtra, Odisha and Tamil Nadu.

India and Climate Change

India has a wide range of climate. It is possible to experience temperatures between minus 35 °C and plus 40 °C on any day of the year depending on where you choose to be. Certain regions are extremely arid with negligible rainfall, whereas others, like coastal areas and dense forests of the North-east and the Western Ghats, have high humidity and heavy rainfall. The seasonal distribution also varies because the country has some of the world's highest snow-capped mountain ranges in the Himalayas but also plains, plateaus, hilly terrains, deciduous forests as well as mangrove forests, deserts and low-lying marshlands. In the past hundred years, the average maximum temperature has risen by one degree, and at this rate certain coastal land areas in some regions, particularly on the Eastern coast around Puri, could get permanently inundated by rising sea waters. The Eastern coastlines and the Southern Peninsula are vulnerable to frequent storms with gale force winds, cyclones and occasional tsunamis.

In August 2018, the unprecedented inundation of Kerala and Karnataka in the South and Nagaland in the North-east wreaked havoc and reminded everyone of the urgency and significance of addressing issues related to climate change. Yet, there were parts of Gujarat, Rajasthan, Madhya Pradesh and West Bengal that suffered from drought during the same period. Extreme rainfall events (more than 100 mm in a day) are increasing at a decennial growth rate of 6% during the period 1901–2018. India has engaged seriously with actions under the UN Framework Convention on Climate Change and in developing guidelines for implementing the Paris Agreement on Climate Change. In 2018, the Conference of Parties (COP 24) at Katowice also witnessed India's continued support to international commitments. This augurs well for Indo-Finnish potential collaboration on matters of climate change and has potential to be expanded beyond bilateral benefits towards developing third-country business as well.

The Indian Economy's Trajectory

Trade and foreign direct investments play an important part in India's economic growth. According to India's National Accounts Statistics, the ratio of gross fixed capital formation to GDP rose from 26.5% in 2003, to a high of 35.6% in 2007, and slid to 26.4% in 2017. The growth rate of capital spending by the government (at current prices) increased from an average of about 7% in 2012–13 to over 21% in 2015–16. The share of private corporate sector in total investment increased from 36% in 2011–12 to 41% in 2015–16 making it the largest sector investing in the economy.

The Economic Survey 2017–18 provides details of new infrastructure investment outlays many of which will involve the private sector. In roads, these include new national highways (NHs), for converting state highways (SHs) into NHs. As of September 2017, the length of roadways was 115,530 km of NHs along with 176,166 km of SHs and 5,326,166 km of other roads. A new umbrella programme, '*Bharatmala Pariyojana*' (meaning Circumambulatory India Garlanding Scheme) for holistic highway development, is progressing well. Indian Railways is also expanding capacity and performance. During April–September 2017, Indian Railways carried 558.1 million tonnes of revenue earning freight. About 425 km of metro rail systems are operational and about 684 km are under construction in various cities across India.

In ports, cargo traffic handled at major ports during 2017–18 was 643 million tonnes. Under the Sagar Mala Programme for port-led development along Indian coastline, 289 projects worth €31 billion are at various stages of implementation. In telecom, under 'Bharat Net' and 'Digital India' programmes aimed at converting all of India into a digital economy, by 2017, the number of subscribers had reached 1,207 million (502 million in rural areas; 705 million in urban areas). In civil aviation, the growth rate was 16% on a passenger base of about 130 million with new initiatives on air services, airport development and regional connectivity with the UDAN scheme with an affordable fare level. In power, the installed power generation capacity in the country reached 330,861 MW in 2017 and there is a target of 100% electrification by 2019 with a new scheme, Saubhagya (Pradhan Mantri Sahaj Bijli Har Ghar Yojana).

The response from foreign investors speaks for itself. According to the Economic Survey 2017–18, the FDI equity inflows grew by 8.7% during 2017–18. Total FDI inflows grew by 8%, i.e. US$60.08 billion in 2016–17 in comparison with US$55.56 billion of the previous year. This was the highest FDI inflow ever for any particular financial year. In 2017–18, till September, the inflow of total FDI was US$33.75 billion. In terms of share in FDI equity inflows, Mauritius, Singapore and Japan have been top three countries in India contributing 36.17, 20.03 and 10.83% of the total FDI equity inflows during 2016–17.[4] In terms of the sectors receiving FDI equity inflows, services (finance, banking, insurance, etc.), telecommunications and computer software and hardware have been the top three sectors with a share of 19.97, 12.80 and 8.40%, respectively[5] (Chap. 08, Economic Survey 2017–18).

The policy environment in India has maintained the direction of economic liberalisation and growth despite changes in the character of coalitions that formed the government between 1991 and 2014 when the BJP came to power with its own majority. Macroeconomic, industrial, financial, trade and fiscal policies have been stable, consistent and predictable, and there has not been any major economic crisis since 1991. Company law reform, implementation of competition policy, simplification of asset restructuring, introduction of nationwide general sales tax, rationalisation of tax rates including GST slabs, speeding up of bankruptcy and insolvency procedures, allowing foreign participants (foreign institutional investors) in both equity and debt markets, removing restrictions in foreign direct investment, reduction in tariff and non-tariff barriers, and an exchange rate policy sensitive to market conditions are some of the important reforms that have provided enterprises a more liberal operating climate.

---

[4]The FDI inflows to India from Mauritius and Singapore contain inflows from many other countries that are routed through these two countries for fiscal advantages and ease of control.
[5]http://mofapp.nic.in:8080/economicsurvey/pdf/120-150_Chapter_08_Economic_Survey_2017-18.pdf.

The direction of policy changes is transparently predictable. Government policies are expected to accelerate development by balancing what markets can do with where the government needs to intervene for the well-being of weaker and poorer sections of society by providing resources for sanitation, health care, education and basic infrastructure services with social safety nets for the economically disadvantaged.

The changing economy is characterised by shifts in the pattern of consumption by households. The consumer expenditure surveys conducted by NCAER reveal that this is so for both urban and rural households. This is reflected in the high growth sectors of organised manufacturing activity which are petroleum and plastic products, food products, transport equipment and chemicals and pharmaceuticals. If we go by gross fixed capital formation rubber, plastic and petroleum products followed by wood and wood products (including furniture and fixtures) and beverages, tobacco and related products are the other groups representing the highest growth of investment (gross fixed capital formation, GFCF). Energy (in the form of the oil bill) dominates India's imports, although capital goods also feature prominently. The European Union and the USA are the largest trade partners for India, but China is emerging as an important source of imports as well as a destination for exports. Even the traditionally important partner, Japan, has been overtaken by China in volume of trade.

The Indian Capital Market has expanded manifold since the liberalisation of the Indian Economy in 1991, and there are several hundred public issues every year that raise capital in the form of equity from the public and institutional investors. In the 12-month period 2017–18, there were 214 public issues that mobilised about €17 billion from the public. The benchmark index of the Bombay Stock Exchange (BSE), BSE SENSEX, stood at a high of 36,778 points as on 1 February 2019, witnessing a gain of 24.2% from its closing of 29,621 points on 31 March 2017. NIFTY 50, the benchmark index of the National Stock Exchange (NSE), closed at a new high of 10,893 points on 1 February 2019, witnessing a gain of 18.7% from its closing of 9,174 points as on 31 March 2017.

Compost Heap of Indian Politics

In the country section on Finland in this chapter, the political spectrum of parties was described together with their declared manifestoes. This is difficult to replicate in describing Indian parliamentary politics for three reasons. First, the number of political parties is large (2,044 in 2018) and there are numerous strong regional parties alongside national parties. Secondly, besides the central government and the Parliament of India in New Delhi, there are as many as 29 elected state governments with assemblies to make laws and 7 union territories—some of which also have elected assemblies that can make laws. Thirdly, the Finnish parliamentary system is unicameral, whereas the Indian system is bicameral with representation in the Upper House (Rajya Sabha) also playing a part in voting on proposals requiring majority support from both houses of Parliament and the representation in the Rajya Sabha is indirect on the basis of seats held in the State Legislative Assemblies.

Yet, the Indian system is unitary, not federal, with residuary powers vesting in the union unlike the USA where residuary powers vest in the states. Anyone intending to do business in India should get familiarised with what subjects are legislated exclusively by the centre and which subjects are only legislated by the states. There is also a Concurrent List of subjects on which the centre and the state can both make laws. We will return to this in Chap. 7 after discussing institutional diversity. For now, to understand the shifting sands of alliances in Indian politics, we may use the analogy of a compost heap in ferment to point out the following elements around which coalescing crystallisations can be noticed:

Heap 1 The Congress and its 'allies of convenience' proclaiming commitment to secular ideology, inclusive growth, pro-human rights protection for minorities with a nationalism notion grounded in pluralism packaged with expectations that the voters are eternally grateful for the Congress-led freedom struggle for India's independence as the basis for family claims to continuing dynastic control over the party; tainted by allegations of scams in coal block allocations, telecom spectrum auctioning and defence deals, institutional capture and role of party leaders in allowing Sikhs to be killed in Delhi the 1984 backlash after Indira Gandhi's assassination by her Sikh bodyguards.

Heap 2 The Bharatiya Janata Party (BJP) and its allies with great emphasis on national security, pro-poor schemes, resource allocations for infrastructure, promise of cleaner water, hygiene and sanitation, promises around ease of doing business, claims to clean administration alongside allegations by the opposition parties of crony capitalism. Hindutva nationalism as ideology (cow protection, promises of building a Hindu temple for Rama on the site of the disputed land where a mosque was destroyed in 1992) and exercise of state power to silence protests, curtailment of labour rights, student protests and a declared anti-immigrants stance. Tainted by the killings of Muslims in the Gujarat riots and in police encounters widely believed to have been staged despite acquittals of accused because 94 prosecution witnesses did not depose in court. For the first time in India's electoral history, there is no elected Muslim in the majority party's parliamentary representation.

Heap 3 Socialist parties of various hues and vintages such as the Samajwadi Party (which can also be considered as a caste-based party in Heap 4) and the West Bengal-based Trinamool Congress with proclaimed commitment to justice for all and rule of law, secularism and development agenda; appeal to motherhood, strengthening communities at the grass roots, declared concern for dignity and humanity for all, empathy for immigrants. Several political parties in this heap are tainted by allegations of supporting private profiteering, financial scams, mining concessions and preventing candidates from registering as candidates in local elections.

Heap 4 Caste-based political parties such as Bahujan Samaj Party and Rashtriya Janata Dal broadening their support base to include all; special promises for backward classes and castes and an inclusive society with a socialist ideology;

pro-farmers, pro-workers. Tainted by allegations over nepotism, corruption from previous spells in governance and hoarding black money. Seat adjustments and alliances between parties in Heap 3 and Heap 4 are quite likely in national elections.

Heap 5 Regional parties such as Telugu Desam, DMK, ADMK (factions of the AIADMK), Akali Dal, Biju Janata Dal, YSR Congress, Nationalist Congress Party and Aam Aadmi Party with a stake in allying for power with national coalitions proclaiming a pro-poor development agenda, focus on regional issues, with a history of populist announcements for farmers, women, consumers, particular communities. Tainted by allegations in corruption scandals and flexibility for compromises and horse-trading. Alliances and seat adjustments of Heap 5 parties with parties in Heaps 1 and 2 are more likely, but it is also possible that some of these could ally with parties in Heaps 3 and 4.

Heap 6 Communist parties trying to renew the appeal of democratic communism independent of Russia and China with a support base from peasants, workers and particularly tribal communities with a reputation for clean administration and good governance but lacking in money power to canvass in elections.

The spectrum of Indian political parties is largely groupable in coalitions around these six heaps. The intelligent reader would be able to identify when the time arises who is in which heap because Indian politicians are very flexible. As the saying goes, 'A week is a long time in politics'. When an election result does not produce a clear majority, horse-trading ensues involving inducements of ministerial berths or straight cash as the norm. It is anybody's guess whether the 2019 general elections will produce a majority for any party or whether a hung parliament will witness a scramble for coalition formation in which a national or regional leader could well emerge as a compromise candidate for the position of Prime Minister. Whatever be the outcome, governments with political parties of all hues have remained committed to the long-term economic policy agenda ushered in 1991. And this is why investors and businesses need not expect any radical shifts in economic policy. We leave open for now, the question of how to relate to these heaps that would be discussed further in Chap. 7.

The well-being and prosperity of inhabitants of any small open economy like Finland and any large semi-open economy like India with a backlog of development agenda both depend much on the business know-how of managers of enterprises and public systems to seed and harvest technical and social innovations in international value chains. How, at what cost and with what pace firm access missing markets in world trade can make a difference to reaping scale effects from new designs of cross-border value chains. 'Made in Finland' or 'Made in India' can be less relevant than 'Made by Finland' or 'Made by India' if benefits from cross-border inflows of factor incomes (wages, profits, interest, rents) exceed private and public costs incurred for production, marketing and delivery. However, very little is known about how, and how much can be globally harvested by Finland and India from trade-substituting investments and collaborative innovations seeded through local, regional and national initiatives and support mechanisms for players bilaterally in the two territories and through bilateral and plurilateral collaborations in third countries. Firms in both countries have hitherto mainly emphasised boosting their own manufactured exports to the exclusion of other modes of international business. Manufacturing technologies are migrating rapidly, and the flexibility inherent in the cross-border dispersal of value chains in a more open environment for trade in goods militates against reliance on manufacturing for sustaining competitiveness except in cases of input-dependent industries located for such reasons. New product-service linkages formed on the basis of combining advantages of aggregation, arbitrage, adaptation and assimilation will make the difference between arenas of sustainable competitiveness and beachheads of collaboration for new synergies.

EU countries that face the twin burden of demographic shock and small domestic markets have the greatest urgency to increase their international flows of goods and services. Finland is the first EU member state to undergo demographic transition, and dependency ratios in more than half of its local communities are beyond sustainable levels. The fertility rate in Finland is well below a replacement rate, and local communities such as Miehikkala are offering incentives to mothers who deliver babies to grow in the community. The stressed sub-national fiscal transfer mechanisms and highly uncertain returns from commercial exploitations of investments in high-technology and knowledge-intensive business services could push Finland into a downward spiral due to a demand-constrained scenario and a 1–2% growth rate per annum in GDP which is considered good by European standards. Due to the limited size of its domestic economy and sluggishness in markets in its neighbourhood (with the exception of Russia), Finland's high-tech investments can be justified only if leveraged by international flows from afar. The problem is aggravated if Finland's capacities created in technologies are treated akin to a sunk cost that cannot be salvaged due to a demand-constrained scenario instead of being regarded as productive assets to be developed further. On the supply side, EK is complaining of skill shortages within the country that coexist alongside chronic unemployment affecting one in every three educated persons below the age of 35, after over half of the adult labour force over the age of 50 has prematurely exited the labour market.[6]

India is not without its problems either despite being one of the top five countries of the world in economic size (as measured by purchasing power parity dollars) and in its rates of growth. The buoyant demand in India for competitively produced industrial goods and knowledge-intensive services has attracted large investments of foreign direct investment that now exceed portfolio fund flows. The most important constraint to faster growth in India is infrastructure (roads, railways, ports, airports, communications and power). The need for creation of new supply capacities for transport infrastructure, energy and environment, machine tools, manufactured consumer goods and the development of new technologies in ICT,

---

[6]Disguised unemployment in the form of further higher education, rotational short-term half-yearly jobs to continue drawing average earnings from wage-earner funds for another two years and an unusually high medical invalidation rate among those above 50 in age to draw early pensions are disturbing signs in a welfare state that provides free education and health care.

logistics, energy exploration, mining, aerospace, biotechnologies, nanotechnologies, telematics, etc., requires productive investments to develop and use new technologies and scale up to compete as a global manufacturing and service hub in a range of industries in a supply-constrained scenario. The obvious complementarities between Finland and India merit a closer look. What started out as a premise of 'unlikely twins' has shown up synergies that definitely merit serious prospecting.

Paired country studies of trade and investment potential at a disaggregated level discussed in Chaps. 2 and 3 reveal more than sub-national sectoral analysis from two-digit analysis because boundaries of sectors and clusters have become elastic. Finland's direction of trade has diversified beyond Germany, Sweden and Russia, traditionally its biggest trading partners, but the success in geographically diversifying its non-EU trade has been modest and achieved at the cost of burgeoning adverse trade imbalances in goods trade with USA and China. India's direction of trade has shifted away from Europe towards USA, China, the Middle East and East Asia. These developments make it both necessary and worthwhile to analyse the potential synergies between Finland and India in a historical context loaded with many years of mutual disinterest.

The practice(s) of business and the conceptualisation of practices can lead to the establishment of existing traditions as norm or their canonisation in doctrinaire forms without space for exploring other promising paths of the possible by removing impediments in the way of policies and practices needed to succeed in crossing into new horizons. Project modalities with soft targets are the *sine qua non* of Finnish internationalisation based on advocacy of gradual 'incrementalism' in which Finnish firms tend to delay entry. The entry costs are afforded mainly by large and medium firms able to sustain higher costs of such gradual incrementalism in what they perceive to be high-risk environments. Finnish managers have been slow to grasp that successful firms have to get more out of their entire organisation comprising all stakeholders and in arenas of contestation with institutional contexts different from their own. Indian businesses have also been slow to prospect business opportunities in Nordic Europe partly because of comfortable avenues of growth in the domestic market but also because they have tended to look mainly to English-speaking countries for low-hanging fruit in doing business abroad in the Middle East, Africa and Southeast Asia.

Industry–Academia–Government Partnerships

A significant part of R&D in both countries is done through business–government partnerships and business-academia collaborations through higher education institutions and research laboratories. However, such partnerships are organised very differently in the two countries. The government-to-government, academia-to-academia and business-to-business relations between Finland and India can be strengthened in three ways:

- There is a need to support an ongoing process to know where the shoe pinches businesses and the rest of society in the two countries and to examine what may be done about it. This is best done with action research and dialogues through the creation of an institution spanning both countries where all three constituents, governments, business and academia are represented as partners in the cause of Finland–India Economic Relations to mitigate policy impediments and practical hurdles.
- The awareness deficit about the other country's institutions, culture, practices and more specifically the gap in knowing where synergies can be beneficially prospected at micro-level requires constant updating, information sharing and knowledge creation. Access to knowledge about the social and technological innovations in the two countries is a prerequisite for designing sustainable value chains and structuring organisations as containers of hope for economic value.
- It is impossible to plant an economic orchard in India's institutional desert if the people do not develop a sense of belonging and commitment to the communities of habitat they reside in. It is equally impossible to preserve Finland's welfare system if it deteriorates into an economic graveyard where the interests only of residents in the national capital region of Helsinki are safeguarded. The recognition of this truth which is not so self-evident would go a long way in supporting what Finland and India can seek from and extend to each other on the basis of collaborations.

The resource bases and opportunity horizons in the two countries differ in stark contrast to the point of potential complementarity. It can be profitable to explore that. To quote Moominpappa in the Finnish fantasy book 'Exploits of Moominpappa' by Tove Jansson, are you curious to open "a new door to the Unbelievable, to the Possible, a new day that can always bring you anything if you have no objection to it"?

References

Ahonen P (1995) Restructuring Finland, Administrative Science, 1995 C 1. Working paper series, University of Tampere

Grundström E, Lahti VM (2005) The India phenomenon and Finland. Background study for Sitra's India programme, SITRA, Helsinki

India Office Records (1858) Her Majesty's Proclamation. British Library, London: L/P&S/6/463 file 36, folios 215–16

Mathur A (1998) Finland-India Economic Relations: a twinning study of trade and investment potential. ETLA, Helsinki. Reprinted 2002

Mathur A (2002) Indo-French Economic Relations. Working paper 87, ICRIER, New Delhi

Mathur AN (2007) Finland-India Business Prospects 2007–2017, Indian Institute of Management Ahmedabad, March 2007

Mathur AN (2008a) Distant neighbourliness: Finland's fast expanding relations with India. Paper presented at the workshop on Finland–India economic relations, Helsinki University of Technology, Otaniemi, Finland, 28 August 2008

References

Mathur AN (2008b) When the Twain Meet: a twinning comparison of enmeshing clusters between Finland and India. In: 11th TCI conference 2008, University of Capetown, South Africa

Mathur A, Mattila S (2009) India–Finland economic and technology cooperation: expanding frontiers, new horizons, transforming arenas. An invited background paper for the 15th technology summit of the confederation of Indian industry with Finland, New Delhi, India, 25–28 November 2009

Mattila S (2008) Multi-content revelation through dialogue processes: a study in understanding the hermeneutic primary task of small groups in the context of Finland and India. Doctoral dissertation, Tampere University of Technology, 2008. Publication 738, Tampere University of Technology Press, Tampere

Porter M (1991) Know Your Place, Inc, pp 1–3. Available at http://www.inc.com/magazine/19910901/4825.htm/

Tharoor S (2016) An era of darkness: the British Empire in India. Aleph, New Delhi

World Bank (2017) World development report. World Bank, Washington

World Trade Organization (2017) Annual report 2017. WTO, Geneva

Chapter 2
Business Opportunities in India

> *There is a way between voice and presence where information flows.*
>
> Rumi

Abstract In this chapter, business opportunities in India are discussed. The analysis of opportunities is primarily prospected from the perspective of Finland and Finnish businesses. These opportunities could also be availed by firms from other countries capable of building Finland–India value chains or extending these opportunities for value constellations involving businesses in countries beyond India and Finland. There is also an exploration of how the universe of business opportunities identified may be approached together with prospects for technology transfers, trade, trade-substituting investments and product-service linkages. Modalities including modes of entry and mobilisation of resources and responses needed are also examined.

Introduction

When Finland enjoyed trade surpluses as a small open economy, there was no need felt to go far to unfamiliar places and risk averseness prevailed. Finland generally enjoyed a favourable balance of trade with the value of its exports exceeding imports until 2005. This has changed. Since 2006, Finland has a negative balance of trade with imports exceeding exports every year except for 2010. Finland's negative balance of trade is contributed primarily by imports from Russia, China, Germany and Sweden. In the composition of trade, this is due to oil imports, machinery imports and imports of chemicals and pharmaceuticals. It would help Finland to examine whether this direction of imports is optimal by considering alternative sources at least for those imports that can be sourced from elsewhere at better prices.

The value of trade in goods between Finland and India compares poorly with the potential and also with the magnitude of trade of these countries with other partners. Neither Finland nor India has the other country among its top ten trading partners.

The level of bilateral trade has not reached a threshold where either country could regard the other as an important source or destination country based on the current strength of economic ties.

There are four ways of mapping the universe of business opportunities that await Finnish business in India. First, attention can be given to Finland's worldwide exports to compare these with India's list of imports to identify where Finland exports to the world but not to India or where exports to India are significantly smaller compared to Finland's worldwide export shares. Secondly, we can find out with analysis, the revealed comparative advantage of Finland in exports to India across all sectors of economic activity classified by the Standard International Trade Classification (SITC), Harmonised System (HS) of Commodity Description to show up potential profitable trade in all possible items to any desired level of disaggregation. This would cover goods trade, and product-service linkages can then be prospected using the International Monetary Fund (IMF)'s Extended Balance of Payments system that tracks services. Thirdly, opportunities arising from the development agenda of projects that are already financed or committed by the Government of India from internal public finance outlays and multilateral assistance from the World Bank and Asian Development Bank also deserve attention. The advantage here is obvious. The institutional customer already exists supported by purchasing power. Fourthly, we can study the business profiles, portfolios and trajectories of the top 500 companies of Finland (in the Talouselämä list of 500, the T-500) and the top 500 companies of India (in the Economic Times list, the ET-500) and identify synergies among potential partners in the disaggregated SITC codes where revealed comparative advantage from either side has been established. The fourth way is presented as potential pairings discussed in later chapters (Chaps. 7 and 8) of this book.

Finland's Exports to the World and India

Finland's exports to world and to India are concentrated in a few sectors. From Table 2.1, it can be seen that about 82% of Finland's worldwide exports and 91% of Finland exports to India are within just 14 SITC codes: mineral fuels and oils (27), organic chemicals (29), plastics and articles thereof (39), wood and articles of wood (39), pulp and paper products (47 and 48), Iron and steel and their articles (72 and 73), copper and articles thereof (74), nuclear reactors and boilers (84), electrical machinery and equipments (85), vehicles other than railway or tramway (87), optical, photographic, cinematographic instruments and parts or accessories thereof (90) and miscellaneous goods (99).

Among these, Finland's exports to India are so small as to count as zero in the above table in three categories: (27) mineral fuels, mineral oils and products or their distillation; bituminous substances; mineral waxes; (44) wood and articles of wood;

Table 2.1 Sectoral shares of Finland's exports

SITC HS code	Code description	% share in total exports to world	% share in total exports to India
27	Mineral fuels, mineral oils and products or their distillation; bituminous substances; mineral waxes	11	0
29	Organic chemicals	2	3
39	Plastics and articles thereof	4	4
44	Wood and articles of wood; wood charcoal	4	0
47	Pulp of wood or of other fibrous cellulosic material; waste and scrap of paper or paperboard	3	2
48	Paper and paperboard; articles of paper pulp, of paper or of paperboard	13	15
72	Iron and steel	6	7
73	Articles of iron or steel	2	0
74	Copper and articles thereof	2	2
84	Nuclear reactors, boilers, machinery and mechanical appliances; parts thereof	13	21
85	Electrical machinery and equipment and parts thereof; sound recorders and reproducers, television image and sound recorders and reproducers, and parts and accessories of articles	9	30
87	Vehicles other than railway or tramway rolling stock, and parts and accessories thereof	5	3
90	Optical, photographic, cinematographic, measuring, checking, precision, medical or surgical instruments and apparatus; parts and accessories thereof	4	3
99	Miscellaneous goods	6	3
Total shares		82	91

wood charcoal; and (72) articles of iron or steel. An analysis of major exports from Finland to the world and India reveals the following active two-digit codes:

(a) **Mineral fuel and oils (27)**: minerals and mineral products from tar and bitumen (2710), electrical energy (271,600). Finland does not export these to India regularly.
(b) **Organic chemicals (29)**: phenols; phenol-alcohols (2907), oxygen function amino-compounds (2922), heterocyclic compounds with nitrogen (2933), nucleic acids and their salts (2934), and other organic compounds (2942). In this SITC Category (29), sub-categories acyclic alcohols (2905) and ketones and quinone (2914) are not regularly exported to India.
(c) **Plastics and articles thereof (39)**: primary forms polymers of ethylene (3901), polymers of propylene or other olefins (3902), cellulose and its chemical derivatives (3912), tubes, pipes and hoses (3917), self-adhesive plates (3919), other plates, sheets, films (3920 and 3921), other articles of plastics (3926).

(d) **Wood and articles of wood; wood Charcoal (44)**: wood sawn or chipped lengthwise (4407), plywood veneered panels (4412), builders joinery and carpentry of wood (4418).
(e) **Pulp of wood or of other fibrous cellulosic material (47)**: chemical wood pulp soda (4703), wood pulp obtained by mechanical and chemical preparations (470,500).
(f) **Paper and paperboard; articles of paper pulp (48)**: newsprint (4801); uncoated paper and paperboard (4802); uncoated kraft paper and paperboard (4804); other uncoated paper and paperboard (4805); vegetable parchment (4806); paper/paperboard coated on one or both side (4810); paper, paperboard, cellulose wading (4811).
(g) **Iron and steel (72)**: ferro-alloys (7202), ferrous waste and scrap (7204), flat rolled products of stainless steel of different width (7219 and 7220), flat rolled product of other alloy steel (7225). In this SITC code (72), ferro-alloys (7202) of Finland have potential but have not been exported to India yet.
(h) **Articles of iron or steel (73)**: tubes, pipes and fittings (7307); structures (7308); sanitary ware and parts (7324); other articles of iron or steel (7326). In this SITC code (73), Finland has not yet exported any iron or steel tubes, pipes and hollow profiles in open seam or welded, riveted or similarly closed items in Sub-category 7306.
(i) **Copper and articles thereof (74)**: copper waste and scrap (7404), copper plates and sheets (7409), copper tubes and pipes (7411). In this SITC code, sub-categories copper mattes; cement copper (7401); refined copper (7403) have export potential too but are not yet exported to India. The volume and value of copper plates and sheets in Sub-category 7409 exported to India are also well below Finland's share in world exports.
(j) **Nuclear reactors and boilers (84)**: turbo-jets, turbo-propellers (8411); centrifuges (8421); other lifting, handling, loading or unloading machinery (8428); other moving, grinding, levelling and scrapping machinery (8430); parts and accessories (8431); other agricultural or horticultural machinery ((8436); machinery for making pulp of fibrous cellulosic materials (8439); automatic data processing machines and units (8471); machinery for sorting and screening (8474); taps, cocks and valves (8481); and transmission shafts (8483). Finland has not yet exported to India in Sub-category 8436: other agricultural, horticultural, poultry/bee-keeping machinery with mechanical/thermal equipment; poultry incubators and breeders.
(k) **Electrical machinery and equipments (85)**: electric motors and generators (8501); electric generating sets (8502); electrical transformers, electric generating sets and rotary converters (8504); electric laser or photo light beam (8515); electrical parts for telephony/telegraphy (8517); records, tapes and other recorded media (8524); electrical apparatus for switching (8536); and electronic integrated circuits (8542) 8504.
(l) **Vehicles other than railway or tramways (87)**: motorised vehicles (8703), motor vehicles for transport of goods (8704), special purpose motor vehicles (8705). Finland has not yet exported to India in sub-categories 8701: tractors (other than tractors of heading 8709) and 8703: motor cars and other motor

vehicles for transport of persons (excluding 8702) and racing cars. People in India following Formula 1 know of Kimmi Raikkonen and his 2018 victory, but not many would know that Finland exports racing cars.

(m) **Optical, photographic, cinematographic instruments (90)**: apparatus based on the use of X-rays (9022); hydrometers, thermometers (9025); instruments and apparatus for physical or chemical analysis (9027); oscilloscopes, spectrum analysers (9030); measuring or checking instruments (9031); and automatic regulating or controlling instruments (9032). In this SITC code (90), instruments and appliances used in medical surgery and in dental/vet applications, scientific electromedical apparatuses and sight-testing instruments (9018) are being exported to India, but the potential is far from saturated.

While the above analysis enables track missed trades and business opportunities of Finnish exports to India in line with Finland's world export trends on items in India's import list, it is possible to independently establish and verify the SITC codes where Finland has a potential revealed comparative advantage for exports to India. A modified version of the revealed comparative advantage (RCA) methodology based on the Balassa index had been developed for undertaking paired country comparisons for trade in goods in the context of researching foreign presence of companies from Belgium and India (Veuglers and Mathur 1993). This methodology was developed further in the context of paired twinning comparisons of trade and investment potential for other countries, France and Finland (Mathur 1998, 2002, 2007a).

In order to verify whether Finland has a comparative advantage in a sector, a revealed comparative advantage index (RCAfj) was conceptualised at the four-digit, six-digit and eight-digit level of disaggregation using data for the years 2014–2017 sourced from the Directorate of Commercial Intelligence and Statistics of the Ministry of Commerce, Government of India and cross-checked against data from four other sources, the Tradedx database of the Centre for Monitoring Indian Economy (CMIE), data from the Department of Customs of India and Finland, Tilastokeskus, the Statistical Centre of Finland, Eurostat database of the EU and the Direction of Trade Statistics published by the International Monetary Fund.

The revealed comparative advantage index was conceptualised in the following way similar to how this was done in previous studies (Veuglers and Mathur 1993; Mathur 1998, 2002, 2007a):

$$RCAfj = \frac{Xfj/Xf}{Xfji/Xeuji}$$

where

Xfj Exports of Finland in sector j
Xf   Total exports of Finland

The numerator, by definition, cannot exceed 1

Xfji Exports of Finland to India in sector j
Xeuji Total exports of EU to India in sector j

The denominator, by construction, cannot exceed 1.

When RCAfj was found to be larger than 1, the Finnish export share of the Indian market for this industry or sector at the appropriate level of disaggregation was regarded as exceptional compared to the expected export share of Finland, which implied that Finland has some unexploited advantage in this industry. Where Xfji = 0 or indeterminate, the item was retained. Items exported to third countries by both countries (e.g., gas cylinders for liquified gases and elisa kits) have also been taken into consideration for investment analysis.

The scope of the potential does not rely on RCAs alone because RCAs can get distorted by intra-firm arrangements involving transfer pricing, inter-firm non-compete contracts and inter-firm joint product developments. In some cases, they make more sense when analysed alongside services. This is especially so after 2005 when GATS services trade liberalisation triggered trade-substituting investments for innovations in products, processes, technologies and knowledge-intensive product-service linkages in cross-border value chains. With this caveat, the SITC codes where Finland has a revealed comparative advantage (RCAF) for exports to India at two-digit level are presented in Table 2.2.

Table 2.2 Potential Finnish exports to India based on Revealed Comparative Advantage of Finland (RCAF)

SITC HS code	Code description	RCAF values
22	Beverages, spirits and vinegar	9.53
23	Residues and waste from the food industries; prepared animal fodder	3.57
25	Salt; sulphur; earths and stone; plastering materials, lime and cement	4.70
28	Inorganic chemicals; organic or inorganic compounds of precious metals, of rare-earth metals, or radioactive elements or of isotopes	7.3
29	Organic chemicals	2.06
30	Pharmaceutical products.	2.99
32	Tanning or dyeing extracts; tannins and their derivatives; dyes, pigments and other colouring matter; paints and varnishes; putty and other mastics; inks	13.87
34	Soap, organic surface-active agents, washing and lubricating preparations, artificial and prepared waxes, polishing or scouring preparations, candles and similar articles, modelling pastes, 'dental waxes' and dental preparations	37.60
38	Miscellaneous chemical products	2.66
39	Plastics and articles thereof	16.69
40	Rubber and articles thereof	9.81
43	Furskins an artificial fur; manufactures thereof	6.65
44	Wood and articles of wood; wood charcoal.	113.57
47	Pulp of wood or of other fibrous cellulosic material; waste and scrap of paper or paperboard	4.82
48	Paper and paperboard; articles of paper pulp, of paper or of paperboard	4.33

(continued)

Finland's Exports to the World and India 51

Table 2.2 (continued)

SITC HS code	Code description	RCAF values
49	Printed books, newspapers, pictures and other products of the printing industry; manuscripts, typescripts and plans	6.96
59	Impregnated, coated, covered or laminated textile fabrics; textile articles of a kind suitable for industrial use	1.43
63	Other made up textile articles; sets; worn clothing and worn textile articles; rags	10.07
64	Footwear, gaiters and the like; parts of such articles	2.07
68	Articles of stone, plaster, cement, asbestos, mica or similar materials	1.73
69	Ceramic products	2.58
70	Glass and glassware	6.22
71	Natural or cultured pearls, precious or semi-precious stones, precious metals, metals clad with precious metal and articles thereof; imitation jewellery; coins	1.6
72	Iron and steel	17.07
73	Articles of iron or steel	24.54
74	Copper and articles thereof	5.17
75	Nickel and articles thereof	7.36
76	Aluminium and articles thereof	2.13
79	Zinc and articles thereof	44.14
81	Other base metals; cermets; articles thereof	7.58
82	Tools, implements, cutlery, spoons and forks, of base metal; parts thereof of base metal	21.19
84	Nuclear reactors, boilers, machinery and mechanical appliances; parts thereof	40.65
85	Electrical machinery and equipment and parts thereof; sound recorders and reproducers, television image and sound recorders and reproducers, and parts and accessories of articles	17.65
86	Railway or tramway locomotives, rolling stock and parts thereof; railway or tramway track fixtures and fittings and parts thereof; mechanical (including electromechanical) traffic signalling equipment of all kinds	1.66
87	Vehicles other than railway or tramway rolling stock, and parts and accessories thereof	16.82
89	Ships, boats and floating structures	18.44
90	Optical, photographic, cinematographic, measuring, checking, precision, medical or surgical instruments and apparatus; parts and accessories thereof	19.01
91	Clocks and watches and parts thereof	3.75
94	Furniture; bedding, mattresses, mattress supports, cushions and similar stuffed furnishings; lamps and lighting fittings, not elsewhere specified or included; illuminated signs, illuminated nameplates and the like; prefabricated buildings	18.30
95	Toys, games and sports requisites; parts and accessories thereof	2.99
99	Miscellaneous goods	26.66

An in-depth disaggregated analysis was undertaken at four-digit, six-digit and eight-digit levels to look for items and trends that could be missed by limiting the analysis only to those products that get highlighted at the two-digit level of analysis. Product categories at a four-digit disaggregated level where Finland has a comparative advantage in exports to India are listed in Annexure I. Further analysis from the four-digit disaggregated analysis is presented in Annexures II–IV. A comparison was then made with the composition and direction of India's imports from EU in these categories to confirm the potential. The high-value items exportable from Finland to India are listed in Annexure II together with an indication of items already being exported wherever the value exceeded €10 million. The Indian imports from EU that Finland exports worldwide are listed in Annexure III. Among these, the high-value Indian imports from EU where Finland exports to India are listed in Annexure IV.

Deepening studies were carried out to identify for whole industries and for specific firms and locations, the gaps where synergies are strongest and where the structuring of investments is most profitable. In the first phase, a baseline study of Finland–India trade was completed by extracting complete data for all SITC codes down to eight-digit disaggregation from the databases of the Centre for Monitoring Indian Economy (CMIE) and the Directorate General of Commercial Intelligence and Statistics (DGCIS). Action research methodologies were used, and 'listening posts' convened in Finland and India to share the results of the baseline study to which representatives of business, governments and academia alongside consumers and potential investors were invited to listen to their hopes, wishes, concerns and anxieties expressed.

Concurrently, case studies were researched at enterprise level in the SITC codes 48, 84 and 85 that emerged as the most promising categories of mutual interest to Finland and India. Among others, a Finnish company based in Lahti that faced an internationalisation imperative and had to choose between China and India was researched as a case study (Mattila and Mathur 2007) to raise more hypotheses about cost-benefit ratios in Finland's global harvesting of income flows of locally seeded innovations through global techno-commercial exploitation through collaborations in India in the technology service sector. These inquiries were supplemented through questionnaires, checklists and interviews in both countries to understand trade patterns in respect of:

(a) Goods that comprise the largest share in exports of Finland to India at two-digit, four-digit, six-digit and eight-digit levels of disaggregation.
(b) Goods with high rates of growth in imports by India by identifying such goods with the highest inter-temporal increases in the preceding three years at four-digit, six-digit and eight-digit levels of disaggregation.
(c) Goods that comprise the largest shares in the import basket of India.
(d) Goods exported by Europe to India that feature in Finland's exports but not to Finland's exports to India.

India's chemical imports of organic (28) and inorganic (29) chemicals are sourced mainly from EU countries with Germany, Belgium, UK, France, Netherlands, and Sweden being the major source countries. In 2016–17, India imported €621 million of organic chemicals (SITC 28) and €1,809 million of inorganic chemicals (SITC 29) from the EU. Finland's share was less than €4 million in organic chemicals and about €12.5 million in inorganic chemicals, well below its potential. Finland's distinct comparative advantage can be exploited here. The items where the comparative advantage reflects most strongly are cobalt oxides (2822), chlorates and bromates (2829), sulphates (2833), hydrids and silicides (2850), anisic aldehyde (2912), formic acids (2915) and phosphoaminolipids (2923) where some exports are already taking place. Zinc oxides (2817) and titanium dioxides (2823) are not yet exported from Finland to India, and underutilised capacity in search of export markets exists in Finland for both categories. Under-represented segments include phosphoric acid (2809), oxylene (2902), acetones (2914), halides (2918), amino-compounds (2922), betamethasone (2927) and alkaloids (2940).

In pharmaceutical products (ITC Category 30) where EU exported about €854 million of products in 2016–17, Finnish firms, despite RCAF pointing to good export potential, had a share of only €6 million. Finnish firms have secured a share of the Indian market only in pigments (3212), industrial enzymes (3507) and pregnancy confirmation kits (3822). Conspicuous by complete absence in Indian import shares are Finnish firms in fertilisers (a joint venture in Gujarat partly compensates), resins (3506), photographic and cinematographic goods. Severely under-represented sectors include antibacterial serums (3002), bandages (3005), paper industry preparations (3809), platinum catalysts (3815) and industrial monocarboxyls (3823).

In 2016–17, the value of Indian imports from Europe of wood and wood articles (44) was €163 million in which the Finnish share is negligible although Finland has potential to export based on RCAF. In Category 48, Finland's share was about €90 million in India's imports of €974 million from Europe. Finland has a large 20% market share in newsprint (4801), a 44% market share in dyed printing paper (4802), a 17% share in writing paper (4802) and a 9% share in plywood (4412). These shares are under contestation by firms from Germany, France, UK and Sweden. The increase in Indian paper and paperboard import tariff requires firms to consider creation of manufacturing capacity versus exporting. In pulp (47), Finnish firms do not have any shares of European exports to India in many lucrative segments like dissolving grades of chemical wood pulp (4702). Finnish exports to India are rather small in currency note paper (4802), sanitary paper (4803), filter papers (48054001), felt papers (48055000), cable and condenser papers (48057003), insulating papers (48103901), stationery papers (48173009), facial tissues (48182000), sanitary napkins (48184000), corrugated board (48191001), paperboard stationery (48209000) and printed papers and board (48211009) all of which have potential.

Modest shares disproportionate to Finnish comparative advantage relative to other European countries are also notable in non-dissolving grades of chemical wood pulp (4703), sack kraft paper (48042900), kraft paper and paperboard (48044900), art paper of less than 150 gsm (48101101), plastic laminated papers (48113909), corrugated board cartons (48191009), cones (48194000) and printed calendar blocks (4911). Finnish paper and paperboard products are well represented in exports to India in three segments: adhesive papers, lightweight graphic papers and bituminised papers where they have better market shares than products from Italy, UK, Germany and Sweden. For instance, Finland accounts for 62.8% of EU's exports to India of impregnated papers.

There are 358 paper mills in India. Many of these were initially set up with small capacities due to capital import constraints and capacity constraints under the licensing system. A phase of expansion and consolidation together with associated modernisation is going on. Current demand for paper and paperboard exceeds supply by 40% in most segments. The return on net assets even at their inefficient scale is between 12 and 28% for the firms and represents a profitable opportunity for right-scaled new investments. Here is an excellent opportunity for both trade and trade-substituting investments.

In the category of glass and glassware (70), there is an acute shortage of capacity (thereby, also of domestic supply) in the Indian market of sheet glass, float glass, safety glass, insulating glass, vacuum glass, electrical glass, ophthalmic glass, laboratory glass, glass cubes and mouldings and preservation glass, 75% of which is imported from Europe. The trade value of imports in this category from Europe is about €136 million. Finland is a major EU exporter in all of these and yet does not have any share of the Indian market. French firms have established manufacturing units in India during the last two decades. Finnish exports to India in this category are currently limited to glass fibres, glass wool and rear-view mirrors.

In the category of iron and steel products (72 and 73), Finland's exports to India of stainless steel billets (7218), speciality nails (7317) and flat rolled products (7208) correspond to expectations. The trade value of imports from Europe in this category was €2,382 million in 2016–17, but Finnish exports to India were barely €20 million. Finnish firms have not yet tried to penetrate the Indian market in machinery belt fasteners, heavy gauge products, powders, alloys, railway rails and have miniscule shares in medical springs, pins and needles, nuts, screws and bolts and steel angles. It is noteworthy that Norway, Sweden and Denmark have higher shares than Finland here.

In category 74 (copper and articles of copper), every EU country exports copper alloy foils and copper fittings to India with European exports to India of €379 million. Finland's share of exports to India in copper tubes and pipes and waste scrap is currently about €16 million could be increased. Finland's share of the Indian import from Europe (€576 million) of aluminium and aluminium products (Category 76) at €7.5 million can also be increased. The same holds for zinc and zinc products (79) where import from Europe is about €9 million and where Finland's share is negligible. Finland has potential to export aluminium foils (7607) and zinc wire (7904) that are regularly exported from Europe to India. The Finnish share in Indian imports of unalloyed aluminium and unwrought zinc could also be significantly increased. In cobalt alloys (8105), Finland already has a 27% share in India's imports from Europe, but the trade in tungsten bars and rods (8101) and titanium articles (8108) is small and could be increased. There is also a huge potential for Finland to export lithium to India or begin to produce lithium batteries in India because India has announced a complete shift to electric cars by 2030.

The largest shortfall against expectations arises in the sector classification mechanical appliances, reactors and boilers (84) where Finland's production capacity and exports are particularly well developed. The trade value of imports from Europe in this category is €6,067 million, of which Finland's share is less than €148 million. Finland has negligible shares of India's EU imports of bulldozers (8429), forest machinery (8432), dairy machinery (8434) and machine tools (8456–8465). Finland also has small and modest shares in Europe's exports to India in central heating boilers (8403), furnaces (8416 and 8417), calendaring and rolling machines (8420), fibre cellulose pulp machinery (8439), tool holders (8466), construction machinery (8474), injection moulding equipment (8477) and transmission bearings (8483). The Category 8429 mentioned above includes items with very high RCAF for Finland in self-propelled bulldozers, angle dozers, graders, levellers, scrapers, mechanical shovels, excavators, shovel loaders, tamping machines and road rollers.

In water boilers (8402), 98% of Indian imports from Europe are sourced from Belgium, Germany and Italy. Finland has the residual 2% share. Similarly, Finnish products have successfully penetrated the Indian market but not yet developed more than a 2% share of Europe's exports in gas generators (8405), hydraulic jet engines and pneumatic motors (8412), liquid pumps (8413), vacuum pumps and industrial blowers (8414) and ball and roller bearings (8482). The successful Finnish products in this category with rising shares in India's imports from Europe are engine parts and piston rings (8409), oil refining equipment (8419), centrifuges (8421), escalators, elevators, work trucks (8431), paper machinery (8441), industrial appliances (8479), pressure valves (8481) and fluid couplings (8483). Snow ploughs and blowers are also an important Indian import item where USA and Canada are the only countries presently involved in exporting to India.

The demand for electrical machinery in India is growing with exponential expansion in the energy sector and in energy-intensive industries favouring captive generation. Motors (8501) constitute an important import item in the category electrical machinery (85). All EU countries with the exception of Greece, Portugal and Ireland export to India in this category. The trade value of European exports to India in this category was €3,568 million in 2016–17. Finland has a well-developed production and export sector here, and this is a promising opportunity area both for trade and trade-substituting investments. Finland's strength is well represented through Wärtsilä Diesel and others in electricity generation sets (8502) and generator parts (8503) with Finnish shares ranging between 25% and 53% of all Indian imports from the EU for different capacities of generators with one notable exception. In the 5000–10,000 KVA range, the Finnish share is zero because Germany has cornered 100% of this EU trade with India. Finnish shares are also low in electrical transformers (8504).

In telecom, Nokia mobile phones were a runaway success, but its networks business in the Indian market hardly took off. In networks, Nokia was a late entrant (compared to Ericsson, Motorola, Siemens and Telstra) was not well prepared for the competitive bidding of contracts and lost many contract bids. It recovered to win one bid for the city of Chennai (previously known as Madras), in 1996. Finland's share of European telecom equipment exported to India remained unusually low until the consolidation of this business of Nokia with Siemens Networks. In 2019, the potential is in 5G digital network business. In cellular phones (8525), Sweden, Germany, UK and Denmark have larger shares of India's imports from the EU. Finnish exports to India of aerial reflectors (8529) and printed circuits (8534) are strong and growing.

In the category locomotives (86), Finland's comparative advantage is in cargo containers (8605) where it already has 5% of the market share of India's imports from Europe. The growth in cargo containers continues with rising trade volumes, and new ports and airports, and as domestic interstate trade shifts to greater use of containers. It is a fiercely competitive market with firms from Germany, UK, Netherlands, France, Belgium, Denmark and Italy competing with Finnish firms for shares of the growth. The trade value of European imports in this category was about €145 million in 2016–17, but Finland's exports to India in this category in the same period was less than €1.25 million.

In the category Road vehicles and parts (87), India being the biggest two-wheeler manufacturer in the world imports large volumes under this head. The trade value of European imports in this category was €1,267 million in 2016–17, but the Finnish share was only €1.2 million. The comparative advantage of Finnish firms is strong in bicycle parts (8714) where Finland also imports bicycles from India. EU firms from Germany, France, Italy, Netherlands and the UK are currently involved in sharing this market. Finnish firms might need to increase their market share to maintain a critical minimum presence in this category. India's tractor production has not kept pace with demand. The reason is that tractors are used as multipurpose vehicles (not only as farm implements) in rural areas where road network density is limited. Europe's exports of tractors to India are growing despite competition from domestic manufacturers in India. Finnish firms have a 4% share of this import from Europe and one Finnish–Indian joint venture. Under ship, boat and floating structures (89), Finland's comparative advantage lies in floating structures that require to be broken up and its 2% market share quite accurately reflects the static nature of this trade.

Another promising category is medical, measuring, optical and other instruments (90). The trade value of imports from Europe in this category was €2,308 million in 2016–17, but Finnish exports to India in this category in the corresponding period were less than €20 million. Finland has a particular advantage with medical apparatuses (9018) and X-ray machines (9022) which do not yet account for significant shares. The demand for medical and surgical instruments and laboratory and scientific instruments and industrial valves is growing rapidly in India. FDI-led investments here are also augmenting domestic capacity and competing with exports. Furniture (94) is another category where Finland's exports are less than €1 million and where Finland has distinct advantages and many brands offering good quality. The recent arrival of the Swedish IKEA with its first outlet in Hyderabad and the announcement of more outlets indicates that there is promising potential here.

Discovery of new applications is also more likely in the Indian market due to its diversity. To take just a few examples:

- Sensor technologies of JMK and KSV in Finland are presently limited to weight and ash sensors for the paper industry. The growth of fibre optics where India is a world leader in certain technologies provides opportunities for non-traditional applications in addition to electronics.
- The eclectic nature of the Indian construction industry could lead to new applications for technologies in cements, floorings, adhesives and structural bondings.
- Anti-vibration technologies in metalastic products—another Finnish stronghold—have vast applications in the railways and in factory automation.
- Windpower is being developed along the coast of Orissa, Andhra Pradesh, Tamil Nadu, Gujarat and Maharashtra and solar energy technologies being diffused throughout India on an unprecedented scale. Swedish and Danish firms are already in the market.
- There are megaprojects of major urban renewal in Indian cities funded by the World Bank to modernise the sewerage and waste treatment, particularly solid waste. Finnish firms like Nerox have opportunities here.

A list of knowledge and technology-intensive services structurable in Finland or India as trade-substituting investments for mutual trade or for third countries has been prepared for a more detailed investigation in progress. The service trade in the identified areas already occurring cannot be known without another kind of analysis involving income flows. As noted by me in a previous publication (Mathur 2007b available at www.oulu.oaka.fi as it was first presented at a seminar in Oulu, Finland), in service trade, there is nothing tangible or visible that crosses international borders. There is also no commodity description as in goods which carry a customs tag. Another big difference is that activities in GATS Modes 2, 3 and 4 occur within national jurisdictions. In order to track flows of factor incomes, it is possible to use the International Monetary Fund's Extended Balance of Payments System to obtain a measure of flows, and the foreign affiliates' trade in services can be added later. Once actual flows of services are determined, a revealed comparative advantage index for services can also be developed (as described in Mathur 2006), but no one has as yet developed and put to use such an index. For now, the RCA analysis completed for the 500 biggest companies by sales turnover of Finland (The Talouselämä 500 List) and India (The Economic Times ET-500 List) is presented in **Annexures IX and X respectively.**

Finland–India Trade

During the period 1999–2011. Finnish exports of goods to India trebled and India's exports to Finland doubled. Altogether, Finnish exports to India grew to more than three times the size of India's exports to Finland by 2012–13, increasing the trade gap. Between 2012–13 and 2017–18, Finland maintained a trade surplus with India but the gap reduced (see Fig. 2.1).

Fig. 2.1 Finland–India Trade 2012–18. *Source* Tilastokeskus, Finland

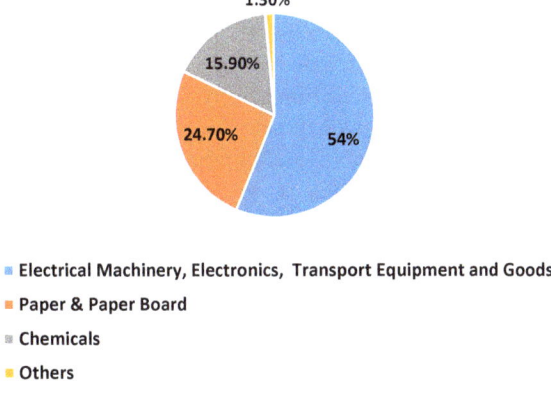

Fig. 2.2 Composition of Finland's exports to India in 2016–17. *Source* Tilastokeskus, Finland

The composition of Finnish exports to India is shown in Fig. 2.2.

Potential Finnish Exports to India by Specific Items

In the case of Finland, more than 90% of trade gets covered from disaggregation of the most important two-digit-level codes, but less than 70% of Indian exports to Finland can be tracked in a similar manner. In both cases, for Finnish trade-substituting investments and for Indian trade-substituting collaborations, some of the most attractive and fast-growing synergies and opportunities were discovered only from multilevel analysis taking into consideration more factors.

There is demand in India for Finnish branded consumer products in food and beverages with rapidly growing sales of Finnish crisp bread, chocolates, cheese, confectionaries, Finnish berry liqueurs, wines, vodka, enzyme preparations and animal feeds, and these are in short supply meriting expansion. The Indian market for Finnish branded consumer products in such food and beverages is so large that volumes would justify both technology transfers and scope for manufacturing subsidiaries and joint ventures.

Consumer durables

Consumer durables like belt-buckles, hand tools for plumbing, carpentry, masonry, nail cutters, thermometers, kitchenware, glassware, hot and cold taps, floor coverings and wooden furniture are just a few examples in the wide range of Finland's designed products. In these, licensing and franchising could be an entry modality, besides manufacturing locally through subsidiaries or joint ventures. However, firms such as Oras, Lundia and Iittala, to mention just a few, are not yet doing business in India and when contacted revealed that they had not examined opportunities in India. Also, design collaborations (for consumer and industrial products) between Finnish and Indian industry offer bright prospects. This has been demonstrated by pioneers such as Fiskars that made the leap to do business in India and have been very successful.

A wide range of industrial goods exported in small quantities has scope for production in India by Finnish firms through technology transfers to joint ventures or wholly/partly owned subsidiaries. These include pistons, pumps, engines, machine tools, burners, gas generators, gas turbine parts, high-pressure hydraulic pumps, centrifuges, cranes, gears, shafts, audio-visual equipment for cinema and media, security equipment, electrical machinery, spectrometers, spectrophotometers, prefabricated low-cost housing, rockdrills and speciality papers. Machines for working with glass, rare-earth metals lithium, scandium, yttrium, mercury, cobalt and tungsten, have been exported from Finland to India in small quantities, and these and other radioactive minerals could increase trade volumes considerably. The Finnish chemical industry has been exporting colours, dyes and pigments for white paint like titanium dioxide and also a wide range of inorganic chemicals. Small quantities of pharmaceutical products and intermediate formulations and growing volumes of LDPE polyethylene and cellulose derivatives belong to the promising items.

Among items belonging to the list of promising Finnish exports to India are tableware, kitchenware, hot and cold taps, toilet articles, floor coverings, special purpose tyres, casks, barrels, tubs, vats, glass chimneys, and steel structurals for the construction industry, rudders for boats and ships, threaded nuts and washers, padlocks, rockdrills, industrial scissors and blades. In each of these, a trade-substituting investment involving services in India that enables factor incomes to flow back to Finland may be more profitable than manufacturing the item in Finland at a much higher cost and exporting the item to India until the day when the competitive edge of the item in price and quality is completely lost.

Two of the most interesting sectors for Indian firms to benefit from Finnish technology are energy and environment and infrastructure (e.g., dozens of new airports, hundreds of thousands of kilometres of highways, and numerous cargo handling, ship repairing, warehousing, container terminal projects to improve turnaround time of Indian ports from 3.5 days to 10 hours, new telecom services and several metro rail projects are underway). These are noted in a later part of this chapter. Finnish firms have not yet taken a big role in the build–operate–transfer (B-O-T) or in the build–own–operate (B-O-O) modes except as subcontractors or suppliers of equipment. According to the latest available information, sectoral investment growth rates in India are remarkably high (Economic Survey 2017–18[1]) in several areas such as mining, manufacturing, construction, transport, storage and communication.

The most noticeable changes have occurred in Category 48 (Paper and Paperboard) and Category 84 (boilers, pistons, pumps and engines). New export

---

[1]In covering economic development and its opportunities, this chapter draws on official information reported in the Economic Survey 2017–2018, published by the Ministry of Finance, Government of India. Further details are available at http://mofapp.nic.in:8080/economicsurvey/.

items in Category 48 (such as electrosensitive paper, vellum and parchment papers, braille paper) bear testimony to the growing sophistication of the Indian market to need new sub-categories never previously exported from Finland to India. In Category 84, machine tools, punching, shearing and turret machines, industrial burners, gas generators, piston engines, marine propulsion engines, outboard motors, aircraft engine parts, piston rings, gas turbine parts, high-pressure hydraulic pumps for gases and liquids, industrial fans, heat exchange units, centrifuges for chemical industry, hoists, pulleys and tackles, boring machinery, cranes, paper machinery, glass machinery, gears and shafts, electric inverters, machinery for power generation, transmission and distribution, arc welding machines, soil heaters, telephony and telegraphy equipment, signalling and traffic control equipment, photo-sensitive transistors audio-visual equipment for the film industry, and security surveillance equipment including inobtrusive metal detectors, optical instruments, geophysical instruments, meteorological instruments, thermometers, flow meters, spectrometers and spectrophotometers, medical, dental, veterinary furniture and barbers' chairs, prefabricated buildings and furniture are the most promising items that indicate large and rapidly growing volumes to be expected over the next decade. Metal scrap (from copper, zinc, aluminium, iron) and wastes that cannot economically be reprocessed in Finland also exhibit high annual growth rates of exports to India.

New Opportunities for Finland–India Trade

Thus, there are five different kinds of new opportunities in Finland–India trade:

(a) Completely missed opportunities in goods trade for reasons not clear or simply neglect as already identified in a previous section.
(b) Goods trade opportunities relevant to Indian markets tested as viable and growing but far from saturated. Tableware, kitchenware, hot and cold taps, toilet articles, floor coverings, bovine hides and skins, pinewood, special purpose tyres, casks, barrels, tubs, vats, pressure containers for compressed gases, glass chimneys, and steel structurals for the construction industry, rudders for boats and ships, threaded nuts and washers, padlocks, rockdrills, industrial scissors and blades, handtools used by artisans, mechanics and semi-skilled labour in plumbing, carpentry, electrical works, masonry are among the new items in the Finnish export basket to India.
(c) Trade-substituting investments in goods trade for buyback arrangements that would increase volumes, value and profitability for players involved. Although 70% of India's exports to the EU consist of manufactured goods, this is a miniscule proportion (about 5%) of all manufacturing in India. Besides the basket of traditional items (textiles and clothing, nuts and fruits, tea, gems and jewellery), there has been a growth in Indian exports to Finland in iron and steel, instruments, travel bags and packaging materials and travelgear, furniture,

chemicals, pharmaceuticals and nutraceuticals. Trade-substituting investments are feasible in such areas.

(d) Product-service linkages to leverage technology and knowledge-intensive investments on a scale that would transform directions of trade for one or both countries for high-value items in which trade exists.

(e) Product-service linkages to leverage technology and knowledge-intensive investments by techno-commercial engineering of new options unrelated to bilateral trade on a scale that would justify collaborations for third-country markets.

An intriguing aspect of Indo-Finnish trade that has not so far been discussed is the occasional occurrence of the same or similar items in both lists—the list of Finnish exports to India and that of Indian exports to Finland. At one level, there is nothing unnatural in this because firms in the same line of branded manufactured goods compete for consumers with differentiated products in each other's territories. However, in the case of Finland and India, most of the trade consists of unbranded commodities or industrial goods. Actually, in certain items, the direction of trade is changing. In Chap. 1, the example of X-ray machines that Wallac began exporting from Finland to India in 1997 was discussed as an illustration of late internationalisation. Since 2006, X-ray machines (called Roentgen machines in Finland) were exported from India to Finland and they were not made by Wallac. The window of opportunity to internationally exploit an innovation in a competitive mode is indeed finite, and the time span is reducing all the time. This creates incentives for enterprises with pioneering technologies to collaborate for manufacturing in ways that their presence in foreign markets (and in this case in their own domestic market) does not get jeopardised. In a world where governments committed to open world trade can no longer erect tariff and non-tariff barriers to keep out competition, this is critical. The same situation also presents opportunities to create new product-service linkages through trade-substituting investments for mutual markets or of a scale even larger, for worldwide markets.

Enterprises that export manufactured goods are usually not constrained by unique geographical considerations of soil, climate, etc. They can often be better off with trade-substituting investments in the other territory. In some cases, it may still be worthwhile to continue with exports on cost and profit considerations. In other cases, majority investments and joint ventures may be more advantageous. The incentives for scaling up trade-substituting investments are greater when directions of exports can widen or when the domestic demand is large and sensitive to price. Trade-substituting investments can create more jobs in both countries (Mathur 2007b).

New product-service linkages can be innovated. Knowledge-intensive business services (**KIBS**) can affect demand patterns with new product development, new services, positioning new product-service bundles, with high-value services and avoiding competition in unbranded commodities. This cannot be analysed from past trends. Foresight and courage are required to design initiatives capable of credibly developing new alternatives for decision-makers to accept new supply chains and new ways of doing. The prospect of India becoming a supply chain hub is far from saturated.

GATS-supported services trade enables business opportunities for reconfiguring product-service linkages. The development and diffusion of new technologies, new products, new management processes, new organisational systems and new logistical structures require services before products can be made and delivered. Further, certain services directed at people's minds or bodies or to things have to be organised to be both produced and delivered in the same real time. A related aspect is that the same service may be possible, in some but not all cases, to be deliverable in alternative modes of service supply. The efficacy with which service delivery is organised with regard to cost, quality and reliability makes a difference to the design and sustainability of value chains. Table 2.3 indicates the empty white spaces available for twelve categories of GATS services under four modes of service supply with examples.

Table 2.3 GATS-enabled services trade

	Mode 1: cross-border supply (CBS)	Mode 2: consumption abroad (CA)	Mode 3: foreign commercial presence (FCP)	Mode 4: Movement of Natural Persons (MNP)
1. Business services	Document translation services	Legal representation	Branch office/ Subsidiary/ Affiliate	Representative agent/ Technician
2. Communication services	Broadcasting/ podcasting/ email/ WhatsApp/ Skype	Creative services for advertising	Call centres, media offices, newspaper publishing	Exhibitors
3. Construction and related engineering services	Product designs, site planning	Landscape surveys, training	Site office for project management	Consultancy
4. Distribution services	Logistics tracking	Distribution contracting	Distribution agencies	Traders of the bag
5. Educational services	Distance Learning	Exchange students	Campuses abroad	Visiting teachers
6. Environmental services	Sensors conveying information	Safari, forest visits	Himalayan Research stations, adventure camps	Scientists conducting research abroad
7. Financial services	Accounting and tax return preparations	Funds managers	Banking services	Actuaries and assessors
8. Health related and social services	Radiology reports	Medical procedures, surgeries	Hospitals abroad	Doctors and surgeons visiting patients

(continued)

Table 2.3 (continued)

	Mode 1: cross-border supply (CBS)	Mode 2: consumption abroad (CA)	Mode 3: foreign commercial presence (FCP)	Mode 4: Movement of Natural Persons (MNP)
9. Tourism and travel related services	Travel planning	Travel to tourist destinations	Hotels, restaurants abroad	Tourist guides/ trip organisers
10. Recreational, cultural and sporting Services	Netflix movies, telecasts of sports events	Travel to museums, theatres, operas abroad	Cultural centres, Stadia	Athletes to compete, singers to perform
11. Transport services	Insurance, logistics planning	Fuelling, maintenance abroad	Garages	Drivers
12. Other services not included elsewhere	e-commerce	Therapy abroad	Law firms	Journalists

The 48 boxes in the above table can be business-to-business (B2B) services or business-to-consumer (B2C) services or government-to-government services (G2G). G2G services are especially important for innovations related to science and technology in fields where the major initiatives involve governments and public–private partnerships as in health care, public hygiene, sanitation, sewerage, waste management, water management and other fields of public systems management. Certain attractive business opportunities related to infrastructure development (highways, ports, airports) in India are only available on a build–operate–transfer (BOT) or build–own–operate (BOO) basis. The capabilities to create and manage services become an important part of such endeavours. There are competitive bids coming up for new airports, new cargo handling capacity in deep sea ports and highways. Projects involve participating in global tenders and building capabilities for them.

Finnish Priorities: Too Few or Too Many?

Finland invests about 3.5% of its GDP in research and development. This is mostly technology seeding, and it calls for aggressive international harvesting. Does Finland have too few priorities being actioned in India or too many? From Finland's absence in many arenas of action in India such as infrastructure development, creative services, health care and education, it would seem that there are too few priorities with much left outside its radar. Yet, from the way business delegations go around in India, be it Finpro Chief casually inviting Bollywood to film in Lapland (for the nth time with little result to show for it) or Finnfund Chief urging Pune to be declared as a twin city of Tampere (with negligible incremental investment in either direction to show for it after years of such bonhomie and considerable reception fatigue at the local chamber of commerce in Pune that graciously hosted several delegations), it also appears that there are too many actors tripping over each other and chasing too many priorities. The declared sectors of Finnish interest in India have changed with time. Initially, these were limited to telecom, electronics, IT-enabled services, offshoring and outsourcing, infrastructure and logistics (business from new roads, ports and airports), food processing in megafood parks, a Nokia park for its flagship company, medical devices, environmental technologies and carbon credits, forestry, paper machinery, construction and project goods.

According to the Finland–India Business Guide, there are Finnish firms present in India *"through subsidiaries or joint ventures with local companies"* and that *"about a hundred Finnish firms export to India or operate on the market through local representatives"* (Embassy of Finland 2016). The Finland–India Business Guide names Finnish Companies in India, of which some, like ABB (of Sweden), Andritz (of Austria), Ahlström Asia Pte. Ltd. (China), Perkin Elmer Inc. (U.S.A.) and GE, are not Finnish companies.[2] The revised count of Finnish companies in India having subsidiaries or joint ventures or branches based on verification of this Finnish official list is fewer (excluding those with only representative agents or liaison offices to scout for business). The prominent Finnish players included Kone in elevators (with a 30% share of the market), Wärtsilä in diesel generator sets (with 70% share of the market), Huhtamäki and Eltete in paper and packaging. Elcoteq is a recent entrant in electronics with a hub in Bangalore, while Thermo Electron Oy has established a branch office in Mumbai. Projects have attracted Metso Minerals for marketing its road-building equipment and mining drills. The Finnish IT service company, TietoEnator, established a wholly owned subsidiary in India. There are many other Finnish companies that are discussed in a later chapter.

The Finnish trade site in India (http://www.finland.org.in/trade.htm) notes Finland's interest in outsourcing and offshoring IT services to India. This comes across as quite a compelling reason for Finland because heavy ICT investments were made in Finland on the assumption that Finland would lead the way in the EU as a model ICT hub from where value-added services could be structured for the whole world. This was a myth. As noted by me in a previous publication (Mathur 2005), the importance of ICT arises from evidence that international trade in

---

[2]Consistency requires that 'traders of the bag' be distinguished from 'traders of the tent'. It is one of the travesties of globalisation that multinational firms operate in foreign countries under flags of convenience different from their true identities. Is a Swedish or Austrian or American firm to be counted as Finnish in India just because it also has some business in Finland? Does a Finnish firm's investment in China become Finnish simply because it partly carries a Finnish name (like Ahlström Pte. of Shanghai) and is such a Chinese company's presence in India to be regarded as Chinese or Finnish? For the sake of bilateral clarity in Indo-Finnish economic relations that would govern reciprocity in 'national treatment' for GATS, a limited liability company must be regarded as an artificial juridical person of a particular territory and it would be misleading to consider a company as 'Finnish' in India if it did not exist in India as a Finnish subsidiary or joint venture or if its branch in India did not have some direct ownership or control from a company in Finland.

intermediate goods facilitates access to key inputs for domestic production processes and contributes to the competitiveness of individual industries. In ICT produced manufacturing (ICTPM), the EU average consumption of ICTPM inputs to produce one monetary unit of ICTPM goods is 0.262, while for Finland this coefficient takes up the value 0.366 (European Commission 2005, pp. 54–55). The Eurostat New Cronos input–output tables reveal that productivity of highly skilled value-added ICT in Finland is the lowest in the European Union (European Commission 2005, p. 62, Table IV.21). Further, only Greece and Portugal rank lower than Finland in overall terms of GDP contribution per hour worked (O'Mahony and Van Ark 2003, p. 20, Table 1.2) and the labour productivity growth in Finland is negligible despite severe job cuts.[3] Yet, Finland's value-added shares of ICTPM and ICT producing services (ICTPS) are above the average of the EU which suggests that Finland's ICT sector, despite lacking competitiveness, was somehow supported.[4] One important dimension of the ICT crisis is the movement away from high-cost software development in Finland presciently noted by researchers conscious of the role ICT expansion played in economic recovery in regions like Tampere during the 1990s (Kasvio 2005, p. 11).

Opportunities Financed by Government Outlays and Multilateral Assistance

The first category of traditional development discourse for the government-led business opportunities in India has been around food, clothing and housing (colloquially referred to as *roti, kapda aur makaan*). This covers businesses around increases in agricultural productivity from the use of tractors, farm equipment, irrigation canals, dam construction, drip irrigation and hydroponics, irrigation management, use of fertilisers, investments in both domestic and export capacity augmentation for garments, fabrics, textiles, carpets and rugs, home furnishings, house construction, sewerage systems, sanitation and waste disposal.

The second category in the development discourse is around energy, safe drinking water, water harvesting and conservation, water supply, roads

---

[3]During 1995–2001, Finland's annual growth rates of labour productivity exhibit a skewed distribution. The highest growth rates were in electronic valves and tubes (60%), office machinery (43.6%) communications (12%) and financial intermediation (8.7%), whereas labour productivity declined in education, health care, research and development, scientific instrument making, transport equipment, construction, mining, radio and television receivers, hotels and catering, shipbuilding and repairs, insurance and other business activities (O'Mahony and Van Ark 2003, pp. 126–127).

[4]During the 1990s, about a third of Finland's growth in GDP could be attributed to Nokia. This changed. From 2001 onwards, Nokia expanded its activities abroad rather than in Finland. However, its draft on national assets, public outlays and community resources of Finland continued to remain considerable and became disproportionate to what it was contributing to Finland.

(colloquially referred to as *bijli, pani aur sadak* referring to electricity, water and roads). This includes, conventional non-renewable (coal, oil, gas) and non-conventional renewable sources of energy such as hydro, nuclear and solar, attention to water pollution in wells, rivers, lakes, groundwater table and expansion of roads infrastructure including flyovers, toll roads, inter-city highways, and roads to enable children to go to school, workers to get to workplaces, and citizens to be able to access markets, facilities, institutions that would truly be emancipatory for democratic functioning and well-being.

The third category of discourse now emerging is around education and health care for all, job creation beyond minimum support guarantees and support for enterprising through telematic connectivity. The launch of a new public healthcare scheme and new financial incentives for innovation, enterprising, contribution to augmenting public goods and access to information for enterprise decision-making belong in this category.

Let us take a look at some of the government schemes reported by the Economic Survey 2017–18. The Government of India is trying to provide 24×7 reliable and quality power supply to all. The Deen Dayal Upadhyaya Gram Jyoti Yojana (DDUGJY) scheme of 2015 promised 100% village electrification by 2019. Another Saubhagya scheme initiated in September 2017, for universal energy access targeted last mile connectivity. As per Saubhagya portal of Rural Electrification Corporation, out of 181 million rural households in the country, 142 million (about 78%) of rural households had been electrified by January 2018. The social impact of this and the potential for new economic activities that this can now spawn is mind-boggling. This kind of transformation of villages into small towns with facilities comparable to larger urban settlements can now generate new potential for growth and connectivity because the skills of people would become connected and marketable. With this, there would be new demand by households and by businesses in new regions which could not have supported many activities previously.

Climate change initiatives are a promising new avenue. About 18% of India's electricity generation was from renewable energy sources in 2017. The International Solar Alliance (ISA), launched by the Prime Minister of India and the President of France on 30 November 2015 in Paris, became effective from 6 December 2017. ISA is a coalition of solar resource-rich countries located fully or partially between the Tropics of Cancer and Capricorn harnessing solar energy. ISA is the first International intergovernmental international organisation headquartered in India. Currently, 46 countries have joined, and of these, 19 countries have ratified the ISA Framework Agreement. ISA is a trillion-dollar opportunity in solar energy. Would Finland join in collaborating with India or miss out on it? As I write, I am aware of how Fortum of Finland is prospecting these opportunities but that is only the tip of proverbial iceberg.

India's solar energy initiatives are pioneering in nature because India possesses pioneering solar technologies in solar energy storage and business opportunities are available among potentially 121 countries that can be part of the ISA. As part of implementing the National Action Plan on Climate Change (NAPCC), eight national missions have been launched in India covering solar energy production and storage, energy efficiency, agriculture, water, sustainable habitat, forestry, Himalayan ecosystem and knowledge creation.

The members will collectively contribute $1 trillion by 2030 to the ISA. Additional resources committed by India to ISA include Rs. 1 billion for ISA fund corpus and annual expenditure grants of Rs. 150 million per annum for the period 2016–17 to 2020–21. Additionally, the Government of India has provided for US $2 billion line of credit (LoC) to the African countries. France has committed an additional €300 million for solar projects across ISA member countries.

The Economic Survey 2017–18 notes that as part of the mission on strategic knowledge on climate change, India has established eight Global Technology Watch Groups in the areas of renewable energy technology, advanced coal technology, enhanced energy efficiency, green forestry, sustainable habitats, water, sustainable agriculture and manufacturing. India is one of the few countries where, despite ongoing development, forest and tree cover have increased transforming country's forests into a net sink in contrast to the declining forest cover in forest-rich countries such as Indonesia and Brazil.

Water Pollution

The National Mission to Clean the Ganga River along its length of more than 2,500 km is one of the major challenges to combat water pollution in North India. This is an excellent opportunity to prove existing Finnish technologies that have been used in water bodies of Finland so that many more projects of similar nature that are on the anvil would generate a stream of business opportunities. The expertise so proven would be in demand in many countries including China, Egypt and Brazil that are struggling to clean their rivers and lakes.

Air Pollution

Air Pollution is one of the most intractable challenges in India due to road dust, construction dust, garbage accumulations, crop residue, biomass burning and vehicular and other emissions. The practice of crop residue burning responsible for about a third of the air pollution in North India is associated with the use of combine harvesters—machines that harvest, thresh and clean the separated grain altogether. The labour saving, time saving and cost saving leave behind 30–35-cm-long stalks and stubble that is burnt.

The economics of agri-technology incentivises the increasing air pollution. The rental cost of a combine harvester is just Rs. 800 for 0.4 ha. The cost of stubble removal per hectare is Rs. 3,500 per hectare. So instead of bundling residues as fodder, a one rupee matchbox can be used to just burn it. A solution and a system are both required. Finland has a well-established system of bagging and recycling crop-waste although it is only seasonal in July–August. Here is something that could be scaled up for India.

Make in India

The 'Make in India' programme launched in 2014 aims at making India a global hub for manufacturing, research and innovation and integral part of the global supply chain. The only two Prime Ministers present at the inauguration in India were the Swedish and Finnish Prime Ministers. The Swedish Prime Minister spoke of the fast-expanding Swedish-Indian collaborations in various fields. The Finnish Prime Minister spoke about Finland's SLUSH event and invited those present to visit SLUSH.

'Make in India' is an opportunity to link up with the government identified ten 'champions sectors' that have potential to become global champion, drive double-digit growth in manufacturing and generate significant employment opportunities. The sectors that have been identified are **capital goods**, auto and **auto components**, defence and aerospace, biotechnology, pharmaceuticals and **medical devices**, chemicals, **electronic system design** and **manufacturing (ESDM)**, leather and footwear, textiles and apparels, food processing, gems and jewellery, new and renewable energy, **construction**, **shipping** and **railways**. The **bolded** ones are the sectors in which Finnish enterprises have solutions, products, services and technologies.

Make in India but Made by Finland and India

In telecom, there is potential for setting up manufacturing of semiconductors and fabrication of chips in India where skilled technical labour force in India and low-cost high-quality R&D can be combined with the technology strengths of Finland. There is a need in India for more than ten naphtha cracker plants of 750 thousand tonnes each together with downstream facilities. The widespread use of cement and steel in construction and other industrial applications that have high growth rates is of interest to Finnish firms and to Indian firms for joint ventures that could also lead to collaboration for new plants in third-country markets, especially in other Asia and Africa. There is no government restriction to trade on manufactured steel in India except for high-grade iron ore exports to be channelled through Minerals and Metals Trading Corporation (MMTC) and the National Minerals Development Corporation (NMDC).

Roads Infrastructure

The *Bharatmala Pariyojana*[5] mentioned in Chap. 1 is a new scheme for highways development for optimising freight and passenger traffic. Critical infrastructure gaps are being bridged with development of economic corridors, inter-corridors and feeder routes, National Corridor Efficiency Improvement, border and international connectivity roads, coastal and port connectivity roads and greenfield expressways. The target is 24,800 km in the first phase 2018–2022 with an outlay of Rs. 535,000 crores (Rs 5350 billion). There is much scope to bid for executing projects and also to function as part of supply consortia.

New Airports

India is one of the fastest growing domestic aviation markets in the world and is already the third biggest worldwide. Eighteen new airports are at various stages of being built in the country, which include Mopa in Goa, Navi Mumbai, Shirdi and Sindhudurg in Maharashtra, Bijapur, Gulbarga, Hassan and Shimoga in Karnataka, Kannur in Kerala, Durgapur in West Bengal, Dabra in Madhya Pradesh, Pakyong in Sikkim (already functioning), Karaikal in Puducherry, Kushinagar in Uttar Pradesh, Dholera in Gujarat, and Dagadarthi Mandal, Bhogapuram and Oravakallu in Andhra Pradesh. 'Site clearance' has also been granted for five greenfield airports: Machhiwara in Punjab, Itanagar in Arunachal Pradesh, Jamshedpur in Jharkhand, Alwar in Rajasthan and Kothagudem in Telangana (as reported in the media by Times of India[6]). Business opportunities in airport construction extend to all the navigational equipment, cargo handling systems and other infrastructure that an airport complex requires. The liberalisation of air services with the proposed India–Afghanistan Air freight Corridor and the Air Services Agreement between India and Serbia require new systems and standards for cargo handling. Many new international airports are being built with 74–100% foreign equity participation allowed for the construction and management under build–operate–transfer (BOT), build–operate–lease–transfer (BOLT), build–own–operate (BOO) or lease–develop–operate (LDO).

---

[5]As described in official documents on the Government of India website http://pibphoto.nic.in/documents/rlink/2017/oct/p2017102504.pdf.
[6]https://timesofindia.indiatimes.com/business/india-business/india-fastest-growing-domestic-aviation-market-globally-economic-survey/articleshow/62695189.cms?utm_source=contentofin.

Shipping

Shipping is another priority sector where many projects supported by government funding have been announced. Nearly 95% of India's trade by volume and 68% by value is shipped by sea. India had a fleet strength of 1,374 ships in 2017 with Shipping Corporation of India (SCI) having the largest share of the tonnage handled at 34%. Around 443 ships handle India's overseas trade and the rest cover coastal trade.

To encourage the growth of Indian tonnage, the government has reduced the GST from 18 to 5% on bunker fuel used in Indian flag vessels, provided parity in the tax regime to both Indian and foreign seafarers, and simplified ship registration, and chartering permission rules. In India, shipbuilding and ship-repair facilities are both abundantly available. There are 27 shipyards with 6 under central public sector, 2 under State governments and 19 as private. Traditionally, the shipbuilding industry was dominated by South Korea, China and Japan, but this is changing as India is strategically located on the international trade route with a long coastline of about 7,500 km and 14,500 km of potentially navigable waterways.

Nine Indian ports have been benchmarked to international standards to reduce dwell time, transaction time and ease congestion. A new Sagar Mala Programme has been launched to reduce logistics cost for international and domestic trade, and 508 projects at an estimated investment of more than Rs. 8,000 billion have been identified for implementation over the next 20 years. These projects are being implemented primarily through the private players or PPP mode. From 2018 to 2022, new projects of about Rs. 100 billion would be inviting bids annually. Masterplans have been made for all major ports.

For Inland Waterways Transport (IWT), the 'Jal Marg Vikas Project' on River Ganga to connect Varanasi and Haldia, a navigable distance of 1,380 km, has been announced. On the River Brahmaputra, Ro-Ro services have begun between Dhubri and Hatsingimari in July 2017 on an Inland Waterways Authority of India (IWAI) vessel. Under the National Waterways Act, 2016, another 106 additional inland waterways have been declared as National Waterways (NWs) and work is being taken up on the Barak River, on Cumberjua, Mandovi and Zuari in Goa, River Rupnarayan and Sunderbans in West Bengal and on the Alappuzha–Kottayam–Athirampuzha Canal in Kerala and on the River Gandak. To reduce the logistics cost of cargo and facilitate passenger movement between North East and the rest of India, MOUs have been signed with Bangladesh. Here is another area where Finland's expertise with waterways (lakes, canals, locks) has potential to be used.

Telecom

The telecom sector in India is buoyant as an outcome of spectrum management, 'Digital India', a government programme, is an ambitious one for expanding the scope of the digital transactions for knowledge- and information-driven society. In 2017, there were 1,207 million subscribers with wireless telephony accounting for over 98% of the connections. The mobile industry in India currently employs more people than the population of Finland. But the telecom sector also faces debt piles, price wars, reduced revenue and irrational spectrum costs. Jio, a new entrant, has disrupted the market with low-cost services. More disruptions are to be expected with the universalisation of optical fibre networks as part of the Digital India initiative. Finnish firms have experience of the rise and fall of Nokia and also of high penetration rates and how connectivity enabled revolutionise public services and governance in Finland. That valuable experience could be useful as India prepares for the next phase of the digital revolution.

Oil and Gas Projects

About half of India's 26 sedimentary basins covering an area of over 3 Million km^2 spread over onshore, shallow water and deep water lack adequate geoscientific data. Evaluations of un-appraised areas are required, and about Rs. 2,933 crores have been committed on this project being implemented by Oil India Limited (OIL) and Oil and Natural Gas Corporation (ONGC).

Refining Capacity in India is second largest in Asia after China. The biggest crude refinery in the world is in India, and India is emerging as a refinery hub with refining capacity exceeding demand. On the National Gas Grid, an additional 15,000-km-long pipeline network is being developed. The government has approved partial capital grant of Rs. 51,760 million (40% of the estimated capital cost of Rs. 29,400 million) in September 2016 to GAIL for constructing 2,650 km Jagdishpur-Haldia and Bokaro-Dhamra Pipeline (JHBDPL) natural gas pipeline project, popularly known as Pradhan Mantri Urja Ganga of Eastern India. This project will connect eastern part of the country with National Gas Grid and will ensure the availability of clean and eco-friendly fuel, natural gas, to the industrial, commercial, domestic and transport sectors in the States of Uttar Pradesh, Bihar, Jharkhand, Odisha and West Bengal. According to the information in the public domain from the Ministry of Petroleum website, these pipeline projects would support the revival of three fertiliser plants in Gorakhpur (UP), Barauni (Bihar) and Sindri (Jharkhand) along the route.[7] These developments are of interest to Finland which is both an infrastructure builder and a net energy importer.

---

[7] http://petroleum.nic.in/sites/default/files/AR16-17.pdf.

In conclusion, there is no dearth of business opportunities in India. With more exports to India and less expensive imports, Finland can improve its overall balance of trade. When returns are generated on trade-substituting investments, that would also lead to an improved balance of payments with growth in factor incomes from abroad. In partnering with the Government of India, the public sector and private enterprises in India, new directions of business can arise. The geographical footprint of Finnish business can reach hitherto unserved and underserved markets with new value propositions particularly in other countries of Asia, Africa, South America and the Middle East.

References

Embassy of Finland (2016) Finland-India business guide. Team Finland, New Delhi

European Commission (2005) EU sectoral competitiveness indicators, Brussels

Government of India (2018) Economic survey 2017–18. Ministry of Finance Department of Economic Affairs Economic Division, New Delhi

Kasvio A (2005) Future challenges of information society development. In: Anttiroiko A-V, Kasvio A (eds) From industrial city to informational city: analysing the dynamics of local economic and social regeneration with a special emphasis on the city of Tampere. Tampere University Press

Mathur A (1998) Finland-India economic relations: a twinning study of trade and investment potential. ETLA, Helsinki (Reprinted 2002)

Mathur A (2002) Indo-French economic relations: a study of trade and investment potential. Indian Council for Research on International Economic Relations, New Delhi

Mathur A (2005) The future of international business in the Tampere Region. In: Kasvio A, Anttiroiko A-V (eds) eCity: analysing the efforts to generate local dynamism in the city of Tampere to meet the challenge of changing global economy. Tampere University Press, Tampere

Mathur A (2006) Institutional factors governing choice of GATS modes for services supply. In: ANZIBA 2006, conference proceedings, University of Wellington, New Zealand 16–18.11.2006

Mathur AN (2007a) Finland-India business prospects 2007–2017. Indian Institute of Management Ahmedabad

Mathur AN (2007b) Why some unemployed are unemployable? Challenges for Policy Research in Finland and India. In: Conference proceedings, second EU-EFA international conference, 7–9 Sept 2007, Oulu

Mattila S, Mathur AN (2007) Oilon, case number IIMA/BP/336, Case Bank. IIM, Ahmedabad

O'Mahony M, Van Ark B (2003) EU productivity and competitiveness: an industry perspective: can Europe resume the catching-up process?. European Commission, Brussels

Veuglers R, Mathur A (1993) Foreign presence of Belgian companies, Onderzoeksrapport 9327, K.U. Leuven

Chapter 3
Business Opportunities in Finland

You cannot cross the Sea by standing and staring at the water.
Rabindranath Tagore

Abstract This chapter presents a schema of how business opportunities in Finland may be explored together with the identification of prospects for trade, trade-substituting investments and product-service linkages. The analysis uses the same methodology of constructing a revealed comparative advantage index as done for business opportunities in India in Chap. 2. Modalities including modes of entry and mobilisation of resources and responses are also discussed.

Introduction

There is an enormous lack of awareness about business opportunities in Finland among business leaders, entrepreneurs and managers abroad, including India. There are also blind spots in the Indian mindsets about viable business models in Finland because of sticky beliefs that a business model successful in India must work everywhere else. This kind of hubris has been shattered in numerous instances as close by as in neighbouring Nepal and in developing countries of Africa. And by now there are tens of such failures of Indian investments in Finland because investors did not appreciate the nature of opportunity or failed to understand how the business model for the same product or service required to be organised quite differently in Finland. Yet, others who paid attention to detail and developed capabilities have experienced much success in investments from India in Finland and in trade with Finland.

This chapter discusses what business opportunities in Finland may be approached with the identification of prospects for trade, trade-substituting investments and product-service linkages. This chapter draws on previous papers by the author (Mathur 2006, 2007a, b, 2008a, b, 2009; Mattila and Mathur 2009) presented at seminars in Finland in Helsinki, Turku, Jyvaskylä and Oulu and at international business conferences in Wellington, New Zealand and Capetown, South Africa. A multilevel analysis has been undertaken with regard to the following:

(a) Goods that comprise the largest share in exports of India to Finland at two-digit, four-digit, six-digit and eight-digit levels of disaggregation using the SITC HS codes of the international classification.
(b) Goods with high rates of growth in imports by Finland have been identified.
(c) Goods that comprise the largest shares in the import basket of Finland have been examined regardless of origin and were already referred in Chap. 2 for the purpose of pointing to possibilities in Finnish trade diversification by country of origin that would improve its balance of trade, considering that over 60% of Finnish imports are currently from expensive sources.
(d) Goods imported by Finland which feature in India's exports to the EU, but not to Finland.

In value, India's worldwide exports are about four times the exports of Finland to the world. But in goods, exports of India to Finland are less than exports of Finland to India as discussed in Chap. 2. Indian exports to the world and to Finland are concentrated in a few sectors. About 76% of India's worldwide exports and 70% of exports of India to Finland are limited to a few SITC codes such as cereals (10), mineral fuels and oils (27), organic chemicals (29), pharmaceutical products (30), plastics and articles thereof (39), cotton (52), articles of apparel and clothing accessories (61 and 62), natural or cultured pearls and articles of gems and jewellery (71), iron and steel and their articles (72 and 73), nuclear reactors and boilers (84), electrical machinery and equipment (85), vehicles other than railway or tramway (87) and aircraft, spacecraft and parts thereof (88). The sectoral shares of India's exports are shown in Table 3.1.

Table 3.1 Sectoral shares of Indian Exports

SITC HS code	Code description	% share in total exports to world	% share in total exports to Finland
10	Cereals	3	0
27	Mineral fuels, mineral oils and products or their distillation; bituminous substances; mineral waxes	21	2
29	Organic chemicals	4	5
30	Pharmaceutical products	4	13
39	Plastics and articles thereof	2	2
52	Cotton	3	0
61	Articles of apparel and clothing accessories knitted or crocheted	2	7
62	Articles of apparel and clothing accessories not knitted or crocheted	3	6
71	Natural or cultured pearls, precious or semi-precious stones, precious metals, metals clad with precious metal and articles thereof; imitation jewellery; coin	14	6

(continued)

Table 3.1 (continued)

SITC HS code	Code description	% share in total exports to world	% share in total exports to Finland
72	Iron and steel	3	4
73	Articles of iron or steel	2	8
84	Nuclear reactors, boilers, machinery and mechanical appliances; parts thereof	5	8
85	Electrical machinery and equipment and parts thereof; sound recorders and reproducers, television image and sound recorders and reproducers, and parts and accessories of articles	3	6
87	Vehicles other than railway or tramway rolling stock, and parts and accessories thereof	5	1
88	Aircraft, spacecraft, and parts thereof	2	2
Total % share		76	70

Indian Export Potential to Finland

Analysis was also done by constructing a similar but modified revealed comparative advantage index (RCAI) for India as constructed and analysed for Finland in Chap. 2. Indian production and export base is highly diversified with respect to the EU-28, but it has failed to grow to substantial volumes or diversify with Finland. India has had an adverse trade balance with Finland in goods trade for years and this itself poses some constraints to exports and imports. The strongest export sectors of India were analysed with respect to the aggregate of exports to Nordic countries and the aggregate of exports to the EU by identifying all articles of traded value above €1 million where an EU-28 country or at least two out of Sweden, Denmark and Norway are involved as destinations provided the item belongs to Finland's import list. The composition of India's exports is summarised in Table 3.2 (this is based on disaggregated figures available for 2017).

Table 3.2 Composition of India's exports to Finland

Food and beverages	6.5%
Minerals, gem and jewellery	3.0%
Chemicals and pharmaceuticals	21.0%
Manufacturing goods incl. textiles, engg.	44.0%
Others	25.5%

Source Tilastokeskus, Finland

Two-digit SITC codes in which India has Revealed Comparative Advantage (refer Table 3.3 below) are: cereals (10), oilseeds and oleaginous fruits (12), animal or vegetable fats and oils (15), preparations of vegetables, fruit, nuts or other parts of plaints (20), residues and waste from the food (23), salt, sulphur, earth and stones (25), Mineral fuel and oils (27), inorganic chemicals (28), organic chemicals (29), pharmaceutical products (30), essential oils and resinoids (33), soap, organic surface-active agents (34), albuminoidal substances (35), miscellaneous chemical products (38), plastics and articles thereof (39), raw hides and skins (41), wood and articles of wood (44), pulp of wood or other fibrous cellulosic material (47), paper and paperboard (48), printed books and newspapers (49), cotton (52), man-made filaments (54), articles of apparel and clothing accessories (61 and 62), articles of stones, plaster, cement (68), glass and glassware (70), natural or cultured pearls, jems and jewellery (71), iron and steel (72), articles of iron or steel (73), copper, nickel and aluminium articles thereof (74, 75, and 76), nuclear reactors and boilers (84), electrical machinery (85), vehicles other than railway or tramway (87), optical, photographic, cinematographic instruments (90), Furniture, bedding, mattresses (94) and Miscellaneous goods (99).

Table 3.3 Potential Indian Exports based on Revealed Comparative Advantage of India (RCAI)

SITC HS code	Code description	RCAI value
10	Cereals	14.41
12	Oilseeds and oleaginous fruits; miscellaneous grains, seeds and fruit; industrial or medicinal plants; straw and fodder	8.39
15	Animal or vegetable fats and oils and their cleavage products; prepared edible fats; animal or vegetable waxes	2.92
20	Preparations of vegetables, fruit, nuts or other parts of plants	1.35
23	Residues and waste from the food industries; prepared animal fodder	10.59
25	Salt; sulphur; earth and stone; plastering materials, lime and cement	2.50
27	Mineral fuels, mineral oils and products or their distillation; bituminous substances; mineral waxes	6.48
28	Inorganic chemicals; organic or inorganic compounds of precious metals, of rare-earth metals, or radioactive elements or of isotopes	1.31
29	Organic chemicals	4.13
30	Pharmaceutical products	3.24
33	Essential oils and resinoids; perfumery, cosmetic or toilet preparations	9.14
34	Soap, organic surface-active agents, washing and lubricating preparations, artificial and prepared waxes, polishing or scouring preparations, candles and similar articles, modelling pastes, 'dental waxes' and dental preparations with a b	2.04
35	Albuminoidal substances; modified starches; glues; enzymes	6.65
38	Miscellaneous chemical products	3.58
39	Plastics and articles thereof	8.17

(continued)

Table 3.3 (continued)

SITC HS code	Code description	RCAI value
41	Raw hides and skins (other than furskins) and leather	1.93
44	Wood and articles of wood; wood charcoal	1.59
48	Paper and paperboard; articles of paper pulp, of paper or of paperboard	2.45
49	Printed books, newspapers, pictures and other products of the printing industry; manuscripts, typescripts and plans	4.05
52	Cotton	1.66
54	Man-made filaments	4.68
61	Articles of apparel and clothing accessories, knitted or crocheted	1.00
62	Articles of apparel and clothing accessories, not knitted or crocheted	1.51
68	Articles of stone, plaster, cement, asbestos, mica or similar materials	1.39
70	Glass and glassware	1.78
71	Natural or cultured pearls, precious or semi-precious stones, precious metals, metals clad with precious metal and articles thereof; imitation jewellery; coin	2.81
72	Iron and steel	11.83
73	Articles of iron or steel	1.44
74	Copper and articles thereof	3.12
75	Nickel and articles thereof	11.19
76	Aluminium and articles thereof	9.67
84	Nuclear reactors, boilers, machinery and mechanical appliances; parts thereof	29.46
85	Electrical machinery and equipment and parts thereof; sound recorders and reproducers, television image and sound recorders and reproducers, and parts and accessories of articles	11.20
87	Vehicles other than railway or tramway rolling stock, and parts and accessories thereof	10.25
90	Optical, photographic, cinematographic, measuring, checking, precision, medical or surgical instruments and apparatus; parts and accessories thereof	2.01

Items on Finland's import list that India exports to the EU and where EU shares of Indian exports are significant have been identified. India's exportables to Finland are detailed in Annexures V–VIII. Annexure V lists high-value RCAI led Indian exports to the world importable by Finland. Annexure VI lists high-value RCAI led Indian exports to EU that is also on Finland's import list. Annexure VII lists the top ten Indian high-value exports to Finland at the four-digit disaggregated level. Annexure VIII lists high-value Indian exports to European Union importable from India by Finland. Many of India's exports are consumer goods. The concentration of wholesale and retail trade in Finland poses an institutional impediment which is discussed in Chap. 8 for ways around them.

The disaggregated analysis reveals the following situation:

(a) **Under Cereals (10)**: Rice (1006) is the only Indian export to Finland under cereals and the quantity was so small that it doesn't show up at the two-digit level.

(b) **Under Minerals (25 and 26), Mineral Fuel and Oils (27)**: Petroleum oils and oils obtained from bituminous sources (2710) is India's only export to Finland in this category. Other potential items like marble and calcined coke where EU's share is over 75% of India's worldwide exports (and both are imported by Finland), Indian exports to Finland are zero. Trade in slate, cut granite and mica powder exists but Indian share of Finnish imports of these are small. It is rumoured that this is controlled by import cartels. Other items with export potential are bentonite clays, building stones, mica flakes, titanium ores and concentrates, unprocessed ilmenite.

(c) **Under Chemicals (29 and 38)**: Heterocyclic compounds with nitrogen (2933), Nucleic acids and their salts (2934), halogenated, sulphonated, nitrated derivatives of products of heading 2912 (2913), Antibiotics (2941 are already exported to Finland. Finland's imports of sodium and sodium products (like Silicates) from India are significant. But cyclic hydrocarbons (2902) which have an 18% share in India's exports to the world in this category have potential to be exported to Finland and have not yet been exported. With the exception of parachloroanilene (2921), Finland's share of EU imports from India could be larger in all items.

Other items with export potential are chemicals such as manganese sulphate, cyclic hydrocarbons like toulene, nitrogenated hydrocarbons, menthol, benzyl alcohol, methyl and ethyl ketones, ketone alcohols and ketone aldehydes, phosphoric esters, amino sulphonic anilines, and folic acid and pigments such as reactive blues, vat yellows, acid browns, solvent orange, solvent reds, azoic blacks, optical whiteners and printing inks.

(d) **Under Pharmaceuticals Products (30)**: Medicaments (excluding items of 3002, 3005/3006) for therapeutic uses in measured doses or in packing for retail sale (3004) are being exported to Finland without 'Manufactured in India' markings in Business-to-Business sales. Most of the Ibuprufen sold in Finland is from India, but the packets don't mention that. There is enormous scope to export many other Indian generics directly to Finland instead of via Germany. The Finnish government has been encouraging the prescription of generics as a policy and the resistance points are from old trade links and suppliers, their friendly procurers in Finnish pharma and the aggressive promotion by incentivizing doctors in Finland to prescribe patent-expired trade-marked branded generics by pharma companies from North America and Germany. For example, Zovirax sells in Finland at forty times its actual price as the generic acyclovir would cost from India. Bacibact sells at ten times the price in Finland as the generic equivalent would cost from India. Indian pharmaceutical industry should work in collaboration with the Finnish authorities to reduce the cost of medicines in Finland that would have favourable effects not only for consumers but also for Finland's negative balance of trade with Germany.

In pharmaceuticals, with the exception of trimethoprim and amoxycillin, EU accounts for 28% of India's exports of medicines. Finland imports chloramphenicol, cephalexin and eyedrops from many countries, but the quantity of Indian imports is small.

Pharmaceutical products such as penicillins, ampicillins, amoxycillines, erythromycins, cephalexins, streptomycins, cefoxitins, cephalosporins, ofloxacins, macrolides, corticosteroid hormones, cefadroxil, diloxanide furoates, cimetidines, famotidines, liver extracts, ayurvedic medicines exported as neutraceuticals, menthol crystals, gonadotrophins, luteinising hormones, anti-fungal, anti-amoebic, anti-helminitic and anti-protozoal drugs, omeprazole, lansoprazole, analgin, paracetamol, ibuprofen, tenoxicam, meloxicam, captopril, enalapril, lisinopril, perindopril, ramipril, verapamil, nifedipine, amlodipine, lacidipine, bandage gauzes, surgical dressings, dental cements and filings, dentrifices are traditional Indian exports to Finland. These indicate such high growth rates that it seems likely that these exports are intended also for other EU markets than Finland.

(e) **Under plastics (39), Rubber (40) and Leather (42)**: other articles of plastics (3926), other plates and sheets of plastics (3920), articles for the conveyance of packing of goods (3923). India's exports to the world (but not to Finland) include Polymers of propylene or of other olefins, in primary forms (3902), and polyacetals, other polyethers epoxide resins (3907) which have potential to be exported to Finland.

In the Code 40, the only significant Indian exports to Finland in the category of rubber and rubber products are synthetic rubber (4002) and conveyer belting (4010). Latex sponges have potential where the average annual order has been just 280 kg—too small to ascertain sustainable profitable trade. Micro-organism cultures from India in demand in Germany, Sweden, Italy, Netherlands and Portugal are not exported to Finland at all. Finland is under-represented in EU shares of Indian exports of polyester film, perfumery, plastic kitchenware and tableware (3924), hospital sheeting (4005), rubber forms (4008) and hoses (4009). Surgical gloves (4015) are an item of Indian exports to all EU countries except Finland.

In Code 42, conventional Indian exports of leather and leather goods where EU import shares are very high include processed leather, leather cases and bags, jackets, gloves and other leather manufactured goods. Finland's imports from India in this category are tiny with the exception of leather bags. Indian footwear is a major export item to the EU. EU accounts for Indian export shares of 80% for leather footwear, 50% for rubber footwear and 30% for waterproof footwear but Indian firms have failed to establish any significant shares of the Finnish market. In hats, Indian firms have done better, but Finnish imports from the Baltics compete aggressively for market shares in this category.

(f) **Under Cotton (52)**: Cotton sewing thread (5205), cotton Yarn (5205), and woven fabrics of cotton (5208, 5209, 5211), are exported to Finland. Two sub-categories cotton, not carded or combed (5201) and woven fabrics of cotton, containing <85% cotton, mixed mainly with man-made fibres weighing >200 g/m^2 (5212) also have potential to be exported from India to Finland.

(g) **Under Articles of apparel and clothing accessories, Knitted or Crocheted (61)**: Women or girl suits (6104), T-shirts, singlets and other vests (6109), other garments not knitted or crocheted (6114). Men or boys shirts, knitted or crocheted (6105), babies garments and clothing accessories, knitted or crocheted (6111) which have begun to be exported to Finland in small quantities have high potential to expand exports. Here, exports from Bangladesh, Turkey and China compete with Indian exports and there is also trade diversion of Indian exports via Germany and Sweden.

In fabrics, with the exception of yarn, only silk, wool and cotton fabrics are India's potential exports to Finland and current shares are very small. The targeting of Finland as an export market for carpets, textile floor coverings, braids, embroidered silk and cotton lace has not yet been done. Finland imports small quantities from India of these articles and EU countries including Norway account for about 65% of the Indian exports in this category. Finland is also a growing market for manufactured textiles, knitted fabrics, cotton ensembles, trousers and shorts, shirts, blouses, underpants, panties, bathrobes, t-shirts, jerseys, babies garments, track suits, hosiery, shawls, coats, men's suits, women's suits, ski suits, scarves, bedlinen, table linen, bedspreads, towels, ties and cravats. All these are already exported from India to Finland, but the volume of exports is very small compared to other countries of the EU including Sweden, Norway and Denmark. Items currently exported from India to Finland in high volumes are bras, corsets and stockings. Items conspicuously missing are blankets, boatsails, raincoats and swimwear which Indian firms are yet to begin exporting to Finland although EU shares of India's worldwide exports of these are 75% for blankets, 40% for boatsails, 55% for raincoats and 20% for swimwear. In all these categories, Swedish imports are eight times the value of Finnish imports although the differences in the size of the market are not so much.

(h) **Under Articles of apparel and clothing accessories, not Knitted or Crocheted (62)**: Women or girls blouses (6206), Women or girl suits (6204), track suits, ski suits (6211), shawls, scarves, mufflers (6214) are already exported from India to Finland and exports are growing. There is also potential for exports of Men's or boys' suits (6203), Men's or boys' ensembles, jackets, blazers, trousers, bib and brace overalls, breeches and shorts (other than swimwear) (6205) which have so far been exported only in tiny quantities.

In textiles and clothing, Indian exports to Finland that have high potential on the basis of past trends, and growth rates of recent years, include mulberry, raw silk, silk embroidery threads, woven silk and wool fabrics, cotton grey yarns, cotton shirtings, cotton fabrics, bed linen, furnishing fabrics, handloom fabrics, dyed woven cotton fabrics, denim, coir mattresses, textured polyester yarns, dyed parachute fabrics, polyester and mixed fabrics, spun yarn, cotton twine, carpets of silk, wool, laminated fabrics, rugs (of kelem, schmks, karamanie and smlr varieties), druggets, cotton corduroy pieces, velvet fabrics, quilted wadding, duvets, overcoats, anoraks, cloaks, ski jackets, ready-made garments (trousers, shorts, bibs, suits, jackets, blazers, ensembles, dresses, skirts, kurtas, kurtis, blouses, innerwear, bathrobes, T-shirts, jerseys, pullovers, cardigans, sweaters, tracksuits, swimwear, hosiery, shawls), raincoats, umbrellas, handkerchiefs, scarves, caps, ties and cravats, curtain fabrics, pillowcases, napkins, mosquito nets, cushion covers, and footwear.

(i) **Under natural or cultured pearls, gems and jewellery (71)**: Diamonds whether or not worked (7102), silver (7106), base metal (710700), gold (7108), articles of jewellery (7113), imitation jewellery (7117) already feature in India's exports to Finland. In gems and jewellery, India does not export any pearls or silver filigree to Finland although both are imported into Finland from Russia which itself imports these from India. Precious and semi-precious stones (7103), non-industrial diamonds (7102) and articles of precious and semi-precious stones (7116) are routed from India to Finland through Russia and the UK and do not feature significantly in bilateral trade statistics.

Finland does not have a culture of using 22- or 24-carat gold in jewellery and the trade in this category would be much greater if Indian exporters positioned 14-carat and 18-carat gold jewellery and silver jewellery in Finnish traditional styles. Gems and Jewellery are among India's strong export sectors worldwide. In gems and semi-precious stones, emery and garnets are the most important items in exports to Finland. Exports to Finland indicate a trend towards increased flow of diamonds, topaz, aquamarines and jewellery. Some of the 'Kalevala collection' of Finnish gold, silver and bronze jewellery that people buy in Finland out of patriotic reasons and cultural heritage and which is also popular with tourists to Finland is already made in India.

(j) **Under Iron and Steel (72)**: Ferro alloys (7202), flat-rolled products of iron or non-alloy steel with different widths (7209, 7210, 7211), bars and rods of stainless steel (7221, 7222), wire of stainless steel (7223) are already exported from India to Finland. But semi-finished products of iron or non-alloy steel (7207), flat-rolled products of iron or non-alloy steel, of a width of 600 mm or more, hot-rolled, not clad, plated or coated (7208) which are not yet exported from India to Finland also have potential.

(k) **Under Articles of Iron or Steel (73)**: Tubes, pipes of different forms (7303, 7306, 7307, 7308), chain and parts there of (7315), screws, bolts, nuts (7318), table kitchen or other domestic article made of iron or steel (7323), other cast articles of iron or steel (7325), other articles of iron or steel 7326) are already exported and have high potential because India has emerged as a hub for auto components and other spare parts of machinery. Tubes, pipes and hollow profiles, seamless, of iron (other than cast iron) or steel (7304) and other tubes pipes of iron and steel (welded, riveted, etc.) having circular external diameter exceeding 406.4 mm (7305) which are not yet exported from India to Finland also have potential. There is trade diversion of Indian exports in this SITC Code and exports reach Finland via Germany and Russia.

Metals and metal manufactures are an underdeveloped trade category with a strong presence in both countries. Finnish imports from India comprise tubes and pipe fittings, bars, rods, angles, transmission belting, needles, stainless steel articles, non-malleable cast-iron articles, and leaf springs and these exports could grow quite fast because product standards are well established from India's exports of these items to every EU country. Significant omissions here are roller chains, threaded bolts and nuts, screws, washers, zips and the quantities of Finnish imports from India of cutlery, tungsten carbide tips, steel wires hand tools, saw blades, wrenches, hoists and escalator parts have remained small. Extruding dies, centre lathes, lightning arrestors and builder's hardware are the fastest growing Indian exports to Finland in this category.

(l) **Under Nuclear Reactors, boilers, machinery and mechanical appliances (84)**: Engines and motors (8412), pumps for liquids (8413), machinery, plant or laboratory equipment (8419), parts and accessories (8431), machinery for sorting and screening (8474), machines and mechanical appliances having individual functions (8479), taps, cocks, valves (8481), transmission shafts (8483) are already exported from India to Finland, but there are many glaring omissions in this category. Steam or other vapour generating boilers (other than central heating hot water boilers capable also of producing low pressure (8402), spark-ignition reciprocating or rotary internal combustion piston engines (8407), compression ignition internal combustion piston engines (diesel or semi-diesel engines) (8408) and automatic data processing machines and units (8471), which are not yet exported from India to Finland at all have considerable export potential. Among items exported to Finland in small quantities which have potential for increase are centrifuges, including centrifugal dryers; filtering or purifying machinery and apparatus, for liquids or gases (8421), and dish washing machines; machinery for cleaning or drying bottles or other containers; machinery for filling, closing (8422).

The market in Finland for Indian manufactured products from mechanical engineering industries is poised to grow during the next ten years as firms in Finland begin to procure more and more of their intermediary requirements outside the EU. The goods of particular interest would be steel plates, sheets and strips, chromium bars and rods; angles, shapes and sections of various alloys of nickel, iron, chromium; electrode quality stainless steel wires, pipes used in oil and gas pipelines, galvanised iron and stainless steel flanges, couplings, elbows, sleeves; fencing wires, wire meshes, threaded nuts, lifting and hoisting chains, needles, pins, stainless steel utensils, parts for earth-moving equipment, steering and rudder equipment for ships and boats, aluminium sheets and strips, aluminium foils, door and window frames, gas cylinders for liquefied gases, pliers, pincers, tweezers, spanners, wrenches, vices, clamps, industrial cutting knives, tungsten carbide tips, hinges, sign plates, marine propulsion turbines, industrial boilers, steam turbines, parts of mechanical appliances, grinding and polishing machines, non-electric braille typewriters, pneumatic tools, industrial valves, ballasts for fluorescent lamps, static convertors, microwave ovens, lamps, sound amplifiers, capacitors and semiconductor devices, optical fibre cables, insulation fittings, shock absorbers, integrated circuits, motorcycles, bicycles and their parts, contact lenses, spectacle lenses, hydrographic instruments, catheters, syringes, surgical knives, cannulae, pantographs and drawing instruments, X-ray (Roentgen) machines, musical instruments, office furniture, watches, sports equipment like golf clubs, golf balls, footballs, gymnasium and athletics equipment, sports nets, tennis and badminton rackets, and fishing rods, hooks and tackles.

(m) **Under Electrical machinery and parts thereof (85)**: Electric motors and generators (8501), Electrica l transformers (8504), electrical ignition or starting equipment (8511), electric, laser or other light photo beam (8515), electric parts for line telephony/telegraphy (8517), disc, tapes (8523), transmission apparatus for radio (8525), electrical apparatus for switching or protecting electrical circuit (8536), insulated wires and cables (8544) are already exported from India to Finland. Here, exports of South Korea compete with Indian exports because there is a free trade agreement between EU and South Korea covering this category. The market in Finland for Indian manufactured products from electrical and optical engineering industries have bright prospects.

(n) **Under Vehicles other than railway or tramway**: Motor cars and other motor vehicles (8703), special purpose motor vehicles (8705), parts and accessories of the motor vehicles (8708), tractors (8701) and motorcycles and cycles (8711) which are not yet exported from India to Finland also have potential.

(o) **Under Aircraft, spacecraft and parts thereof (88)**: Other aircraft, for example helicopters, aeroplanes, (8802), drones, parts and accessories (8803) that India exports to the world also have potential to be exported to Finland but in this category there have been miniscule Finnish imports from India.

Primary Products Neglected in Indian Exports to Finland

India is among the world's biggest producers of dairy products, poultry products, nuts, fruits, vegetables and cereals with surplus over requirements in many items. With non-tariff barriers such as phytosanitary barriers getting removed or better regulated with more transparency due to initiatives at WTO, a wide range of products such as flower buds, cut flowers, bouquets, foliage, ornamental fish, preserved vegetables, dried vegetables, dried onion powder, pepper, spices like cardamom, cinnamon, nutmeg (that Finland imports from England and the Caribbeans), coconuts, cashew nuts, walnuts, dates, figs, pineapples, avocados, guavas, mangoes, bananas, oranges, papayas and fruit pulp can be exported from India to Finland in large volumes. This would be constrained only by the oligopsonistic nature of the Finnish consumer market which is dominated by three players, the S-Group, the K-Group and Lidl.

Traditional Indian exports like tea, coffee, basmati rice textiles and clothing, and pharmaceutical products can also grow in volume and value. Here, importers in Finland and exporters from India can target the whole of Nordic Europe, the Baltics and Germany through Finland. There could be logistical advantages in doing so for the new items mentioned in the preceding paragraph and the traditional Indian exports.

Among animal products, significant Indian exports to Finland are boneless bovine meat (0202) and feathers and skins (0505). The only other product in this category imported into Finland from India in a very small quantity is live fish. Finland's neighbours Sweden and Norway import all of these, Additionally, they import pomfret fish, mackerels, cod, lobsters, shrimps, molluscs, oysters, and mussels which Finland in turn imports from Sweden and Norway. Natural honey is a major Indian product exported to France, Germany, UK, Italy, Netherlands but not to any of the Nordic countries. In food items such as honey, exporters may have to give attention to the tastes and preferences in Finland (for example, Manuka honey, or Egyptian Clover or other organic honey varieties and not the highly sugary Dabur and Patanjali honey).

Among vegetable products and processed foods, 65% of Indian exports of flower bulbs and flowering plants and 75% of cut flowers is to EU including Netherlands, but exports to Finland are negligible. A small quantity of teas and coffees, frozen vegetable mixes, cashew nuts, natural gums and resins is exported to Finland. Processed mangoes and instant coffee are two items where Finnish shares of Indian exports to the EU are significant. Although EU shares of Indian exports of walnuts is 75%, bananas 22%, seeds and spices 55% fruit juices 26%, other fruit preparations 57%, Finland's share in EU imports from India in all these categories is near zero.

Small quantities of certain items have been newly exported from India to Finland by traders in inter-firm trade. Some of these that have high potential to grow to large volumes include olegnus fruits and oilseeds, camphor oil, mustard oil, garlic oil, spices oil, clove oil, plant extracts used in perfumes and cosmetics, hair dyes, xanthium gums and oleoresins (fenugreek, turmeric, celery, nutmeg, clove, capsicum), belladona extracts used in medicated dressings, pasta, jams, jelly, marmalades, edible preparations from fruits and nuts, sauces and condiments.

Potential Unconventional Indian Exports to Finland

Unconventional items that have an export potential from India to Finland include toys, candles, cinefilm, fungicides, mosquito repellants, textile reagents, paint solvents and thinners, prepared culture media for micro-organisms, laboratory diagnostic reagents, ethylene, propylene and styrene polymers, urea resins, silicons, rubber and plastic tubes, pipes and hoses, linoxyn floor coverings, vinyl chloride bags, cassette tapes and floppy discs (blank and music), plastic tableware and kitchenware, gloves and mittens of different types and for various uses ranging from housecleaning, gardening, industrial uses to surgery in hospitals; radial summer tyres for cars, bicycle inner tubes, rubber contraceptives, surgical drapes, leather and skins of goat, sheep, lamb, harness and saddlery for horses and dog coats, bags of leather including travel bags, purses, wallets, vanity cases and satchels, jute bags, other articles of jute and coir, jewellery boxes, belts and bandoliers, clothes hangers, mosquito nets, neem- and sandalwood-based herbal toothpastes, soaps, creams, and neutraceuticals.

Other manufactured goods where Indian exports to Finland exist and could grow are computer accessories, connectors, chemical plant machinery, industrial valves, loudspeakers, electromagnets, software, insulated cables, diodes and transistors, scooters and bicycles, musical instruments, stuffed toys, footballs, golf balls, fish hooks, gymnastic and athletic equipment and handicrafts.

Indian traditional export items such as gems and jewellery, clothing, textiles leather products and spices have entered the Finnish market and this was expected. But the top 20 exports of India to Finland account for less than 60% of India's exports to the world. This means that the Indian export basket to Finland is different relative to what India exports to the rest of the world. There are also differences from what India exports to other EU countries. Indian exports to Finland of edible preparations, preserved vegetables and fruits and pharmaceutical products are high relative to India's exports of these commodities to the EU-28.

The RCAIs with respect to Finland appear to be in a flux with eleven out of forty SITC codes having lost their RCAIs. Fewer new products have since achieved an RCA value of above 1.0 to replace them. These changes in the RCAIs point to changes both in the direction and the composition of Indian exports. Apart from textiles and primary sector products, consistency can be noticed in RCAIs in the India's chemical and pharmaceutical products with respect to Finland. However, India's high RCAIs in many of the technologically advanced sectors are not yet reflected in India's exports to Finland. There are also items of electrical machinery that are exported which are not signalled by RCAIs.

The sectors or commodity groups in which exports to Finland are occurring without RCAI are:

- Electrical machinery/electronics
- Boilers
- Plastics/products

Trade can occasionally develop in patterns that are specific to the complementarities between partners or strengths of each economy. Certain sectors of economic activity deserve special mention in prospecting potential of Indian exports to Finland because they can be mobilised as supply chains with initiatives from either end. Wherever value addition is required or claimed before an Indian export item reaches the point of final consumption, there exists scope for opportunities to do that value addition as part of 'Make in India' for mutual benefits to enterprises in both countries.

It is remarkable that even in Category 48 (Paper, Paperboard and Printing), traditionally a well-established Finnish export goods category, there are certain specific niches where India exports to Finland and these exports can be increased. These are handmade paper for gift-wrapping, letter-writing, and other uses; duplicator stencils, envelopes and other paper stationery, corrugated paper and paperboard boxes, paper bags and paper board sacks, accounts book registers, paper tags, bobbin spools used in paper plants, wrapping paper, decorative laminates, greeting cards, printed wall and desk calendars, diaries and pocket calendars and printed posters.

In environment technologies, Indian firms could tie up joint ventures with Finnish firms because Finland is listed in Annexure I of the Kyoto Protocol, and this enables Finland to buy carbon credits from a developing economy like India. The Ministry of Environment and Forests of the Government of India has approved about 200 projects under the Clean Development Mechanism (CDM). A similar approach could be made by private firms as well as in public–private partnership mode for afforestation with carbon sequestration. India's National Forest Policy targets forests and tree cover of a third of the total land area. Despite modest success, India has achieved forestation in only about a quarter of the land area as yet. There is scope for Indian counterparts to invite Finnish forestry on the lines of India's Swedforest project with Sweden for trade in carbon credits.

India-based suppliers are in a position to compete for 40% of the global potential market in automotive components due to their advantages in factor costs, availability of skilled, engineering manpower and maturity of the domestic supply chain (McKinsey 2018). India has an advantage in skill-intensive segments of the industry and a deficit in the input components many of which are imported from Europe. SASA, the Scandinavian Automotive Suppliers Association, has an agreement with ACMA for sourcing and stocking auto components from India, for supplying Scandinavian countries. Opportunities exist for collaboration in engine development, alternative fuel technologies such as electric cars (India has announced abolition of petrol and diesel-fuelled cars by 2030).

Vehicle styling and infrastructure for automotive testing is another area of potential mutual collaboration. India already exports to Finland the Alto and Santro models of cars manufactured in India by Maruti Udyog and Hyundai, respectively. Finland–India Economic Relations can further involve export of electronic components and spare parts with potential for trade-substituting investments. The involvement of Finland is feasible also in renewable energy technologies such as hydrogen technology, technology for lithium car batteries for electric cars and adoption of environmentally friendly technologies.

Indo-Finnish collaborations involving 'Made by Finland and India' can make supply chains cost-efficient and improve supply chains in Europe, besides joint ventures in other developing country markets of Asia and Africa. In the years ahead, manufacturing in India will upscale for economies and increase its share in exports worldwide, also to Finland. The areas of complementarities in high-technology products with product-service linkages would grow the most and make it attractive for Indian and Finnish enterprises to collaborate for third-country markets besides the EU.

From the foregoing analysis, it may be noted that there exists considerable scope because the trade potential itself is presently largely untapped. Trade-replacing FDI is another alternative that merits examination. The case for this is stronger for Finnish firms because of India's large market size, differences in product cost structures and a higher income elasticity of demand in India compared to Finland. For Indian firms, Finland represents an untapped market with established and predictable patterns of continuing imports. As a point of entry into the Nordic and Baltic region, and the EU, Finland could also attract FDI from large Indian firms with needs to sustain links in the EU and on its fringes to the East and to Norway. The uncertainties over Brexit find about 900 Indian firms that access the EU single market through their affiliates in the UK scrambling for relocations.

Potential for Trade-Substituting Investments

An interesting item that would illustrate trade-substituting potential is "pressure containers for compressed gases" that features in both lists—Finland to India and India to Finland. If skills are available at both ends and can be shared, the item could be made with the better of the two technologies in a socio-technical system that makes techno-commercial sense. Such an item points to the opportunity for collaboration at enterprise level through trade-substituting investments.

Industrial production indices indicate that global competitiveness has been achieved by India in generic pharmaceuticals, speciality chemicals, automotive components and textiles. The States of Gujarat, Tamil Nadu and Maharashtra reflect these industries strongly in their industrial profiles. The inflow of foreign investment at the Vibrant Gujarat Summit in a single week in January once in every two years is comparable to Slush, Finland's annual event for attracting venture capital for innovation. There could also be collaboration potential here for exports to Finland and rest of the world. Finland was not represented at the Vibrant Gujarat Summits of 2017 and 2019 although other Nordic Countries Sweden, Denmark and Norway participated.

It is expected that investments in petrochemicals, gas pipelines, power, port development, marine technologies, science parks and development of special economic zones for exports would be benchmarked competitively to international standards in India. There is scope for Finland and India to partner in these as well. There has been a discussion about developing locations as science parks for biotech and life sciences also in Finland to link into international knowledge business opportunities from intellectual properties created. A government-to-government approach has been made by Finland to India for joint research and development in science and technology. As these produce results, there could be fresh impetus for joint collaborations in public–private partnerships for biotechnology and nanotechnology applications. Finland's growing businesses are mostly technologies that can be leveraged internationally and regional hubs have specialised towards these (Mathur and Mattila 2009). Examples are hubs for molecular biology and biocentres in Oulu, functional food technologies, biotechnologies and pharmaceuticals, maritime technologies, media and culture in Turku, wellness technologies, paper machinery technologies and energy and environmental technologies in Jyvaskylä, etc. Small and medium enterprises with niche technologies from Finland would have tremendous prospects of raising capital and organising commercial production in India if they learn to collaborate and structure their international business opportunities in India where the constraints are supply-led, not demand constrained as in Finland.

Finnish Industrial Structure

Finnish models of industrial structures and markets are typically constructed (by policy-makers, firms and researchers) on the assumption of vertical clustering with assured linkage effects (that occur with a lag) engineered through subsidies and linkage incentives brokered between the clusters through Finnish banks and parastatal funding institutions. In such a model, there is a high dependence on handholding by the State and its parastatal agencies. This has an effect not only on trade but also on the oligopolistic nature of industry in Finland. This is gradually changing with recent decisions on restrictive trade practices by the national competition authority.

Challenges for Indian Firms

The challenges for Indian firms seeking business opportunities in Finland arise from the peculiarity that enterprises in India are able to participate in the worldwide boom in services from within the domestic economy. India has become a procurement zone for services enabled by telematic connectivity and a competitive locale for structuring value-adding hubs where products and services can be bundled together not only for the domestic market but also for foreign investors, buyers and market-making intermediaries. Paradoxically, although incentives for doing business abroad, for instance in Finland, have increased, initiatives are seldom taken by Indian firms, with the notable exception of IT firms.

Large Indian industrial houses have mainly looked to countries other than Finland, including to neighbouring Sweden, Denmark, Norway and the Baltics. If the decision not to consider doing business in Finland were the logical outcome of informed evaluations or market forces unhindered by the dynamics of asymmetric information, this chapter would not be needed. Paradoxically, it is precisely because Indian firms seldom prospect synergies with potential partners in Finland and vice versa that makes it interesting and worthwhile to find out what is being missed.

Indian Priorities: Lethargy or Red Tape?

As a business destination in Europe, Finland was historically crowded out by other European locations where English, French or German is spoken. Indian firms didn't need to do business with Russia through Finland because they had direct links. Finland was regarded as a high-cost country from where only industrial goods' requirements were sourced. The psychic distance was so great that very few traders developed Finland as a destination for traditional Indian exports. Finland always had very few foreigners and it was never easy to obtain even a tourist visa for Finland. No large Indian business firm ever established a subsidiary or branch in Finland until the IT boom. Trade was also intermediated through Germany (traditionally the largest trading partner of both Finland and India), Russia, Sweden and the UK.

During 2005–07, at least six firms (five of which were from the Indian IT industry), Wipro, Tooltech, TCS, Zensar, Blue Star Infotech Limited and Sasken established offices in Finland where they were already doing body shopping for Nokia and a few other clients. However, the number of Indian companies having foreign commercial presence in Finland has remained small and was estimated to be about 30 in 2018. This count does not include clearing and forwarding agents acting on behalf of Indian traders or counterparts or projects of a temporary nature (like Siemens India executing civil contracts in Finland) or a small number of private proprietary Finnish firms established as small family businesses (mainly shops and restaurants) by Indians living in Finland.

The prospects of Indian businesses in Finland need not be analysed by Indian household consumption statistics. Nor by India's manufacturing output growth statistics or by concentrating mainly on primary commodity exports simply because conventional RCAs are highest in primary products. The past trade pattern can be an unreliable predictor of future trade and trade-substituting investments enabled by the explosion in services, intra-firm trade and new modes of entry including foreign commercial presence. In the case of Indian exports to Finland, the conventional method of calculating RCAs does not provide a meaningful result at two-digit level because RCAs are less than 1 for seven of the top 20 export items, all of which are manufactured goods. The interpretation by Bhide et al. (2006) that Finland may represent a kind of lead market for items where RCAs are yet to develop sounds naive because the conventional RCAs as conceived by them may never increase to more than 1 if the pattern of trade has developed by a different logic at a disaggregated level.

For instance, in specialisations by Finnish firms as suppliers of other manufactured goods, value-adding may require imports to technical specifications or due to contracts concerning joint product development and marketing. This seems to be the case for boilers, aircraft parts, auto components and electronics. This can also be due to the differences in price ratios such as those of oil to electricity, particularly when solar power is almost at grid parity in India. For these reasons, Finland–India synergies are better explored at four-digit and eight-digit levels of disaggregation in order not to get swayed by superficialities observed from the data at two-digit level.

The SITRA-NCAER study (Bhide et al. 2006) was quite optimistic in imagining that Finland could be a source for "actual marketing and brand creation of Indian textiles globally". Finland has not been able to market and create a global demand for its own Marimekko products except to a limited extent in Japan and North America. In fact, Finland is not known for development of any consumer brands abroad with a few exceptions such as *Angry Birds*, *Fiskars*, *Nokia* and *Finlandia Vodka*. Rather, it is known for its outstanding industrial technologies and high-technology products. Similarly, the perception that Finland can help businesses buy carbon credits is correct but its capacity to provide environmental solutions for water purification and wastewater treatment is in specific niches. There are a number of lakes in Southern and Eastern Finland which are industrially polluted and Finland has not cleaned them yet. Low-cost solutions from India or joint Indo-Finnish solutions may have potential here. Collaboration on water pollution remedies can spawn better Finnish methods to clean the Ganga River in India while Indian improvisations (jugaad) can make the cleaning of Finnish Lakes techno-commercially feasible so that the kind of unresolved water management issues in Finland can also benefit and collaborations are not viewed as one-way help schemes.

The local-global dialectic in local communities and regions can be further investigated to understand the new emerging economic geography of contacts between Finland and India. This would be useful from the perspective of how business know-how influences cost-benefit analysis for global harvesting of locally seeded innovations in both territories. The status of business know-how with regard to international business development requires to be specifically addressed with regard to entry modes for the structuring of investments in services for Finland, India and third-country markets.

The prerequisites for feasibility of services internationalisation will be better understood with the exploration of links between local-regional, regional-national, regional-global, and national-global to identify business know-how as it exists and the gaps to be addressed. Reciprocity in 'equal national treatment' could affect the choice of how partnerships are structured. The emphasis on services could lead to innovations in pedagogic designs for sharing of business knowledge in sustainable networks of the future, including public–private partnerships involving universities, business schools, chambers of commerce, consortia of small and medium enterprises, and governments at national, regional and local level in both countries to share knowledge creation to mutual advantage.

Made by India and Finland or Made in Finland/Made in India?

'Made in Finland' or 'Made in India' is less relevant than 'Made by Finland' or 'Made by India' as long as benefits from cross-border inflows of factor incomes (wages, profits, interest, rents) exceed private and public costs incurred for production, marketing and delivery. Firms in both countries have hitherto mainly emphasised boosting their own manufactured exports to the exclusion of other modes of international business. Manufacturing technologies are migrating rapidly and the flexibility inherent in the cross-border dispersal of value chains in a more open environment for trade in goods militates against reliance on manufacturing for sustaining competitiveness except in cases of input-dependent industries located for such reasons.

As noted in Mathur (2007b, 2008c), accessible at http://www.oulu.oaka.fi, services constitute a large segment of national economies compared to manufacturing in both Finland and India (54% in India; 65% in Finland) and the tradable scope of services has expanded. The General Agreement on Trade in Services (GATS) envisages cross-border supply of services (Mode 1), consumption abroad (Mode 2), foreign commercial presence (Mode 3) and Movement of Natural Persons (Mode 4) as the four modes of service delivery under equal most favoured nation (MFN) treatment among all World Trade Organisation (WTO) member countries. The ten-year transitional period that permitted departures from GATS ended on 31. 12.2004. Cross-border Supply (Mode 1) is the only mode that belongs to the exclusive EU competence according to a judgement of the European Court of Justice.[1] The other three modes require bilateral prospecting between individual EU member countries and non-members like India.[2]

---

[1] European Court (1994), Opinion of the Court of 15th November 1994. Competence of the Community to conclude international agreements concerning services and the protection of intellectual property-Article 228(6) of the EC Treaty. Opinion 1/94. http://eur-lex.europa.eu/LexUriServ/LexUriServ.do?uri=CELEX:61994V0001:EN:html.

[2] This is the reason why the *High Level Trade Group (HLTG) mandated by the India-EU summit in New Delhi on 7.9.2005 to launch negotiations for a comprehensive trade and investment agreement that could presumably also cover GATS services has not produced anything implementable, to date, and is unlikely to do so in future. Countries like Finland that keep waiting for an EU-India pathway lose out to others including their neighbours Sweden, Denmark and Norway who have developed strong bilateral ties with India without waiting for an EU-India deal.*

The effects on investment, employment and incomes are thus poised to exhibit asymmetric country effects within the EU. EU's principle of subsidiarity would cause further distress in proximate communities and regions because solutions require actions by firms and policy-makers in sub-national spaces to link with distant cross-border locales for product-service linkages in international business.

New Opportunities for India-Finland Trade

There are five different kinds of new opportunities in India-Finland Trade:

(a) Completely missed opportunities in goods trade for reasons not clear or simply neglect as in a whole range of primary products and consumer products manufacturing including consumer durables.
(b) Goods trade opportunities relevant to Finnish and Indian markets tested as viable and growing but far from saturated.
(c) Trade-substituting investments in goods trade for buyback arrangements that would increase volumes, value and profitability for players involved.
(d) Product-services linkages to leverage technology and knowledge-intensive investments on a scale that would transform directions of trade for one or both countries for high-value items in which trade exists.
(e) Product-services linkages to leverage technology and knowledge-intensive investments by techno-commercial engineering of new options unrelated to bilateral trade on a scale that would justify collaborations for third-country markets.

GATS-enabled services trade is another avenue for prospecting product-service linkages. India's success with exporting engineering products to Sweden involved attention to bundling of services. For instance, TEGA organises maintenance and time-bound response to breakdowns for all its mining equipment installed in Sweden. The development and diffusion of industrial products require implementation of new logistical structures and services before products can be delivered. The procurements and warehousing of R-Kioski in Finland can be organised by an Indian enterprise from Bengaluru only because the firm is not only able to signal interventions but its services go further into enabling services required to be triggered and organised in Finland. The efficacy with which services delivery is organised with regard to cost, quality and reliability makes a difference to the design and sustainability of value chains. Certain kinds of services cannot be organized. For example, medical and para-medical services that require language skills to be delivered in Finland can be organized from Estonia, but not India. Yet, this does not prevent Indian enterprise from organising such deliveries in Finland with Estonian or Finnish collaboration. Table 3.4 indicates the empty white spaces available for the twelve categories of GATS services under the four modes of services supply.

Table 3.4 GATS-enabled services trade

	Mode 1 cross-border supply (CBS)	Mode 2 consumption abroad (CA)	Mode 3 foreign commercial presence (FCP)	Mode 4 movement of natural persons (MNP)
1. Business services	IT services	Body shopping in IT	Branches/ affiliates/ subsidiaries	Independent professionals
2. Communication services	Digital media	Creative services consultations	Advertising agencies	Independent journalists
3. Construction and related engineering services	Virtual designing	Turnkey Consultancy	Project offices	Surveyors, map-makers
4. Distribution services	Electronic deliveries	Licensed distribution	Investment in distribution networks	Exhibitors at fairs
5. Educational services	Distance learning	Exchange students	Campus programmes abroad	Visiting teachers
6. Environmental services	Climate/weather information from sensors	Site visits	Research stations eg: in the Arctic	Independent researchers
7. Financial services	e-commerce	Foreign portfolio investing	Brokerage agencies abroad	Havala traders/ Angadia couriers
8. Health-related and social services	Access to personal medical records and radiology reports	Medical tourism	Clinics/ hospitals/ contract management outsourcing	Specialists visiting
9. Tourism and travel-related services	Air BnB bookings	Cultural and eco-tourism	Travel agencies	Tour leaders
10. Recreational, cultural and sporting services	Music, films streamed	Performances like operas, concerts, watching sports events	Stadia, racing tracks, concert halls, etc.	Artists and sportspersons visiting for events/ performances
11. Transport services	Ticketing, back-office accounting	Car rentals	Ski lifts, cruise ships	Drivers, operators, technicians
12. Other services not included elsewhere	Call centres	Physiotherapy	Spas	Masseurs

In the list of Indian exportables to Finland, tractors were identified in a preceding part of this chapter as an item completely missed. Before anyone begins to ship out tractors or even to scout out for customers in Finland for Indian tractors, it would be necessary to do homework related to operational regulations in Finland for tractors, whether the idle capacity of tractor manufacturing in Finland has any next best use or would continue to compete with imports on the back of domestic subsidies, and the possibility of entering the EU single market through a sales and distribution agency capable of locating prospective customers beyond Finland. Each of these activities would cut across services (of types 1, 4, 6, 11 in Table 3.4) above to be performed before the first tractor is exported or a trade-substituting investment activated.

The potential for expanding India's exports to Finland is vast and far from saturated. Yet, the greatest potential in business opportunities in Finland is beyond trade through foreign direct investments in Finland for the entire EU market. That would enable Indian firms to overcome the liability of foreignness as well as the liability of outsidership and be credible in a different way than if all value creation was done only in India. Product-service linkages are the most promising of ways to develop this by blending India's strengths in services with Finland's infrastructure, especially for high-technology products that require not only a good product but also great service to compete in world markets.

References

Bhide S, Mukhopadhyay D, Singh D (2006) Prospects for India-Finland cooperation, SITRA Report 62, Helsinki

European Court (1994) Opinion of the court of 15th November 1994. Competence of the Community to conclude international agreements concerning services and the protection of intellectual property-Article 228(6) of the EC Treaty. Opinion 1/94. https://eur-lex.europa.eu/legal-content/EN/TXT/HTML/?isOldUri=true&uri=CELEX:61994CV0001 Accessed 20 Jan 2019

Mathur AN (2006) Institutional factors governing choice of GATS modes for services supply. In: ANZIBA 2006, conference proceedings, University of Wellington, New Zealand, 16–18 Nov 2006

Mathur AN (2007a) Finland-India business prospects 2007–2017, WP2007-03-01. Indian Institute of Management, Ahmedabad, Mar 2007

Mathur AN (2007b) Why some unemployed are unemployable? Challenges for policy research in Finland and India. In: Conference proceedings, second EU-EFA international conference, Oulu, 7–9 Sept 2007

Mathur AN (2008a) Distant neighbourliness: Finland's fast expanding relations with India. Paper presented at the workshop on Finland-India economic relations, Helsinki University of Technology, Otaniemi, Finland, 28 Aug 2008

Mathur AN (2008b) When the Twain meet: a twinning comparison of enmeshing clusters between Finland and India. In: 11th TCI conference 2008, University of Capetown, South Africa, 28 Oct–2 Nov 2008

Mathur AN (2008c) Prospects for scientific research collaborations in ICT and biotechnology between Finland and India. In: FIER listening post colloquium-II, Tekes-Finpro-Academy of Finland, New Delhi, 25 Nov 2008

References

Mathur AN (2009) The elephant and the swan: Finland-India synergies. Paper presented at the research seminar at the Turku School of Economics, 23 Apr 2009

Mathur AN, Mattila S (2009) Competitiveness and collaboration in high-tech clusters: the strategic management of intellectual capital and organisational knowledge by Ajeet Mathur and Sari Mattila. Presented at the 12th TCI annual global conference, 12–16 Oct 2009, Jyväskylä, Finland, Conference track on "Learning clusters—adapting to the new competitiveness scenario"

Mattila S, Mathur AN (2009) Competitiveness and collaborations in internationalising clusters: scope for co-evolving and leveraging capabilities in business education clusters of Finland and India. Presented at the 12th TCI annual global conference, 12–16 Oct 2009, in the track "Learning clusters—adapting to the new competitiveness scenario", Jyväskylä, Finland

McKinsey and Company (2018) The auto component industry in India: preparing for the future, September. https://www.mckinsey.com/~/media/McKinsey/Featured%20Insights/Asia%20Pacific/The%20auto%20component%20industry%20in%20India%20preparing%20for%20the%20future/ACMA%20Vertical_Onscreen_Final.ashx Accessed 20 Jan 2019

Chapter 4
Managing Finland–India Cultural Differences

> *You never really know your own culture until you are abroad.*
> Anonymous
>
> *The world is a chain, one link in another (is-dinja katina, holqa go ohea)*
> Old Maltese Saying

Abstract Managing cultural differences is an important aspect of international business. This chapter introduces the distinctive cultural nuances of Finland and India and explains cultural dimensions on which Finland and India differ. Cultural differences have implications for boundaries of tasks, time, territory, technology, sentience and understanding in designing organisations, developing leadership styles and reinforcing management policies and practices. In order that dialogues of the deaf are avoided, negotiating stances, norms, beliefs, predispositions and values cherished by Finns and Indians are also discussed.

Introduction

Cultural differences manifest in learned habits, inter-generational recipes of living, patterns of behaviour that are reinforced in particular contexts, in ways how responses to visual, auditory and olfactory stimuli are shaped, and in how mindsets influence reinforcements of attitudes, beliefs, norms and values. In the Finland–India context, there is high likelihood of misunderstandings if cultural differences are not acknowledged and managed (Kirra 2000; Joutsimäki and Mathur 2006; Waqar 2011). These differences have implications for being sensitive to the needs of leadership and management with regard to organising systems boundaries of tasks, time, territory, technology, sentience and understanding. National groups can be distinguished on dimensions of religion, ethnicity, culture and language which are the four elements around which identities of nationhood get crystallised. Climate can be added as a fifth element that influences culture. Languages are windows to cultures and the foremost difference between Finland and India arises from language.

Language

Finnish became an official language in Finland alongside Swedish in 1902. About 94% of the population speaks Finnish as the first language and Swedish is spoken as first language by about 4–5% of the population. The Finnish national identity is itself inextricably tied to the Finnish Language. There is a popular saying in Finland: 'We are not Swedes and we don't want to become Russians and so let us be Finns' (from Finnish *'Ruotsalaisia emme ole, venäläisiksi emme tahdo tulla, olkaamme siis suomalaisia'*). This gained currency and credibility by the distinguishing feature of a unique distinct Finno-ugric language tradition.

The Finnish language is not a Germanic language. It is claimed that it is also not Indo-European although this is debatable. Correspondences with Finnish have been found in both Tamil and Sanskrit. Finnish researchers like Asko Parpola and Simo Parpola have been at the forefront of trying to decipher the last remaining undeciphered ancient script in the world–the Indus Valley Script. Although Finnish, Hungarian and Estonian are all Finno-ugric languages, only Finnish and Estonian are mutually intelligible. Finnish is also related to Karelian spoken in what is now Russian occupied Karelia and along the Finnish–Russian border. Spoken Hungarian sounds just like Finnish but the vocabulary is so distant as to be completely unintelligible. Estonians understand more Finnish than Finns understand Estonian. This is partly due to popularity of Finnish television programmes in Estonia but not the other way around. Another reason is that Estonian is an older purer strain that enables later evolved strains to be recognised, but Finns have not needed to stay in touch with older strains and forms.

The Finnish language is written in the Roman Alphabet, but there are no Finnish sounds associated with the letters b, c, f, w, x and z. In other words, although the word Finland starts with the letter F, there is no letter 'F' in Finnish and Finland is a word derived from 'vinland' by the Swedes. Finnish words are pronounced exactly as spelt. There are three extra letters, ä (pronounced as the a in adjunct), å (pronounced as the a in ball) and ö (a distinctive sound similar to but not exactly as 'eu'). I have yet to master the 'ö' and 'y' sounds myself and appearing as they do in the Finnish expressions 'Hyvää päivä' for Good Day (a common greeting) 'Hyvää yötä' for 'Good Night', this can be a source of much amusement to Finns listening to foreigners speaking Finnish. The fictional language of the elves invented by J. R. R. Tolkein for 'The Hobbit' and 'The Lord of the Rings' is based on Finnish as is the universal language, Mänti, invented by the autistic savant, Daniel Tammet. Tolkein's Quenya is like an Elvish Latin that follows Finnish grammar and its literary form was used for poetry, in songs, for lament, and for magical spells.

Finns speak in monologues and do not interrupt when some else is speaking except to acknowledge non-verbally or by low-decibel short intakes of breath. A Finn would not normally think aloud and would speak only when what is wished to be conveyed has been fully formulated inside the mind. So, there can be silent pauses in between an ongoing conversation and slower reactions than in cultures where cues are quickly taken and responded to. There is no concept of small talk in

Finland and everything spoken is to convey information or to seek information and very rarely to express feelings, emotions, mood or affect. "We mean what we say and we do what we mean" would capture the underlying tonality in Finnish expressions. If you turn off the sound and observe a native Finnish speaker, you can observe that on completion of every sentence, the mouth is fully closed and the lips brought together before opening the mouth again for the next sentence.

There can be long spells of silence in Finnish conversations. This propensity for silence is easily misunderstood and care needs to be taken to recognise its special characteristics as part of everyday communication and business communications. Finns are generally cautious towards questions, invitations, new information and tend to view anything strange with circumspection and cynicism. Since the Finnish national identity was itself coalesced around language, it is hardly surprising that Finnish researchers have been prolific in drawing attention to the importance of language in international business (Piekkari 2014).

The Finnish language has no future tense or gender, and the present participle is rarely used. Although a glossary of some of the important Finnish words and expressions has been provided in this book at the end, many Finnish words cannot be effectively translated into English. This is because the concepts or notions they embody or symbolise do not exist elsewhere. For example, while I have attempted to provide English equivalents to words such as *sisu, pesänjakaja, selvitysmies, munakauppa, talkoot, isännöinti, talonmies, vahtimestari, amanuenssi, nimikirja*, all of these are unique and important Finnish concepts but with no real equivalence in other language traditions and cultures. Many English words too cannot be translated properly into Finnish because they do not pass the filters of the Finnish cultural values. For example, small talk, tacit know-how, substance, entrepreneurship, assertiveness, leadership, scholarship, collaboration (as distinct from cooperation) are difficult to translate into Finnish. The use of English becomes an unsatisfactory way of accommodating world views of national groups who are linguistically, culturally and psychologically remote from each other. The speech culture of Finland is quite distinctive when compared with other Europe (Wilkins and Isotalus 2009).

The best way to experience Indian linguistic diversity is to look at a currency note of denomination 100 or 500 and to examine how many different languages are used to indicate the value of the currency note. Besides the 17 official languages listed from the list in the Eighth Schedule of India's Constitution which would be found stating the denomination of the currency note, there are more than 500 other languages and dialects in India. Although Hindi was proclaimed as the official language of the Government of India, the Constitution also accords official status to English as the other official language of the Government of India. States are free to legislate official languages within their own jurisdictions. English remains the link language for all of India although strictly speaking, official communications can be made in any official language. Consider what can happen. If someone from Chennai writes a letter in Tamil to an addressee in Assam, the recipient is within rights to respond in Assamese but it is not going to be easy for the communication in Tamil to be understood in Assam and for the reply in Assamese to be understood in Tamil Nadu. Most likely they would use English. This stirs up controversy from time to time. In Southern India, linguistic division of states was forced by political movements leading to the creation of Andhra Pradesh and Telangana (for Telugu speakers) and Karnataka (for Kannada speakers). When the new metro line was inaugurated in Bangalore (Capital of Karnataka) in July 2017, there were violent protests over the Hindi signboards that were placed alongside Kannada and English and the Hindi signboards were eventually removed.

All judicial proceedings in the Supreme Court and High Courts are required to be conducted in English in India. Yet, four states, Bihar, Madhya Pradesh, Rajasthan and Uttar Pradesh have obtained permission to hear cases in Hindi in their High Courts and the Madras High Court in Tamil Nadu allows cases to be argued in Tamil. All parliamentary laws are drafted in English (with Hindi translations). In Finland, official work of the government can only be carried out in Finnish or Swedish although companies like Kone and Nokia switched the official company language to English and several others are following suit. Exceptionally, '*joikku*' (sami laments) are permitted to be used by Samis of Finnish Lapland.

Post-independent India adopted the three language formula in India's education policy requiring all students to learn English, Hindi and a national/regional/foreign language. So, anyone who has studied in school in the past 70 years is likely to speak three languages, including English. However, since States of the Union have authority to decide on school curricula (including medium of instruction) and the priority to be assigned to three languages, certain states like West Bengal persisted with Bengali as the first language introducing other languages at later stages of school education. So, the standard of spoken and written English varies greatly in different parts of India.

Religion

In Finland, nature worship and ancestor worship have historically been part of religious traditions evidenced by archaeological finds from the bronze age and the red ochre period corresponding to the fifth millennium B.C. Nature worship is still practised in Finland by various groups, including but not limited to the reindeer-herding Samis and Shamans. In the twelfth century, Catholic Christianity spread with the arrival of Papal missionaries backed by Sweden after Finland was made part of Sweden in 1155 under St. Hendrick, the first Bishop of Åbo (Turku). The Catholic influence was dominant until the formation of the Kalmar Union in 1397 when Queen Margaret of Denmark united Norway, Sweden (of which Finland was then a part), and Denmark. From being predominantly Roman Catholic, Finland changed when the Protestant Reformation made Lutheranism the State Religion in 1593. Finns have a healthy respect for the Church, but the majority do not participate regularly in its activities. Yet, quite many Finns marry in the church have children baptised and confirmed and may opt for a Christian burial for themselves and their relatives. And the Finnish Church does reach out to non-members, including foreigners, as part of its community outreach.

In the present times, the Evangelical Lutheran Church and the Finnish Orthodox Church (modelled after the Greek Orthodox Church) are the two officially recognised religions that are entitled to official support from a share in taxation of their adherents. The Lutheran influence predominated after the collapse of the Kalmar Union with King Gustav Wasa of Sweden ruling over Finland. The Finnish Orthodox Church is strong in Eastern Finland with the monastery at Valamo as its Centre. The Upsenski Cathedral in Helsinki consecrated in 1868 is a monument from the Russian period and yet also a functioning Finnish Orthodox church as part of the Diocese of Helsinki. The Upsenski Cathedral became an autonomous part of the The Ecumenical Patriarchate of Constantinople in 1923 after Finnish Independence and is one of the major tourist attractions. There are also tiny minorities of Catholics, Laestardians, Buddhists, Hindus, Muslims, Jews, Confucians in parts of Finland. Finnish rationality in everyday life including business draws very little from religion. Systems and institutions that have evolved are 'secular' in character in the European sense of the word 'secular' that signifies the absence of religious influence.

In India, theistic religious traditions have co-existed alongside atheistic and agnostic traditions. The Republic of India has no official religion. The majority of strands in Indian philosophy to this day are non-theistic. Yet, religion plays an important part in Indian culture giving a multi-religious flavour to Indian secularism [that observes the principle of '*sarva dharma sambhava*' (any religion may be followed) and '*panth nirapekshata*' (equal treatment of all faiths)] in contrast to non-theistic secularism in many parts of the world. How did this happen? The Indian civilisation has been open to all faiths over a long period of time. Despite short periods of inter-religious violent strife and opposition to particular faiths by certain Rulers and political parties, the general norm is one of tolerance for the practice of all faiths. Religious freedom is guaranteed by the Indian Constitution. This can occasionally create controversies on whether places of worship or pilgrimage run by religious sects are private institutions or public places where constitutional guarantees of equality and dignity can be enforced. In October 2018, in the case of the Ayappa shrine in Sabrimalai, Kerala, the Supreme Court of India adjudged that the age-old convention restricting the entry of women of menstruating age to enter the shrine was wrong but the temple custodians have appealed against this judgement and there has been considerable public outroar and opposition embarrassing the State Government of Kerala that has responsibility to uphold law and order when it has tried to implement the Supreme Court Judgement. About 55 women were able to enter the shrine in the first three months after the verdict.

Practically, all the world's religions and religious denominations within them are present in India. There are Hindus, Muslims, Christians, Sikhs, Jews, Jains, Buddhists, Parsis and many others. Hinduism is not a congregational religion and contains atheistic as well as agnostic and theistic traditions. Actually, Hinduism cannot be regarded as a religion at all being an umbrella term to cover a broad array of philosophical and cultural traditions with some common elements such as acknowledgement of *ahimsa* (non-violence), *karma* (as you sow so shall you reap) as values; the belief that death is an event and not a finality; tolerance and welcome to *atithi* (which literally means whomever or whatever turns up without *tithi* or appointment date, unexpectedly); and faith in the unity and indivisibility of nature and the cosmos (symbolised by *Vasudhaiva Kutumbakam*, the notion that the whole world is one solidaristic community) and adherence to *dharma,* the notion that actions should be inspired by what ought to be done and not by what fruits or consequences they would bring. Varma (2004) provides an erudite introduction to what 'Being Indian' involves.

From our perspective, it would be useful to locate the influences that religious identity and religions in Finland or India have for business life, work life, and in general, for quality of life. This may be done in two steps, following Habermas's taxonomy: first by locating the religions along two axes: whether a religion is theocentric or cosmo-centric, and whether a religion is world-affirming or world-negating emphasising the other worldly (Table 4.1).

Two examples would suffice to indicate the significance of religion in business life. In India, the belief that death is an event was unconsciously instituted into the laws of company formation where there was originally no exit policy provision except for a weakly existing provision for closure and liquidation. At the time new economic reforms in 1991 lifted the veil of oligopolistic protection of licenses and brought intensified competition, and increased the risk of going out of business for the weak and inefficient, firms that had already collapsed and not functioning had been in the process of getting closed for long periods. Some of them were awaiting closure for more than 55 years! The thinking was that once a company was created it would always exist. If a private enterprise failed, it deserved to be nationalised for another lease of life and if it failed as a nationalised enterprise, then it ought to be privatised and given another incarnation. There were firms like Inchek Tyres that had been nationalised as National Rubber and later re-privatised when it continued to be loss-making. The new Companies Act in India has exit provisions. It is expected that failed companies that are unviable can now be be closed swiftly and assets restructured although it goes against the culture to treat any death, even a company death, as a finality.

Table 4.1 Classifying faiths

	World-affirming	Other worldly
Theocentric	Lutheran Christianity Zoroastrianism	Catholic Christianity Orthodox Christianity Islam Judaism Theistic Hinduism (Shaivite/Vaishanavite) Vajrayana Buddhism
Cosmo-centric	Agnostic/Atheistic Hinduism (charvaka, samkhya, mimansa) Sikhism Jainism Sufism Confucianism Shinto Shamanism	Mahayana and Hinayana Buddhism

In Finland, business and religion do not mix. The business ethos in the context of Evangelical Lutheran Christianity is quite pragmatic in dealing with change and does not dwell over guilt or sin nor delay closure of an unviable enterprise by seeking to establish who is to blame or what is at fault when a firm has ceased to be viable. In fact, statutory auditors are mandated to draw attention to the need for closure when more than half of net worth remains eroded for more than two years. In India, consumer research points to the influence of religion on consumer behaviour.

In Finland, public policies favour a strong civic sense with public investments for nurturing human capital on the principle of equal opportunities for all. In India, there is a constitutional guarantee for equality but there are enormous backlogs from historical legacies when caste and religion were factors for discrimination. The caste system in India had its origins in the '*varna*' system with horizontal differentiation of vocations. These morphed over time into occupational categories that deteriorated into becoming a hereditary ossification which assumed hierarchical overtones. Abolishing the notion of caste in independent India was not considered adequate because restorative justice demanded extended protection and reservations in education and workplaces for groups that were classified as scheduled castes (SC) and scheduled tribes (ST). The scheduled tribes were those parts of the population excluded from the mainstream that lived in forests eking out a marginal existence and being treated as outside civil society during the British period when they were treated as criminals. Initially, the reservations were meant to be in place only for the first ten years of the republic. But they continued. Continuance of reservations for SC and ST brought about demands from other backward classes (OBCs). Then, due to protests and contests in courts, exclusions were introduced for 'creamy layers' of protected classes. This came about from a Supreme Court Judgement in September 2018 that excludes reservations for the 'creamy layer' of people who were categorised as SC/ST/OBC. The latest tweak is inclusion of another 10% of economically backward classes in reservations for government jobs and places of study in public educational institutions. India is probably the only country where groups agitate to be declared 'backward' and classified so for availing quotas in job recruitments and for places in higher educational institutions.

An interesting feature of caste and class in India is that when missionaries converted some of the underprivileged SCs/STs/OBCs to Christainity or Islam, the caste and tribal identities did not dissolve. Paradoxically Christianity and Islam accepted castes so that India is probably the only country where Christians and Muslims also belong to castes!

Time

Despite the vast expanse of India's geography and big differences in sunrise and sunset times, India functions in one time zone, the Indian Standard Time (IST) every day of the year, regardless of season, winter, summer or monsoon. IST is

5.5 h ahead of Greenwich Mean Time (GMT). The fraction comes from the fact that IST is not derived from GMT but from India's own meridian from the time of the first stone observatory in Ujjain, and later from a notional central station using positional astronomy. Finnish winter time is 2 h ahead of GMT and 3.5 h behind Indian time; Finnish summer time is 2.5 h behind Indian time. Finns generally think in terms of a 24-h clock instead of a.m. or p.m. Summer time in Finland begins from the last Sunday in March and ends on the last Sunday in October.

Finns value punctuality and regard lateness as an insulting lack of concern and consideration for others. In both countries, it is highly valuable to seek appointments well ahead. Indians appreciate punctuality but do not expect to follow time punctually because uncertainties in the environment such as traffic conditions and unforeseen obstacles are real possibilities. When invited to anyone's home for a meal, it is considered polite in India not to arrive on the dot but to arrive 15–30 min later than the scheduled time! Last-minute re-scheduling of appointments is common in India. Some government officials in India keep business leaders waiting for long periods. Requests from government officials and business partners for impromptu meetings at odd times are not uncommon. Business is not conducted on national holidays and religious festival holidays in India. In Finland, business is not conducted on weekends, on any designated holiday and in vacation periods.

The Finnish notion of time is linear, whereas the Indian notion of time is polychronic and cyclic. A customer at a service outlet in Finland is used to being served one at a time, whereas in India it is not uncommon that a doctor, government official, bank manager, or salesperson could be attending to many customers/clients at the same time. In Finland, there is a clear demarcation of work time, free time, hobby time, and family time. The Indian tendency to treat all categories of time to be collapsible or stretchable is a source of much irritation between Finns and Indians working together.

One of the crucial impediments in connecting even mutually interested parties in Finland and India is the travesty of conflicting cycles of time in the respective calendars. The periods that are least conducive for one side appear to be the most attractive to the other side for travel to do business. Finns are accustomed to planning their activities well in advance and arrange their work and activities week by week. Weeks from January to December are numbered 1–52, and week numbers are used as the unit of reference when consulting with each other after the new year's diaries (what Finns call *kalenteri* or calendar) become available around September. In India, new year's diaries become available only in December and the national almanac (*Rashtriya Panchang*) is seldom available before February because it pertains to the period April to March, not January to December. The festival holidays and holiday periods are marked and well defined in the Finnish Calendar. The Indian business cycle begins in April and ends in March of the following year. This keeps professionals busy with accounts closures and completion of activity cycles in March and commencement of the new cycle until early April.

The Indian Almanac, organised by the Lunar Calendar, from April to March becomes available in February but the long list of Gazetted Holidays for the calendar year January to December is usually made known in the last week of December for the following calendar year January to December. Organisations are required to observe four designated national holidays, 15th August (for Independence Day), 26th January (for Republic Day), 2nd October (for Mahatma Gandhi's Birthday) and 10th November (for Prophet Mohammed's Birthday) The date of the last of these varies year to year by the lunar calendar and the date mentioned is for 2019. Organisations also select from the long list, other holidays, in consultation with their employees. Thus, other holidays can vary from organisation to organisation and also from State to State. Only after holiday lists are agreed, working days are knowable.

There are also numerous New Year's days. In 2019, besides the English New Year's Day on 1st January, the following New Year's Days were notified in India's Official Almanac, called *Rashtriya Panchang*: Tamil New Year's Day, Pongal (15th January), Indian New Year's Day (22nd March), Sindhi New Year's Day (6th April), Bengali New Year Day (15th April), Parsi New Year's Day (17th August), Jewish New Year's Day (30th September), and Hejira New Year Day (1st September). Each of these would be a holiday observed by some people in various parts of India.

There is also a system of availing 'restricted holidays' by personal choice on any two days in a long list of restricted holidays. Since holiday lists differ from State to State, and organisation to organisation, and even person to person, it is useful to plan visits and meetings after checking holiday lists.

Since the Indian Government Budget is laid before Parliament every year on 1st February, businesses get busy with lobbying for policy changes in January. In February, they remain busy making sense of how the developments in the economy and budget proposals that affect taxes and subsidies would impact their businesses. Summer sets in around March after the festival of Holi in most parts of India. Foreign trips are typically planned for the summer months May–June–July. In March, Indian businesses are busy with year-ending activities that involve making up of shortfalls in plans and closing the books of accounts and also planning for the New Year starting April. By the time they get set in April, its Easter time in Finland and the first quarter is over. There is only a small window between Easter and May Day, the important 'vappu' labour day holiday which is on 1st May in Finland. In 2017 after a gap of five years, the Finnish and Indian governments managed to revive the Indo-Finnish Joint Commission during this period! The Finnish side had planned for activities around this meeting from the previous autumn. The Indian side had also thought of similar activities but none could be planned because the planning cycle after the government budget was made in February that could enable expenditures to be authorised and resources to be released proved too short.

With Vappu, Finns get busy welcoming the Spring and preparing for summer after the winter thaw and looking forward to the long summer holiday period of Finland by completing whatever chores, commitments, work and activities are required. In Finland, the school term finishes in end May or early June and families plan vacations in three batches—June, July and August. It is in this unwelcome period that requests from Indian counterparts for meetings proposed for June–July begin to arise because this is the period those in India who can do so would wish to escape the summer heat and get to cooler climes. If we look at visits from India to Europe of Ministers, Chambers of Commerce delegations, business leaders and bureaucrats from India, the largest number happen during this period and ritually or hastily held events typically lead nowhere, despite statements of good intent or memoranda of understanding signed mainly to justify such visits.

Finns typically return from their long summer vacation by mid-August and the third quarter of the Calendar Year in India is half over by this time. Meanwhile, the monsoon would also have arrived in India and there would be floods in some parts and drought in other parts keeping government officials busy and rendering travel logistics uncertain and disturbed and flights turbulent. The Onam and Ganesh Chaturthi festivals would rule out two-to-three weeks during August–September.

Finns plan official travel abroad during late September/early October. The Finnish tradition is to travel to sunny destinations when it gets dark in Finland. Not only personal travel but also official business is scheduled taking this into consideration. This is termed '*aurinko matka*' (travel to sunny places) that marks the beginning of the festival period in India with Durga Puja in the East, and Dussehra-Diwali in the rest of the country. In 2017, the Durga Puja period was in the last week of September culminating in Diwali on 19th October. And, it was precisely during this period that Finland sent a minister accompanied by a business delegation to India! In 2018 too, the festive period was celebrated from 4th October onwards with Dussehra on 18th October and Finnish government officials planned their travel to India in that period.

There is again a small window after Diwali, the festival of lights and before Finns begin to celebrate their 'little Christmases' (*pikku joulu*) days in early December. But often, Indians returning from the Diwali festivities would catch up with work and be ready to travel abroad again around mid-December. That is when Finns are extremely busy completing their pending work to be able to celebrate Christmas with their families. Finnish Christmas celebrations are at their peak two days before 25th December. And Indian business delegations tend to land up in Finland around 20th December expecting engagements when normal services are winding down and people have left or are leaving for the Christmas break. In 2017, the Mahindra Group that acquired the Finnish Holiday Club Resorts in 2013 and has lost money from these operations for four consecutive years decided that it would bring over 200 heads of travel agencies from India to Finland to acquaint them with tourism potential and services in Finland and their acquired holiday club facilities precisely at that time!

By the time, Finns return to full swing work after Epiphany in the second week of January, Indians would be getting busy with Makar Sankranti and Pongal and Lohri and Kite Festival around 14th January in different parts of the country. Then, the budget cycle repeats in India with Holi, the festival of colours, and Ugadi to follow while Finns get busy with Skiing vacation weeks by rotation in Lapland.

So is there a way out from this vicious cycle? Yes, of course! But it would require Finns and Indians to take any one of two feasible stances: first, to plot the dates and periods to be avoided with full awareness and consideration of the other side; or second, to sacrifice traditions to make themselves available whenever business exigencies arise or demand. The latter may be possible for Indians who by virtue of sheer diversity could find some talented and responsible people not observing particular festivities to interface with potential business partners, but this is not easy to implement in Finland because everyone including family members throughout the country have the same common dates for all festivities. It would be stressful for families not to have family members participate and contribute to the activities, traditions and work involved around particular traditions. For instance, Finns scrub and clean their homes and shop and cook themselves and visit graveyards to pay respects to their dear departed at Christmas time. It is inconceivable that any family members would withdraw from such collective endeavours.

Sentient Boundaries and Authority Relations

Finns value autonomy and the self-reliant individuality to make decisions concerning their role, goals, budgets and targets within secure collectivities to which they belong. This is possible because formal systems are anchored in planning processes and structures where division of responsibilities and authority is well defined. In India, individuals are always second-guessing what their hierarchical superiors would approve before expressing views, opinions, decisions because powerbases are fragile and volatile, objectives are not stable or consistent, and motivations driving decisions can be in a flux much of the time. This can be annoying for Finns just as Indians would find it exasperating to be pinned down to commitments or horizons at an early stage of discussions.

In India, success and failure and challenge are usually attributed to environmental forces with family and kinship needs often driving rational processes towards irrationality. In Finland, personal factors and task-related role responsibilities are always kept apart. Finns consider it polite to directly say 'No' than to beat about the bush, whereas Indians would never say 'No' but avoid saying 'Yes' when in doubt. Since 'No' is not expressed clearly, foreigners in India should not assume something has been agreed just because 'No' has not been voiced. It is important to be sensitive to note silent passive objections in India and in relating to Indians. With a strong institutional structure of social security, Finns are able to face adversity squarely, whereas Indians tend to rely on family or kinship or collegiate networks to cope with fears and anxieties related to failures.

There is a difference in Finland between contexts characterised by teamwork and those that require resource allocation where hierarchy matters. Hierarchy is played down in all routine tasks that are continuous in nature as opposed to tasks that require commitments to workplaces, development, and new investments. Many workplaces in Finland would routinely have a morning meeting to share views on some of the ongoing challenges over a cup of coffee. Recruitment processes receive considerable attention and arouse processes as part of internal politics. In India, processes tend to be multi-layered and some of the layers may be invisible or secretive. Networks are important in both Finland and India, but they operate differently. In India, networks thrive on goodwill accumulated over a period of time with reciprocity. Trust comes into play as a matter of honour and deserved consideration that could flow from status or accumulated obligations even across generations. In Finland, networks function as a means of informal syndication for transactional and relational advantages sought in competition or cooperation with other such syndicates.

Traditional male chauvinism in India is weakening rapidly with more educated and talented women entering the workforce. This has already happened in Finland where gender equity is the highest in the world. But the processes are quite different. In Finland, equal opportunity entitlements and state support to maternity, childcare, incentives for fathers to participate in childcare are the drivers. These enable females all over the country to claim high participation levels in education and workplaces regardless of family backgrounds. In India, the women availing higher education and preparing for careers even though many in number (maybe even more than in Finland in absolute numbers) come from a narrower set of backgrounds where parents were able and willing to support them financially, emotionally, intellectually. Their advancement involves taking risks in going far from home when local opportunities are limited and infrastructure for safe transportation can be quite lacking. Housing away from the parental home for single women remains a challenge in India because owners of residential accommodation can be reluctant to let out apartments to single women.

The locus of authority at workplaces can shift to acknowledge different power bases. Union density in Finland is high because unemployment insurance contributions are held in wage-earner funds controlled by unions that guarantee average earnings if laid-off or retrenched. The status of shop stewards is high, and they are usually consulted on all important matters that could affect or change workplace relations, employment levels, bonuses and incentives and working times, or the work environment itself. In India, bosses in workplaces are conscious of hierarchy and so-called management prerogatives and tend to bypass consultations if they can. Collective bargaining happens in India only when there are trade unions that demand collective bargaining because there is no statutory requirement of workers' participation in management. The recognition of trade unions for collective bargaining is statutorily mandated only in Maharashtra under the Maharashtra Recognition of Trade Unions and Unfair Labour Practices Act, 1970. The State of Madhya Pradesh has also adopted a similar law and with the bifurcation of Chhattisgarh from Madhya Pradesh, it may also apply there.

The adversarial union-management relations typical of Indian or Anglo-American workplaces are absent in Finland. In Finland, the aristocracy of labour used to be workers in the paper industry. Many of the deals that have been later adopted elsewhere were first struck in the paper industry. In Finland, the legislation on employees' participation in management was circumvented by preserving the traditional role of shop stewards in collective bargaining instead of the compulsory mechanism of works councils. The craft unions in Finland were never direct successors of the guild system. But there is more concentration in employers' associations than in workers' associations. In other words, there could be several workers' associations involved in multi-tier bargaining with a solitary employers' union that structures itself for all the tiers but remains united. All categories of workers, including scientific and professional employees join unions in Finland because there is multi-tier bargaining over work, working conditions and remuneration packages and also because wage-earner funds for unemployment insurance have been traditionally controlled by unions. But this is changing.

In India, union power has weakened continuously since the 1990s and union densities and union power are both in decline (Mathur 1991, 1994). Unions have been largely limited to workers in factories, mines, plantations, big shops and establishments, and in public sector utilities like railways, power plants, postal services, banks and other government departments. Many unions exist only notionally and lack capacity for effective countervailing power. In India, unions play no part in administering unemployment insurance from salary deductions into funds as in Finland. Union-management relations in India are characterised by adversarial bargaining, multiplicity of competing unions, and poor enforcement of labour laws. Management prerogatives are preserved by employers at times with fierce contestations. In circumstances where loss of a workplace is a ticket to economic death, employers exercise power both over the collectivity of employees and also over the propensity of the government to intervene through forms of conciliation, mediation, arbitration, adjudication and enforcement of provisions.

The sectoral specialisation of technical universities in Finland and also in other universities, business schools and vocational education institutions has been encouraged by the government. Yet, 'the role of civil society is restricted' and 'professional communities do not have a societal significance beyond the established structures of the power blocs and their typical firms' (Lilja and Tainio 2005, p. 47). Competition over new investment opportunities is moderated by formal and informal inter-bloc coordination processes. Mutual adjustments are discussed and made at 'neutral meeting places' where inter-group policy-making is done. This kind of mutual adjustment is not so evident at the Nordic level. Finns have been complaining for a long time of how difficult it is to negotiate with Swedes. There are radically different consultative practices elsewhere in Europe and certainly in countries like India where there is also 'psychic distance' and 'cultural distance' involved. The psychic distance between Finland and India is asymmetric. Indians believe Europe is close by but Finland is far. Finns believe that Finland is close by from India but India is far from Finland. When Finnish Ambassador Aapo Pölhö addressed business leaders in Ahmedabad, he began his presentation by highlighting how Finnair takes just 7 hours to reach Finland by flying the Northern route to emphasise that Finland is close by and welcomed Indian investors. An hour later during Q&A, when he was asked why there had been hardly any new Finnish investment in the previous five years, he replied that India is very far from Finland! Dutta (2015) has studied the formation of psychic distance among Finnish professionals in India.

Protocol is an important part of sentient boundaries in Finland and India. Wearing neat and clean clothing appropriate for the season's climate and weather in Finland is of paramount concern to keep warm and dry in a cold climate known for high precipitation most of the year. Finns (men and women) dress conservatively but formally in suits for business meetings and reciprocating likewise is a sign of mutual respect. The weather plays an important part in what to wear. A long coat and hat and scarf and gloves are the norm in winter conditions with snow boots (and an extra pair of shoes to change into once inside an office building); a waterproof jacket and cap and scarf with rain slickers are useful for the autumn; and caps and light jackets for the summer/spring. In India, business suits are the norm for most formal occasions regardless of the season. Women wear business suits or Sarees with a shawl or jacket over it with a cardigan underneath for the cold season. Hotels and convention centres typically keep their airconditioning levels very cold in summer to make it comfortable for suit wearing in hot tropical conditions. Foreigners unaware of this who turn up in clothing suitable for the hot weather would end up shivering.

Finns of all ages and genders generally greet each other with a firm handshake, maintaining eye-contact and a slight nod of the head. 'Hyvää päivää' is the formal way of greeting along with the handshake and less formal are 'Hei' and 'Terve'. 'Moi' is an informal way of greeting without a handshake, especially in central Finland. Hugs are reserved for friends and relatives. In India, shaking hands is common but men usually wait for a woman to offer her hand if she is willing to shake hands. And a woman needs to be careful in offering her hand to men who may be reluctant to shake a woman's hand because some conservative Hindus, Muslims, Jains and Sikhs may want to avoid public touching contact with a woman. The traditional Indian greeting 'Namaste' works everywhere and is best done by joining both hands, with fingers together pointing in the direction of the person or persons being greeted and then speaking out 'Namaste'. Without the gesture, the greeting is empty and would only draw laughter. The significance of the greeting is in its message *'Now all my five senses signified by the fingers of both my hands joined together are turned to you'*.

In business settings in Finland, the honorific Mr./Mrs./Ms. followed by surname is common at the first meeting and thereafter depending on the relationship people may switch over to first names or continue with the more formal way of addressing. Introductions are made with full name without academic or professional titles in Finland but titles are valued in India and should always be used.

Indians do not have surnames in the same way as Westerners are accustomed. Conventions vary widely. Hindu names like mine include a first name (Ajeet) which is a given name followed by a surname (Narain) and a third name signifying the community or clan (Mathur) or place (Mathura) from where the clan originated. In Kerala, among Christians, the first name can be the given name and the middle name is the family name with a biblical surname to follow (as in Ittiyavira Kallivayalil Abraham where Kallivayalil is the family name which may be synonymous with the homeplace with the same name). In some parts of South India, first the name of the place where the person was born is mentioned followed by the father's name (as in Calcutta Ranganathan Jagannathan who would be known as C. R. Jagannathan, where Jagannathan is the given name). Muslim names may carry the father's name at the end (as in Saeed Bin Jung, where it means Saeed son of Jung). Sikhs are generally hailed by their title and first name (as in Dr. Prabhjot for Dr. Prabhjot Singh) because they would all have Singh (if male) and Kaur (if female) as their surname. Some Sikh names have a third name to signify a place or a clan or an honorific as in Neki or Talwandi. Parsi surnames often signify occupations such as Carpenter, Daruwala, Cardmaster, Contractor. People have conjectured whether the trajectory of Indian politics might have been different if the Parsi whom Indira Nehru married had the surname Daruwala instead of Gandhi. To this day, quite many people would imagine that Indira Gandhi was somehow connected to Mahatma Gandhi, whereas she acquired the surname from her Parsi husband, Feroze Gandhi.

No gifts are given in business meetings in Finland, especially not when meeting for the first time. Personal gifts when visiting someone's home in Finland can include flowers, a small handicraft item, a book, or a packet of coffee or bottle of wine. In India, the conduct of business is accompanied with much hospitality and it would be good to be prepared to reciprocate with small gifts such as handicrafts, flowers, chocolates in order not to be left feeling obligated when hospitality is extended or gifts are received. Guests invited to Indian weddings often give an envelope to the couple containing currency notes or gift cheques in odd denominations such as 11 and 101. In India, gifts are not opened in the presence of the giver. When invited to a meal to someone's home in India, it is polite to appreciate the meal but it would be rude to thank for it. Rather one should invite back the person to convey that the relationship is valued.

Misunderstandings can easily arise over gifts in Indian business and work situations. A young multinational executive posted in Jabalpur visited his stockist in Nagpur and on return home found that his car had been filled with oranges. Infuriated at what he perceived was a bribe proffered, he sent his car with his driver back to Nagpur the same evening to return the oranges. The stockist was so offended that he reported this by telegram to the Chairman of the Company. What the newcomer could have done is to reciprocate with a small piece of Jabalpur marble handicraft item on his next meeting with the stockist.

Task Boundaries

In Finland, risk averseness is high with institutionalised norms that favour planning for all tasks. This implies that even operational cycles of known regular periodic activities would have positions of planners associated with them. In new projects, almost the first people to be employed are planners. There are reasons for such systematic and meticulous planning by Finnish organisations. Efficiency is valued because employee costs are high and organisations are lean. The same employee may be required to complete various tasks during the year and unless tasks of roleholders enmesh in a timely way, economic efficiencies are not achieved in teams involving intra-group cooperation and inter-team coordination. The Finnish CEO of Holiday Club Resorts, Iiro Rossi put it succinctly, 'I have only three accountants who handle all the range of work; accounting, financial analysis, VAT returns, payouts, etc. of so many sites and this means planning what is to be done when. In Mumbai, in our sister organisation there are thirty accountants and the boss can easily suddenly ask one or two of them to produce some new kind of financial analysis by the end of the day. I can't do that'.

Planning is at a discount in India where the plethora of unpredictable events and happenings are quite common. In such a millieu, priorities get reset all the time. This places more importance on hierarchies to assign and confirm priorities in India. Information is received openly and there is very little scope for privacy or confidentiality. Information spreads like wildfire. The processing of information is always associated with passions and beliefs making objective facts less persuasive than in Finland.

In Finland, the search for 'objective facts' is valued over 'subjective opinion' even when valuable opinions are expressed by experts with experience. For example, the Rector of the University of Tampere, Krista Varantola was reluctant to initiate discussions for institutional collaboration with India's top-ranked business school IIM Ahmedabad (that features in all world rankings above every equivalent Finnish institution) because she was not aware of IIM Ahmedabad and would not believe the word of the only Indian Professor in the University. The same Rector was willing to accept a proposal for Faculty Exchange with something called Bombay School of Business (operating out of a single room in a Bombay suburb) because there was a favourable internet report about the latter.

Finns are cautious about information that has not been channelized through Finnish authorities. This applies to all kinds of authorities: government, boards of management, company representatives, even professional journals. Establishing credibility for new relations or strange ideas must take precedence over exploration of synergies. For example, Finnish Surgeons were reluctant to adopt a surgical procedure such as the double-incision procedure for compound fractures that was widely discussed as superior in the world-renowned journal 'The Lancet' because the Finnish Medical Journal had not published a favourable article about it. The 'not invented here' syndrome comes up often when there is no credible reference point within Finland. At the same time, gullibility can run riot once something new has caught the imagination and excitement to the extent that many unproven, untested, new medical procedures such as botox treatment for internal organs once introduced became 'normed' quickly, only to be discarded after a short period of time when they were found to be dangerous.

In formal systems in Finland, decision-making is preceded by written proposals that are circulated in advance for opinions to be expressed. But the proposals themselves are seldom circulated without approval of the higher authorities. So effectively, minutes of meetings can be drawn up before the meetings have taken place. There are many informal ways of consulting colleagues before formal proposals are made. On matters that are transactional, phone calls are common. On matters that require deliberation or deep thinking, and an egalitarian ethos, the office sauna or coffee lounge are fora for discussions. It is difficult to behave as an elitist when nude in a sauna. In companies, where women in senior positions need to be included, towels are used in the lounge space outside the sauna rooms. Even the Finnish government budget when its being made is discussed in the Parliament Sauna.

Space Boundaries

The notion of what Indians and Finns regard as their personal space differs. Finns consider 1–1.5 m around themselves to be personal space (for Indians it is 0.75m), and it would make them uncomfortable to have another person within this space unless the person was a close relative. This has implications for relating to Finns in business and social settings and also for arranging seating for business meetings so that comfort levels are not violated. On buses, trains, planes and in elevators, personal space is compromised and this is compensated for by not relating. So there is neither an expectation nor any norm for any conversation among strangers to occur. This is unlike the situation on Indian trains or buses where people introduce themselves and try to relate. For Finns that is a new experience to adjust to the social density in India just as Indians unused to privacy are known to have concluded that Finns who would silently keep to themselves in public places love 'loneliness'. Interior spaces in Finnish buildings are quite standardised in shape and size-enabling interior fittings and fixtures to be manufactured to those standards. This is true for offices and homes, including living rooms, workrooms, kitchens, and bathrooms.

Workspaces in Finland are ergonomically designed and are adjustable for personal differences. The main principles of architectural design are functionality, simplicity, aesthetics and heat insulation unlike in India where key architectural principles are waterproof roofing, ventilation, economy, and aesthetics, particularly the aesthetic science of *Vaastu* (Indian equivalent of the Chinese *feng shui*). In Finland, glass, metal and wood are widely used, whereas in India, bricks, tiles, cement concrete and wire-meshing are used a lot. The organisation of spaces in which people live and work affects how people think, feel and act. Finnish workspace design provides comfort, security, well-being and insulation from cold, dust, noise. Indian workspace design encourages interactions, contact with environment and other people, creation of storage space for files, papers and other artifacts and favours ventilation adequacy and economic cooling.

A lot of Finnish business interaction is conducted over phones and the World Wide Web. In India, while these modalities are used, face-to-face meetings remain important and business discussions over phone would be possible generally only after the parties have met and got acquainted. Business meetings in India are conducted outside business offices in hotels, clubs, professional associations, and occasionally, also in homes and at all times of the day until late evening. In Finland, it is unthinkable to schedule business meetings outside office hours.

Special Characteristics of Finnish and Indian Cultures

The question of whether nations as collective groups of people are cultures in themselves or whether they have a core meta-culture that is collectively reinforced is controversial. There are many frames and numerous concepts by which cultural taxonomies have been portrayed. Popper (1972, pp. 106–152) proposed three descriptors: (1) the world of physical objects, (2) mental states or what may be termed 'pictures-in-the-mind', and (3) thoughts believed to have an objective basis. Anthropological notions of culture lean on studying human relations and relatedness through windows such as language, and reinforcements observed of values, norms, beliefs and attitudes.

In contrast, semiotic notions provide different lenses, especially useful in high-context societies because they rely on object relations, non-verbal communication through symbols and symbolism, and rely on accurate interpretation of intent. In Finland, the semiotic approach is more useful to understand both the micro-cultures and the macro-culture because homogeneity is a pervasive feature of the society. This is contrary to the claim by linguists from the anglo-saxon tradition such as Morrisson and Conaway (2006) who wrongly describe Finnish culture to be low-context and high-content. One easy way of verifying this in any culture is to examine the size of documents that signify agreements. In low-context cultures, agreements and contracts are typically large in size as in the USA or the UK or India. The Indian Constitution is the world's longest text and the Indian Companies Act, the world's biggest piece of legislation of any kind. In high-context cultures where much can be assumed or is societally institutionalised such as in Japan or Finland, agreements and contracts have very little text and focus on core essentials rather than mountains of small print.

To begin with, ethnic homogeneity in Finland is among the highest of all national groups in the world despite the Swedish–Finnish–Sami cleavage. But that is not all. Most people born in Finland and grown up there have been genetically part of a largely inbreeding population. They would also share in common exposure to a homogenous monoculture reinforced around climate, family structures, school systems, religion, retail commerce in terms of experiences of shopping and of institutions such as health care, social security, welfare state guarantees, and the police. It should not surprise anyone that this would produce quite similar ideas, ideologies, norms, values, beliefs and attitudes. The advantage of this is in ease of standardisation of forms, structures, systems concerning all aspects of life including professions and business activities.

Finland was ranked among the top five countries in the World Happiness Report 2017. Yet, it has been speculated that Finno-Ugric genes may account for greater susceptibility to depression, suicides, alcohol abuse and marriage failures (Lehtonen 1993; Osgood et al. 1975). According to these researchers, Finns devalue themselves easily and serene sadness is more prevalent than joy. Finns tend to fall through societal safety nets because emotional support at times of acute distress and trauma is generally sought within families or from paid professionals that include priests and therapists who are available only by appointment. Salaried social workers and half-way homes have been provided by the Welfare State but not everyone can be connected to them in emergencies. The best route is often via the police or emergency services of hospitals.

The cold weather and long winters limit outdoor social interaction of people to sports. The low density of population (about 16 people per square kilometre) enabled habitations to be spaced out and expand the comfort zone for personal space. But there are differences. In Western Finland, the inhabitants live in scattered housing where they can hardly see their neighbours. In Eastern Finland houses are bigger, habitations were more compact, and extended families not uncommon. Trade and Commerce were more important in the East than in the West. Traces and residues from this can be noticed even today. People in the East are more sociable and talkative while the people in the West are reticent and shy.

In Chap. 5, the Nordic Welfare State Model is explained. One of its features, the high female labour participation rate is maintained by keeping the education level of women among the highest in the world and encouraging dual-earner nuclear families without endangering the birth and child-rearing of future potential taxpayers. There has never been any Finnish aristocracy in Finland with the exception of titles like baron (with a coat of arms) conferred by the Swedish Crown during the period when Finland was part of Sweden. There has also not been any underclass destined to stay poor. Social stratification is based on professions and occupations and solidaristic fraternal networks created by families or through sports, cultural or other outdoor activities of common interest. Neighbourhood or locality plays no part in this with two notable exceptions. In Helsinki, the Töölö locality was traditionally the abode of elites and quite many important decision-makers in business and government who reside within a small geographical area know each other. The second exception is the Ostrobothnian community of Laestardians who are a close-knit community around their own culture and religious beliefs. The Lutheran Church to which the majority of the population is affiliated has much less influence on the common people or business life and its numbers are declining.

Deal and Kennedy (1982) proposed another way of categorising micro-cultures by onion peeling from the outer layers of communication patterns to identify the iconic heroes that are held up as role models, then look at rites or rituals that the people engage in and finally decode the core values of a culture from these. Nurmi and Uskvärav (1994) described this for layers of Finnish and Estonian culture.

According to Nurmi and Uskarav, silence and closeness to nature are part of the communication pattern; 'independence in a structure' is a core Finnish value; the sauna, skiing and wandering in the forest are the national rituals (being in the forest has metaphorical and ritualistic significance); and, Sibelius, Mannerheim, Paavo Nurmi, Alexis Kivi and Runeberg's fictional character, Sven Dufva and Väino Linna's fictional soldiers in 'The Unknown Soldier' are the prototypes of heroes. To these, I would add Väinämöinen and Kullervo from the Finnish Epic Kalevala, Larin Paraske (symbol of Karelian songs she sang) or the currently more popular Karita Mattila, Car Racer Kimi Raikkonen from Formula 1, Tove Jansson (the creator of Moomins), Tsunami survivor Sauli Niinisto (currently, President), Media

Baron Aatos Erkki, Linus Torvalds creator of Linux, and Industrialist and richest person in Finland, Antti Herlin, Chairman of KONE in a more modern formulation as depicted in Fig. 4.1.

The micro-culture of organisations in Finland is role and task centric with a delicate balance between intra-group and inter-team cooperation orchestrated by hierarchies. This is effective for operations but less able to respond to abrupt changes or transform itself in turbulent environments. There is a risk aversion to experimentation although once something has been proven and accepted it can be implemented very quickly. There is also an enduring conflict between well-established democratic and egalitarian social and political norms in the macro-culture and its incompatibility with hierarchy in micro-cultures. This makes the study of leadership in Finland particularly interesting.

According to the GLOBE study (Lindell and Sigfrids 2007), Finnish leaders score highly on integrity, inspiration, collaborative team orientation and vision. The results did not vary across sectors. Many of the Finnish business leaders have been officers in the Finnish Military which has had an effect on management styles and organisation. Finnish employees seem to paradoxically want both autonomy and authoritarian bosses. When Sari Baldauf, Director on several boards of companies including Nokia was asked what made her management style different, she was

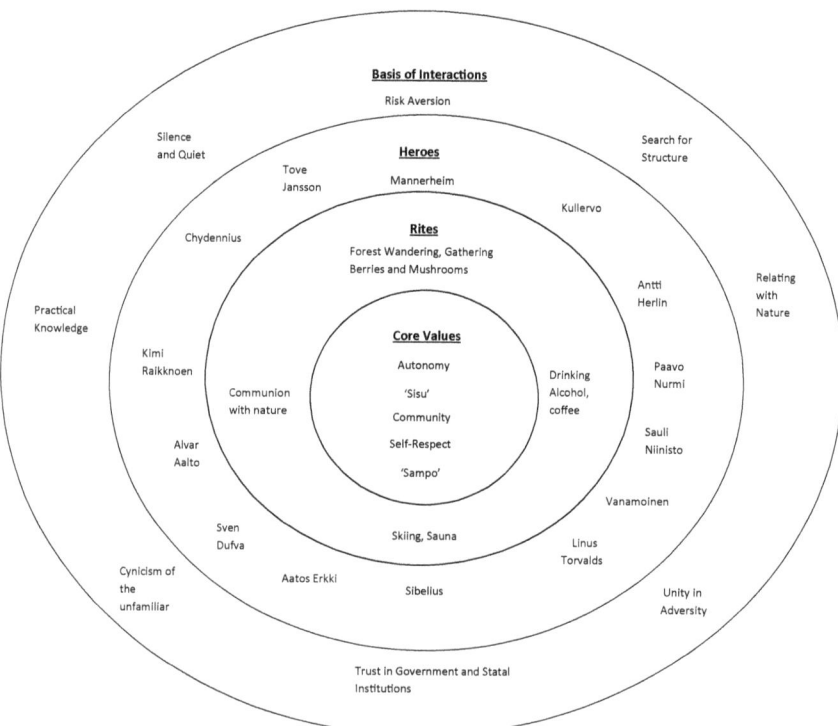

Fig. 4.1 Layers of Finnish culture

Special Characteristics of Finnish and Indian Cultures   119

quite clear in her response 'I haven't been to the army'. Most men in Finland would have done a stint in army service except for a few who would have opted for civil service as conscientious objectors or because they were medically unfit. Women are allowed on a voluntary basis and only a few opt for the experience. This makes civilian leadership styles of men to be adaptations from their army experience, whereas women are generally not so encumbered. It seems that outstanding Finnish leaders are able to bring charisma and energy to their role while drawing on the respect and loyalty of subordinates. Finns hate leaders who would try to micro-manage and curtail the autonomy of functioning for the subordinates by close supervision. This has implications for foreign leaders managing businesses in Finland and also for Finnish leaders abroad in countries such as India where immature dependency on leaders is the norm.

A layered cultural depiction for India in Fig. 4.2 has more elements because of a longer period of recorded history and a larger canvas of geographical area that makes up the national memories. If Fig. 4.1 had been attempted for the whole of Europe, then it would be as cluttered as Fig. 4.2 where the basis of interactions are numerous, heroes have accumulated over time, and rites, traditions and values have got layered over.

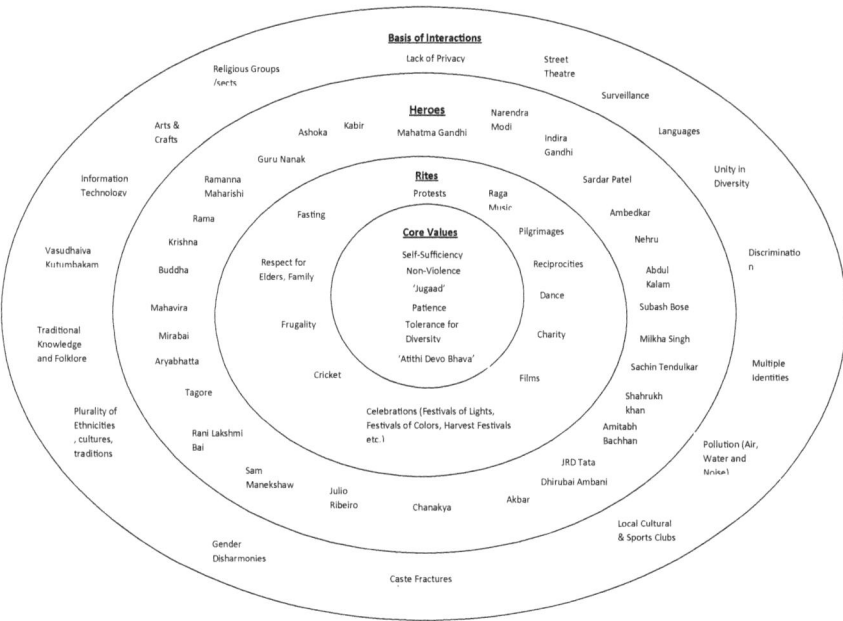

Fig. 4.2 Layers of Indian culture

Social and Cultural Barriers

The extent of cultural contact between Finland and India has been limited. Mental distance rather than geographical distance accounts for it. India is pictured as an overpopulated country with many poor people, frequent natural disasters like floods, droughts, earthquakes and man-made disasters like boat capsizes and train accidents. Industrial India or Business India is less known in Finland just as hi-tech Finland is hardly known in India except to the cognoscenti. Nokia, until recently, was perceived as a Japanese firm and most people going up and down Kone lifts still have no idea that they are partaking of a Finnish product. Industrial Groups like Nirma, Reliance, Birlas, Goenkas and Murugappa are unfamiliar for commoners in Finland. The Finnish media usually confirms stereotypes by its reporting as does the Indian media that reports a land of ice and snow, forest logging, brown bears mauling trekkers, drunks drowning at mid-summer (Juhannus), rail disasters at Riihimäki, and Santa Claus and his reindeer herds. India also scores poorly on infrastructure, environmental degradation, urban sanitation and public hygiene, chaotic road traffic, air and water pollution and visible poverty.

Beneath the veneer of obvious social and cultural differences that arise from differences in demography, nature, urban habitations, economic development, lifestyles, etc., there are important social and cultural differences that reflect differences in life views and world views and reinforce mindsets of those in pursuit of business opportunities more significantly (Mathur and Mattila 2007). For Finns, relating to India requires tolerating ambiguity and diversity on many dimensions (including organisation structures, management systems, business practices and operating styles) to the extent that any generalisations made are likely to be fundamentally flawed or misleading and where the boundaries of private, personal, social and official overlap. For Indians relating to Finland requires cultivating a degree of goal specificity and tolerance for uniformity and standards borne out of entitlements created by systems and definitive norms around work cultures where the personal and the private domains are designed to be excluded from the social and the social from the official. The most important implication is for decision-making where inclusive practices are the norm in India and exclusive practices the norm in Finland.

In India, entitlements are determined around citizenship, employment and membership of a household, whereas in Finland these are determined around the individual entitlements created by the State which may partly be operated through 'liitot' (associations) and employers in some cases. This has implications for organising marketing (for example, for analysing consumer choices), for organising employment in an industry (for example, for designing a compensation system) and for negotiating private and public contracts. Scanty and superficial inferences from differences in cuisine or faith or language or sports or music do not do justice to the many dimensions of differences that people from the two countries would encounter in the other even in exploring business opportunities.

References

Deal TE, Kennedy AA (1982) Corporate cultures: the rites and rituals of corporate life

Dutta DM (2015) The formation of psychic distance: the case of Finnish managers in India, University of Vaasa

Joutsimäki S, Mathur A (2006) Managing international cultural differences, or doing as the Romans (or Finns or Indians Do? Rev Prof Manag 4(2):1–9

Kirra KM (2000) Finns in interaction with non-Finns: problematic phenomena perceived as critical incidents. J Inter-Cult Commun 3. http://www.immi.se/intercultural/Issue3,April

Lehtonen J (1993) Suomalaisuus, Suomi-kuva ja kanasainvälistymisen haasteet. In: Lehtonen J (ed) Kulttuurien kohtaaminen. Näkökulmia kansainväliseen kanssakäymiseen, Jyväkylän Yliopisto, Viestintäitieteiden laitos, pp 7–30 (in Finnish)

Lilja K, Tainio R (2005) The nature of the typical firm in Finland. In Lilja KL (ed) The national business system in Finland, Helsingin Kauppakorkeakoulun Julkaisuja B-60

Lindell M, Sigfrids C (2007) Culture and leadership in Finland. In: Chhokar J, Brodbeck FC, House RJ (eds) Culture and leadership across the world: the GLOBE book of in-depth studies of 25 societies. Psychology Press, New York, pp 75–106

Mathur AN (1991) Industrial restructuring and union power: micro-economic dimensions of industrial restructuring, ILO-ARTEP, New Delhi, World Employment Programme, Geneva

Mathur AN (1994) The future of trade unions. Indian J Soc Work 2:249–256

Mathur AN, Mattila S (2007) Intercultural learning from 'listening posts': embeddedness, diffusion and evolution of subnational and supranational metacultures in Finland and India. In Manikutty S (ed) Learning, teaching and research in a borderless world. Macmillan, New Delhi, pp 1–20

Morrisson T, Conaway W (2006) Kiss, bow or shake hands. Adams, Mass

Nurmi R, Uskvärav R (1994) Estonia and Finland: culture and management: a conjectural presentation, A-9:1994

Osgood CE, May WH, Miron MS (1975) Cross-cultural universals of affective meaning. University of Illinois Press, Urbana

Piekkari R (2014) Language in international business: the multilingual reality of global business enterprises

Popper K (1972) Objective knowledge: an evolutionary approach. Clarendon Press, Oxford

Varma PK (2004) Being Indian. Penguin, New Delhi

Waqar U (2011) Cross-cultural challenges to expatriates in Finland. University of Vaasa, Vaasa

Wilkins R, Isotalus P (2009) Speech culture in Finland. University Press of America, Maryland

Chapter 5
Managing Institutional Differences in Finland–India Business

> *The task is not so much to see what no one yet has seen but to think what nobody yet has thought about that which everybody sees.*
>
> Schopenhauer

Abstract This chapter distinguishes institutional differences from cultural differences discussed in the previous Chap. 4 and introduces the important institutions in both countries in the context of enterprise formation and structuring business investments, trade and collaborations. There is discussion on taxation systems, labour markets, capital markets, community laws, and liquidation procedures. The Finnish Code-Law-based justice system and India's Common-Law-based justice system are different from each other. The Chapter also familiarises the reader with public systems in the two countries and how that may affect the structuring of investments and risks associated with prosecuting and defending legal actions.

Introduction

Institutions consist of arrangements that societies create and evolve over time. These are influenced not only by unique historical trajectories of how countries assumed autonomy and began exercising sovereign governance. These take shape also from the unique environmental, social, political and economic traverses of how national groups come together to support communities of habitat, professions and vocations, and commit themselves to uniting for reinforcing commonly cherished values, beliefs, norms and attitudes about all the various aspects of life. While cultural evolution plays a part in institutional development, institutional differences are not the same as cultural differences because they involve national policies, strategies, structures of governance including taxation, justice systems and processes of societal functioning for governance, competitiveness and international economic relations around motives, aspirations and powerbases of individuals, groups and entire nation-states.

In this Chapter, enterprise formation and its contexts in Finland and India are presented. There is also discussion on the tax systems, and how the Finnish Code-Law-based justice system and India's common-law-based justice system are very different from each other. This means that special attention is required when prosecuting or defending court actions. This Chapter also explains Finland's welfare state model and how systems support individuals and businesses. This is contrasted with India's model of state intervention for the very poor and how that influences the structuring of investments, in relation to differences in labour markets, capital markets, community laws, and bankruptcy procedures. Actual success and failure cases in Finland and in India are also exemplified.

Enterprise Formation

There has been a convergence of company laws worldwide. Finland's Companies Act and the Indian Companies Act have both been substantially amended during the period 2001–2013. The Indian Companies Act is the biggest piece of legislation of any kind in the world. Foreigners establishing companies in India can read the provisions including the small print because it is available in English, besides other official languages. The Finnish Companies Act, like other Finnish laws, is available in Finnish and Swedish, and 'unofficial' translations in English are easily obtained. The important distinguishing features of enterprise laws in Finland and India are worth noting.

In Finland, limited liability companies are of three kinds: private limited company (*yksityinen osakeyhtiö* or Oy), public limited company (*julkinen osakeyhtiö* or Oyj) and European Company (*Societas Europea* or SE when European Council Regulation 2157 came into force). Besides these, partnerships of two or more persons for doing business or owning property and European Economic Interest Groupings (EEIG) are also recognised as partnerships for tax purposes. When partners are personally liable for obligations, such general partnerships are termed *avoin yhtiö* or Ay and where partners agree to limit liability of some partners but not all, it takes the form of *kommandiittiyhtiö* or Ky (Surakka 2012). Business partnerships are not considered separate taxable entities. The net income of a business partnership is determined by rules applicable to corporate bodies but taxed according to the shares of the partnership profits in the hands of individuals. The simplest form of sole proprietor entrepreneurship is referred to as '*toiminimi*'.

In Finland, Representative Agents contract in the name of their Principals. Commission Agents act in their own name and in such cases third parties cannot enforce contracts against the Principals. Branches of foreign companies are registered in the Trade Register maintained by the PRH (Registrar of Companies and Patents). Branches are required to have a representative domiciled in Finland mainly for the purpose of receiving legal notices. Branches are taxed in Finland if they have a permanent establishment, but the foreign company is liable for the obligations of the branch. Annual Returns to the Registrar of companies require the complete annual accounts and reports of the foreign company. This can be avoided by registering a firm as a private limited company known as osakeyhtiö (oy) in Finland. The minimum capital requirement is €2500 and the formalities of establishment are simple and precise. All it requires is a Trade Name, Memorandum of Association, Share Capital, Board of Directors (at least 3), Registered Office Address and the Auditor to be specified. Public Limited Companies require a minimum capital subscription of €80,000. Companies listed on the stock exchange have to be public limited companies. The European Company form (SE) mentioned above requires a minimum share capital of €120,000 and a certain degree of transnationality through formations, through merger, holding company, subsidiary or transformation of a firm with subsidiaries operating in more than one member state of the European Union.

The financial statements and statutory annual report of the Board of Directors require to be presented in Finnish or Swedish but books of accounts, records, minutes of meetings can be kept in any European language, provided a translation into Finnish or Swedish is also made available. Financial statements are expressed in Euro. Finnish GAAP (Generally Accepted Accounting Principles) differs from International Financial Reporting Standards (IFRS). All EU companies listed on a regulated stock market have to maintain accounts in accordance with IFRS but the rest continue to follow Finnish GAAP.

The significant differences between Finnish GAAP and IFRS are:

1. Debt was traditionally considered part of Shareholders' Equity in a limited liability company in Finnish GAAP but now equity would be the residual claimant.
2. Disposals of non-current assets, closures of lines of businesses, dissolution of subsidiaries, mergers can be treated as extraordinary items in Finnish GAAP.
3. In Finnish GAAP, there is a difference in the treatment of depreciation for accounting and tax purposes. The difference between the two is recorded under Appropriations in the profit and loss account, after extraordinary items.
4. Asset Revaluation is allowed only for land and shares in Finnish GAAP.
5. In Finnish GAAP, capitalisation of production overhead as part of inventory carriage cost is allowed but not required even when the amount is significant.
6. Accounting for deferred income taxes is voluntary, so revenues and expenses recorded in different accounting years can change the real profit upwards or downwards in Finnish GAAP.
7. Disclosures of discontinued operations are not required in Finnish GAAP.
8. There are no regulations concerning investment property accounting in Finnish GAAP.

The auditing profession in Finland is supervised by the Finnish Patent Office and Registry (PRH) that authorises Public Accountants to be appointed by large companies (turnover exceeding €50 million, assets over €25 million, more than 300 employees). For other companies, Approved Accountants are authorised by local Chambers of Commerce. Even international auditing firms operating in Finland have to turn to Public Accountants and Approved Accountants for statutory purposes. Finnish Public Auditors and Approved Auditors have the authority to order restructuring of a company or even its dissolution if its net worth falls below half of the paid-up capital for two successive years.

Finland allows acquisitions through purchase of shares or assets. The latter route can exclude all or specified liabilities that would also be acquired if the share route were adopted. Foreign international accounting and auditing firms lack the expertise required for due diligence scrutinies of Finnish companies and often miss out on contingent liabilities and factors that have to do with local networks and commitments or past histories which have a bearing on the future of the firm if it were to be acquired. Light-touch Indian acquisitions of Finnish enterprises such as by Havells (of Sylvania) and Mahindra Group (of Club Resorts) when continuity in top management was arranged have a different trajectory from acquisitions such as WinWinD.

In WinWinD, the change of ownership brought devastating changes in top management and control that bankrupted the firm quite quickly. The new owners of WinWinD did not understand the rigidity of Finnish factor markets (labour, capital, housing, education) relevant to their expansion strategy. In Finland, employees are used to living in owned houses and in communities they have been in for long periods. WinWinD tried to expand by relocating their operations from the Oulu region in the North to the South of Finland in a Swedish-speaking community unmindful of the housing market and Finland's linguistic divide. Employees with housing mortgages found it difficult to move with their families and resettle in the South and the company lost valuable talent.

The economic logic in similar businesses with different business models can be quite dissimilar. In many Finnish acquisitions by foreign companies, acquirers did not invest in understanding the dominant business logic and tried to cut what they believed were avoidable costs to be saved. In the process, they inadvertently cut the lifelines of the business and soon reached insolvency. This has also happened in joint ventures between Finnish enterprises and foreign companies where Finnish enterprises have forced cuts to boost short-term profits and destroyed the long-term gains that would have required patience and courage. This kind of phenomena was noticeable in four biotech and biopharma investments made by Indian investors in Finland-all of which collapsed. Learning from such experiences is important, and these cases have been researched and are in the process of being published separately.

Homogeneity has advantages but the lack of diversity in thinking can be devastating if everyone circulates the same beliefs without anybody questioning them. For instance, Lilja et al. (1992) wrote '*The conclusion remains inescapable that the forest industry remains the dominant industry of the country and nothing seems to threaten its position in this respect*' at a time when Nokia was rising after being restructured with government support. It is even more remarkable that academia was so divorced from business because it was well known to industry and government that the forest industry was planning consolidations and organising to almost flee from Finland by transferring half of the existing capacity to countries outside Finland at this time. Later, the same sense of complacence, arrogance and infallibility resurfaced when Nokia was considered divine and eulogies were being written (for instance, Steinbock 2010) when Nokia was already in deep trouble and poised for freefall.

Payroll issues and Value Added Tax (VAT) registration require to be systematised right at the beginning in establishing a business in Finland. Pension insurance premia and accident insurance premia (including group life insurance and unemployment insurance) are part of social security contributions to be deducted at source. And no billing would be possible without VAT registration and provision for rates as applicable. Insurances for defending or prosecuting legal cases and insurances for professional liabilities safeguarding businesses and professional practices require to be organised at the time of business commencement.

Taxation

Finland has high value-added tax (VAT) rates—among the highest in Europe but below Hungary (27%), Sweden and Denmark (25%). All supplies of goods and services in Finland are subject to value-added tax (VAT). There are three VAT slabs:

(1) 10% for medicines, books, sports equipment and facilities, movies, theatre, cultural performances, concerts, entertainment events, passenger transport services and accommodation services.
(2) 14% for food (including restaurants), animal feeds but excluding drinking water, alcoholic beverages and tobacco.
(3) 24% for all others as the standard rate.

In addition, there are other indirect taxes. Low company tax rates in Finland at 20% (UK at 19%, Ireland at 12.5% and tax havens are lower) co-exist with high individual marginal rates. Individual taxation is higher in Finland than in India at peak rates as well as progressive rates. This has a bearing on the taxation of Finnish managers posted in India and Indian managers posted in Finland. Company taxation rate in Finland (20%) is lower than in India (where it is 25% for company turnover up to Rs 2.5 billion and 30% above that threshold excluding surcharges). There exists a Finland–India Double-Taxation Treaty so that neither Finnish nor Indian tax law would apply; only the Treaty provisions would need to be followed. However, the Finnish authorities may opine in certain situations that Finnish national tax laws supersede the Treaty and make assessments on that basis. The Indian tax authorities also used to contend that Indian national tax laws supersede double taxation treaties but this problem was resolved in a landmark judgement by an Indian Court in November 1998 involving a German Director of an Indian Company where the Court decided that Double Taxation Treaties supersede national laws and foreign directors of Indian companies are not taxable in India.

The peak marginal tax rate for individuals (30%) in India corresponds closely to the corporate tax rate in India (in two slabs, 25% and 30% and both have been lowered in recent years). There is a huge wedge of 33–35% between the Finnish company tax rate (20%) and the highest individual marginal rates (53–55%). In customs duties, the peak customs tariff rate in India has been lowered to 10% (with few exceptions like agricultural goods and motor cars) and the effective average tariff rate is 6.3% for most categories (including all capital goods) and have been totally eliminated in some cases. In Finland, the peak customs tariff rate is 17% but customs duties on food stuffs and textiles and clothing is higher. Finland is committed to maintaining EU tariff rates.

Finland has abolished wealth tax. Thus, domestic corporate bodies are subject to wealth tax in India but not in Finland. In India, the effective tax on royalties and technical services fee was reduced from 50% to 20%. The tax rate on income of branches of foreign firms is 48%. Two ways to lower the tax burden are adherence to bilateral treaty or by incorporation. Tax holidays have been announced in India for investments in power generation, ports, refineries, waterways development and for backward areas. These benefits are available to incorporated entities, but not to licensors of know-how. Additionally, there are tax-free zones adjacent to ports and airports for export-oriented manufacturing units where customs duties are not levied. This has been done to encourage exports from special economic zones many of which are near ports.

Finns have a high expectation from authorities for public goods and services because payroll taxes and indirect taxes are both higher than the European average. For direct taxes, there is a three-tier tax system with three tax authorities in Finland, each with its own jurisdiction. These are municipalities (communes), central government (the State) above certain threshold of income and the Evangelical-Lutheran and Orthodox Churches (the Churches can claim their levy only from members). Each of the authorities is entitled to their shares from income tax. The shares of taxes paid by corporate bodies in Finland are considerably below the average for OECD countries, whereas the taxes levied on individuals are higher than the OECD average. The share of social security contributions is relatively low by international standards. Some social insurance schemes are administered by the private sector, and these contributions that were not previously counted in tax statistics are now counted in OECD tax statistics.

Individuals and resident corporate bodies and estates of deceased persons are liable to tax on their entire income from Finland and abroad. The concept of chargeable income is very extensive. Non-residents in Finland are taxed at a flat rate of 35% of income if they have been less than six months in Finland. Married persons are taxed separately on their respective incomes unless they jointly carry out farming or earn professional income jointly or if either has unearned income beyond a specified limit. The Pensions Act and the Sickness Insurance Act require additional deductions from individual incomes at source.

There are two broad categories for taxation of entities: (1) corporate bodies and (2) partnerships and undistributed estates. Corporate bodies include limited companies, co-operative societies, savings banks, associations, mutual insurance companies, foundations, institutions, or any other similar legal persons. Dividends received by companies or co-operative societies from other companies or co-operative societies are tax exempt.

In India, the fiscal domain for communities such as urban local bodies and panchayats is weak. Municipalities collect house tax. States have authority to levy taxes such as excise duties on alcohol, taxes on petrol and diesel and stamp duty on real estate transactions. The General Sales Tax (GST), India's equivalent of the European VAT, has replaced central and sales taxes in 2017. There are four slabs of GST Rates 5, 12, 18 and 28%. This is likely to be rationalised to just two slabs of 5 and 15 and the 28% slab is being eliminated according to the Finance Minister's statement in December 2018. Income tax from individuals, partnerships, companies and other entities is collected by the central government. There is a system in place under periodically constituted Finance Commissions on revenue sharing between the Central Government and State Governments.

International Taxation in Finland and India

The Finnish statutory tax laws applying to cross-border economic relations determine whether, to what extent and how Finland taxes. Finnish tax authorities interpret these to imply that only the limits are circumscribed by other international tax law rules and regulations, including tax treaties for the avoidance of double taxation. This has been done to secure the extra-territorial tax powers of Finland in cross-border contexts and to limit international double taxation. Hence, instead of starting from a double taxation treaty, one should first read the following Finnish tax provisions: Income Tax Act (TVL) Sections 9 to 13; 45–49, and 76–77; Act on Assessment Procedure (VML) Section 31; Inheritance and Gift Tax (PerVL) Section 4; and Business Income Tax Act (EVL) Section 7. For non-residents, it would be useful to read the Act and Decree on the taxation of income and wealth of a Person Subject to Limited Tax Liability (*Lähde VL and Lähde VA*) and the Act on Elimination of International Double Taxation (*MenetelmäL*).

Finnish Tax treaties are simultaneously international agreements and a part of Finland's domestic law. The five main European Commission (EC) directives on direct taxes apply in Finland which could be relevant for some enterprises connecting their Finnish investments with other incorporated entities (Helminen 2016). These are:

1. The EC Parent-Subsidiary Directive on the tax treatment of inter-corporate dividends implemented in EVL [Section 6a] and [Lähde VL Section 3(5)].
2. The EC Merger Directive concerning company reorganizations implemented in EVL [Section 52 (a) to (g)].
3. The EC Interest-Royalty directive concerning inter-company interest and royalty payments implemented in Lähde VL [Section 3 (a) to (f)] and MenetelmäL [3 (5)].

4. The EC Savings Directive concerning interest income implemented in Lähde VL[Sect. 3(7)] and MenetelmäL [Sections 4(4) and 5(2)].
5. The EC Directive 1164/2016 lays down rules against tax-avoidance practices that directly affect the internal market to be implemented from end of the year 2018.

Finland and India have double taxation avoidance agreements with each other and with many other countries. India has generally used the UN Model Tax Convention, whereas Finland has used the OECD Model Income Tax Convention. Finland and India have double taxation treaties for the avoidance of double taxation since 1961 when the OECD model did not exist. The later treaties between Finland and India have features from both the UN and OECD Model Convention (of 1992 which is an update of the 1977 and 1963 versions). The key concepts are contained in the definitions of 'residence' (the criteria of home and economic livelihood read with the 183-day rule for determining fiscal domicile) and 'source state' for different kinds of incomes. The Vienna Convention on the Law of Treaties signed in 1969 contains the general rules of interpretation of international treaties including tax treaties (Articles 31 to 33). Finland and India have both ratified this Convention. There are two ways that double taxation is avoided in Finland: by exemption or by credit.

The taxation of business income of corporate entities involves correlative adjustments in justifiable cases of transfer pricing. Finland has accepted Article 9(2) of the OECD Model that refers to correlative or corresponding adjustments for the purpose of eliminating international double taxation caused by transfer pricing adjustments in some of its treaties. But Finland has also reserved the right not to include such a provision in its treaties, so it is necessary to check this from time to time. The Act on Assessment Procedure [VML Section 89 (3)] can be applied for the purpose of correlative adjustments.

According to Finland's tax treaties including the double taxation avoidance treaty with India, the source state has unlimited taxing right of royalties if the right or property in respect of which royalties are paid is effectively connected with a permanent establishment which the income recipient has in the source state for its business. This is in accordance with Article 12(3) of the OECD Model.

Salaries from employment abroad of Finnish Residents are totally exempt from Finnish taxation if a Finnish Resident works abroad for a continuous period of at least six months (EPL Sections 9 and 13 and SVL Chapter 18 Section 4). If salaries paid relate to vacation periods spent in Finland (for example, a Finnish Resident employed abroad spends summer vacation and Christmas vacation in Finland with vacation earned on grounds of work abroad), salaries remain tax exempt (KVL 1991/141 and KVL 1996/41).

Both resident and non-resident tax-payers can apply for a binding advance ruling regarding income tax subject to a charge from the provincial tax offices in Finland. India also allows this through a Central Authority for Advance Rulings in New Delhi. Finnish tax offices have authority to rectify tax assessments they have made. In India, rectification requires a formal request to a specified Appellate Authority. Tax appeals against Finnish tax office assessments can be made to Assessment Adjustment Boards but they have to be made quickly. The time limit to appeal in tax cases is 30 days concerning binding advance rulings and three years after the tax year in cases of regular assessment. Decisions on incomes taxed in a year January-to-December become available by the first week of December the following year. This means there are two more years up to December the year after a tax decision has been made. Assessment Adjustment Board Decisions can be appealed at Provincial Administrative Courts by residents within their jurisdiction and to Helsinki Administrative Court by non-residents. Appeals against decisions of Provincial Administrative Courts can be made to the Supreme Administrative Court. Care must be taken to strictly follow any timelines stipulated for appeals in decisions of Assessment Adjustment Boards and Provincial Administrative Courts. Decisions in cases of appeals are often made based on written submissions of the parties without oral hearings.

There have been several irritants arising from the Finland–India Double Taxation Avoidance Agreement (FIDTAA). According to the FIDTAA, the source country of the income has right to tax royalty income, but the business income can be taxed only in the residence country, unless there is a permanent establishment in the source country. The payments from the purchase of software are royalty and assessed in taxes. The same income could also be included in the worldwide taxable income of the Finnish company and taxed accordingly in Finland. Finland does not credit the taxes paid in India, because in Finnish interpretation the consideration constitutes royalty only if the transferor grants to the transferee the right to use the copyright of the product. Finland follows the interpretation of the OECD Model Tax Convention and considers income from the purchase of software a normal business income taxable only in the resident country, if the copyright of the software has not been alienated. This confusion led to Nokia's tax dispute between Nokia and the Government of India. However, in this case, Nokia had neither paid taxes in Finland nor in India on the relevant amount of assessed income that accrued in India. The matter was finally settled by mutual agreement when Nokia paid up its tax dues to India after more than a decade and an interest waiver was extended by India at the request of the Finnish government.

Employment Contracts

In Finland, employment contracts can be oral, written or electronic. Collective agreements can bind present and future employers or employees who were not parties to the agreements. The Working Hours Act limits the working to a maximum of eight hours a day or forty hours in a week. Regular weekly working can be flexible provided the average weekly hours over a 52-week period do not exceed 40 hours. Two kinds of terminations are envisaged in Finnish Law: on individual grounds which relate to conduct and performance of an individual employee, or on collective grounds if there is a downturn in the economic activity or output requirement of the enterprise. For such justified terminations, there are no exit costs except for notice-period pay.

In India, there is a plethora of legislation covering conditions of work, employment security, collective bargaining, remuneration and social security. The Government of India proposes to rationalise Labour Acts by revising and simplifying relevant provisions of existing laws into four labour codes, viz Code on Wages, Code on Industrial Relations, Code on Social Security and Welfare, and Code on Safety and Working conditions. Since Labour is a concurrent subject on which legislation can be adopted by the National Parliament as well as by the State legislatures, the Labour Law provisions vary from State to State. Even the proposed simplification has progressed faster in states like Gujarat, Rajasthan and Madhya Pradesh where the same political party that held majority in the National Parliament during 2014–18 was also in the majority in the State legislatures. Since then, the Congress opposition has formed the new State governments in Rajasthan and Madhya Pradesh, and it remains to be seen whether labour laws would be changed.

In India, labour standards and decent work, Freedom of Association and Collective Bargaining and employment security are limited to those who are protected by labour laws. There are three levels of protection. First, there are labour standards and decent work protocols that pertain to industrial establishments which cover all workers in factories, shops and establishments and mines and plantations. The Factories Act, Shops and Establishments Acts, Mines Act and Plantation Labour Acts and the rules framed thereunder prescribe in great detail the safety, hygiene, working hours, and other conditions such as prohibition of child labour.

The second category concerns laws on minimum wages, payment of wages, bonus, provident fund and pensions, gratuity, and health insurance for various categories of workers including casual labour and contract labour. In this category, the Contract Labour (Regulation and Abolition) Act, 1970 prohibits the engagement of contract labour on perennial nature of jobs. The temptation to violate this provision to save on wage costs is not worth the trouble it would eventually bring. The definition of 'industry' in India is very wide (following the Supreme Court Judgement in the Bangalore Water Supply and Sewerage Board Case versus Rajappa in 1978 available in the 1978 All India Reporter page 548) and all systematically carried out activities where people work to produce goods and services that have economic value are covered. This, when read with another Supreme Court Judgement that 240 days of work (even non-continuous) within any period of 365 days constitutes permanency can lead to situations that establishments have to accept contract labour as permanent employees with retrospective effect paying them equal pay for equal work as for other regular employees.

The third category concerns changes at the workplace (statutorily 21 days' notice is required under Section 9A of the Industrial Disputes (ID) Act 1947 and Standing Orders under the Industrial Employment Standing Orders Act, 1946), and security of work, income, jobs, and employment are also protected under the ID) Act, 1947. The ID Act is the most important labour law in India because it entitles individual 'workmen' (the term includes women) to raise disputes that can be compulsorily adjudicated in Labour Courts and Industrial Tribunals. The ID Act also regulates layoffs, retrenchments and closures prescribing compensation and notice periods. In establishments where 100 or more workmen are employed, prior permission from the government has to be obtained for layoffs, retrenchments and closures. The ID Act also prohibits terminations except for misconduct and even misconduct terminations during the pendency of an industrial dispute require government approvals.

Management Style and Practices

Conventionally, Finnish managers of enterprises have been drawn from commercial or technical backgrounds and MBA education is a recent development. This has led to a widespread belief in Finland that technology or accounting is sufficient to drive management processes effectively. Profitability and Liquidity take priority over sustainable growth and long-term returns. According to Nurmi (1994), management ideas that favour individual responsibility within a planned structure are well received, but there is resistance in Finland to collaborations, joint ventures, organisation development involving less structured ways of teamwork. To quote Nurmi, *'Finns are better at guerrilla warfare than in teamwork'*. Since the 1990s, the priorities have shifted from recruiting talent for the long-term to short-term work contracts, downsizing and outplacements. In India, MBAs and engineer-MBAs are well represented in managerial talent pools alongside specialists and generalists.

Support to Finnish Enterprises for International Business

There are many institutions involved in Finnish external economic relations and trade. In the central government, there are two ministries, the Ministry of Employment and the Economy and the Ministry for Foreign Affairs. The Ministry of Employment and the Economy supports internationalisation as part of industrial policy. Policies on innovation, energy, internal market, competition and employment also affect external economic relations. The Ministry for Foreign Affairs, through the network of Finnish Embassies and Consulates, influences the business operating environment 'through trade policy, public diplomacy and prestige and promotion services' (as officially declared on Finnish official website www.valtioneuvosto.fi). This approach steers a careful tightrope walk between the state-aid outlawed by the EU competition policy and the exceptions tolerated on grounds of permitted national needs.

There are several agencies that function under the Ministry of Employment and the Economy. These include Finpro, Centres for Economic Development, Transport and the Environment, Finnvera, Tekes and Invest in Finland (which is being integrated into Finpro). In addition, the Ministry of Employment and the Economy provides budgetary support to bodies such as the Finnish–Russian Chamber of Commerce. Development Cooperation Agencies under the Ministry of Foreign Affairs include Finnfund and the business partnership programme Finnpartnership.

The Centres for Economic Development, Transport and the Environment and the domestic networks of Finpro, Finnvera and Tekes are now being encouraged to direct companies to other service providers. This kind of orchestrated support is a distinctive feature of the Finnish institutional framework and notable by its absence on the Indian side.

There is a high level of trust and cooperation between businesses and government in Finland. Both local and national governments are committed to supporting industry, subsidising and subventing export marketing, innovations through earmarked fund allocations and also through parastatals created for this purpose such as Tekes, SITRA, VTT, and Finpro. Tekes (part of Business Finland since 2018) plays a key role in passing on know-how from international sources to Finland and in building connections between Finnish players and international value networks. But this has also led to considerable waste of resources. Studies by Venetoklis (1999) on outcomes of subventions granted to business firms by the Ministry of Industry and Trade (erstwhile, KTM) and by Koski (2008) and Koski and Pajarinen (2010a, b) for Tekes funding have shown that business subsidies in Finland have few correlative outcomes and that the selection of projects is irrational and their suitability cannot be justified in many cases.

Business–Government Interface

The degree of business–government cooperation and mutual consultations at the firm level is higher in Finland than in India. Domestic businesses have developed influence mechanisms in both countries but these differ. In India, firms, and competing chambers of commerce, competing industry associations and competing management associations develop industry-wide or region-wide proposals for consideration in which the media plays a part in informed debates reported daily with wide participation from those concerned. Consultations usually involve a much larger segment than the protagonists because it includes people from all walks of life who have an opinion to express. In Finland, business–government discussions have defined fora in the form of state-sponsored associations and state-defined structures and closed-door discussions are the norm.

Finland did not have a Constitution until 2000. It had managed to get by with four separate laws covering government authorities, ministerial responsibility, public administration and powers of taxation. Since 2000, when the Finnish Constitution was first made, the Courts, in the code law tradition, were not unduly concerned to refer to it in interpreting the laws. Over time, the Constitution could acquire some weight if Courts find provisions of specific laws to be in conflict with constitutional provisions. Further, there is still no scope of judicial scrutiny of executive decisions under writ jurisdiction in Finland because the Constitution does not have any provision for writs. Complaints against government decisions would have to be made under Public Law in specified lower courts and tribunals. Hence, commitments made by the Finnish government and Finnish Local Authorities are usually implementable without the kind of challenges that can arise in India as envisaged in the Indian Constitution under Articles 226 (directly to High Court) and Article 136 (directly to Supreme Court). This is explained in more detail in Chap.7. India also accepts public interest litigation, and there is also a right to information law. Unlike in Finland, the central government and State governments in India cannot make decisions without being subject to judicial scrutiny demandable by even a single person in public interest litigation, without any requirement of *locus standi*. These features are not there in the Finnish system. Another difference is that the Indian Parliament enacts a considerable quantum of new laws every year, but the Finnish Parliament is not so prolific in law making. But institutional changes are much more frequent in Finland than in India. In Finland changes disseminate rapidly through high digital connectivity which is reliable, whereas in India digital connectivity is a painpoint in all public systems. Systems are often adopted before they have been user-tested. Even internal portals of large-scale consumer interfacing systems such as the postal system and the banking system suffer from disruptions daily.

Finnish firms find it difficult to estimate entry costs for India. The bureaucratic maze of India is the major formidable barrier to trade and investment. State governments eager to draw investment and promote employment and stimulate local economies help traders and investors (domestic and foreign) by taking some responsibility to facilitate matters and insulate foreign investors from its worst features. Bureaucratic corruption exists but is neither so demanding nor so rampant as made out by intermediaries acting on behalf of foreign companies who often pocket the money they claim to pass on. The constitutional structure of India provides effective and speedy remedies. The degree of discretionary power of bureaucrats has been substantially dismantled and is increasingly subject to judicial scrutiny. Corruption scandals are actually affirmations that the judiciary actively intervenes and a free media reports such happenings making recurrence of deviations from norms less likely.

Legal Systems, Transparency and Disclosure

The differences in the legal systems of the two countries pose several difficulties, but these are surmountable. Finnish Law follows the code law justice system derived from Germanic-Roman origins with Swedish incorporations that are implemented in ways that are a fusion of Swedish legislative and Russian bureaucratic influences. India has a plurality of co-existing justice systems and Indian jurisprudence draws heavily from traditions of natural justice in the common law tradition with admissibility of public interest litigation.

In the common law tradition of India, traditions, precedents from previously decided cases on points of law carry weight and the judiciary has to justify departures from past precedents or follow them. Thus, it is important to examine past precedents where Supreme Court precedents carry more weight than High Court precedents. In the Code Law tradition, each case is decided on its own merits, relying on the statutory laws and provisions expressly stated. But EU legislation and case laws now have important effects on interpretations by Finnish Courts of Finnish Law too.

India lacks a uniform civil code, but the code of civil procedure is the same throughout the country. The Finnish 'loser pays' principle is not followed in India. Usually, parties bear their own costs. In India, much of the time, parties approaching courts are mainly interested in obtaining interlocutory orders in the form of injunctions and stay orders or in getting these vacated because the actual hearing and judgements can take a very long time with plenty of adjournments for all kinds of reasons. There is no equivalent of the law of injunctions in Finland, and there are no adjournments once a case is taken up for hearing. So, parties have to invest right at the beginning in preparing for the whole case for being heard properly with an eye on good quality final judgements from courts of first instance. This is all the more important in Finland because a High Court in Finland relies on the records of the Court of First Instance and would rarely order a retrial. There have been occasions when Judges in Courts of First Instance have destroyed the tape-recorded proceedings in their courts before appeals could be heard. The Supreme Court of Finland admits only a small proportion of appeals for hearing. The institution of the Ombudsman in Finland partially offsets the inadmissibility of writ jurisdiction and public interest litigation but commercial cases would normally fall outside that purview.

Transparency of trading regimes is well established in Finland but not in India where discretionary authority vests in a plurality of concurrent jurisdictions. The transparency of investment regimes is well established in India (and enforceable by law against the Government) but not in Finland where such matters are interpreted politically, case-to-case. All laws and rules in India are available in English. However, Finnish Law (Suomen Laki I and II) is only available in Finnish and Swedish and the authorities have not yet provided all the laws of Finland in English. For instance, important basic laws such as tax law for firms are inaccessible to foreign investors except in Finnish and Swedish or by sourcing the information from one of the Big Five consulting firms. The entry costs of a business investment in Finland thus become higher for foreign firms requiring basic information for business investments than the corresponding entry costs for India. The attractiveness of reaching the entire EU market with a business entry in Finland makes it worthwhile to spend that as an investment in knowing and overcoming the liabilities of outsidership.

Access by foreign firms to publicly maintained data (for example, disaggregated census data) is freely available in India, and most data are transparently accessible. In Finland distributive trades are highly concentrated and secretive, and it is prohibited by law to maintain lists of names and addresses except for approved purposes. Equality of national and foreign entities is part of the constitutional frame in India, whereas inequality by exclusion from associative support structures and denial of equal treatment is still a feature protected by many Finnish laws that are now being modified to comply with EU laws and directives.

The Indian Companies Act is the most voluminous single law of any kind in the whole world and disclosure requirements to comply with standards of transparency are constitutionally governed. This eliminates the risk of information inadequacy on supply and demand for all investors in any market but it places a heavy burden of paperwork on companies comparable to China. Trade, though unhindered by any significant tariff barriers on either side, is still constrained by non-tariff barriers including bureaucratic paperwork at India end to a degree inconsistent with Finnish business culture and the prevailing trust between Finnish businesses and Finnish government.

Business Practices and Commercial Laws

In the Finnish perception, there exist structural constraints to developing business in India. Small Finnish companies have many excellent technologies, processes and products but may not have the resources by way of knowledge and expertise to study business opportunities and to develop them. In large firms, decision-making is slow and knowledge about India is also limited as evidenced by the nature of representation and business links made to date. Contract negotiations require an understanding of payment terms, interest costs, margins, logistics of delivery, local taxes and levies and liabilities which are very different in Finland and India.

In marketing industrial goods and services, the host governments and firms adopt policies based on supply constraints in India and demand constraints in Finland. Imports into Finland are regulated by three national laws even after the EU accession on grounds such as 'apprehension of disorder of an economic sector' (ulkomaankauppalaki of 1994); under enabling provisions for import equalisation taxes, special taxes (for example, automobiles), inspection (for example, electronics), prohibition of foreign labelling (Tullilaki of 1978); and the enabling provision to discriminate between Finnish standards, international standards and something called 'Finnish international standards' with 'Standardisoimisliitto' setting up effective non-tariff barriers (Haapaniemi 1998). The new Finnish Competition Law (Kilpailulaki 948 of 2011) has remedied some of these anomalies.

The home-country policies in India provide incentives to 'Swadeshi' (domestic value-addition by both foreign and local firms) on the back of a large domestic market, whereas in Finland capital flows inwards and outwards are freer than in India. The Finnish Foreign Exchange Control Act has been repealed and the Indian equivalent FERA also replaced by the Foreign Exchange Management Act(FEMA). With the rupee having become convertible for all trade and current account transactions, there is no shortage of foreign exchange in either country. Capital injections still demand long-term strategies that can sustain growth and profitability of FDI, keeping in mind fluctuations in the Euro-rupee rates of exchange.

Foreign control of Finnish equity has been traditionally restricted if the turnover of the firm was beyond €1 billion or employment size crosses 1000 employees. There is no such stipulation in India. There are restrictions on foreign ownership of real estate in Finland, but many of these have been removed to comply with EU accession. India has also removed such restrictions by enabling foreign investments in asset management companies. Finland has not yet implemented the EC directives on agency commissions and continues to have its own law (Kauppaedustajista Laki). There is no law to protect distributors except the archaic provisions of the 1929 Contract Act. Sole and exclusive distributor agreements are regarded valid in Finland though neighbouring Sweden invalidated them to comply with EU law (Gustafsson 1998).

Unlike India's stock exchanges that are a ready source of capital to domestic and foreign companies, the Finnish stock market is small and has not been a significant source for raising capital for new companies. Rather, the Finnish stock market serves as a market for facilitating mergers and acquisitions and bankruptcies. Its silent system of trading (HETI) is non-transparent. Finnish laws traditionally discouraged competition in the domestic economy and permitted oligopolies. To the extent that penal provisions existed for abuse of dominant position, the maximum fine was set at FIM 4 million, but the heaviest fine ever imposed was FIM 13,400 until the hefty fine on Valio in 1998 that has since raised the penalties for abusing dominant position.

Vertical cartels are allowed under Finnish competition law and the European Commission has recently extended this privilege to all member countries defining criteria for it. EC's approval to the merger of IVO with NESTE was made conditional to divestment in subsidiary GASUM which held a monopoly on sales of natural gas in Finland. Further, the duty structure on mineral oils was found violative of Articles 8 (2) and 8 (3) of Directive 92/81/EEC. There is no separate Finnish statute on mergers and acquisitions (M & A) as in other Nordic countries. The Finnish Companies Act is the enabling law on procedures for M & A and the Securities Trading Act has flagging requirements. These correspond to the equivalent provisions under The Companies Act and the Securities and Exchange Board of India (SEBI) law in India.

Intellectual property rights protection is weaker in Finland than in India. Both countries are members of the World Trade Organisation (WTO) and signatories to the Berne Convention but Finland has limited the applicability of international law for foreign copyright holders. Disseminated work is reproducible in Finland without copyright protection and Finnish state-sponsored organisations like *Teosto* and *Gramex* are authorised to reproduce authors they do not represent. Finland is now a member of the European Patent Convention which would override its own patent law. The restrictions under the Finnish Patent Law (patenttilaki of 1967) that a product once marketed in the EU cannot be patented in Finland no longer apply. This has obvious implications for a wide range of Indian pharmaceutical products that are often first marketed in Germany or the UK.

In Finland, consumer protection laws exclude industrial consumption. No product liability accrues as long as the manufacturer has complied with rules of Finnish public authorities. In India, the statute on consumer protection covers all categories of consumers and the definition of product liability is expansive. Under Finnish law, the jurisdiction of a dispute arises where the seller is located, whereas under

Indian law it arises where the cause of action has arisen. Arbitration clauses would also require to be structured for the eventuality of disputes because Finland and India are not 'reciprocating territories' for the implementation of court judgements. The present practice is to opt for Stockholm or London or Paris for arbitration.

Investment Incentives and Disincentives

Investment incentives to foreign investors in India include all the incentives available to domestic investors plus many more available only to foreign investors. This is the reason for considerable round-tripping of investments via Mauritius. Investment incentives in Finland are attractive, but it is not always clear whether these can be availed by foreign investors. Normally, all companies incorporated in Finland would be eligible. These include cash grants, equity investments, cheap loans, tax benefits, funds for development in identified regions called development areas and structural adjustment areas, employee training and export subsidies for 50% of marketing costs. Indigenous entrepreneurship in Finland is weak, and there is enormous potential for synergies here. However, there is some doubt regarding the continuity of Finnish incentives, particularly those that are violative of the EU accession Treaty obligations. The European Commission has opened proceedings against Finland for its subsidies to steel, transport, mining, shipbuilding, synthetic fibres, motor-vehicles, fisheries and agricultural produce.

Exit Policies

In Finland, the exit policies are well laid out and there exist institutions and systems for every stage of a process of closure or insolvency involving auditors, lawyers, notices, announcements in newspapers, and liquidators for the distribution of assets.

In India, the Insolvency and Bankruptcy Code became law in 2018. Now, the Committee of Creditors (CoC) invites resolution proposals and the applicants can then select one of the plans. The text of the new law is available at www.ibbi.gov.in . The new law clarifies who are eligible to submit resolution plans. In the typical Indian drafting tradition (that follows the Upanishadic way of *neti, neti*, not this, not this), the new law does not state who all are eligible to submit resolution plans but declares those who are ineligible to submit resolution plans: '(i) an undischarged insolvent; (ii) a 'wilful defaulter'; (iii) a borrower whose account has been identified as a non-performing asset for over a year and who has not repaid the amount before submitting a plan; (iv) a person convicted of an offence punishable with two or more years of imprisonment; (v) a person disqualified as a director under the Companies Act, 2013; (vi) a person prohibited from trading in securities; (vii) a person who is the promoter or in the management of a company which has indulged in undervalued, preferential, or fraudulent transactions; (viii) a person who has given guarantee on a liability of the defaulting company undergoing resolution or liquidation, and has not honoured the guarantee; (ix) a person who is subject to any of the above disabilities in any jurisdiction outside India; or (x) a person who has a connected person disqualified in any manner above'.

The object of the law is to prevent undesirable persons from bidding for the debtor. The stringent conditions mentioned above could also make present owners ineligible to submit proposals. The law also envisages that an entire board of directors of a company that is under restructuring or insolvency can be replaced by a new cadre of 'insolvency professionals' who can be judicially authorised. In all stressed assets, a resolution plan would typically involve significant haircuts on the parts of the financial and operational creditors. Thus, allowing a promoter to bid without restriction could have resulted in the moral hazard that an owner could first drive a firm into insolvency and then buy it back at a discount. The law enables the Committee of Creditors to avoid imprudent transactions, while retaining the liberty to adopt the best resolution plan proposed.

References

Gustafsson Leif (1998) Business laws in the Nordic Countries. Norstedts Tryckeris, Stockholm
Haapaniemi H (1998) Business Laws of Finland in Leif Gustaffson ed. Business Laws in the Nordic Countries, Norstedts Tryckeris, Stockholm
Helminen Marjanna (2016) Finnish International taxation, 2nd edn. WSOY, Vantaa
Koski Heli (2008) Public R&D subsidies and employment growth-microeconomic evidence from Finnish firms. Research Institute of the Finnish Economy, ETLA, Helsinki
Koski H, Pajarinen M (2010a) Supply, complementarities and repetitions of public support in Finland, discussion paper 1217, The Research Institute of the Finnish Economy, ETLA, Helsinki
Koski Heli, Pajarinen Mika (2010b) Access to Business subsidies: what explains complementarities and persistency? discussion paper 1226. The Research Institute of the Finnish Economy, ETLA, Helsinki
Lilja Kari, Räsänen Keijo, Tainio Risto (1992) A dominant business recipe: the forest sector in Finland. In: Whitley R (ed) European business systems. Sage, London, pp 137–154
Nurmi R (1994) Management in crisis, working paper 2, Turku School of Economics and Business Administration, Turku
Steinbock Dan (2010) Winning across global markets: how Nokia creates strategic advantages in a fast-changing world. Jossey-Bass, New York
Surakka A (2012) Access to Finnish law, 2nd Updated edn., Sanoma Pro, Helsinki
Venetoklis (1999) Process evaluation of business subsidies in Finland, Research Paper 58, Government Institute for Economic Research, VATT, Helsinki

Chapter 6
Bridges for Finland–India Business

> *It doesn't matter whether a cat is white or black, as long as it catches mice.*
>
> Deng Xiaoping

> *Out beyond ideas of wrongdoing and rightdoing there is a field. I'll meet you there.*
>
> Rumi

Abstract This chapter introduces questions of interest to business enterprises and policy-makers in the context of building bridges for structuring Finland–India business. The bridges and modalities are asymmetric because of the cultural and institutional differences discussed in previous Chaps. 4 and 5. There are also differences on other dimensions such as planning processes, stakeholder involvement, competition policies, ease of doing business, nature of contracts, trust in public–private partnerships, and the scope for statal and parastatal involvement in private business in the two countries. Four gateways are discussed in this chapter B2C (business to consumers), B2B (business to business), B2G (business to government), and G2G (government to government). The chapter also notes Finnish companies that already do business in India and Indian firms that do business in Finland as exemplars who have bridged the chasms and can inspire others.

Introduction

The gateways, bridges and modalities for structuring Finland–India business are asymmetric because of the differences in the two countries with regard to business orientation, risk-taking, aspirations, size, competitiveness, contractability and tolerance for ambiguity. There is also the question of trust in public–private partnerships and the Finnish practice of statal and parastatal involvement even in private businesses. Broadly, we can visualise four gateways that would encompass most of the canvas of economic relations. These are B2C (business to consumers), B2B (business to business), B2G (business to government) and G2G (government to government).

© Springer Nature Singapore Pte Ltd. 2019
A. N. Mathur, *Finland–India Business Opportunities*,
https://doi.org/10.1007/978-981-10-8019-7_6

Four Important Questions

In paired comparisons of Finland and India, four questions of interest to business firms and policy-makers arise in the context of bridge-building:

Q.1 What is the scope for mutual or global harvesting of income flows from innovations seeded through techno-commercial collaborations between Indian and Finnish firms in the technology services sector after taking competitiveness into consideration?

Q.2 How do enterprises in the two countries take into consideration differences in business laws, institutions, organisation structures, public systems and management processes in reaching out to business opportunities in the other territory and for third-country markets?

Q.3 How may we estimate the potential of bilateral services trade in the 12 categories of GATS services and determine which of the GATS entry modes are preferable in the different categories?

Q.4 Do policies of the two governments and practices of Finnish firms in India and Indian firms in Finland converge or leave voids in bridging institutional differences for structuring business investments abroad?

The first question above can be probed with reference to the analysis in Chaps. 2 and 3 by estimating where trade-substituting investments are sustainable and noting the degree of competition by existing firms with capacities not only in Europe and India but also in markets worldwide. This would require techno-commercial evaluations of alternative innovative technologies because it would be myopic to proceed on the basis that one good innovative technology is the best.

For the second question, the discussion in Chaps. 4 and 5 covers the basic essentials to be taken into consideration over cultural and institutional differences. Bridge-building here would require sensitivity and courage among potential business partners reaching out to each other across country borders to explore, discover, design and learn from doing. Policy-makers also have an important role here.

The third question above has no straightforward answers. It is possible to estimate service flows from net invisible in the balance of payments, but historical flows can be an unreliable indicator of future potential alternatives because creativity is at play here. With the advent of 'big data' as a digital driver, there is a stranglehold of 'winner takes all' business models. These are the business models that Google, Amazon, Facebook, Microsoft, Alibaba, Uber, AirBnB, Netflix, Tencent and Twitter are evolving. Disruptions will continue to occur across all modes of service supply, not only the direct effect on Mode 1: cross-border electronic services.

Mode 2: Consumption abroad involves tangible or intangible services. Since these services can be directed to people or to things, they are amenable to bundling and repackaging. They also involve consumer education, customer training, and know-how enhancements for service providers. In the Finland–India context, they can be expanded if there is greater mobility of people between the two countries and irritants around issues such as travel visas are sorted out. India, unilaterally, included Finland in the select group of countries whose nationals can obtain visa on arrival in India. But even professional delegates from India to international conferences in Finland face difficulties in obtaining visas. Doctors from India attending a medical conference were recently denied the possibility of spending a few more days as tourists in Finland something that would have both raised awareness about Finland and brought tourism revenues to Finland. This is strange because India is not a country from where Finland gets asylum seekers. Rather, the professional migrant Indians, particularly educated/skilled youth, IT professionals, scientists, engineers, business leaders have been contributing to Finland as residents essentially at the invitation of Finnish universities, Finnish companies, Finnish project consortia such as the one building the nuclear plants and Indo-Finnish joint ventures. Long-term settlers of previous eras were largely shopkeepers and Indian cuisine restaurant owners.

In Mode 3: Foreign commercial presence, the main bridges are built by B2B and B2C activities by firms that foster dependent services enabling professionals to cross-borders for short stays as well as longer, indefinite stays. In the Finland–India context, it is noteworthy that one of the largest foreign national groups in-migrating to Finland in 2017 was Indians taking up roles in dependent services and for tertiary education. This also points to the need to examine Mode 4: Movement of natural persons that bring new skills, new perspectives and new ways of thinking and doing from abroad. In this context, the fourth question assumes significance because there is much that policy-makers can do to facilitate bridges. In a later part of this chapter, I discuss how 'Business Finland' is being created as a platform and leave open for now the question of whether such a platform would work effectively if it were only a bridge for business in one direction.

The Paradox of Competitiveness and Collaborations

Competitive business circumstances in the world enable players to configure value constellations in numerous alternative ways. An evaluation of the competitive position of existing and potential service businesses requires judgements about the capacities of societies as a whole, because relative competitiveness of nations changes over time. An intriguing part of the Finnish puzzle is that contrary to competitiveness perception surveys portraying Finland as the most competitive nation in the world, and corruption perception surveys regularly highlighting it as the least corrupt, the net annual inflows of private foreign direct investment into Finland reveal a declining trend according to the Central Bank of Finland (Suomen Pankki) annual reports since 1995, despite inflows from sales of marketable stock of existing businesses by Finnish firms.

Regions cannot prosper without business growth but businesses can thrive bypassing regions. Research into the predicament of Finland's local communities pointed to the need for restructuring and consolidation of communities at risk, but also that such restructuring, while necessary, would not be sufficient without addressing the internationalisation imperative (Mathur et al. 2003). The paradox is that perceptions of Finland being the most competitive nation have not raised foreign investments in Finland, while incentives to globally compete abroad backed by public subsidies have reinforced pride and created a norm among Finnish firms of 'bowling alone' trying to compete, seeking cooperation rather than collaboration.[1] The dearth of collaborations is fourfold: between firms and communities at home in Finland, between Finnish firms and Indian firms abroad, between Finnish firms and communities of habitat and communities of practice in India; and between Indian firms and communities of habitat in Finland.

Foreign Business Investments by Indian Firms

Multinational subsidiaries of foreign firms (mainly British, American, German, Swiss and Dutch) like Unilever, BAT, ICI, Proctor & Gamble, Nestle, Siemens constitute one set of 'Indian' firms with foreign business partnerships made between their Indian subsidiaries and foreign firms including but not limited to their principals. The second set consists of Indian family business houses that diversified away from trading into manufacturing after independence and developed highly diversified portfolios. The exceptions were groups like Tatas, Birlas, Dalmias, Thapars that started manufacturing activities before 1947. Both these sets mainly made partnerships either for technical collaboration to source know-how or promoted joint ventures in India with foreign equity participation. A third set consists of public enterprises established by the Government of India in the 1950s and 1960s to develop the basic industries involving imports of plant and machinery as well as development of technologies beyond technology licenses and import of equipment. A fourth set emerged in the 1970s when firms like Bajaj Auto, Asian Paints, Reliance and Nirma founded by indigenous first generation entrepreneurship geographically spread out beyond the shores of India to establish branches and companies (each one of them is a world market leader for its brands). Additionally, there have always been trading houses and a growing number of non-resident Indians in Europe and elsewhere who made business investments.

Although the last category, traders and trading houses (estimated to be about 12 million) consist also of traders in textiles, gems and jewellery, minerals, metals, tea, coffee, spices, a growing number (about 1 million) have made industrial investments in incorporated entities for producing and marketing goods and services. There are also representative offices, branches and subsidiaries of Indian companies of the four sets identified above all over the world, but mainly in USA,

---

[1]The word 'collaborate' reflecting a joint endeavour with a commonly agreed primary task is not much used in the context of international relations in Finland. Finns speak of 'cooperation' by which it is meant that two or more parties could agree to singly undertake performance commitments for respective tasks in a coordinated manner to benefit from exchanges made possible by such coordination.

Continental Europe, and South-East Asia. In Finland, there are 95 firms owned or co-owned by Indians or Indian or non-resident Indian corporate entities. These include Indian restaurants, consultancy firms, publishing houses, textile firms, design firms and trading agencies.

Firms in India have begun to defy the conventional logic that exports should be ventured only after local demand has been met. For example, the bi-axially oriented polypropylene-film company Polyplex exports 70% of its manufacture. Arvind Mills exports 48% of its textile production. Cosmo Ferrites exports 45% of its metallurgical production in manganese and zinc ferrites. Ranbaxy exports 45% of its pharmaceutical output. Innovassynth (a born global Indian firm) exports 100% of its goods and services.

The profitable public sector contributes about 29% to India's GDP. In the public sector, 75 of its most profitable firms have the advantage of size, infrastructure, managerial acumen, financial muscle and global reach. They are most strongly represented in chemicals and petrochemicals, minerals and metallurgical, metals, fuels, electronics, aerospace and heavy engineering. Their new projects include new fertiliser plants, investments in new mines, in petrochemicals, petroleum and natural gas exploration and refining, construction of ports and airports and thermal and hydel power plants.

B2B and B2C Bridges from India to Finland

The experience of firms that have commenced foreign commercial presence or attempted foreign commercial presence is always insightful to firms that tread in the same direction later. The discourses around these that catch the attention of policy-makers and the general public can facilitate processes or dampen new initiatives. There are also occasionally other factors to consider. For instance, in 2009, there was enormous Finnish interest in India and Indian interest in Finland when the largest ever delegation of Finnish business leaders accompanied Minister Mauri Pekkarinen to India. The follow-up to this is another story. In 2010, Finland posted its largest ever balance of trade surplus with China due to some extraordinary one-time deals. For all the ten years before that and the eight years after that, Finland has had negative balance of trade with China but this singularity gave Finnish decision-makers the idea that they were succeeding in China more than in India and the interest in India waned.

Wipro and Sasken communication technologies were among the first Indian IT companies to invest in Finland through acquisitions. These two IT collaborations sparked euphoria and a kind of India-mania in Finland which did more damage than good to Finland–India Economic Relations. Finnish parastatals like the Finnish Innovation Fund, SITRA were intrigued by the Indian acquisitions in Finland and hailed it as something remarkable. SITRA hailed it as an 'India phenomena' (Grundström and Lahti 2005). However, instead of setting up or supporting business research projects in Finnish universities or Indian Institutes of Management to study the nature and scope of synergies that could be facilitated across promising sectors, the task of exploring these so-called India phenomena was contracted out by SITRA to a British agency, Demos. The report by Demos (Bound et al. 2006) was scanty on facts and abundant in scepticism. It eulogised Finland and derided India. Since it confirmed prevailing prejudices, it was welcomed by SITRA and Vesa-Matti Lahti Manager at SITRA enthusiastically added his foreword endorsing it. Anyone unfamiliar with British biases against India and interested to know should read Durant (1930) before entrusting an India evaluation to agencies of its former coloniser. The facts provided by the then Indian Ambassador in Helsinki who invested time hosting the DEMOS and SITRA team at several Wine and Cheese evenings were largely ignored when the report was eventually produced.

Here are some gems about India from the DEMOS-SITRA Report:

"India is a paradoxical country. Statistics – *while important* – *can sometimes be misleading*" (p. 12)

[This, in a country that has one of the world's best national statistical organisations supported by institutions such as the world renowned Indian Statistical Institute]

"*In a country so huge that even if 90 per cent of the population believe one thing or behave in a particular way, it still means that over 100 million people – still nearly twenty times the population of Finland – do not.*" (p. 12)

[The relevance of this remark is hard to fathom. India was the world's first country to launch a periodic national household survey for statistics based on random sampling]

"*It is also important to realise the paucity of reliable statistics available about India.*" (p. 12)

[India is one of the few countries where the vast Central Statistical Organisation regularly publishes statistical series on all aspects of the Indian economy. Official Statistics of India are verified, accepted and published by the World Bank and, International Monetary Fund (IMF). UNCTAD's World Investment Report also annually publishes detailed Indian investment data with analysis. The Centre for Monitoring Indian Economy's CMIE database has been available since the 1970s and in an era with electronically available databases such as TradeDX, it is strange that a SITRA contractor would have such a biased opinion and that SITRA would accept and publish such a report without proper peer review]

"*It is always worth maintaining a healthy degree of scepticism about grand claims made for the country.*" (p.12)

[This is almost a racist remark!]

The main actors in Indian business are traders who have something to export and import and industrial firms that manufacture and market products and services and source capital goods or know-how or find destinations for their exports. Firms need to establish business to business links. Annexures of this book provide ready data on which to act. For example, category 7415 threaded bolts and nuts where 50% of Indian export is to EU and export to Finland is zero although exports to Sweden exist, an Indian firm could now identify industrial customers in Finland and provide samples and quotations knowing that the odds are very favourable. A more detailed analysis of industries and firms could pinpoint specific firms also. If India's Triveni Sheet Glass was to expand into production of float glass and automotive glass which it presently imports from Japan, the information in this book enables identify Finland as a source country and to reach Tamglass in the Kyro Group with some simple trade enquiries.

In 2019, there were about 30 Indian firms (excluding shops and eateries registered as companies) actively present in doing business in Finland. The notable IT companies among them are HCL, Infosys, ITC Infotech, Larsen & Toubro Infotech, Sasken, Sonata, TCS, Tech Mahindra and WIPRO. In healthcare diagnostics and biotech, Labsystems Diagnostics, Systems Biology and Trivitron are the prominent ones. Havells in electricals, Wipro Infrastructure Engineering in construction and Mahindra Group are three large Indian firms that have made a name for themselves.

The process of developing the mutual synergies may be accelerated by investing in knowledge and management development. Since both countries have a number of institutions and large firms, chambers of commerce, management and industry associations, business schools, technology institutes and economic research agencies public and private, any and all of these could do this without Government intervention. The role of the two governments in promoting their institutions with investments for such mutually beneficial synergies could help both countries greatly and should not be excluded. The EU-India Economic Cross-Cultural Programme is another new bridge that now exists.

B2B and B2C Bridges from Finland to India

There are more Finnish firms doing business in India than Indian firms doing business in Finland. Some of the Finnish firms have used affiliates and subsidiaries in other countries to invest in India. Finnish firms in India are generally doing well. They could all be doing even better. They themselves constitute bridges to India for other firms, from Finland to India and also from India to Finland. These comprise the first spearheads of Finnish internationalisation to India and the learning from their experiences is important for them and for others. It is essential to know what obstacles they have faced and their unsolved problems that remain challenges to be addressed. There are also Finnish firms doing business with India and Indian firms doing business in Finland among those that have not yet established foreign commercial presence in the form of an establishment.

In the first wave of Finnish investments and partnerships in India, Kone and Wärtsilä were among the most prominent. Kone established itself in India in 1984 and is the leading elevator company in India, headquartered in Chennai. Wärtsilä came to India in 1986 and became a household name in an era of power cuts with its diesel generating sets. Metso (formerly, Valmet) has been in India since 1992 and is a diversified enterprise in mining engineering, construction, pulp and paper machinery, energy, power, chemicals and petrochemicals and has two factories in Alwar, Rajasthan and Ahmedabad, Gujarat. Huhtamäki has two subsidiaries and through them, thirteen factories with a range of food and beverage packaging products in Mumbai (Maharashtra), Silvassa (Dadra & Nagar Haveli), Hyderabad (Telangana), Rudrapur (Uttarakhand), Parwanoo (Himachal Pradesh) and

Bangalore (Karnataka). Oilon, a manufacturer of burners partnered with Thermax, a boiler manufacturer and co-generation solutions provider in Pune to establish a Finnish joint venture Ecopower (later renamed an Oilon Company) for R&D in combustion engineering economies in Lahti, Finland.

In the recent decade, some of the more dynamic Finnish firms among the later entrants in India that are expanding their business rapidly deserve special mention. Cargotec is one of the most successful Finnish firms in India with cargo handling solutions and products under contract with ports and offshore installations. Chempolis is active in biomass conversions and recycling of agri-waste. Fortum has acquired a 5 MW solar power plant in Rajasthan and another 10 MW solar power plant in Madhya Pradesh that has been connected to the grid in 2015 as the first project to be commissioned under the National Solar Mission. Jotwire, together with Ouneva Group of Finland is among the Finnish firms that have recognised the potential of using Indian manufacturing as a hub for worldwide markets for a wide range of electrical and electronics products out of a factory in Manesar, Haryana. WMI Konecranes is one of the fastest growing Finnish companies in India with cargo-handling equipment and solutions. UPM has a joint venture with Anika called India Recypa for waste paper recycling since 2007 and is rumoured to be prospecting a site for a paper mill.

Nokia (formerly Siemens Networks that was acquired by Nokia and initially renamed Nokia Siemens Networks and then renamed Nokia) remains in India after the original Nokia (in the mobile phones business) sold its mobile telephony business to Microsoft. Another Finnish firm Lindstrom is active in rental work wear and has quickly spread to ten Indian cities. Maillefer Extrusion has a wholly owned subsidiary with wire, cable, pipe and tube extrusion technologies in Vashi, Maharashtra. Normet, a technology services provider has a subsidiary company in Noida, Uttar Pradesh. Ojala has an 80% owned subsidiary in Kanchi, Tamil Nadu for making sheet and flat bars for the energy and environment engineering industry. Outokumpu in metal engineering business has a wholly owned subsidiary in India in New Delhi and custom bonded warehouses in Mumbai, besides offices in Chennai, Pune and Vadodara, Gujarat. Outotec in minerals and metal processing technologies has an Indian subsidiary in Kolkata, West Bengal for services in engineering, designing and procurement. Stera has a wholly owned subsidiary with a factory in Chennai for making mechanical, electrical and electronic components.

Some of the other notable ones are also worth mentioning. Abloy with its high-security locks has a subsidiary in Chennai. Ahlstrom is active in speciality papers and non-wovens with a factory in Gujarat. Betonimestarit has a joint venture with Simplex Prefab Infrastructure with a factory in Khopoli, Maharashtra. Sartorius Biohit Liquid Handling has a subsidiary in Chennai, Tamil Nadu. Dinex Ecocat, an exhaust gas catalyst converters manufacturer has a joint venture with an Indian partner in Faridabad, Haryana. Ecosible is in e-waste processing in Ambattur, Tamil Nadu. Elematic, in the business of precast plants has a factory, in Alwar, Rajasthan. Eltete, in transport packaging materials, has a factory in Vapi, Gujarat. Ensto, an electrical engineering company has a subsidiary in Gurgaon, Haryana. GEMCO Kati is a joint venture in mining, construction and exploration in

Chandrapur, Maharashtra. Nirafon, that manufactures acoustic cleaning systems, has a joint venture, Harley Nirafon in Kolkata, West Bengal. Immo Group has four procurement subsidiaries in India for importing to Finland leather goods, carpets, handicrafts and fashion accessories. Incap has a factory in Tumkur, Karnataka for making printer circuit board assemblies. Kemppi has a wholly owned subsidiary in Chennai with a factory for making welding equipment. Valkeakosken Betoni has a joint venture with the Indian VME Group in Chennai for making precast concrete products for the construction industry.

There are several Finnish companies offering services in Mode 3: Foreign Commercial Presence. Mirasys has registered a greenfield company, A & J Intelli Systems in Gurgaon, Haryana for its security and surveillance technology business so that it has equal treatment with other Indian companies for a slice of the video surveillance business. Konecranes is active in India for engineering design services in Pune, Maharashtra. CITEC is active in project management services for the energy sector. Sanako in language learning operates in New Delhi under contracts with the University of Delhi and schools such as Delhi Public School and Modern School. Cadmatic has a wholly owned subsidiary for software solutions and engineering design in Thane, Maharashtra. Rannikon koneteknikka (RKT) has a wholly owned subsidiary in Bofo Solutions for turnkey solutions in Pune, Maharashtra. Elomatic has a joint venture with Pharmalab India for turnkey engineering services to pharma and biotech industries. In process control and defect detection, Stresstech has a wholly owned subsidiary in India in Navi Mumbai, Maharashtra. Tieto has an offshore IT services unit in India serving global customers out of the MIDC Kharadi Knowledge Park in Pune, Maharashtra. Valmet (reborn from the demerger of Metso in 2013) has two subsidiary companies in India, Valmet Chennai and Valmet Automation offering engineering services and solutions for pulp, paper and energy industries. Orion, the Finnish Pharma firm has a wholly owned subsidiary in Mumbai for procuring human and veterinary pharmaceuticals and active pharmaceutical ingredients from India in B2B sales. Aspectum has a subsidiary in Gurgaon, Haryana as a service provider.

More Finnish companies can do business in India by investing in building capabilities for managing businesses in environments different from what they are accustomed. There is no substitute to management education, learning by doing and consolidating the learning from doing, and through concept development in firms and institutions of higher education. In Finland, there are many universities, technology institutes, vocational training colleges and firms that offer export marketing courses and related courses. However, there is a need to develop comprehensive postgraduate management education institutions and in-house management development centres for international business development in enterprises. In Finland, there is a dearth of economic policy research institutions with capabilities and resources to research and understand economies and business potential with developing countries such as India to advise the Finnish policy-makers. The recent announcement in October 2018 by Finland to establish the Helsinki Graduate School of Economics is an excellent initiative in this direction. In the words of

Finnish Prime Minister, Juha Sipilä,[2] *"there is a growing demand for economics expertise in the planning and impact assessment of policy measures. Political decision-making requires high-quality assessments of impacts on the economy and society"*.

The task of preparing Finnish managers for opportunities in India could begin by building knowledge resources about the Indian economy, maintaining data sources and data links and learning how to use Indian databases for specific Finnish industries, sectors, firms, technologies, products and services. The cost of doing this could be prohibitive for most single enterprises except the large ones and so the small ones require to be helped by the creation of a network under the auspices of a public institution.

Research support is another solution. For example, if Eco-S Oy with its price tag of $20–$60 million for a mini paper mill with a capacity of 80,000 tonnes per annum which will employ 70 people is looking to develop Indian business, opportunities identified in this book could serve as a starting point. From the information in this book, the entrepreneur knows straightaway the range of products in his product category (48) that are feasible. All that would be needed would be to consider the techno-commercial feasibility by adding some more information. In this case, the plant can be based on straw and agro-fibres or require an urban area of one million population to use recycled fibres according to the calculations. The calculations to be redone would be of fibre recovery in a lower paper per capita country such as India, but import potential would need reckoning too. It would also involve an estimation of how many such plants might be needed so that the initial planning and execution builds a stream of orders executable every year. From an observable shortfall of 40%, it would be noticed that there is an immediate need for twelve such plants and this demand would grow. If attention were to be concentrated to States with the speediest implementation, the choice would be Gujarat (where such plants already exist for recycling paper brought from abroad to its ports), Andhra Pradesh or Madhya Pradesh or the North-eastern states. To avail of a five-year tax holiday, a joint venture for manufacturing under Build-Operate-Transfer arrangements with a local partner in a backward agricultural area within reach of an urban habitation of 2 million such as Jagdalpur, Itarsi or Indore (in Madhya Pradesh) or Vijaywada, Hyderabad or Vishakapatnam (in Andhra Pradesh) could be a way ahead.

This could be repeated by building a second plant before transferring the first enterprise to a joint venture or to an Indian collaborator on preagreed terms. If preferred, newsprint could be produced and marketing handled through a marketing company or directly with large customers by building a marketing organisation with a profit to net worth of 26% for the effort. The initial capital could be raised on the Indian stock market to augment promoters' capital. In the event of oversubscription (a likely scenario), the promoters' capital would be saved. This opportunity may

---

[2]http://www.helsinkitimes.fi/finland/finland-news/domestic/15035-new-centre-of-excellence-in-economics-to-be-set-up-in-finland.html.

never arise if the only way prospected were to try and sell the plant from Finland through an agent in India.

Similarly, opportunities can be developed for a wide range of Finnish technologies, processes and products. Sectors where identified end-users exist are easiest because sectoral demand and supply shortfalls are known and can be forecasted accurately. Firms making buyer decisions and star trading houses involved with imports can be directly targeted as can a range of producers who have an incentive to license know-how to expand existing product ranges with ready-made marketing networks. At a more sophisticated level, new products (and processes and technologies behind them) could be test marketed in urban centres like Ahmedabad, Bangalore, Hyderabad and Cochin before being offered to Indian partners.

The problem with half-baked assessments is that they can thoroughly mislead policy-makers and the public in general. For instance, in evaluating Nokia in India, the Demos report (Bound et al. 2006) did not critically examine what was really happening. All credit was given to Nokia for a stellar performance in India and none to the Indian business environment in the following lines (p. 13):

> Nokia inaugurated its manufacturing facility in Sriperumbudur, Chennai, India in March 2006. From the beginning of building to the first phone rolling off the production line took only 23 weeks. It was an important moment - Prime Minister Matti Vanhanen and Jorma Ollila, Chairman & CEO of Nokia were there to see it happen. Ollila said "India is amongst the top 5 telecom markets in the world. Setting up this manufacturing facility in India reiterates our long term commitment to the Indian market." The Chennai manufacturing facility currently employs 1,100 people and expects to significantly expand its work force in India over time. Nokia will invest approximately €120 million in the plant, which will serve the growing demand for mobile handsets in the Asia Pacific region.

The reality that India provided a customs duty exempt special economic zone to Nokia in Sriperumbudur and all its supply chain partners like Perlos, Foxconn and Tietoenator (now renamed Tieto); that the State government of Tamil Nadu paid 50% of the salaries of workers engaged by Nokia by generously, although unlawfully, acceding to Nokia's request for mis-classifying a large number of qualified technicians who already held engineering diplomas as apprentices under the Apprenticeship Act (half of an Apprentice's salary is paid by the government); and that Nokia was dodging taxes in India (which remained unsettled until 2018-long after the Nokia factory in India was shut down) were glossed over.

What Has Been Done and Further Research Envisaged

The largest 500 companies of Finland (in the Talouselämä-500 list, the T-500) and the largest 500 companies of India (in the Economic Times-500 list, the ET-500) have been listed in Annexures IX and X, respectively, with identification of four-digit level SITC codes from which potential synergies can be quickly found horizontally for collaboration and vertically for designing value chains on the basis of RCAs. More research requires to be undertaken in all the identified sectors at the firm level and at the sectoral level to make an inventory of existing capacity and know-how and to examine cost and profit streams of different linkable alternatives including an examination of trade versus other forms of trade-substituting collaborations as value constellations.

Cost-benefit analysis to examine techno-commercial feasibilities of alternative forms of structuring investments are also required to determine what technologies, processes, products match best with different forms of investment structuring in Finland–India value chains, and the extent to which third-country firms or markets may be involved. Investment location analysis for specific projects at enterprise level can help identify preferred locations and methods of project management to bundle technology and organisation together in socio-technical systems in a scientific manner since almost everything can be changed about a manufacturing investment except its location. For the high growth sectors identified such as infrastructure development, forestry, engineering, transport, energy and environment, potential participation in the value chain ought to be mapped to precisely determine what opportunities are likely to arise and where and when. The viability of a simplified system of trade between the two countries with databanks accessible from either end ought to be examined.

The research done for this book has found affirmative evidence for vast trade potential between Finland and India in a number of sectors and in many product categories of such sectors. Both countries are found mutually under-represented in EU-India trade with respect to their revealed comparative advantages. A small fraction of potential trade is found actualised. Trade diversion via Germany, Russia, Sweden, UK and Norway partially accounts for the low level of economic contact at enterprise level. The investment linkages noticed from trade analysis and trade-substituting potential require to be studied more deeply before they can be confirmed. In a number of industries, foreign direct investment appears a more appropriate form of structuring investments than exporting.

Investment potential awaiting entrepreneurial interest and exploration is identifiable in several growth sectors. These investments could translate into microeconomic opportunities for the actors directly involved in profiting from them and confer indirect benefits through their employment and income streams for many others with multiplier effects. Apprehensions regarding vast differences on social, institutional and cultural dimensions are valid. However, many myths about improbability of microeconomic linkages can be speedily dispelled by learning from doing. Opportunities identified could also be systematically pursued by deepening studies through scientific analysis of techno-commercial and socio-technical feasibilities at the sectoral level for specific technologies, processes and products. The bundling of product-service linkages and trade in services with knowledge-based investments merits an in-depth follow-up research study. The knowledge-intensity of demand-constrained Finnish capacity and India's supply-constrained pace in addressing the enormity of India's development agenda and market potential present unusual synergies.

Government to Government Business (G2G)

The first trade agreement between Finland and India was made on 29 June 1967. This was followed by an exchange of notes in 1974 (!) establishing the Indo-Finnish Joint Commission that met irregularly and was practically defunct. On 25 March 2010, Finland and India entered into a new AGREEMENT ON ECONOMIC COOPERATION[3] for developing and intensifying mutual economic cooperation on the basis of reciprocity and benefit, and for maintaining a satisfactory legal framework for Finland–India relations with due regard to all the laws in the two countries. There were four explicit aims[4]:

1. Promote activities aimed at the development of bilateral economic cooperation;
2. Support and develop business contacts;
3. Facilitate the expansion of bilateral trade and investment and promote economic and investment opportunities in their respective countries;
4. Reinforce cooperation for the enhancement of economic relations between the contracting parties.

The pillars of economic cooperation envisaged under this agreement are:

(i) Exchange of information on economic development and bilateral trade, economic plans, forecasts and strategies;
(ii) Exchange of information on laws and regulations relating to trade and economic cooperation;
(iii) Inform each other about existing possibilities concerning trade fairs, exhibitions, entrepreneurial missions and other promotional activities;
(iv) Facilitate the exchange of experts, technicians, investors and business representatives of the public and private sectors;
(v) Explore and promote joint business possibilities in third countries arising from partnership between Finnish and Indian companies;
(vi) Address any other questions relevant to maintaining and intensifying trade and economic relations between the contracting parties.

This agreement revived the Indo-Finnish Joint Commission (that had not convened in years) to promote, oversee and coordinate the cooperation between Finland and India and tasked the Joint Commission to:

1. Undertake discussions on the development of bilateral economic relations;
2. Identify new possibilities for further development of economic cooperation;
3. Draw up suggestions for the improvement of terms of economic cooperation between enterprises of contracting parties;

---

[3]Source: https://commerce.gov.in/writereaddata/trade/India%20Finland%20AGR.pdf and www.mea.gov.in.
[4]Source: https://commerce.gov.in/writereaddata/trade/India%20Finland%20AGR.pdf.

4. Discuss problems that could hinder the development of trade and economic cooperation as well as any other issues arising in the implementation of this agreement; and,
5. Make recommendations for the implementation of this agreement.

Joint Working Groups (JWG) were envisaged to be established within the framework of the Joint Commission. The sessions of the Joint Commission are supposed to be convened once every two years, or more often, if required, alternately in Finland and in India. In the same year, 2010, a memorandum of cooperation on road transport[5] was also negotiated and signed by the Governments of Finland and India with the aim of institutionalising technical and scientific cooperation in the fields of road transportation covering the following fields:

- Highways/roads construction, operation and maintenance;
- Planning and information management system for road administration;
- Finnish and Indian technical rules and legislative instruments concerning toll roads construction and managing;
- Forms of private investments attraction for the field of public/private partnership for the construction and upgrading of roads including procedure for competitive bidding, supervision and implementation;
- Road traffic safety;
- Road data bank systems including methods for collecting input data;
- Road and highway maintenance/upgrading strategies including adopted systems and road maintenance equipment;
- Implementation and management of upgrade/new construction road (highway) and bridge projects;
- Road and bridge technology;
- Staff training;
- Intelligent transportation systems;
- Intermodal transportation;
- Transportation for the mobility disabled; and,
- Other fields of mutual interest.

This agreement explicitly provided for promoting and developing relations between enterprises (consultancy and engineering companies in the field of roads, manufacturers of equipment, material and other products for the sector), with the purpose of arriving at industrial cooperation agreements and transfers of technology. The forms of cooperation envisaged were development of working programme containing the topics of cooperation, the specific projects to implement and the foreseen activities comprising:

---

[5]Source: Memorandum of Cooperation on Road Transport between Finland and India (copy of original text obtained by the author from the Embassy of India, Helsinki).

- Exchange of scientific and technical information, documentation and research reports with particular attention to computer systems for planning, design, management and maintenance processes;
- Exchange of information about construction and maintenance technologies and work methods;
- Sharing research experience and developments in other fields of road transport;
- Mutual consultation, exchange of experts, scientific and technical personnel and trainees, the extent of which to be mutually agreed upon by the two parties;
- Joint organisation of symposia, seminars and other meetings;
- Other forums of cooperation as mutually agreed.

The financing mechanism was left open with forms and costs for individual activities of cooperation to be decided upon in each particular case in accordance with the laws and regulations of India and Finland with each country taking responsibility for international travel expenses of its representatives. In order to promote and activate the institutional cooperation, an Indo-Finnish Joint Working Group has been established and tasked with developing and updating the working programme and implementation of the working programme providing for contact between the parties.

A big hurdle to Finland–India Economic Relations has been lack of basic awareness among the people of both countries about the other country. A cultural agreement between Finland and India had been made around the time when the first Double Taxation Avoidance Agreement was signed in 1983. This cultural agreement had also included 'science' which provided the window to negotiate and sign a new agreement[6] on scientific cooperation in 2008 aimed at promoting mobility of scientists and high-level experts to include:

(i) Sharing experiences in national research, development and innovation policies and programmes of each country;
(ii) Exchanging scientific and technological information and documentation;
(iii) Drawing the attention of potential partners directly involved in industrial research and development in their respective countries to possibilities for cooperation with the other country;
(iv) Facilitating the identification of specific projects or partnerships between Finnish and Indian companies and initiating contacts between researchers, research organisations and companies through visits, workshops and seminars;
(v) Facilitating the mobility of researchers, scientists and high-level experts;
(vi) Facilitating the creation of joint commercial and non-commercial initiatives.

This agreement envisaged the creation of a Joint Committee/Group of experts on Cooperation in Science & Technology for ensuring that the objectives are achieved with the following functions:

---

[6]Source: Agreement on Scientific Cooperation between Finland and India (Copy of Original Text obtained by the author from the Ministry of External Affairs, Government of India, New Delhi).

(a) Considering the policy aspects relevant to the implementation;
(b) Identifying areas of mutual interest on the basis of the priority interests;
(c) Reviewing the progress of the implementation; and
(d) Effecting follow-up and proposing specific measures to enhance cooperation.

Article 6 of the agreement provided for "separate protocols/arrangements to be worked out by Finnish and Indian partners participating in a collaborating activity under this agreement which bears commercial, business or other proprietary aspects, for safeguarding their intellectual property rights involved in such activity and the dissemination thereof. The protection of intellectual property rights is supposed to be in accordance with the respective national laws and regulations as well as the relevant international agreements to which Finland or India are parties".

There is also a confidentiality clause in Article 7 that all appropriate measures would be taken to protect all information bearing commercial, business or other proprietary aspects and communicated between the parties as provided for by their respective national laws and regulations. By subsequent supplementary agreements, India's Department of Science and Technology as well as India's Department of Biotechnology and their Finnish counterparts Tekes and the Finnish Academy have made agreements for mobility of scientists to participate in projects in either country.

The 18th Session of the Finland–India Joint Commission was held in Helsinki on 19th–20th April 2017. Recent initiatives taken by the Government of India like 'Startup India', 'Make in India', 'FDI Policy', 'Ease of Doing Business', 'Digital India', and 'Smart City' were discussed as these have the potential to expand all the four gateways, especially on trade in services and product-service linkages. Noting that bilateral trade between the two countries was about €1 billion, both sides recognised that the level of direct investment between India and Finland was still modest. Finland is a stable, knowledge and solution-based economy, where expertise and professional skills are widely available. This makes the country an ideal test ground for new solutions and technologies. Investing in Finland offers an opportunity to raise investor companies' competence and know-how.

Correspondingly, 'Startup India', a flagship initiative of the Government of India, focuses on innovation and design. The new investor-friendly policy allows FDI up to 100% through the automatic route, in most sectors/activities. The 'Make in India' initiative to make India a global manufacturing hub is another programme to foster innovation, skill development, protection of intellectual property and manufacturing infrastructure. In this campaign, the Government of India facilitates, assists and handholds investors to ensure that they are able to establish and operationalise their industry and business in India without facing hurdles and systemic delays. Twenty-five priority sectors have been identified for growth under the campaign. Another recent initiative is the 'ease of doing business' where emphasis has been laid on simplification and rationalisation of the existing rules and introduction of information technology to make governance more efficient, effective, simple and user-friendly.

India's then Minister of State for Power, coal, new and renewable energy and Mines, Piyush Goyal, visited Finland in November 2016. In his meeting with the

Prime Minister of Finland, there was a discussion to initiate an Indo-Finnish minister-led energy, investment and mining dialogue. Based on this platform, several contacts both at expert level and senior official level have taken place with a view to enter into concrete cooperation. All these positive developments were to encourage more Finnish companies to be interested in India as an attractive, stable and safe business and investment environment for Finnish businesses.

New and renewable energy is one of the most active and potential fields of G2G, B2G and B2B collaborations. Mutual interest to develop Indo-Finnish collaboration in renewable energy is reflected by the memorandum of understanding (MoU) between Indian Ministry of New and Renewable Energy and the Ministry of Economic Affairs and Employment of Finland signed in October 2014 during the State visit of India's President to Finland. The MoU and the established Joint Working Group on renewable energy offer a governmental framework and a platform for joint projects and collaboration activities between Finnish and Indian companies, research organisations and officials. The first JWG meeting was held in February 2015 in New Delhi.

The potential fields identified are joint development projects and business ventures around solar, biomass and biofuels, waste-to-energy and circular economy, efficient and flexible energy technologies for smart energy production and distribution, electric mobility and charging. Both sides have agreed that in order to enhance bilateral collaboration on renewable energy, they would take initiatives in the following sectors:

(a) To study cooperation possibilities in wind forecasting.
(b) To study the potential for launching R&D&I cooperation and bilateral funding mechanisms in mutually interesting areas.
(c) To hold further discussions on potential areas and forms of collaboration, for example organising seminars, workshops and networking events.

Finnish companies have been welcomed to participate in India Solar Mission. Fortum is the first Finnish firm that accepted the invitation and is involved with two solar projects already. India is phasing out petrol vehicles by 2030 and Fortum is among the companies that is building charging stations for electric vehicles. Its first charging station was inaugurated in October 2017 when Finnish Minister Kimmo Tiilikainen led a 'Team Finland' visit to India. with a 25-member business delegation from the energy, cleantech, bioeconomy, technology and environmental technology sectors.

Cleantech, Water and Waste Management

The development of clean technologies, such as energy efficiency, water and waste management and treatment and their support are also part of G2G initiatives that would pave the way also for B2G and B2B gateways in this arena. Bioeconomy, clean solutions and circular economy are Finland's innovation and industrial policy priorities. Most of the Finnish companies operating in India are working in the fields of cleantech. Finnish Researcher Larikka (2012) has published a study of Cleantech business opportunities in India for Finnish enterprises. Finnish Cleantech solutions are based on efficient, competitive market-based solutions, which reduce emissions in the environment. Technologies, processes and expertise developed in Finland can be transferred and applied globally in four applications:

- Sustainable waste management;
- Municipal wastewater sludge treatment;
- Value from organic waste—Biorefinery;
- Wastewater treatment and management of industrial effluents.

The Joint Working Groups (JWG) have become a platform for networking potential Indian and Finnish partners, both public and private organisations and companies, and for initiating joint projects. The Finnish Meteorological Institute (FMI) has long-lasting collaboration with The Energy and Resources Institute (TERI) in India and has recently completed a successful first project with the Indian Meteorological Department (IMD). The FMI is also discussing possible collaboration with the Indian electricity grid sector. VTT, the Technical Research Centre of Finland, has initiated research and development collaboration in India in many areas of energy and environment.

Science, Technology and Innovations

In science, technology and innovation, India's Department of Science and Technology (DST) and the Department of Biotechnology are collaborating with Finland's Ministry of Economic Affairs and Employment, Tekes and the Academy of Finland. The governmental agreement on Science and Technology signed in 2008, the Joint Committee (JC) established in 2009 and the Indo-Finnish Joint Working Group (JWG) on Innovation established in 2010 serve as an umbrella and platform for networking and joint calls. The start-up and venture funding event Slush has attracted three Indian start-up companies. Mutually important areas of collaboration are cleantech, information and communication technologies (ICT), electronics, manufacturing, health and biotechnology.

The Academy of Finland now has active interaction with DST and DBT both bilaterally and multilaterally at the EU-level, e.g. in the Inno-Indigo-ERA-NET. Many fields of research (e.g. solar energy, nanomaterials, synthetic biology) have been supported, and joint Finnish-Indian research projects have produced cutting edge research and publications. Renewable energy has been an important recent theme in bilateral collaboration. The jointly funded projects between Finnish universities and governmental research institutes and Indian research organisations are also progressing.

VTT participates as the representative of Finland in the Strategic Forum for International Science and Technology Cooperation (SFIC) between Europe and

India in the working groups: Environment/Water and Energy. VTT and Indian CSIR (Council of Scientific and Industrial Research) are both members in the Global Research Alliance. The focus of VTT's research and development projects in India is on energy and environment, health and well-being, ICT and electronics, as well as science and technology policy research. VTT is looking for direct contacts to Indian industrial companies in order to bring innovative solutions to their challenges through Hackathon events.

Education and Skill Development

On higher education and research, there is a memorandum of understanding between the Indian Institutes of Technology (IITs) and a Consortium of Finnish Higher Education Institutions. The partners at this stage are IITs in Mumbai, Gandhinagar, Hyderabad, Kharagpur, Kanpur and Roorkee and, from the Finnish side, Aalto University, University of Jyväskylä, Tampere University of Technology, University of Tampere, University of Turku, Lappeenranta University of Technology, University of Helsinki and University of Oulu, Åbo Akademi University and University of Eastern Finland. In February 2017 Aalto University School of Science and IIT Madras signed an agreement for Joint Doctoral Program/Double Degree Program for Ph.D. education. Due to contraction by consolidation, the number of institutions in the Finnish Higher Education Consortium has reduced. Tampere University of Technology is now part of the University of Tampere.

The network of Finnish vocational institutions has now become active in India. The overall objectives are to respond to the competence needs of the labour market and to promote the cooperation between training and enterprises. The network will increase the mobility of teachers, trainers and students between the countries as well as to enhance opportunities for work-based learning. Finland has expressed interest in participating in a dialogue between the Finnish and Indian administrations, on governing skills and extending the dialogue to the education and training leading to professional qualifications.

Finnish universities of applied sciences are interested in developing and deepening existing cooperation with Indian higher education institutions, especially in the fields of student and staff exchanges and joint research, development and innovation projects. Finnish Universities of Applied Sciences (the erstwhile polytechnics) are increasing the number of Indian students in their English-taught degree programmes. But at present, India and Finland do not have an agreement focusing specifically on Educational Exchange. A MoU on the mutual recognition of qualification between Finland and India is on the anvil. The volume of exchange student mobility between higher education institutions in India and Finland is rather small at about 30 students in both directions.

There are further possibilities to explore mutual discussions and cooperation in the following sectors:

- Mutual recognition of skill qualifications between both the countries,
- Benchmarking of skill standards in Finland and India,
- Identification of areas of collaboration in apprenticeship for different sectors especially with Finnish companies in India and Indian companies in Finland,
- To scale up the working with 17 Finnish vocational institutions which are active in India (the Salpaus Consortium that visited India in 2005–06 was the first such and the action research study of Mattila (2008) studied that entire process documenting the insights from that experience which paved the way for more involvement of Finnish vocational institutions in India),
- Post-doc researchers in the area of applied research in bioeconomy.

Information Technology and Telecommunications

Promoting sustainable ICT solutions in developing smart cities as well as encouraging investment and technology partnerships for developing broadband networks and applications, wireless and mobile applications, cloud computing and IT manpower training are also G2G initiatives that can lead to more B2B business. Fostering the availability, production and use of reliable and safe ICT's in the markets is the most significant way of increasing cybersecurity.

Transportation: Roads, Railways, Aviation and Shipping

Smart mobility and innovations for future transportation are important for both sides. There have been amendments in the bilateral air services agreement allowing direct flights to important new destinations in India. This can bring India and Finland closer to each other. The modernisation of Indian Railways through design of wagons and components, institution of fog-lights and anti-vibration metalastic couplings, safer foot overbridges, dry toilets, hygiene and sanitation improvements, waste management can all benefit from Finnish products and services. The Railway Design and Standards Organisation of India can also produce prototypes of devices that can be used by the Finnish Railways if officials of the two railways begin to converse for improvements at both ends. India has much to learn from the quality of Finnish roads and how road-building may be improved in India Finland's shipyards and India's shipyards have different advantages to offer the other side. Port infrastructure is another field which can benefit from new models of collaboration.

Cooperation in Textiles Sector

India is an important trading partner for Finland in textile and fashion industry and new projects are underway in circular economy, meaning economic reuse of recycled textiles and clothes, as well as innovations in this domain around recycling cloth to produce new yarn and cotton-type yarn from wood-based raw materials. Textile Machinery is another promising area where Finland and India can combine their advantages, especially for third-country markets.

Tourism Cooperation

In 2015, Visit Finland was merged into Finpro, Finnish Trade Promotion Agency, that has a presence in New Delhi. India has no tourism office in Finland yet. The nearest India tourism office located in Amsterdam undertakes tourism promotional activities in Finland. It conducts road shows/workshops/seminars in various cities of Finland to create awareness about India in the Finnish travel trade. India Tourism, Amsterdam, participates in MATKA (Trade Fair) held in Helsinki every year to attract the trade and consumers of this market. India Tourism office prints the brochures and publicity material in Finnish language for distribution and organised a Know India Seminar in Helsinki in November 2016.

Tourist traffic between the two countries at about 15–20 thousand each year for the last few years is rather small. Finland has also not yet attracted the Indian film industry to shoot films in exotic locales of Finland. To further promote tourism between the two countries certain measures could be undertaken:

- Exchange of relevant data and statistics;
- Familiarisation tours by inviting the travel writers/photographers/film-makers to each other's country;
- Exchange of visits for promotion of tourism cooperation by sending delegations consisting of representatives of travel agents, tour operators and hoteliers etc.;
- Exchange the details of the training facilities available in the field of tourism, hotel management, catering technology, etc.;
- To explore possibilities of promoting the exotic locales of Finland in each of its four seasons as filming locations for Indian movies;
- To explore the possibilities of promoting investment in the field of hotel industry tourism and infrastructural development (India allows 100% FDI in hotel sector);
- To explore the possibility of entering into memorandum of understanding in the field of tourism cooperation.

The multilateral Trade Facilitation Agreement (TFA) became effective on 22 February 2017 when the WTO obtained the two-thirds acceptance of the Agreement from its 164 Members. India had ratified the TFA in April 2016. Due to the increasing importance of trade in services, India has taken the initiative to launch discussions on an agreement for facilitating trade in services, as a counterpart of the goods-specific Trade Facilitation Agreement (TFA). A draft text of such an agreement has been tabled by India on 23 February 2017 at WTO. India's proposal aims to address numerous border and behind-the-border barriers across all modes of supply, as well as procedural constraints, which are impediments to the realisation of the full potential of services trade. These impediments limit the benefits of trade in services especially for SMEs and small exporters worldwide. Most industrial products today are sold together with a service contract, and it is important to include services such as maintenance and repair in framework agreements at G2G level. E-commerce is very important for both Finland and India and the Information Technology Agreement (ITA) awaits being applied comprehensively to all product categories—including all telecommunication equipment.

Non-Tariff Barriers and Protection of Bilateral Investments

G2G initiatives are also required in many other areas. Provisions of mandatory testing and local content requirements in the telecom sector constrain Finnish firms in India compared to local producers. Finland has non-tariff barriers due to which fresh fruits and vegetables, as well as processed and packaged food items exported from India to Finland experience difficulties. India has adopted a new model bilateral investment treaty text and all extant agreements whose initial period was over had been terminated by the Government of India. This also affects the bilateral investment protection treaty with Finland that would end, unless renewed, in 2019.

Trade Promotion Measures

The relationship between the Finnish research and innovation system and international business needs strengthening. OECD has urged Finland to examine new ways of developing public–private partnerships. A critical bottleneck is enterprise-level productivity in small and medium-sized enterprises (SMEs) and start-ups for enabling them to grow and compete globally. In response to this, the Team Finland concept has changed dramatically in recent years (Ministry for Foreign Affairs of Finland 2016). The Team Finland network is a locus of convergence for all government-funded services of export promotion and internationalisation services provided for Finnish companies. In November 2016, the Finnish government decided to reorganise Team Finland operations and services in two stages. The purpose of this change *"is to support the Government's ambitious objective to double the exports of small and medium-sized enterprises by 2020"* (according to the announcement made in Finnish on the Government of Finland's Ministry of Economic Affairs and Employment http://www.tem.fi/).

The first stage of the reform consisted of measures that can be implemented and carried out within a short time frame. These included redefinition of Team Finland services to respond to the actual needs of Finnish companies, integration of services provided by municipalities, regions and local government, introduction of a service voucher to support internationalisation efforts, and integration of Tekes's and Finpro's program activities.

In the second stage, the government together with key interest groups representing Finnish Business assessed the needs for possible structural changes. Based on this analysis, the government decided in March 2017 to combine Tekes and Finpro into a new platform with the label 'Business Finland'. On 28 December 2017, the government appointed a Board for Business Finland for the term from 1 January 2018 to 31 December 2019. The board is chaired by Pertti Korhonen who headed Tekes, the Finnish Funding Agency for Innovation. Tekes and Finpro were joined from the beginning of 2018. Business Finland brings all services related to innovation funding, exports, investment and tourism promotion under the same roof. This is the G2B Bridge. It is estimated that about 650 experts from various agencies and the Ministry have been transferred to the new organisation, Business Finland. Abroad, cooperation of Business Finland with the Ministry of Foreign Affairs is leveraged through Finnish diplomats serving abroad. This is the G2G Bridge.

The hope is that the entire life cycle of the growth and internationalisation of companies can now be tracked. The Finnish government support would begin at the product development stage, extend to testing of business models and continue until commercial introduction abroad. The responsibilities of the units of Tekes and Finpro, which are Export Finland, Invest in Finland and Visit Finland, shall remain but the way to organise and provide the services is being harmonised for better support to growth-oriented companies aspiring to internationalise.

A variety of funding options are available for Finnish companies seeking growth potential in India. Finnvera, the official Export Credit Agency of Finland, and its subsidiary Finnish Export Credit Ltd provides financing services for the exports of Finnish companies to India. The range of support provided covers small transactions to major infrastructural projects. Additionally, Finnvera provides financing for Finnish SMEs for investments involving India. Finnpartnership promotes companies' internationalisation through its business partnership support facility and provides assistance in identifying business partners. Support is also granted to import from developing countries, development of vocational training and technological pilot projects. Indian companies seeking business partners and opportunities in Finland can make use of Finnpartnership's matchmaking services free of charge. Finnfund, the Finnish Fund for Industrial Cooperation Ltd, provides long-term risk capital for companies running projects that make use of Finnish technology or expertise and which support economic and social development in India.

The Finnish India Trade Association in Helsinki mainly consists of small immigrants running shops, pizzerias and restaurants and tiny export–import trade largely around diaspora sales of cultural and nutritional products. The Indo-Finnish Business Forum in India is also limited to a narrow set of Finnish players. There is scope for evolving both of these to new thresholds of engagement and participation.

G2G and B2B Joint Efforts

The combined endeavours of Government and Business, the latter through chambers of commerce in Finland and India from time to time, have not resulted in many mentionable new mutual investments. The follow-up research with all the companies that were represented in these endeavours reveals that not even 2% of the firms involved succeeded in making new business connections between Finland and India. The causes identified are:

1. Inadequate prior preparation to understand the nature of business opportunities to be prospected and the questions to ask;
2. Culture Shock;
3. Loss of interest in exploring and developing relations with prospective business partners on the assumption that information exchange at first meeting should suffice;
4. Hardly any follow-up to examine alternative solutions to the first hurdles encountered.

The biggest Finnish delegation to ever visit India was in November 2009 when Minister for Foreign Trade Mauri Pekkarinen led a delegation consisting of 138 leaders of Finnish business enterprises right after the 2008 global financial crisis that produced a growth slowdown amounting almost to a mini-recession in Finland. But the Black Swan event in 2010 when just for that one year Finland registered unusually big trade with China (and a trade surplus too) on the back of a few large plant commissionings in the paper and pulp sector, interest in following up on the 2009 business discussions waned and hardly any new Finnish investment in India arose from that visit.

The Confederation of Indian Industry (CII), in partnership with Team Finland, organised the India–Finland FIND conference on 15 October 2013 with the objective of exploring opportunities for cooperation between both the countries. The inaugural session of the conference was addressed by Alexander Stubb, Minister for European Affairs and Foreign Trade of Finland, Panabaka Lakshmi, Minister of State for Petroleum and Natural Gas, Government of India and Mr. Aapo Pölhö, Ambassador of Finland to India. The same was followed by business-to-business meetings between the Indian companies and the Finnish Delegation. A similar conference was also organised by CII in Mumbai.

The CII organised the Conference on Promoting Economic Engagement between India and Nordic Region of Europe on 21 February 2014 in New Delhi. Dr. E. M. Sudarsana Natchiappan, Minister of State for Commerce and Industry, was the chief guest at the conference which was attended by all Nordic Ambassadors and Diplomats, including Finland. There was a broad consensus that bilateral trade between India and the Nordic region, at US$ 6.3 billion was far below its potential. The attendees highlighted sectors such as steel, pulp and paper, auto components, pharmaceuticals, IT and ITES, biomass, trade and tourism that had enormous growth potential. The meeting never got around to discussing why there was so much difference between the Nordic countries in relating to India when many of their competitive advantages were similar. For instance, there was no discussion on why Swedish firms had preferred trade-substituting investments over trade in many sectors or why this pathway had not been adopted by more Finnish companies. In the case of Denmark, it was understandable because there were bad vibes in India's political relations with Denmark over Denmark's refusal to extradite a terrorist who had dropped bombs in Eastern India and escaped to Denmark. But there was no such hurdle in Finland–India relations.

It is disconcerting that sometimes the mutual interest that is announced is more show than substance. A CII CEOs Delegation accompanied the President of India during his visit to Finland in October 2014. The 20-member delegation participated in business sessions with counterpart organisations in Finland and also met several key officials and agencies responsible for promoting trade and investments. During this visit, it was announced that there were more than a dozen agreements signed (and incidentally, a similar number was announced from the President of India's visit to Norway around the same time). A week later when I visited the Joint Secretary, responsible for relations with Finland in the Ministry of External Affairs New Delhi, the Ministry had a difficult time even finding these agreements. Even after heroic efforts, the ministry could only retrieve a few of them. But pictures of the then President Pranab Mukherjee with Santa Claus were available. Later, I was able to get a few more of the agreements from the Finnish Ambassador in New Delhi but even there the complete set was unavailable. Months later, I retrieved a few more in their draft form at the Embassy of India in Helsinki. Finally, I probably have the complete set but this made me wonder if any other office within the two governments does.

The Federation of Indian Chambers of Commerce and Industry (FICCI) has institutional agreements with Finland Chambers of Commerce and Industry, Finnfund and Finpro and is working with both Indian Embassy in Helsinki and Finnish Embassy in Delhi in promoting business linkages by optimally utilising the services of FICCI Bisnet division, a specialised agency mandated to promote such connects. FICCI led a 19-member business delegation to Finland coinciding with the visit of Pranab Mukherjee, then President of India on October 14–16, 2014. A number of business interactions and site visits were organised during the visit for the business delegates. Arrangements for cooperation in nuclear and radiation safety and the atmospheric environment were agreed in principle.

The FICCI led a 17-member business delegation accompanying Piyush Goyal, the then Minister of State for Power, Coal, New and Renewable Energy and Mines, to Finland on November 3–5, 2016 and had business sessions with the Finnish counterparts. Immediately after this visit, Matti Anttonen, Deputy Minister for External Economic Relations at MFA, led a business delegation to India in areas of renewable energy and infrastructure on November 8–11, 2016. They had meetings with a number of key figures in administration in New Delhi, in Indian companies, and academia in Gujarat.

The Ministry of External Affairs, Government of India, CII and the Nordic Missions in India, jointly organised the India-Nordic Conclave on Smart Cities on 7 March 2017 in New Delhi. The Conclave had participation from all Nordic countries, including Finland. The Conclave provided the stakeholders from India and Nordic a platform to discuss the most recent innovations, trends, challenges and opportunities in India with regard to solutions for the challenges of new Smart Cities in India.

The first meeting of Indo-Finnish Business Working Group on Energy & Mining arranged by FICCI and the Embassy of Finland in New Delhi on 10 March 2017. This convened business executives from 10 Finnish and 13 Indian companies under joint chairmanship of Finland's Ambassador Nina Vaskunlahti and FICCI Chairman Pankaj Patel. Markku Keinänen, the new Deputy Minister for External Economic Relations at MFA, held consultations on topical trade policy issues in New Delhi on April 6–7, 2017. Later in the year 2017, India's Minister of State for External Affairs also visited Finland. There was another Finnish business delegation led by Deputy Minister of Economic Affairs, Petri Peltonen, to New Delhi on 25–27th of April 2017. FICCI hosted a business session for Mr. Peltonen along with a 17-member business delegation on 26 April 2017 in New Delhi. In addition, FICCI organise structured B2B meetings for the Finnish delegation.

With so much activity, some bridges between India and Finland already exist and more can be designed. It is said that people do not learn from others' experiences and that we learn only from our own experiences. In the next two chapters (Chaps. 7 and 8), we explore practicalities of organising for business in India and Finland by gaining something from the experience of those who have learnt from doing regardless of whether they succeeded or failed. It is as important to understand how not to do business as it is to know the realms of the possible and Koski has pointed out limitations of the Finnish business subsidy model succinctly (Koski 2008). It is also necessary to understand better the ecosystem and trajectories in the two countries and the unique challenges that they involve.

References

Bound K, Leadbeater C, Miller P, Wilsdon J (2006) The new geography of innovation: India, Finland, science and technology. Sitra Report 71. SITRA, Helsinki

Durant W (1930) The case for India. Simon & Schuster, New York. Strand Book Stall, Mumbai Reprint, 2015

Grundström E, Lahti VM (2005) The India phenomenon and Finland. Background study for Sitra's India programme. SITRA, Helsinki

Koski H (2008) Public R&D subsidies and employment growth-microeconomic evidence from Finnish firms. ETLA, Helsinki

Larikka M (2012) Strategic alliances as an international entry strategy: Finnish Cleantech SMEs and the Indian Market. University of Turku

Mathur AN, Ryynänen M, Nystedt A (2003) Communities at risk, Series A1: Studies 48. University of Tampere, Tampere

Mattila S (2008) Multi-content revelation through dialogue processes: a study in understanding the hermeneutic primary task of small groups in the context of Finland and India. Doctoral dissertation, Tampere University of Technology, 2008. Publication 738, Tampere University of Technology Press, Tampere

Ministry for Foreign Affairs of Finland (2016) Finland's development policy. Government Reports to Parliament Series, Helsinki

Chapter 7
Organising for Business in India

> *To a frog that's never left his pond the Ocean seems like a gamble,*
> *Look what he's giving up:security, mastery of his world, recognition!*
> *The Ocean frog just shakes his head,*
> *I can't really explain what it's like where I live,*
> *But someday I'll take you there.*
>
> Rumi

Abstract Foreign firms have difficulty making sense of the complexities, diversity and ambiguities that they encounter in institutional interfaces in India. The crowds, the traffic, the pollution and the contradictions they need to resolve in everyday life add to the challenges. The centre-state duality in governance that affects industrial projects in India, the cultural contestations and argumentativeness that are widespread, the passive aggression, the cut-throat competitiveness and the idiosyncrasies of different groups would all be amusing if they were not also disturbing and frustrating. This chapter introduces the essentials of constitutional, legal, political, economic and social systems, organisation structures and typically Indian management styles and processes that can be exasperating to the uninitiated.

Introduction

Even a zealously proud Indian would hesitate to claim that it is easy to do business in India. Despite improvements in India's rank in the ease of doing business indicators published by the World Bank, any foreigner in India would come across certain difficulties that are known and predictable. Even stepping out from any Indian megacity's international airport terminal brings you face to face with crowds, pollution, traffic chaos and a level of hygiene and sanitation which can be a shock. The newness in interfacing with Indian infrastructure and resources, unfamiliarity with institutions and the climate can all add up to make the liabilities of foreignness and outsidership quite formidable. So despite opportunities, there is a definite need to understand, prepare and develop capabilities for engaging with challenges of doing business in India. Many of the challenges, obstacles and frustrations of enterprises—both domestic and foreign—have to do with lack of awareness of the labyrinths or being underprepared for coping with and responding to the institutional peculiarities and legacies, the vast diversity of management styles and commercial practices in different parts of the country and the complexity of structures, non-transparency of systems and obtuse processes that could involve exercise of discretionary authority by the politicians and the bureaucracy.

Chapters 4 and 5 already pointed to the cultural and institutional differences that need managing in the context of organising. It would be simply wrong to subsume all of these differences under the black box of 'Indian culture' or consider India as being in a stage of transition about to reform. The whales of Asia (Japan and China being the other two, besides India) have continuously demonstrated that they are not about to change their way of doing business anytime soon. Cries for and proclamations of reform have led to changes in appearance without substantial transformations. Anyone playing the waiting game would gain little in waiting and would only be taking the risk of missing out and being pre-empted and outcompeted from opportunities that beckon.

Understandably, Finnish firms have difficulties in doing business in India and with Indians. There are two fundamental difficulties. The first has to do with the orientation and expectations of Finnish firms and the mindsets of business leaders and managers who have grown up in the Finnish culture and worked in the Finnish business environment. The second set of challenges have to do with India and what one may call 'Indianness' in the business context. Making sense of the complexities encountered in laws, business practices, management styles, situational ambiguities is all parts of encounters in institutional interfaces in India. The crowds, the traffic, the pollution and the contradictions that keep popping up in everyday life add to the challenges. The centre-state duality in governance that affects all industrial projects in India, and regional cultural contestations and rivalrous argumentativeness among groups is widespread. The passive aggression, the cut-throat competitiveness and the idiosyncrasies of different interest groups would all be amusing if they were not also disturbing and frustrating.

Then, there is the complex task of choosing an entry mode appropriate for any particular business opportunity and evaluating country risks and political risks associated with it. All organisations involve creation of internal markets in a firm with due regard to factor markets in a host country that can be quite different from the home country. Finally, human talent has to be positioned, developed, recruited from the host and home country and a system of business intelligence relevant to the operations has to be put in place. Let us dwell on all these one by one.

Orientation of Finnish Firms

The practice(s) of business and the conceptualisation of practices can lead to the establishment of existing traditions as norm or their canonisation in doctrinaire forms. This can constrict the space for exploring other promising paths of the possible by removing impediments in the way of policies and practices needed to succeed in crossing into new horizons. These in turn foster beliefs, attitudes and values all of which are sticky and require effort to reflect upon. The performance and international competitiveness of Finnish firms are sensitive to debt gearing, and high investment rates are frequently associated with low returns and high risk (Artto 1995). This makes Finnish firms risk averse. Incrementalism, derived from Johansson and Vahlne's Uppsala model (Johansson and Vahlne 1977), has been the normative model in Finland (Luostarinen 1994). Criteria-based discriminant analysis to distinguish successful firms from failure cases may enable us to confirm or refute the normative value of the incrementalism model, but this has not been empirically tested. Typically, it involves a long phase, stretching to two or three decades before Finnish firms may establish representative agents. In the absence of critical minimum human resource size in the destination country that may be required to plan and execute trade and investments, many opportunities remain undeveloped and evaporate. Later, Johansson and Vahlne revised their model (Johansson and Vahlne 2009) and admitted that the 'incrementalism' notion was partly normative and partly phenomenal, being observed in Swedish companies, and based on the notion of a liability of foreignness that can be bypassed by overcoming what is truly the liability of outsidership.

The Finnish model in practice also assumes that the direction of trade is signalled or determined by the willingness to allocate public resources by the Finnish State to subsidise and support Finnish foreign trade and investment based on opinion formation through lobbies by large firms and associations (Koski 2008). While this delivers results in exports, it does not encourage knowledge-intensive specialisations to be cultivated with reference to structuring investments in other modes. Project modalities with soft targets are the *sine qua non* of Finnish internationalisation based on advocacy of gradual 'incrementalism' in which Finnish firms first delay entry and the entry costs are afforded mainly by large and medium firms able to sustain higher costs of such gradual incrementalism in what they perceive to be high-risk environments. Finnish managers have been slow to accept that successful global firms have long-term horizons and learn to operate in arenas of contestation with institutional contexts different from their own.

The industrial structure of Finland presented many possibilities for geographically diversified internationalisation when the Soviet trade collapsed but Finnish firms were generally hesitant to go beyond Tallinn, St Petersburg or Germany at that time. A part of this hesitation may be attributed to the losses large firms, like Enso, Huhtamäki, Valmet, Amer, Valio and Marimekko, incurred in international business with the Americas–Canada, USA and Brazil in the 1980s and losses Nokia incurred in Europe because of management inadequacies until 1995. In turning to

Asia, structuring investments required the willingness to analyse and tune into the economic logic of a very diverse set of circumstances within and across these countries. The novelty of relating to exotic cultures at a time when the East Asian economic miracle was being prematurely celebrated promoted much state subsidised tourism and contributed to some international business. The discovery of China and Vietnam as markets and Singapore as a location were among the positive developments from this phase of Finland's internationalisation. But India remained neglected.

India's Governance Frame

Anyone visualising engagement with organising to do business in India after attractive opportunities have been identified should at least browse through the Constitution of India and India's Companies Act, 2013, to know when and how to refer to them. Both are lengthy, and it is not necessary to read them cover to cover. But some elements of them require to be familiarised. Since all laws in the country (including Parliament-made laws) are required to be consistent with the constitutional frame and can even be challenged or struck down when so challenged. For this reason, one should never take a legal provision or government notification or informal promise from anyone at face value. Examine whether it stands scrutiny against the principles of the constitution. As a political union of states, India is a sovereign, socialist, secular, democratic republic. Each of these four adjectives describing the republic has their own weight and their own historical legacy and has given rise to features in the governance frame, to people's aspirations, to policies and to practices.

Sovereignty is taken seriously, and since the democracy has not yet matured to a stage where aggression would become taboo, the government and countervailing forces against the government engage in discourses that are not free from strife, conflicts and even violence, despite the respect for Gandhian ahimsa (non-violence). The persistence of sharp economic disparities is itself a form of violence, and I am grateful to the Founder of SEWA, Ela Bhatt, for having drawn my attention to this.

It is essential to be familiar with the Chapters in India's Constitution on Directive Principles and Fundamental Rights, the availability of writ jurisdiction under Article 226, and the Schedules to the Constitution that list which matters would be governed by the central government and which by the state governments. The Union List has 97 entries including national defence, foreign affairs, atomic energy, railways, national highways and waterways, international and interstate trade and commerce, banking, insurance, intellectual property, mines, oilfields and central taxes. The State List contains 66 subjects such as trade and commerce within the state, state taxes, land rights, public health, agriculture, water supply and irrigation. There is also a Concurrent List in which matters can be legislated by both the central government and the state government, and the later legislation would prevail unless countermanded by the centre's legislative authority on the Concurrent List. The Concurrent List has 47 subjects (including criminal law, family law, contracts, economic and social planning, industrial and labour disputes and price control). If a matter is not covered in any list, the Parliament has exclusive power under Article 248 to make new laws. This provision was used to legislate the Consumer Protection Act, 1986. Each state in India has its own political, cultural and social identity, and its communities carry their own customs, traditions. Note that in the seven union territories all matters are governed by the central government.

The governance system in India is based on a system of separation of powers between the legislature, the executive and an independent judiciary. The executive frame rules and regulations after laws have been passed either by Parliament or by a state legislature. The Parliament is bicameral with direct first past the post elections for the Lok Sabha (the Lower House) for demarcated constituencies and a complex system of elections based on indirect proportional representation from an electoral college from the State Assemblies for the Upper House (Rajya Sabha). There is also a system of elections for urban local bodies (municipal councils) and gram panchayats (village-level representative bodies) that can make local laws, adjudge certain disputes and levy property taxes, utility levies, luxury taxes.

Nobody wants to fight legal cases, and businesses may go through an entire life cycle without getting involved in a court case but it helps to be prepared. It is useful to be prepared to defend actions, prosecute legal actions and at least know how the system functions in India. A business would normally identify a legal practitioner or firm at an early stage of business commencement so that in an emergency, there is someone to turn to. The judicial system is based on common law supplemented by statutory laws arising from legislative enactments, contract law and customary laws. Civil cases and criminal cases are heard by different courts of the first instance. Civil cases would normally be heard by subordinate judges under a District Judge, and criminal cases go to a Magistrate or Sessions Judge. Appeals go to the High Court of Jurisdiction.

For cases under special laws as for company securities, company law matters, income taxes, customs duties, excise, labour, industrial disputes, competition policy, there are special courts and tribunals. Appeals from such courts can be also be made first to the High Court of Jurisdiction, and appeals from the High Court can be made to the Supreme Court. In exceptional cases, the High Court can hear a matter directly under Article 226 and the Supreme Court can hear a matter directly under Article 136 of the constitution. Writ jurisdiction, a common law heritage, enables writ of certiorari (for correcting wrong laws, rules, government orders), writ of mandamus (for getting judicial orders against government failures that mandate the government to act in accordance with rule of law), writ of prohibition (for seeking judicial orders to ban perverse acts of commission or omission by government), writ of quo warranto (for obtaining judicial order to question by what authority the government made a decision) and writ of habeas corpus (for judicial order to produce the body in case of illegal detention). Indian courts also accept public interest litigation where anybody may raise an issue in the public interest. There is also a Right to Information Act (RTI) in India under which anyone can demand that the government provide information that is in its possession for the sake of transparency and disclosure. Foreign judgements are becoming part of materials being considered in Indian courts, for instance in proceedings of the Competition Commission of India, and the Income Tax Appellate Authority in matters of international taxation.

Arbitration is used in B2B legal disputes in India and is governed by the Arbitration and Conciliation Act, 1996, that was drafted on the lines of the UNCITRAL Model Law. Arbitration can be used in domestic cases, enforcement of foreign judgements, international commercial disputes, and it also provides mechanisms for conciliation. India has ratified the New York and Geneva conventions on arbitration enabling awards under either of them to be implemented. There is a catch here. This can only be actually done if the jurisdiction in which the award was delivered abroad is a reciprocal jurisdiction notified by the central government. Finland and India are not reciprocating territories as of now. But this can be changed.

Institutional arbitration offers another way. There are four institutions in India, and any one of them can be agreed upon. These are the FICCI Arbitration and Conciliation Tribunal (FACT), London Court of International Arbitration, India (LCIA, India), Indian Council of Arbitration (ICA) and International Centre for Alternate Dispute Resolution (ICADR). The process of arbitration in India takes on average of 12–18 months. Among places for arbitration abroad, London, Geneva and Singapore are popular choices. In a landmark judgement (Bharat Aluminium versus Kaiser Aluminium Technical Services, 2012, 9 SCC 552), the Supreme Court of India has decided that enforcement of a foreign arbitral award can be refused in India only if it is contrary to the fundamental policy of Indian law or the interests of India or to justice or morality with one caveat. A party located abroad may not be entitled to interim relief. Under Indian law, the law of the country that has the closest connection with an agreement in dispute would be treated as the curial law.

Establishing a Business in India

There are many forms of business entities in India. Establishing private limited companies and public limited companies are two of them. A private company needs just two shareholders and is the ideal form for a start-up business activity in India and for joint ventures. There are no restrictions on private companies regarding the nature of activities, nor on how many it employs. The filing, disclosure and compliance requirements for a private company are minimal unlike those for a public company. The Companies Act, 2013, replaced the Companies Act, 1956, and governs the functioning frame for companies regarding how and when to comply with disclosures and norms of those disclosures. There are clear rules on composition of boards, independent directors, requirement of women directors and the functioning of boards and their fiduciary responsibilities. The exit procedures are supplemented by the new insolvency and bankruptcy code. Firms listed on stock exchanges have to follow rules of the Securities and Exchange Board of India. These rules are transparently available from the SEBI official website: https://www.sebi.gov.in/. Companies with a net worth over 500 crores or a turnover greater than 1000 crores or net profit more than 2 crores are obligated to spend at least 2% of their average net profit of preceding three years on corporate social responsibility (CSR) activities.

It is also possible to start sole proprietorships, partnerships, limited liability partnerships, cooperatives, one-person companies and joint Hindu Undivided Family (HUF) businesses. All these options are available to residents. Proprietorships and partnerships by non-residents are also permitted with the approval of the central bank, the Reserve Bank of India (RBI). Non-residents can establish branches and liaison offices of companies already incorporated elsewhere under the Foreign Exchange Management Act, 1999 (FEMA). But branches and liaison offices face more controls, especially with regard to inflows and outflows of foreign exchange.

There are three regulatory bodies involved for inflow and outflow of foreign exchange. These are the Department of Industrial Policy and Promotion (DIPP) in the Ministry of Commerce that frames the industrial policy and issues updates on the FDI policy, the central bank called the Reserve Bank of India (RBI) which makes rules and regulations and periodically issues circulars, notices and clarifications under FEMA and the Foreign Investment Promotion Board (FIPB) in the Ministry of Finance. Investments can be made by non-residents in equity shares, convertible debentures and convertible preference shares of an Indian company, through the automatic route or the government route. Under the automatic route, the non-resident investor or the Indian company does not require any approval from Government of India for the investment. This applies to a wide range of investments, almost everything, except broadcasting, print media, civil aviation, satellites and core investment companies that have to be routed through a specified administrative ministry under the government route for prior approval of the Government of India. Even under the government route, once investment has been permitted, additional investments would no longer require prior approval.

Since 2017, FDI is allowed more liberally. Foreign investment under the automatic route is now prepermitted up to 49% even in the defence sector and private security, insurance, single-brand retail trading, telecom and petroleum refining. Full 100% FDI under the automatic route is allowed in white label ATM operations, financial services, greenfield investments in pharmaceuticals, asset reconstruction companies, railway infrastructure construction, operation and maintenance of suburban corridor projects through public–private partnerships (PPPs)[1], high-speed train projects, dedicated freight lines, rolling stock including train sets, and locomotives/coaches manufacturing and maintenance facilities, railway electrification, signalling systems, freight terminals, passenger terminals, infrastructure in industrial parks pertaining to railway line/sidings including electrified railway lines and connectivities to main railway line and Mass Rapid Transport Systems. Automatic FDI is also allowed in mining (except titanium mining), oil and natural

---

[1]Source: http://dipp.nic.in/sites/default/files/FDI_Circular_2015.pdf.

gas exploration, airport projects, construction development projects (including development of townships, construction of residential/commercial premises, roads or bridges, hotels, resorts, hospitals, educational institutions, recreational facilities, city and regional-level infrastructure, townships), industrial parks and broadcasting carriage services for other than news channels.

Non-resident Indian investments are treated as domestic investments. FDI of 100% is also allowed in all limited liability partnerships. Manufacturers can conduct both wholesale and retail trade including e-commerce. Foreign portfolio investors can invest up to 74% in private banks. FDI up to 100% under the automatic route is allowed in e-commerce, floriculture, horticulture, cultivation of vegetables and mushrooms under controlled conditions, development and production of seeds and planting material, animal husbandry (including breeding of dogs), pisciculture, aquaculture, apiculture, plantations of tea, coffee, rubber, cardamom, palm oil, and olives, and services related to agro and allied sectors. The DIPP website http://dipp.nic.in/ has details of this liberalisation in its policy document dated 28 August 2017 accessible from this website. The small print associated with each sector should be carefully read because tiny provisos exist and a few exclusions exist for certain specific sub-sectors even where automatic FDI has been permitted.

The DIPP policy pronouncements[2] are notified by the Reserve Bank of India as amendments to the Foreign Exchange Management (Transfer or Issue of Security by Persons Resident Outside India) Regulations, 2000 (notification No. FEMA 20/2000-RB dated 3 May 2000). These notifications take effect from the date of issue of press notes/press releases, unless specified otherwise therein. In case of any conflict, the relevant FEMA Notification will prevail. The procedural instructions are issued by the Reserve Bank of India vide A.P. (DIR Series) Circulars. The regulatory framework, over a period of time, thus, consists of acts, regulations, press notes, press releases, clarifications, and all of it is transparently available with regular updates from https://www.rbi.org.in/. It is simple to access when you know what to look for.

There are just a few sectors where FDI is prohibited such as in lottery business, online lotteries, gambling and betting including casinos, chit funds, nidhi companies, Trading in Transferable Development Rights (TDRs), real estate business or construction of farm houses (the expression 'real estate business' excludes development of townships, construction of residential/commercial premises, roads or bridges), manufacturing of cigars, cheroots, cigarillos and cigarettes, of tobacco or of tobacco substitutes. Activities/sectors not open to private sector investment–domestic or foreign are atomic energy, railway operations (other than permitted activities mentioned above), foreign technology collaboration in any form including licensing for franchise, trademark, brand name, management contract for lottery business and gambling and betting activities.[3] Spedding (2016) provides an informative guide for organising business in India.

---

[2]Source: http://dipp.nic.in/sites/default/files/CFPC_2017_FINAL_RELEASED_28.8.17_0.pdf.
[3]Source: http://dipp.nic.in/sites/default/files/FDI_Circular_2015.pdf.

Entry Criteria and Preferred Forms

The entry mode decision for the Indian market involves demand analysis of the existing product range and another demand analysis of the technologies that could foster new products. This is easily achieved by market research and through closer contact with identifiable sets of potential partners and customers, especially in industrial technologies, processes and products. The four principal modes of entry for Finnish firms in India are exporting, exporting and importing, licensing technology and joint ventures. It is also possible to just have branch offices, liaison offices or project offices. In determining the modality, it is important to consider the commercial intent, regulatory constraints and taxation. Branches run the risk of being treated as 'permanent establishments' for the purpose of international taxation. New joint ventures no longer require consent of existing Indian partners except for old collaborations prior to January 2005 where they still require it. This is an anomaly that will hopefully be removed in future. With the removal of limits and restrictions on royalty payments, franchise fees and brand licensing fees, franchises have also become an attractive entry modality.

Finnish firms like Kone, Fiskars, Huhtamäki and Wärtsilä Diesel (all successful Finnish firms in India) found it useful to consider many partners and several alternative locations before making their choices. The preferred mode of the successful Finnish firm has been a wholly owned subsidiary or a manufacturing joint venture with at least 50% participation in equity or a technical collaboration through licensing of know-how. But the list of Finnish manufacturing joint ventures in India is small and has grown modestly in contrast to Swedish joint ventures which have grown tenfold in ten years. Finland's pioneers in collaborative joint ventures consist of Fiskars (with Godrej) for scissors and knives, Huhtamäki (with EID Parry) for confectionaries, Kemira (with GNVC) for special grade fertilisers, Kymen Sukka (with Shiva) for socks, Nowo Development (with Charminar) in textile non-wovens and Kone (lifts and escalators), Wärtsilä (diesel generators, Nirafon for electronics), KWH Pipe (HDPE pipes) through own subsidiaries.

Technical collaborations exist in automatic data processing machines (ABB through own subsidiary), heat recovery (Ahlström with Emmas and Seppo Ralli through Ralli), synthetic fabrics (Metco with SWIL), telecom cables (NK Cables with Vikas), floatation machines, copper technology, smelting (Outokumpu with McNeilly Bharat, Hindustan Copper and Indo-Gulf Fertilisers & Chemicals) and lactose (Valio Engineering with Lacto Protein). New collaborations include Ivo Power with Power Grid, Valmet with Mechano Paper, Eco Technology with JVV and Diapek with Datamatics.

In terms of Dunning's model of FDI (Dunning 1997), the advantage of Finnish firms lies in proprietary intangible depreciable assets that may be exploited only in conjunction with other factor inputs. These are outbid from being constructed in the value chains of the domestic Finnish economy in the absence of scale economies implying access to markets a necessary prerequisite. For instance, the average efficient size of a paper mill has increased to 200,000 tonnes per annum (tpa) and the minimum efficient size of a steel plant is 2 million tpa. When manufacturing capacities and markets are located closer to the customer, the logic of minimising transaction costs begs the question whether returns on technology investments can be efficiently negotiated and reaped from a distance.

Technologies have become like tradable products, and there usually exist multiple sources and many national and international mechanisms for bundling technology and capital together. In a study comparing Japan and Finland, it was found that Finnish research and development investments as a proportion of GDP (at 2.2%) have matched that of Japan for decades but the conversion ratio to techno-commercial exploitation is barely 1% in Finland in contrast to about 50% in Japan. Another study on Finnish firms empirically demonstrated that the process of accumulating dynamic competencies as framed by Dosi and Marengo (Dosi and Marengo 1994) in firm-specific modes would be beneficial only if the results could be used in markets (Leiponen 1996). A later study of Tekes projects revealed that the Finnish conversion of innovation in techno-economic forms remained low (Koski 2008).

A section of Indian entrepreneurs interviewed lamented that Finnish technologies like wood–plastic combinations and furfural technologies could not be developed because of excessive emphasis on trade links instead of knowledge links. They were also critical of what they perceived as inflexibilities of management systems of Finnish firms. The sauna market was cited as an example by Indian hoteliers. Here, the business went to a Swedish firm because the Finnish business representatives were not paid adequate daily allowance for travel by their firm for visits to India (compared to visits to Brazil) and this posed a disincentive to business development. But the sauna market is far from saturated, and there are plenty of opportunities because the hospitality industry is growing at double-digit rates.

Technologies are considered proven when they become techno-commercially successful outside their country of origin. One of the reasons Finnish technologies are not sufficiently supported by investments is that many of them have not been proven outside Finland. The openness of the Indian business to new technologies and the low cost of experimentation presents opportunities to Finnish firms. Technologies implemented in India automatically qualify for funding under development finance such as World Bank's IDA loans for the developing world lowering the threshold costs of worldwide technology diffusion. The preservation and development of innovation capabilities of Finnish firms could thus be enhanced.

The experience of Finnish managers in India is quite mixed. Some of them have taken to India like a duck to water and found trustful supportive business partners and gradually assimilated life and work in a new environment. Others, including some Finnish entrepreneurs and managers from the Finnish companies in India listed in Chap. 6, complained of the time taken to negotiate terms in India, of diffused decision-making, the unreliability of their Indian counterparts in keeping to datelines and the stresses associated with infrastructural inadequacies and paperwork. Some Finnish managers in joint ventures also complained that they were not sufficiently supported in planning and organising for themselves and their families in India in important aspects of life and work. This needs attention too because ease of living in India for expatriates is as important as ease of doing business.

Positioning Talent

There is also a choice to be made whether the management team would be a combination of local talent and expatriates or to rely almost entirely on local talent. This requires policies on how long expatriates would be posted on assignments in India, how their social and economic security in the home country would be safeguarded, and also on the handing over and taking over processes which are crucial for continuity not only for techno-commercial reasons but also for relationships with other actors in the business environment. The delegated authority for communications will have to be established so that managers are not always looking for what to say on the basis of permissions from headquarters and are able to foster credibility among the role sets they relate to in government and business circles.

One of the reasons that Valmet struggled in China during the period 1982–94 was that Valmet managers were not only marooned away from their Finnish moorings but had little support from their home company headquarters to assimilate their lives (including family lives) and work and access social networks. Some of them were so lonely that they turned alcoholics. If Finnish managers have to separate from family life to live and work as singletons in remote places (factories in India can be away from cities), the stresses accumulate. It may also affect the company's governance or performance as Wärtsilä (with so much experience of India) realised after discovering a fraud in their Mumbai office, long after it began to completely depend on a team of Indian managers.

Financing a Business in India

Investible capital that comes to India in the form of foreign direct investment (FDI) is generally unrestricted except for the defence sector on ground of national security and a few other sectors like retailing on grounds that small retailers are not ready for competition from large foreign retail chains. Debt borrowings from abroad are regulated under RBI's external commercial borrowing (ECB) guidelines. Loans, securitised instruments such as fixed rate bonds and floating rate notes, preference shares, buyer's credit, supplier's credit are all treated as debt.

The capital markets in India are regulated by the Securities and Exchange Board of India (SEBI) established by parliamentary statute for development and regulation of securities markets including stock exchanges and other financial intermediaries. Public issues of shares to raise capital require SEBI rules and norms to be followed.

SEBI is mandated to protect the interests of investors, outlaw unfair trade practices and insider trading, and monitor capital issues by public subscription. The Indian Capital Market is one of the oldest markets in Asia. The Bombay Stock Exchange (BSE) was established in 1875 and the National Stock Exchange (NSE) in 1992. There is also a Forward Markets Commission under the Ministry of Finance for the regulation of futures and forward trading in commodities.

Initial public offerings (IPOs) are a source of capital for new firms as well as exits by founding promoter investors. There are three categories of IPO investors. Qualified institutional buyers (QIBs) include mutual funds, foreign portfolio investors, and domestic and foreign venture capital. Individual investors constitute another important category who can bid for up to Rs. 200,000 worth of shares in a public issue. Non-institutional investors (NIIs) that may comprise entities or individuals may also bid for shares. Typically, banks and financial institutions act as underwriters for public issues. However, their underwriting risk does not extend to undersubscription, only to full and timely payment of subscriptions procured by it. All public issues have to follow SEBI guidelines. There are minimum dilution requirement set based on the post-issue capital of a company calculated at the offer price. Half of any public issue has to be allotted to QIBs, and in some cases 75% has to be allotted to QIBs (if a company's net tangible assets are below Rs. 30 million or if its pre-tax operating profit is less than Rs. 150 million or if its net worth is below Rs. 10 million or if the aggregate of the proposed issue and any previous issues in the same financial year exceeds five times the pre-issue net worth of the preceding financial year) because they are considered informed investors. For any issue where QIBs are being allotted 50% of the issue, 35% of the issue is for NIIs and 15% to individual investors. Undersubscriptions in NII or individual category can be made up by oversubscription in the QIB category. If QIBs are to take 75% of an issue, 15% for NIIs and 10% for individual investors would be the distribution.

Intellectual Property Rights (IPR)

The IPR system in India is more than 150 years old and is TRIPS compliant because India is a signatory to the TRIPS agreement on Trade Related Aspects of Intellectual Property Rights, 1995, and has amended all national laws accordingly. IPR protection is available for patents, trademarks and service marks, copyrights, designs, geographical indications, plant varieties protection, trade secrets, domain names and integrated circuit layouts. India is a member of international conventions and treaties such as the Paris Convention on Protection of Industrial Property, 1883, the Berne Convention for the Protection of Literary and Artistic Works, 1886, the Universal Copyright Convention, 1952, and the Patent Co-operation Treaty, 1970.

Competition Policy in India

Indian competition law bans abuse of dominant position, anti-competitive agreements, combinations which cause appreciable adverse effects on competition and regulates mergers and acquisitions. The Monopolies and Restrictive Trade Practices Act, 1969, targeted monopolies to prevent restrictive and unfair trade practices and was primarily made to curb concentration of economic power in the licensing era. This has been repealed and replaced by the new Competition Act. The Competition Commission of India (CCI) is mandated under the Competition Act, 2002, to abide by the principles of 'rule of reason' for promoting business and protecting the interests of markets and the consumers. Amendments in 2007 and 2009 to this act have strengthened its provisions. Horizontal agreements or cartels are not illegal, but suspected defaulters can be required to show that they are not in breach of any of the objects of the Competition Act. In the case of vertical agreements, the complainant has to prove its case before the CCI. The Competition Act provides for appeals against CCI decisions to the Competition Appellate Tribunal. Like its counterparts in EU and in USA, the Competition Act has extraterritorial jurisdiction under Article 32 of the act for anti-competitive activity outside India.

Environment Protection Law

India is one of only three countries after Australia and New Zealand to have a 'Green Court' for the adjudication of environmental matters with jurisdiction over all civil cases where a substantial question relating to environment (including enforcement of any legal right concerning the environment) is involved. The main environment laws cover environmental clearance procedures for industries, hazardous waste identification, environmental audits, limits on effluent and waste discharge, soil erosion, desalination, forest conservation, species extinction and endangered species, habitat fragmentation, depletion of natural wealth, indiscriminate mining, restrictions on industrial activity in eco-sensitive and eco-fragile zones and environment impact assessment requiring prior environmental clearances in respect of specified projects under the Environment Impact Assessment Notification, 2006, issued under the Environment Protection Act, 1986.

Taxation

The Indian tax year is from 1 April to 31 March. The system of taxation is a combination of direct taxes on incomes and indirect taxes where the tax is levied on the producer or seller of goods and services and which would typically get passed on to the consumer. In the case of GST, there is a system of seamless crediting in place. The GST is leviable by both the centre and the states giving a dual GST structure on every transaction throughout the supply chain. Fast track registration has been enabled permitting digitally signed invoicing. Export-oriented manufacturing is exempt from domestic tax laws in the special economic zones (SEZs).

In the case of income tax, different rules are applied to tax on salaries (deducted at source) from tax on capital gains, income from house property, profits and gains from trade or profession and income from other sources. The applicable rates are revised annually based on the Finance Bill along with the Union Budget proposed by the Finance Minister on 1 February. Changes in indirect taxes are given effect immediately even though the Finance Bill tabled in Parliament may be passed on a later date. Businesses need to reserve time to implement price changes on the day of the budget presentation which is telecast live.

Special Features of the Indian Market

Consumers are price conscious and look at 'value for money' closely. Regulatory authorities learn from doing, and learning curve effects can produce some inconsistencies in their decision-making. The media is quite independent, but there is also a lot of 'paid news' which is both a source of opportunity and a reason to be sceptical when reading or viewing news channels. The judicial system is strong but slow. Government contracts involve tenders that go through multiple rounds for technical bids and commercial bids.

Infrastructure is improving, but it is not of the same standard as a developed economy. This should be factored in when calculating time that would be taken for travel and freight transportation. Warehousing would need special care because of pests, water leakages, heat and humidity. Indian markets are both segmented and fragmented requiring attention to product and service positioning, consumer protection laws, and law and order conditions of localities. Business does not have high status because it is perceived as almost synonymous to profiteering. This makes reputational risk a serious matter, and preserving credibility for external constituents would involve constant vigil and communications. Bad news is the currency of the media, and care has to be taken also over residual matters that may become flashpoints.

Business communities are a pervasive feature of the Indian business scene—the Marwaris, Sindhis, Parsees, Khoja Muslims, Chettiars, Baniyas, Gujaratis and similar others, too many to be mentioned, would be found concentrating certain trades and businesses. It would be difficult to make generalisations about India because of the diversity of phenomena on all possible dimensions. It would always be possible to show a counterfactual to any generalisation made about India.

The main advantages in organising for doing business in India are availability of a wealth of natural resources, including minerals, a talent pool of well-educated English-speaking human capital, responsive entrepreneurial communities of practice, a democratic system with an independent justice system, a written constitution of governance and rights, constitutionally guaranteed equal treatment of foreigners, a free media, an organised system of money and capital markets and the automatic route to invest in most sectors for 100% FDI-owned entities. These offset some of the difficulties that have also been candidly discussed in this chapter. There are several good books of a general nature that have been written to introduce visitors to India's culture, business milieu, Indian etiquette and civilisational appeal, tourism horizons and which also provide an overview of the business environment (Parpola 2005; Kumar and Sethi 2005; Padmanand and Jain 2000). But since I have not come across any book that introduces a potential business prospector to organising for doing business in India, this chapter has tried to fill that gap.

The very first research paper on opportunities in the Indian market for Finnish companies was published by Fintra and co-authored by my first Finnish student, Heikki Tulkki (Korhonen and Tulkki 1996). Yet, in 2012, the Academy of Finland's evaluation of Finnish research programme LIIKE noted that there had been much neglect of international business research in Finland (Blackburn et al. 2012). Finland–India Economic Relations had particularly suffered. Between 1996 and 2012, there was hardly any resource allocation for researching the organisation of Finland–India business in either country because as far as international business was concerned, Finland was preoccupied with China and Southeast Asia and India was only prospecting low-hanging fruit in English-speaking countries. There were the SITRA studies which have already been commented upon in a previous chapter as being out of touch with reality and too eager to reinforce prevailing opinions and myths. Some were over-optimistic (such as Bhide et al. 2006; and Grundtröm and Lahti 2005), and some were outright cynical (Bound et al. 2006).

Very few studies researched business organisation in the Finland–India context between 1996 and 2012. These were the baseline study supported by ETLA (Mathur 1998), two studies supported by Liikesivistysrahasto of which one prospected the scope of Finland–India Economic Relations (Mathur 2007), the CIMO-UGC supported action research doctoral dissertation that studied the experience of Finnish investors prospecting for business in India (Mattila 2008) and the study on the business opportunities for Finnish Cleantech SMEs in the Indian market (Larikka 2012). Much more research is required to prospect the organisation of business opportunities in India. Studies are needed from the perspective of developing more understanding of which entry modes would suit what kinds of business investments and in which geographies (in a large country) would ease of business and opportunities best match capabilities. The sets of capabilities that would require to be developed and nurtured would also have to be given attention. Sweden regularly brings batches of Swedish business leaders, entrepreneurs, government officials for management development programmes to the IIMs. But Finland does not. The general information made available by the Embassy of India (2019) in Helsinki, the Finnish–Indian Trade Association (2008) or Team Finland at the Embassy of Finland (2016) in New Delhi is quite basic in nature and outdated. And therein lies the difference. In 2006, the size of Swedish and Finnish business investments in India was comparable. Both have grown since then but Swedish business in India is now about ten times that of Finland.

References

Artto E (1995) Performance and international competitiveness of listed industrial groups 1986—1994: Finland versus Sweden and Germany, working paper W 131, Helsinki School of Economics and Business Administration, 1995

Bhide S, Mukhopadhyay D, and Singh D (2006) Prospects for India-Finland Cooperation, SITRA report 62, Helsinki

Blackburn Robert, Liukkonen Paula, Alasoini Tuomo (2012) Research programme on business know-how LIIKE 2 2006–2009. Academy of Finland, Helsinki

Bound K, Leadbeater C, Miller P, Wilsdon J (2006) The new geography of innovation: India, Finland, science and technology, Sitra Report 71, SITRA, Helsinki

Dosi G, Marengo L (1994) Theory of organizational competencies in England In: RW (ed) Evolutionary concepts in contemporary Economics, University of Michigan Press, pp 157–178

Dunning JH (1997) Towards an eclectic theory of international production: some empirical tests. J Int Bus Stud 11(1):9–31

Embassy of Finland (2016) Finland-India business guide, New Delhi

Embassy of India (2019) India-Finland business links, Helsinki

Finnish-Indian Trade Association (2008) in Finnish. http://www.kauppayhdistys.fi/suomi-intia/news/cemat-raportti–intiassa-voi-olla-suomalaisyrityksen-helpompaa-toimia-kuin-kiinassa-001.html

Grundström E, Lahti VM (2005) The India phenomenon and Finland, Sitra report 56, Helsinki

Johanson Jan, Vahlne Jan-Erik (1977) The internationalization process of the firm: a model of knowledge development and increasing foreign market commitments. J Int Bus Stud 8(1):23–32

Johanson Jan, Vahlne Jan-Erik (2009) The Uppsala internationalization process model revisited: from liability of foreignness to liability of outsidership. J Int Bus Stud 40:1411–1431

Korhonen K, Tulkki H (1996) India as a market for Finnish Business (mimeo), working paper, FINTRA, Helsinki

Koski, Heli (2008) Public R&D subsidies and employment growth-microeconomic evidence from Finnish firms. Research Institute of the Finnish Economy, ETLA, Helsinki

Kumar Rajesh, Sethi Anand Kumar (2005) Doing business in India. Palgrave Macmillan, New York

Larikka M (2012) Strategic alliances as an international entry strategy: finnish cleantech SMEs and the Indian market, University of Turku

Leiponen Aija (1996) Competence, innovation and profitability of firms, discussion paper 563. ETLA, Helsinki

Luostarinen R (1994) Internationalisation of finnish firms and the response to global challenges UNU-WIDER, Helsinki

Mathur A (1998) Finland-India Economic Relations: a twinning study of trade and investment potential. ETLA, Helsinki. Reprinted 2002

Mathur AN (2007) Finland-India business in 2007: context, trends, prospects and challenges, Indian Institute of Management Ahmedabad, March 2007

Mattila, S (2008) Multi-content revelation through dialogue processes: a study in understanding the hermeneutic primary task of small groups in the context of Finland and India. Doctoral Dissertation, Tampere University of Technology, 2008. Publication 738. Tampere University of Technology Press, Tampere

Padmanand V, Jain PC (2000) Doing Business in India. Sage, New Delhi

Parpola Asko (2005) Intian Kulttuuri (in Finnish). Otava, Keuruu

Spedding Linda S (2016) India: the business opportunity. Eastern Book Company, Lucknow

Chapter 8
Organising for Business in Finland

Chance favours only the prepared mind.
Louis Pasteur

What is a prepared mind? It is a ready mind, an open mind, a mind that knows or a mind that maybe just intuits what it doesn't know, questions its own tacit assumptions, and is drawn to inquiries to look more deeply beneath the appearances of things and perhaps behind the conventional narratives about the way things are or aren't the way they were.
Jon Kabat-Zinn

Abstract The notion that business models successful in India can be tweaked and transplanted in Finland is one of the leading causes of business failures of Indian investors in Finland. Those Indian companies that have succeeded engaged in adequate preparations and approached Finland with an open mind to understand Nordic business models, with sensitivity to Finnish management systems, structures and processes and appreciate the cultural and institutional differences. Overcoming the liability of foreignness and the liability of outsidership are two key aspects of foreigners organising for doing business in Finland. This chapter introduces the reader to the business ecosystem in Finland and to the logic of the Nordic Business model for organising to do business in Finland.

Introduction

Foreigners prospecting business opportunities in Finland are often unaware of Finland's institutions and how the trine of national, regional and local authorities affects business initiatives in Finland. Despite the attractiveness of opportunities, support from parastatal agencies to private enterprises and the ease of establishing a business in Finland, not even a patriotic Finn would claim that it is easy to do business in Finland. The rigidity of factor markets (capital, labour, housing, land, etc.) is legendary. The restructuring frequency of domestic enterprises is high, and the failure rate of foreign enterprises (of all sizes) is even higher. It took IKEA (from neighbouring Sweden) decades before it could get land from municipalities to establish itself in Finland. It is amusing that members of the Finnish-Indian Trade Association who are well settled in Finland and most of whom have not much contact with India anymore do not say anything to encourage Indians towards doing business in Finland. But they take pride in circulating opinions that it is easier to do business in India compared to China (Finnish-Indian Trade Association 2008).

The proportion of foreigners in the resident population of Finland at under 2% is the least in the whole world. Overcoming the liability of foreignness (including namial liability of a foreign name) is the first challenge. The Finnish language is the country's distinguishing identifier. The linguistic and religious homogeneity is widespread. This is despite tiny minorities of the Swedish speaking people in Southern Finland and along the Western Coastline and the Samis in the Arctic Circle. There are linguistic hurdles for foreigners to access laws, rules, regulations and participate in civic or economic life on equal terms despite pervasive social equality. But none of these challenges is insurmountable.

For those businesses that are able to overcome the liability of foreignness and the liability of outsidership, the opportunities Finland offers are not only considerable and within grasp but among the best available in Europe. The rewards and incentives are significant, and the arena of action can be functionally vast with oligopoly as the norm, and geographically extensive covering the whole of the European Economic Area. The key to doing business successfully in Finland is to have a sound business idea, to understand the society and its institutions and to rapidly overcome the liability of foreignness and outsidership. This is not achievable by proxy and has implications for mindful presence and for modes of entry.

Paradox of Continuity and Change

According to Tove Jansson's literary character Moominpappa, *'There are some things one can be absolutely sure of: sea currents, the seasons, the rising of the Sun, for example'*. The foundational premise in any Finnish business is that despite risks and uncertainties, planning is important. In Finland, management and control processes require detailed planning to be credible. The Indian way of doing things is to have short planning horizons, to learn from doing and avoid deeply etched recipes. The first tension in Indo-Finnish interactions lies here. The paradox here is that innovations are welcome and change overwhelms continuity in Finnish business firms all the time, but there is an expectation and belief that dynamic capabilities can be evolving in a way that strategy, tactics and operations would always be synchronised and expressible in a roadmap.

Practicalities of Organising for Business in Finland

In Chaps. 4 and 5, many of the issues that are rooted in managing cultural differences and institutional diversity have already been discussed, including taxation and the legal system. As a member state of the EU, the convergence between the Finnish competition policy, intellectual property rights, environmental protection and other such matters with what is prevalent in the EU is profound and does not require as extensive a discussion as Chap. 7 merited on India. Hence, the focus in this chapter is on five important pillars of organising to do business in Finland before introducing the business ecosystem and explaining the waves of changes that are presenting new ways of organising around emerging opportunities.

Language

English is widely spoken by Finns, especially in the cities and towns and in professional circles. In Helsinki, bus and tram drivers are able to converse in English. But Finland's national identity coalesced around the Finnish language. So it is important for foreigners who are planning to have a long-term association in doing business to learn the Finnish language. Even if a professional were to invest in language learning as a part-time effort alongside a day's work, it is possible to reach what is called Level 3 in the language proficiency levels in about two years. A person learning the language would already be able to speak a little and understand something of the language in about six months. A language is a window to a culture, and this is the best way to begin to understand Finnish mindsets. Mingling with people outside the workplace through sports or cultural activities would aid not only the language learning effort but also provide a social network outside the professional network. The liability of foreignness can be mitigated by blending into the country's way of living and working.

Credibility

It is imperative that all business matters from starting a business (whatever its form) to running the business be dealt with timely, cleanly and completely. The patentti-rekisteri hallitus (PRH) is the single window registry for incorporation of business entities, appointment of auditor, submission of annual returns, registration of intellectual properties, and for searches to get information about any business in Finland, including its directors. The staff are helpful, speak English and can provide all the paperwork that requires complying with. Since the level of disclosure is 100%, it reflects very poorly if your potential business partner was to check out your business entity and find that you have misrepresented facts or have not filed annual returns or are in any kind of default. By the same logic, feel free to access the information from PRH if you are planning to do business with another firm to know its state of health.

Taxation

Tax records are public in Finland. Finns take pride in paying taxes properly. Care has to be taken to pay taxes regularly; file returns in time in respect of both direct taxes and indirect taxes such as VAT. If a business is temporarily being suspended, it is essential to apply to be taken off the VAT register (if VAT registration has been done) and it is always possible to get listed in the register again. Otherwise, monthly returns must continue to be submitted even if there was no business income. A tax dispute would require resolution and cannot be left unresolved because the Finnish system has efficient institutionalities to initiate recovery through enforcement. Since official notices from authorities would be in Finnish or Swedish, translation services may be required. The first attempt should be to approach the local authority that has made an assessment if it is believed to be incorrect. In many cases, clarifications can lead to immediate rectifications. But if a tax dispute persists, then you may require the services of a tax lawyer who can represent you before an Assessment Adjustment Board without delay because there is a time limit for handling of such cases.

Banking and Insurance

It is always useful to have a bank account with a Finnish Bank that has direct correspondent link with a bank in your home country. That saves on intermediary bank commissions and also expedites transfers under the SWIFT/IBAN system. In India, it is not the foreign banks or private banks that have the most direct correspondent links abroad but the large public sector banks such as State Bank of India, Axis Bank and Bank of Baroda. In the Finland–India context, the bank of choice is the State Bank of India which has the largest number of branches and a direct correspondent link with Nordea Bank in Finland. For insurances, there are many choices in Finland for general insurance. Individuals resident in Finland should preferably take out legal insurance, medical insurance, travel insurance and professional liability insurance policies with the same insurance company where they have taken out their home insurance policy because then they would have seamless coverage for personal and professional exigencies. The Indian insurance companies, National Insurance and Bajaj Alliance, and the Finnish insurance companies, Tapiola and Fennia, are among the efficient ones.

Community Relations

Every community (municipality) in Finland has its own sense of solidaristic identity. Every community has its own distinctive logo and often also a descriptor such as '*hunaja kaupunki*' or 'honey community' for Akaa and '*mansikka paikka*' or 'strawberry place' for Valkeakoski. The Finnish communities exercise local governance over decisions for new firms over issues such as land leases, subsidised office facilities, sharing in salary costs of labour force/trainees in the interests of promoting employment. A business should be able to articulate its vision, express its hopes and needs and generously support local initiatives that raise the community's well-being. It would be useful for any new business to get acquainted with the local community authorities that deal with support to businesses and labour market registrations. Here, new businesses would discover incentives for locating in the local area and also get access to educated and skilled workforce seeking employment. Often, workers introduced by the employment office from among the unemployed job seekers can be initially engaged for trial periods as trainees with wage costs shared between an employer and the unemployment office's placement budget.

The Business Ecosystem in Finland

The business ecosystem in Finland is quite distinct and unique. It is different from Anglo-American models, practices and styles. Despite being in Europe, Finland's business ecosystem is different from French, German, Hispanic, Italian or Russian ways of functioning and organising. Its resemblance to the Swedish, Danish or Norwegian business ecosystem is also superficial. The fundamental wealth creating mechanisms in the society are anchored in the trine of community, collectivity and collegiality. These are often brokered by the government (through the ministries for foreign trade, labour and economic livelihoods, and finance) and parastatal institutions such as Tekes, VTT and SITRA that shape both factor and product markets. Koski (2008), Koski and Tuuli (2010) and Koski and Pajarinen (2011a) provide an excellent insightful perspective of how the Finnish system functions and how insiders use the system for business development. Foreign commercial presence in Finland as a company would enable participation in this model for firms and for people employed in them even if the capital was to be sourced from abroad.

Basic information for doing business in Finland is available in books such as Liede (2005). But Finnish sources including Team Finland's Finland–India Business Guide (Team Finland 2016) are not written from the perspective of an investor looking into Finland from the outside to examine how business opportunities can be structured in Finland. They also do not deal with 'ease of living' in Finland. Finns would be surprised that Helsinki is considered a hardship posting by Indian diplomats. To fill this gap, there is an interesting Handbook for Survival in

Finland (Matthan and Matthan 2014) that deals with practicalities of everyday life. Matthan and Matthan (2014) bring out several curious sides of Finland. They analyse shopping for daily needs and question whether a high-cost society is the same as a high standard of living society. They also vividly bring out the incestuous nature of insider groups that control access to public resources. Some of what they write is confirmed by Koski and Pajarinen (2011b). Waqar (2011) provides another insightful perspective analysing experiences of expatriates in Finland in engaging with the Finnish business ecosystem.

The Finnish business system is partly based on a common Nordic model which supports social benefits and social services for child care, maternity and paternity alongside a free universal school education system to ensure a high labour participation rate for males and females. Taipale (2014) and Pyrhönen (2015) provide two contrasting perspectives of the way social innovations in Finland that have affected living and work-life. The key aspect of the Finnish ecosystem is the logic to keep consumption demand high with a production system where stimulation of exports with an open economy plays an important role in constantly expanding production possibility frontiers.

The success of Finnish firms has been built on technological excellence combined with risk aversion and risk syndication in business-to-business deals in niche spectra of industrial products in forestry, metals, energy and techno-electronics including telecom. The small size of the economy resulted in high degrees of concentration in consumer markets with few entrenched players and little incentive to develop international brands.

Finnish models of industrial structures and markets are typically constructed (by policy-makers, firms and researchers) on the assumption of vertical clustering with assured linkage effects (that occur with a lag) engineered through subsidies and linkage incentives brokered between the clusters through Finnish banks and parastatal funding institutions. In such a model, there is a high dependence on handholding by the State and its parastatal agencies. Paradoxically, pioneering technologies often fail to be exploited because of this since the wait for market signals can be long and uncertain when neither an enterprise waiting for signals from its government nor the officialdom trying to read signals over long geographical and mental distances may know how, when and where to leverage harvestable innovations. Investments in telecom technologies between 1950 and 1980 could be reaped only after bundling all the public investments and proprietary technologies of Televa and Salora and others into the flagship, Nokia in the 1980s invoking a 1939 law that placed restrictions on Ericsson and Siemens in Finland and protected Nokia from international competition until 1994[1] (Ahonen 1995).

Historically, the 'typical' Finnish firm was a large multidivisional enterprise for the production of intermediate industrial goods (Lilja et al. 1991). This was a legacy

---

[1]*This breathed new life into Nokia when it had no profitable business left in its portfolio having sold all major divisions, one by one, during the 1980s in a decade of decline that culminated with its then Chief Executive committing suicide.*

originally rooted in the economic hegemony as part of Sweden and later Russia and reinforced by war reparations (amounting to 300 billion dollars) forced on Finland after World War II. As capital-intensive raw materials converters, such firms were incentivised to become knowledge-intensive and technology innovating. The nexus of large firms with small and medium enterprises (SMEs) has limited the functions of SMEs as ancillaries, skill providers and project coordinators for the large firms or as local players catering to a limited geographical segment (Lilja and Tainio 2005; Tainio and Lilja 2005).

The transition of the Finnish business ecosystem during the 1990s was triggered by a deep recession and financial crisis following the evaporation of barter trade with the Soviet Union when it disintegrated in 1991. For the first time, many Finnish firms began marketing their products that had hitherto been traded through federated national marketing. In the days of barter trade, the Finnish Oil Refining Corporation, NESTE played a major role because it held the monopoly over oil imports in exchange of which it had authority to offer equivalent exports. Since the central bank also played a role in enabling competitive devaluations, it brokered the production and marketing quotas among firms involved in the barter trade. Potentially rivalrous firms did not really compete with each other in the market place during that period.

The stock market has not played a major role in raising equity capital for Finnish firms. Banks and financial institutions have been the main capital providers to enterprise. Investors in Finland would have to source initial capital from abroad and then leverage that for further funding from Finnish parastatals or local communities or industry-academia consortia if the nature of the investment can justify that in line with Finnish priorities.

The tripolar economic model revolved around three constituencies, businesses, farmers and workers. Each of these constituencies had their own syndication and their own banks. With barter trade abolished and a series of competitive devaluations in the 1990s, there was overheating of the economy due to an asset price bubble. This was sparked by real estate brokers behaving like bankers and bankers behaving like brokers. When the banking crisis erupted, this led to the collapse of one bank (SKOP), and the merger of KOP with SYP to survive as Merita, which later became Nordea. This brought about significant restructuring of the tripolar economic model.

During the same period, there were isomorphic pressures brought about by European integration processes culminating in a series of treaties beginning with the Maastricht Treaty that created the European Union (EU), the formation of the World Trade Organisation (WTO) and the introduction of the Euro. The founding treaties of the European Communities that constituted the European Coal and Steel Community with a High Authority (that later became the European Commission) were essentially aimed at promoting Franco-German peace and security in the Saar and Ruhr regions of Central Europe. The Treaty of Rome, 1957, that brought about the customs union as amended by the Maastricht Treaty (1992), Amsterdam Treaty (2000) and the Nice Treaty (2003) later formed the core of EC Law. Finland joined the EU from 1995 and adopted the Euro since inception of the Euro in 1999.

The EU directives have set limits to the support and aid that governments can provide to firms in their jurisdiction. Despite that, due to the principle of subsidiarity in the EU treaties, the Finnish system is able to provide a lot because municipalities and public institutions have an interest in gaining workplaces by offering free or subsidised infrastructure support in the form of land and buildings. Also, many big firms have established their own financial nests abroad as have the wealthy. The dependence on Finnish bank capital has reduced, but this is also eroding commercial bank profitability. The level of foreign ownership in Finnish financial and non-financial enterprises is rising. How this is happening without significant inflows of FDI is a mystery.

Finnish Business Corporations: Genesis and Trajectory

The first waves of international trade and commerce to impact Nordic Europe came from the Hanseatic League organised from Lubeck (with connections to Hamburg and Bremen) in Germany around 1159 and officially founded in 1356. The Hanseatic League (also known as the Hanse or Hansa, Hansa Teutonica or Liga Hanseatica) was a business syndicate of merchant guilds and their market towns. The Swan Label in Finland in use even today is a legacy of the Hansa trade despite the fact that no town of Finland was officially affiliated with the Hanseatic League. The league was actively trading in Viipuri, Turku, Naantali, Rauma, Raasepori, Häme, Ulvila and Porvoo (Salminen 1999).

The Hanseatic League provided a framework for international economic relations to the Nordic and Baltic regions stretching from Germany and Poland in the East to Viipuri and Turku in Finland and Bergen in Norway in the West. The league aimed to protect merchant guilds' economic interests and privileges across a string of affiliated cities and countries that became trade routes. Some of these trade routes remain important. The Hanseatic cities had their own legal system and even armies for mutual protection and aid. Despite this, the organization was not a State, nor could it be considered a federation of city-states. Only few cities of the league enjoyed autonomy and liberties comparable to those of a free city-state. From its moorings in North German towns in the late 1100s, the league dominated Baltic maritime trade for three centuries along the coast of Northern Europe. Its reach extended from the Baltic to the North Sea and inland during the Late Middle Ages. Eventually, its influence waned after 1450, and finally after 1669, it got subsumed by German nationalism. But the historical connect with Germany has remained, and despite a negative balance of trade, Germany remains Finland's largest trading partner and many Finnish imports from India are being sourced via Germany. There is a huge potential here to organise for Indian exports identified in Chap. 3 that Finland can import directly from India at a lower cost and thereby also reduce its trade deficit. For Indian exporters, this is the low hanging fruit that they could organise to pluck.

From the 1860s when wood chips could be converted into paper, Finland's 'green gold' presented a source of economic value with value-added manufacturing. Repola (which owned United Paper Mills better known as UPM), Kymmene, Enso-Gutzeit and Metsä-Serla were the largest of the paper companies of Finland. UPM merged with Kymmene to form UPM-Kymmene in 1995 and in response, Enso-Gutzeit (originally a Norwegian enterprise that was nationalised by the government of Finland after independence in 1917) and Stora (of Sweden) merged in 1997 to create Stora Enso, the world's largest paper company. The trigger behind these mergers was the amalgamation of KOP (Finnish speakers' commercial bank) and SYP (Swedish speakers' commercial bank). The refusal of the Finnish government to rescue SKOP, the workers' Savings Bank signalled a new era of weaker trade union power and restructuring of paper manufacturing capacity away from Finland became possible.

The strong Finnish paper industry (euphemistically called 'forest industry' in Finland) with about 15% of world market share was instrumental in stimulating demand for other industries such as industrial machinery (Valmet, now morphed into Metso; Ahlström, Rauma Repola and Tampella), sawmills, pulp mills, chemicals, shipping, shipbuilding, road and rail transportation and technology consulting (Jaakko Pöyry and Ekono) with multiplier effects for the economy until the 1990s. But this meant that the macroeconomic policies were influenced by the wishes of influential elites associated with these industries. This also impacted political representation in the medium term. The other impetus came from war reparations to the Soviet Union in the form of manufactured goods contributing to a strong engineering and metallurgical industries in addition to the magnetic pull of the paper industry described above. Ships and Icebreakers were among the products of this era.

The Nokia Phenomenon

When Nokia was expanding in its mobile telephones business, it needed Indian IT prowess but wanted the Indian IT firms that it was contracting with to establish themselves with registered incorporations in Finland for unijurisdictional control. Wipro was among the first in this wave of Indian foreign direct investments when it acquired Rovaniemi-based Saraware for €25 million. Saraware, a company with 200 employees already provided design and engineering services to Nokia at the time. With ownership of Saraware, Wipro established a development centre in Tampere, Finland, in November 2002. Yet, despite being one of the first Indian IT service giants in Finland, Wipro found it extremely difficult to function because they had not prepared for cultural and institutional differences. Wipro expected Finnish employees to be able to work beyond regular office hours at short notice oblivious to the Finnish culture where work time and personal time do not mix.

Sasken was the next Indian IT company that Nokia invited. Sasken acquired the Finnish firm Botnia Hightech for €35.5 million. Sasken expected Finnish employees to be responding to clients in USA and India between mid-summer and mid-August and were surprised that Finland has a long common summer vacation period at that time. The business levers for these Indian enterprises were adaptation and arbitrage, and it was in adaptation that they faced enormous difficulties.

The Rise and Fall of Nokia and the new Nokia

Nordic Mobile Telephony (NMT) based on analog technology made cellular phones possible in 1981. The first NMT phones were car phones. The battery life was short, and they were bulky. Then came miniaturisation where Benefon succeeded in reducing the weight to about 100 grams and the size to less than 100 mm (about 4 inches).

The early adoption of mobile telephony enabled the wide use of telematics for government services. An important aspect of organising for business in Finland would be preparedness to work in and around a high-tech digital society where decision-makers connect quickly, and despite risk averseness, the whole society is capable of bringing about transformations very rapidly. The context is a post-Nokia mobile telephony society struggling to find new 'Nokias'. A word about the old Nokia is therefore pertinent.

The shift from smokestack industry to electronics and telecommunication was associated with Nokia's rise from the ashes after it had reached near bankruptcy and sold off almost all its businesses. At the end of the 1980s, Nokia had eleven business verticals with thirty different businesses with a market capitalisation of less than $1 billion (Tainio and Lilja 2005, p. 68). And it was accumulating losses. Those interested in understanding what brought about Nokia's phoenix-like reincarnation as a telecom, and later networks giant, should read Pertti Ahonen's account of how Finland was restructured during the 1990s (Ahonen 1995) which provides fascinating glimpses of public–private partnerships and startling evidence of how Nokia was rescued. Briefly, the government gave away mobile telephone technology that it had from the days when mobile phones were made in government factories for the Finnish and German army (with German and Swedish technology) during World War II. With technological advances in miniaturisation of integrated chips since that time, the mobile phones could now be made much more compact.

What really kick-started the process was the early deregulation of the telecom industry that enabled Sonera and Radiolinja to build GSM networks alongside existing networks in the early 1990s. For a while, Nordic Mobile Telephony (NMT) and GSM both coexisted and competed. The first Nokia GSM phone was created in skunkworks in Tampere by a small group of Finnish electronicians. This enabled Nokia to raise $3.5 billion in 1993 through private equity placement with a few American institutions and get listed in 1994 on the New York Stock Exchange. In 1998, after Motorola's Iridium satellite telephony project failed to take off, Nokia became the world's leading producer of mobile phones. That Nokia is no more. But like it is said, 'The King is dead. Long Live the King', Nokia Siemens Networks has become a new 'Nokia' and even been renamed 'Nokia'.

The Growth of Finnish Firms Beyond the Forest Sector

This second wave of internationalisation after the initial boom from the paper industry has shown a more lasting effect than even the so-called Nokia effect which is now history after Microsoft acquired Nokia Mobile Phones. The changes in Finland have to do with new institutional features where the power of banks has been replaced by boards and the parastatal institutions are also reassessing their role and interventions vis-a-vis subventions. There is greater participation in international alliances and negotiations over standards, platforms and global arrangements. As a result, information and communication technologies (ICTs) have overtaken the paper industry as Finland's largest export sector and are in turn in the process of transformation for leveraged initiatives in those parts of the world where Finnish enterprise never previously existed. Koski et al. (2001) were among the first to study the scope and limits of Europe's emerging ICT clusters and compared the ICT 'Great Central Banana' of Europe with 'the Small Nordic Potato'.

Due to high-end network capabilities in and around the new Nokia and many others, Indian IT industry is in a uniquely placed advantageous situation to connect with the wave of 'big data'-led businesses that need both IT solutions and networks. There cannot be a better hub than Finland, and it is not surprising that some Indian IT firms have already arrived. The complementarity also arises because Finland's own ICT competitiveness is small and can be expanded only when augmented by high-end IT skills in quality and volume. Organising for this gap involves a combination of Mode 3 foreign commercial presence and Mode 1 cross-border electronic supply. The levers here are aggregation and arbitrage in the short term and assimilation of new know-how from learning by doing in the long term. The appropriate entry modality here would be establishing a wholly owned subsidiary or a greenfield enterprise in the form of a private limited company.

The Finnish gaming industry, the music industry and Finnish intermediation with portals and cloud technology have witnessed considerable growth since 2001. Other such examples include the potential worldwide replication of the Finnish distributed enterprising model in collaboration with an Indian partner, and another is the technological breakthrough that resulted from the joint endeavour between Thermax from India and Oilon from Finland in energy technologies relevant in marine applications and cogeneration solutions involving product-service linkages (Mattila and Mathur 2007). The appropriate entry modality in such cases is establishing a joint venture.

The third wave of changes on the anvil since 2015 involves big data, cloud computing, and new platforms of business-to-business collaboration. These are associated with the emergence of focused international multinational corporations in place of conglomerate types of portfolio-based business enterprises and new sectoral specialisations such as in clean technologies, solar energy, waste recycling, biomaterials, bioenergy and more distributed enterprising. Organising for these can involve new enterprises in Finland and in India.

Media and Multimedia

When the Finnish Journalist, Pia Heikkilä, based in Delhi writes in Helsingin Sanomat (Hesari), the reach is much more than 5.6 million Finns in Finland due to digital editions of Hesari. As of now, there is no Indian journalist based in Finland with the exception of a Malayala Manorama connection in Oulu who writes blogs but not articles in any Indian newspaper. And media is much more than journalism. It includes advertising, publicity, virtual media, multimedia and various forms of online electronic media that form part of the burgeoning communications industry. Comparisons are important to examine the financing of public service companies (from income taxes collected or licensing fees), newspapers that command a price (Finland has about 190 such), of regulation of commercial broadcasting, press freedom and support, access to broadband Internet, smartphones, tablets, choice of newspapers, magazines, print directories, direct mail, outdoor hoardings, displays and the cinema.

Understanding how the fourth estate functions is an important element in doing any business in any country. High-performing countries tend to have active media players and opportunities. At a time when national media markets are converging into a single marketplace connected by Google, Apple, Facebook and Microsoft, politics and economics are both interdependent with media. With multimedia and convergence between various forms of media as witnessed in international trends where news channels, entertainment companies and the film industry have blended into forms that almost blur such distinctions, the time is ripe for the Indian movie industry (Bollywood) or any of the media players to make the leap into the European market through Finland.

Finland has the largest proportion of the newspaper industry publicly traded on the stock market with four of the five biggest Finnish newspapers listed on the Helsinki Stock Exchange. The Sanoma Group, a diversified media conglomerate, controls 30% of the total national circulation with its flagship newspaper, Helsingin Sanomat, that has the kind of independent reporting, quality and coverage comparable to Washington Post in USA, The Guardian in the UK, and The Asian Age, Millennium Post or The Hindu in India. About 23% of Sanoma is owned by the Jane and Aatos Erkko Foundation (which also administers the Erkko family owned shares after the death of Aatos Erkko in 2012) and 10% by Antti Herlin, the business magnate whose family owns Kone Corporation, a major manufacturer of escalators and elevators worldwide (Ohlsson 2015).

The Herlins, through Mariatorp Oy (owned by publisher and Editor Niklas Herlin, brother of Antti Herlin), also have stakes (together with Ilkka-Yhtymä of

Seinäjoki) in the second largest newspaper group in Finland, the Alma Media Group that publishes Aamulehti and Iltalehti and which also owned MTV Oy before divesting broadcasting to the Bonnier Group. Keskisuomalainen and TS Group are the two other big players in the Finnish media market. Sanoma and Alma Media each had more than half a million paid circulation of their newspapers with Sanoma at 499,000 and Alma Media at 457,000 according to the verified figures of 2013. Only Schibsted and Amedia of Norway and Bonnier of Sweden had larger circulations in the Nordic Area. In television viewing, MTV3 (owned by Bonnier of Sweden) and Nelonen (Channel 4, owned by Sanoma) between them lead in Finland cornering about half of the total viewership.

Investment Thinking of Indian Industry

The success of Indian firms, initially in insular and protected markets under the licensing system, was based on access to a large and growing domestic consumer market and limited exports. Now, there is fierce competition among brands and in industrial products, and some firms are getting caught in growth stalls. Indian companies with a growth stall could be examining new opportunities in Europe. Large Indian industrial houses have mainly looked to countries other than Finland, including to neighbouring Sweden, Denmark, Norway and the Baltics. That makes it interesting and worthwhile to find out what is being missed and what new business may be organised and how.

With imports growing faster than exports, India's external balance could make a negative contribution to GDP growth in future years unless exports diversify and returns on outwards foreign direct investment return to India as factor incomes. Another worrisome feature is the decline in organised sector employment in India which can mainly be stimulated through services where the employment elasticities with respect to rates of growth are higher than in manufacturing.

Indian Investments in Finland

The first Indian investments in Finland date back to the 1970s and 1980s when Indian migrants in Finland set up restaurants and ethnic shops in the Helsinki area (Helsinki, Espoo and Vantaa) and in Tampere and Oulu. Oulu also became the site of the first Indian media investment firm established by a member of the Manorama Family that owned the largest selling regional publication in India in the 1980s.

There were several notable joint venture collaborations in Finland between Finnish and Indian enterprises that blossomed in the 1990s and the first decade of the new millennium. These included ventures in publishing, educational conferencing ventures, an R&D collaboration for new designs of boilers and burners

(Mattila and Mathur 2007), and in a range of biomedical engineering and forest industry related enterprises. At that time, Finland was neither on the Indian radar as an important investment destination nor was India regarded as a source of foreign direct investments into Finland. So this was happening without much fanfare and did not even register with the governments as an augury that could have good effects for both countries in future.

Although there are now more Indian businesses in Finland as noted in Chap. 6, organising to connect B2B, B2C and G2G initiatives is still not free from difficulties. In Chap. 9, this is discussed more elaborately. The historical lack of interest has left some inertia despite the flurry of recent G2G bridges mentioned in Chap. 6. This apathy is worth recapitulating.

In the 1990s, when I asked the then Joint Secretary in India's Ministry of External Affairs (MEA) responsible for the Finland desk, the MEA did not even have a complete set of existing bilateral agreements and neither did the Indian Ambassador in Helsinki have a complete set. At my urging, it is to the credit of his successor, Rajesh Nandan Prasad, who diligently compiled the complete set at both ends a few years later. Diplomats could then refresh themselves as to what agreements existed and what more could be done. That paved the way for more cooperation agreements and also the long overdue revision of the double taxation avoidance treaty. At about the same time, when I broached the subject with the then Finnish Ambassador to India, Benjamin Bassin, that Indian investments were beginning to happen in Finland and whether Finland would welcome such investments by providing more information about Finnish business laws to prospective Indian investors in English, he expressed shock and responded with just two words, 'What audacity!' It left me with the distinct impression that the awareness deficit about India in Finland and Finland in India was profound and widespread and not without reasons.

Since then, there have been several Indian investments in Finland that have been discussed in Chap. 6. As part of the Finland–India Economic Relations Project, case studies of Indian investments in Finland are being researched, documented and published separately, to invite reflections from all concerned as to what went well, what did not and why some of them collapsed. These take time because, in many of these, it seems that the Indian investor has a perception so different from his Finnish counterparts that it becomes important to listen to both sides patiently. But one important insight from this work in progress has already arisen. In all cases of failures of Indian investments in Finland, there was inadequate preparation from the Indian side, and along the way, the conversation between the Indian and Finnish partners became a dialogue of the deaf. What distinguishes the successful firms from failures was preparation, learning quickly from doing and taking help from those who know to overcome the liability of foreignness and the liability of outsidership.

References

Ahonen P (1995) Restructuring Finland, Administrative Science, 1995 C 1, Working Paper Series, University of Tampere

Finnish-Indian Trade Association (2008) in Finnish. http://www.kauppayhdistys.fi/suomi-intia/news/cemat-raportti–intiassa-voi-olla-suomalaisyrityksen-helpompaa-toimia-kuin-kiinassa-001.html

Koski H (2008) Public R&D subsidies and employment growth-microeconomic evidence from Finnish firms. Research Institute of the Finnish Economy, ETLA, Helsinki

Koski H, Pajarinen M (2011a) The Role of business subsidies in job creation of start-ups, gazelles and incumbents. Research Institute of the Finnish Economy, ETLA, Helsinki

Koski H, Pajarinen M (2011b) Do business subsidies facilitate employment growth?. Research Institute of the Finnish Economy, ETLA, Helsinki

Koski H, Rouvinen P, Ylä-Antitila P (2001) ICT clusters in Europe: the Great Central Banana and the Small Nordic Potato. Research Institute of the Finnish Economy, ETLA, Helsinki

Koski H, Tuuli J (2010) Business subsidies in Finland: the dynamics of application and acceptance stages. Research Institute of the Finnish Economy, TLA, Helsinki

Liede H (2005) Doing business in Finland. KHT Media, Helsinki

Lilja K, Räsänen K, Tainio R (1991) Development of Finnish corporations: paths and recipes In: Näsi J (ed) Arenas of strategic thinking, WSOY, Helsinki

Lilja K, Tainio R (2005) The nature of the typical firm in Finland. In: Lilja K (ed) The national business system in Finland, Helsingin Kauppakorkeakoulun Julkaisuja B-60, Helsinki School of Economics, Helsinki

Matthan A, Matthan J (2014) Handbook for survival in Finland. Findians, Oulu

Mattila S, Mathur AN (2007) OILON-a case study. IIM Ahmedabad Casebank, Ahmedabad

Ohlsson J (2015) The Nordic media market. University of Gothenburg, Göteborg, Nordicom

Pyrhönen N (2015) The true colours of Finnish welfare nationalism. SSKH Skrifter 38, University of Helsinki, Helsinki

Salminen T (1999) Finland, Tallinn and the Hanseatic League—Foreign trade and the orientation of roads in Medieval Finland. In: Mauranen T (ed) Traffic, needs, roads; perspectives on the past, present and future of roads in Finland and the Baltic Area. Finnish Road Administration, Helsinki, pp 29–37

Tainio R, Lilja K (2005) The Finnish business system in transition: outcomes, actors and their influence. In: Lilja K (ed) The national business system in Finland, Helsingin Kauppakorkeakoulun Julkaisuja B-60

Taipale I (2014) 100 social innovations from Finland. Finnish Literary Society, Helsinki

Team Finland (2016) Finland-India business guide. Embassy of Finland, New Delhi

Waqar U (2011) Cross-cultural challenges to expatriates in Finland. University of Vaasa, Vaasa

Chapter 9
Future Trajectories of Finland and India

> *You think to make your living from tailoring, but then somehow money comes in through goldsmithing which had never entered your mind.*
>
> Rumi

> *The future is that period of time in which our affairs prosper, our friends are true, and our happiness is assured.*
>
> Ambrose Bierce

Abstract This chapter charts out the possibilities and challenges in the future traverse of both countries—Finland and India, and how this can bring new opportunities, but also new risks and new social and political innovations. Finland and India both have their residues as well notable transitions impacting their social and economic traverse. In Finland, the demographic transition is associated with the twin burden of skill shortages alongside endemic unemployment unless employment-intensive knowledge services are leveraged for commercial uses beyond Finland. In India, the demographic dividend period would be ending and service internationalisation would hold the key to new forms of international product-service linkages. Far-reaching political, economic, social and institutional changes are likely to characterise complexities for inclusive governance, raise costs of competitiveness, and require active labour market policies for work and income creation alongside more open international economic relations in both countries.

Introduction

The world is at the cusp of entering the third decade of the twenty-first century with considerable residues and flashpoints. FDI Global investment flows fell by 23% in 2017 (UNCTAD 2018) and according to forecasts, there are very few destinations where inwards FDI continues to grow alongside domestic institutional investors. India is one such.

According to the Economic Survey of Finland (OECD 2018), Finland had a lower GDP per capita in PPP terms than the other Nordic countries and it had a higher unemployment rate and tax rate compared to them. In Finland, the continuing demographic transition is associated with the twin burden of skill shortages alongside endemic unemployment among the young and rising costs for supporting an ageing population. Policies would have to explicitly or implicitly deal with the depopulating areas of the country that could become vulnerable. Finnish Communities at risk (Mathur et al. 2003) could need rescuing. Land prices, costs of housing, and wages can fall. Availability of essential public goods and services including health care and living support to the elderly in small communities would require new forms of organisation and delivery. Technology-intensive employment creating knowledge services for commercial uses beyond Finland would have to be a high priority for 'Business Finland'. Oksanen (2017) raises questions on how traditional links between the labour market and social security provisioning are weakening and models based on "self-employment, platforms, sharing economy and joint providership" may have to be developed.

The demographic dividend of a young population in India has a finite time horizon and is geographically skewed. Benefit transfers to the poor, especially distressed farmers and segments of the population requiring subsidised health care and infrastructural upliftments will continue to require budgetary allocations for at least another decade, possibly two decades depending on the growth rate. India will also continue to have substantial defence and internal security expenditures necessitated by being a country with an army geographically next to an army with a country. There have been many dire forecasts about India. Selig Harrison who presciently predicted the demise and disintegration of the Soviet Union also predicted that the centrifugal forces in India would tear it apart (Harrison 1960). Harrison was right about the Soviet Union and wrong about India. That did not happen and is unlikely to happen. But there are other challenges that can pose serious problems.

India's Challenges

Foremost among these are challenges from environmental degradation (water, air, solid waste disposal, pollution). Air pollution, water scarcity, city traffic congestions and waste management are four problems of India that are at present out of control. The Government of India is doing a lot to solve these challenges but any truthful account would be amiss if it did not draw attention of the reader to this. Nine of the world's ten most air-polluted cities are in India. Air pollution is an unsolved problem, and this health hazard is affecting large parts of North India and also cities in Central and Western India. About 375,000 tonnes of solid waste would require collection and treatment in India daily by 2025.

The water table has precariously lowered in several parts of India. Climate change can cause some of the coastal areas to get submerged with rising sea levels, melt some of the Himalayan Glaciers, and result in floods, to begin with, and then drought. Running water is already rationed in many Indian cities in the sense there is no continuous water supply and households have to store water in personal tanks.

In West Bengal, there is arsenic in the groundwater. The arsenic content in the Kolkata groundwater made it unsafe to drink a long time ago. Water shortages can create stresses for households and also for farmers that grow water-intensive crops like paddy. Efforts are on to recharge the West Bengal water table and redress urban sewerage and drainage systems. In all the urban development near the new Bengaluru airport in Karnataka, there is no piped municipal water supply and water is supplied by tankers. Cities like Mumbai need to accept the monsoon rains as part of seasonal inevitability, not an aberration. Solutions have to be found for drainage of water-logging.

Traffic congestion is severe in all metro cities. Cities like Bengaluru have terrible traffic congestion. The planners failed to anticipate the IT boom and that Bengaluru would become the world's leading IT hub even two decades ago. In Gujarat, the world's fastest expanding cities Surat (the world's diamond hub) and Ahmedabad (a knowledge cluster with extraordinary growth in population by in-migration and public investments and private entrepreneurship) demand urban planning on a scale the world has not previously witnessed. In West Bengal, flyovers have been constructed to cope with the traffic congestions in Kolkata which holds the world record for the least public space in any urban agglomeration at 6% of the space (compared to the city planning norm of reserving 25% area for roads, gardens, parks and open spaces). Bangkok in Thailand is a distant second.

In India, the demographic dividend period would be ending by 2030 except in a few States in the East and North East of India. The median age in India was 28 in 2018. About 12 million working-age persons join the labour market in India every year but the formal sector employment absorption is small at less than 1 million. This human capital crisis is one of the biggest challenges facing India in the two decades ahead before India approaches a stable population level. Attempts to skill people through programmes and schemes can augment the supply side, but active labour market policies would have to be instituted to stimulate labour demand. The reliance on the growth rate to stimulate labour demand as a derived demand will not solve the problem of growing unemployment which has the potential to disrupt social harmony and security in the country. Rising unemployment is depressing wage rates and more than 10 million are being added to the unemployed labour pool annually. The pace of infrastructure development and service internationalisation hold the key to new forms of international product-service linkages.

Four Critical Questions

In twinning paired comparisons such as that of Finland and India, four questions of interest to business firms and policy-makers for the future arise:

Q.1 What would be the long-term scope for mutual or global harvesting of income flows from innovations seeded through techno-commercial collaborations between

Indian and Finnish firms in the technology services sector after taking competitiveness into consideration?

Q.2 How would enterprises in the two countries reach out to business opportunities in the other territory for third-country markets?

Q.3 Which of the four GATS entry modes would emerge as modes of choice for Finland–India business in the twelve different categories of GATS services?

Q.4 How would policies of the two governments and practices of Finnish firms in India and Indian firms in Finland converge or diverge or simply leave voids for structuring business investments?

These questions are not easily answered but need to be kept in view as the future unfolds.

Economic Growth Models

The difference between India and Finland in their respective models of growth will remain. The development and industrialisation process is being telescoped in India. In pursuing self-reliance to the point of mistaking self-reliance with self-sufficiency, initial industrialisation of the Indian economy covered a wide range of industry with a presence in every sector. The new economic policies introduced since 1991 involved significant departures from protectionism. Yet, India is not likely to abandon public planning for the development of infrastructure, energy, transportation, telecom, and urbanisation. But there will be more public–private partnerships. Significant public outlays from national finances are annually allocated for investments in these sectors. This demand translates into investment opportunities and acts like a magnet for foreign investment flows. Business opportunities will remain open to the domestic and foreign private sector except in a few defence and strategic sectors where Russia, France, and the USA may continue to dominate in G2G deals.

In Finland, the small open-economy imperatives alongside the welfare State's commitments on guaranteed minimum thresholds of individual entitlements for private and public goods will involve a balancing act between resources and public actions. For reasons that are well documented in studies (Koski 2008; Koski and Tuuli 2010; Koski and Pajarinen 2011a, b), the economic rates of return on subventions in Finland for innovation and support for new products, business models, international business can be greatly improved.

Paradox of Competitiveness and Collaborations

Competitive business circumstances in the world enable players to configure value constellations in numerous alternative ways. An evaluation of the competitive position of existing and potential service businesses requires judgements about the capacities of societies as a whole, because relative competitiveness of nations changes over time. The Finnish welfare state modulates consumption of wealth generated by economic activities. Discussions about the future of the welfare state with an ageing population and the demographic shock have tended to be inward-looking towards creation of jobs in non-traded services for the care of the infirm and the elderly, or in work such as taxi driving, truck and van driving, kiosk catering, cleaning services, data entry, call centres, automation of business and consumer services such as banking and insurance, services for the enjoyment of the arts and aesthetics for the affluent retired, tourism, and coordination services, temporary work in social services, public health care and education. Yet, banking, primary health care, postal services and bus and commuter services have contracted in Finland. Finland will continue to import several goods (and some services) from abroad which requires attention to collaborative services and foreign direct investments abroad to maintain healthy balance of payments for the future.

Both Finland and India are experiencing changes in the business environment in many dimensions. Indian enterprises lulled by the comfort of a large and growing domestic market also need to wake up to the way the world is changing and others are catching up. 309 out of India's largest 500 companies (by size in sales), in the ET-500 list of companies of 1995 disappeared from the list by 2005 and another 101 declined in their rankings because strategic leadership was not alert to competition and opportunities (Aggarwal 2010).

There is belated, reluctant yet growing acknowledgement that future challenges require combining of technological expertise with high-level business know-how and business competence in both countries. Ten areas of focus can be identified:

1. Knowledge-intensive Business Services
2. Flexible Organising: using global aggregators such as the FAANG (Facebook, Apple, Amazon, Netflix and Google)
3. Inter-firm networks in the global economy that can substitute and complement what single firms do to the point that single firms may diminish/vanish
4. Emergence and development of the electronic marketplace: threats and opportunities
5. Motives and Powerbases of Owners and top management teams
6. New challenges related to governance jurisdictions of globally operating businesses
7. Entrepreneurship and its facilitating environment
8. Future of work and how individuals will locate in the nexus of contracts that populate the continuum from markets to firms
9. The ecological responsibility of enterprises and business management in the global economy
10. The partitioning of tasks in the pulls between competition and collaboration.

In Finland, this process is associated with transformative development of information technology and telecommunications and emergence and maturing of capital markets. The 'old' industrial economy continues its decline in volume and value of production and markets. The nature and structure of the new economy are gradually taking shape in some predictable ways but there are also plenty of surprises. This concerns macro-level phenomena with changes in sectors, markets, networks and societies driven by global forces, as well as micro-level phenomena with changes in the way work is organised, how demand patterns are changing and the initiatives of enterprises.

The evaluations of business acumen by the Academy of Finland provide many pointers. One of the weaknesses noted in Finnish international cooperation is *"that 'international' in Finland tends to be interpreted as American, or close to American, with some consideration of Nordic colleagues"* (Jönsson et al. 2006). The same report also raised other issues: *"One may ask whether there is an overproduction of Ph.Ds, and is the time ripe to expand post doc research funding in Finland?"* and questioned *"whether the quantity of academic publications are the right measure for a programme oriented towards the specific challenges of Finnish companies in a globalised world"*.

Downsizing Trends in Finland

The Finnish word '*supistanut*' (denoting contraction/shrinkage that has taken place) has gained alarming currency in Finland since 2014 with significant contractions of consumer services in public and private sectors. Besides postal services, banking services, and primary healthcare services, universities have shrunk or been consolidated into shrinkage. Bakeries, grocery stores, bookshops and even chains of department stores have shrunk. The legendary Stockmann Department Store sold the country's leading book store franchise '*Akateeminen kirjakauppa*' to Bonnier, a Swedish media company and sold its grocery store business to the S-Group.

During the first half of 2014, many customers were surprised when one of the largest department store chains Anttila and its affiliate Kodin-1 were quite suddenly shut down by the K-Group that owned them. The reportage of this in Kauppalehti (a business daily paper) dwelt at length on the real estate area that was being swiftly emptied in Turku, Vantaa, Espoo and Tampere as if the swift emptying was a great accomplishment (Marja Vehviläinen, Kauppalehti, 9.7.2014). And spokespersons of asset management firms were quoted to convey how wonderful it was that instead of struggling and keeping built area uneconomically occupied, this was being emptied efficiently. But there was no mention of the human tragedy for employees or the shopping woes of customers of neighbourhoods like Espoonlahti or Myyrmanni. This signalled an era where change driven by the urge for more profits is welcomed no matter how painful the adjustments or how great the pain and costs for proximate communities of habitat.

Future Studies

Finland has a long tradition of future studies and of planning. Future studies prospect hopes, challenges, preferences to which planning responds. There have been several doomsday forecasts about the future incapacity of the Scandinavian and Nordic Countries to sustain their Welfare State models (Liu 1996). According to the Future Report (Government of Finland 2018), Finland will adopt a lifelong learning model for all population groups promoting more flexibility in the labour market. Planning in Finland articulates purposes, invokes tripartite cooperation between government, business and academia, and spells out the outlines of policies. According to the Government Programme[1]:

> Finland strives to influence international economic development to attain a stable and balanced development of the world economy and to promote Finland's own commercial and economic interests. The Government will prepare a cross-sectoral action plan on Finland's external economic relations. Implementation of the programme will support employment in Finland, particularly the internationalisation of small and medium-sized enterprises (SMEs).

A Government-appointed Expert Working Group chaired by the Matti Alahuhta, Formerly, President and CEO of Kone Corporation was tasked with examining the Finnish system of promoting exports and internationalisation. The Group concluded that *"effective promotion of Finland's external economic relations required reform of the current model because the economic operating environment had fundamentally changed since the time basic structures were created for the promotion of exports and internationalisation"* (Government of Finland 2013).

A new system has been put in place that focuses on increasing value added in Finland for creating jobs and well-being in the country[2]. There is a new policy for exerting influence in target markets such as India by ensuring a level playing field with international competitors. Resources allocated are not clarified though and the Finnish trade promotion team in Delhi functions from the Swedish Diplomatic Mission. At the turn of the Millenium, the Swedish and Finnish investments in India were at about the same level but Swedish investments in India have since grown tenfold in a decade and a half while Finnish investments are only marginally more than 15 years ago. It remains to be seen if Finnish business in India can be drummed up under a Nordic umbrella.

India was the tenth largest recipient of foreign direct investment with a record FDI of $ 60 billion in 2017 (UNCTAD 2018). In B2B business, India has developed from being a basic goods manufacturer in the decades just after independence to add sophisticated industrial capacity on the back of expanding consumer and industrial demand from the 1980s. India has become not only a large producer hub but also one of the world's biggest markets with significant international investors

---

[1]Publicly available at http://www.valtioneuvosto.fi.
[2]https://um.fi/team-finland-services-offered-for-companies-by-the-ministry-for-foreign-affairs.

and innovation hubs. B2C business and B2B business contribute to each other. The Insight Report 'Future of Consumption in Fast-Growth Consumer Markets: India' notes that the upper-middle income and high-income segments in India constituted a quarter of the households in 2018 and would constitute half of the households by 2030 (World Economic Forum 2019, p. 6). This increase of 128 million consumers in the high- and upper-middle-income groups by 2030 is the magnet for FDI to India by investors who know that there is new effective demand across a whole range of goods and services. In 2030, according to the forecast in this report, there would be 370 million Generation Z consumers of ages 10–25 using smartphones, digital media, digital consumption platforms comfortable with technology-enabled consumption models (World Economic Forum 2019, p. 11). There would be more than a billion Indians using the Internet.

A Finnish government policy document (Government of Finland 2013) acknowledges this by noting that *"Finland cannot build its growth solely on the European internal market but has to seek growth also from emerging countries outside the EU."* Value constellations in international business are organised internationally. This affects the competitiveness of companies and regional clusters and place limits on economic nationalism as a policy.

The increases in global population and economic growth, especially in Asia and Africa, will affect demand for natural resources as raw materials, and publicly funded infrastructure besides shaping the increased deployment of renewable energy, particularly storable solar energy at grid parity prices as part of addressing the challenges around climate change. The demand for environmental technology products and solutions can open up significant business opportunities for Finnish expertise. Finland would require to promote international activities of SMEs at all stages. The growing dependence on knowledge-intensive business services, digitisation, climate change initiatives, sustainable use of resources, southwards migration and ageing of population are trends that will have a profound impact on Finnish economy and business. There would be new opportunities for business activities around environmental and social sustainability. The traditional multilateral trade liberalisation within the framework of the WTO would be largely replaced with bilateral and plurilateral agreements. This would necessitate intensifying closer bilateral cooperation for better utilisation of international value chains.

Team Finland

The core idea of Finland's new network approach is: 'The external economic relations network: Team Finland' (Refer https://team.finland.fi/team-finland-lyhyesti accessed 28.10.2018). The main actors in this network are ministries, embassies, the Registrar of Companies and Patents (PRH), Tesi, Finpro, Tekes, Finnpartnership, Finnish cultural and science institutions, Finnvera, Finnfund and regional networks led by Centres for Economic Development, Transport and the

Environment[3]. The task is to develop an inter-institutional network for deeper cooperation driven by shared purposes. The network launched two collaborative programmes, 'Future Watch' and 'LetsGrow'.

Team Finland's 'opportunities' service, also intends to provide business intelligence. This consists of two elements. Launched in 2017, the Future Watch service specialises in medium-term assesments spanning a time period of 2–5 years. The 'Market Watch' service is for short-term market information for up to 2 years and includes analysis of 'the direct business opportunities available to companies and the risks involved in the political and business environment'. The risk analysis includes publications by the Ministry for Foreign Affairs on political risks in different parts of the world. But the achievements of these initiatives in India have been so far been quite modest. Business opportunities analysed and identified in this book have not yet been prospected.

'Team Finland' requires significant restructuring to be of effective support. In its present form and way of functioning, its expertise for setting goals and actualising priorities is weak. By the Finnish government's own candid admission, "*The Team Finland system lacks foresight and has a poor ability to utilise new opportunities and build partnerships*". (Government of Finland 2013). Finnish enterprises prospecting business in India such as Kone, Wärtsilä, Oilon, Stera and Trivitron succeeded without 'Team Finland'. The resources allocated to actors promoting exports and internationalisation are unlikely to increase substantially and if these continue to be poorly deployed, business customers will not be able to use them. Changes in the international business environment constitute the core stimulus. Especially, changes in how companies approach value chains would need to be tracked in all forms of internationalisation besides traditional exports subventions. In addition to supporting the early stages of the internationalisation processes of SMEs, more attention is required also for supporting companies that have already become established abroad and seek expansions in India.

An oversight mechanism, the Team Finland Steering Group reporting to the Prime Minister, has been established for planning and updating the constantly evolving international strategic initiatives. Shared premises for the Foreign Service and other actors representing Finland will have to be supported for synergies in the trine of operational efficiency, managerial effectiveness and economic diplomacy. Finnish Ambassadors have been made responsible for building and chairing the Team Finland network in countries where they are assigned. These are the persons who require high-quality international business management education for their work in a host country like India alongside participation in IIM networks and regional management associations. Else, the same pitfalls of trying to go 'bowling alone' would be repeated with overreliance on lobby groups such as CII and FICCI. CII and FICCI have not been very successful in mustering much corporate or entrepreneurial participation in business delegations to Finland beyond their own

---

[3]See http://www.vnk.fi/.

office-bearers and bureaucrats. This is not their fault. Unless their membership becomes more aware of business opportunities in Finland, it is unreasonable to expect them to mobilise business leaders for purposes other than sponsored tourism to Finland.

The expectation from Team Finland is that customer care would be holistic and satisfy needs of Finnish companies of all sizes in all sectors and at different stages of internationalisation. Team Finland is also expected to support inwards FDI to Finland. The Growth Channel project of the Ministry of Employment and the Economy is being adopted as the model for developing customer service around public services for stimulating exports and internationalisation. The scope would include financial, consultancy and support services.

One way of strengthening Finnish networks in India would be by increasing awareness of Finland as a nation that never colonised anywhere, a country that not only takes responsibility as a welfare State for its own society but is also genuinely concerned with international initiatives for security and prosperity. Any pilot projects by Finland in the problematic challenges in India ought to be highlighted in all interfaces. For instance, very few people know that there are three pilot projects for waste recovery and recycling by Finland in the National Capital Region.

The thinking that key priority areas for country branding can remain unchanged across all geographies needs reconsideration. Finland can differentiate itself through India specific projects with three main themes: cleanliness (including cleantech, quality of life, a well-functioning society, the Arctic, love of nature), design (products, services, cross-sectoral) and education and competence (including entrepreneurial start-ups). Supporting responsible entrepreneurship can give Finnish companies an additional leverage in India. Synergies benefitting both countries would include quality of education, commercial diffusion of the outputs of the research and innovation systems, and the availability of skilled labour. Finland stands to gain from affordable and undistorted access to procurement of natural resources, industrial intermediary inputs, and sustainable renewable energy investments at competitive prices. And a systems approach would be vital for the continuity of production and smooth-running logistics.

When Finland strives for reducing trade and investment barriers, it would also have to organise reciprocal facilities and accept international standards across a range of sectors and activities. To this day, Finns can get tourist visa on arrival in India but there is no reciprocal provision. Speedpost letters from India cannot be sent to Finland by the postal system. Finland also does not have a system of delivering registered post to addressees and registered post has to be collected from post offices by the addressees.

Horizontal trade policy solutions would have to be supported with sector-specific ones. The commitment to liberalise trade in services would require changes in rules and standards for the development of Internet services, Internet governance and efficient enforcement of the protection of intellectual property. Infringements of foreign IPRs by Finnish enterprises have occurred and come to light such as in the scandalous misappropriations of foreign designs by iconic Marimekko (Nelimarkka 2015), and by Nordea Bank of Niinivaara's patents reported by the Finnish media in Oulu. Such practices would have to be avoided to maintain higher standards of business integrity. The rules and regulations of TEOSTO and GRAMEX, the two parastatal bodies governing rights of authors and artists would have to ensure continuous updating and alignment with intellectual property rights protection under WIPO and WTO's TRIPS agreement.

Public procurement is likely to become more transparent in Europe and open to competition, first in the internal market of the EU and later possibly also across WTO membership. The oligopolistic nature of Finland's suppliers would also require to adapt. The waves for protective creativity and innovation would have to be balanced with the expansion of procurement with attention to prevention of counterfeit goods entering Finland. The growing demand for cleantech products and services worldwide including in India can improve Finland's export horizons and also the scope for participation in new projects as partners and co-investors.

Finnvera is committed to enabling Finnish exporters of capital goods to compete globally with credit lines. However, it would not be adequate for export industry to have access to a well-functioning export financing or subsidising mechanism. The system's risk-taking capacity will have to increase. This would be particularly important to encourage 'Made by Finland' in sectors of special relevance to Finland's industrial policy and to India's industrial policy with outwards foreign direct investment.

The principle of subsidiarity in the European Union requires Finland to go beyond piggy-back riding on EU initiatives with countries outside the EU. Except for cross-border electronic trade, the EU common commercial policy cannot enable expansion of EU-wide arrangements for expanding international business with countries outside the EU. Some preferential trade agreements have been negotiated by the EU by pooling the authority drawn from its membership as in the case of Japan effective February 1 2019, but it is being wrongly referred as a free trade area agreement because it does not cover all trade. There is no point in blaming slowness in outcomes from ongoing fruitless talks for an India-EU free trade area. More bilateral arrangements with India such as the ones made in biotechnology would be the way forward. Finnvera's activities could be directed to promoting the internationalisation of SMEs in India, besides credit insurance to small-scale enterprises. Parastatal agencies such as TEKES and FINPRO (both now part of Business Finland), SITRA, VTT would also need to develop their own management expertise and organising capabilities for doing business in India. Their limited success has bred overconfidence that their existing recipes for doing business abroad are adequate for doing business in India.

Finland's FinNode network was an early example of a successful model for closer ties between Finnish publicly funded organisations in relation to particular countries. The FinNode network succeeded in identifying and promoting new innovation-related phenomena. The FinNode framework included a steering group of the nine partners and a working committee consisting of its four primary members (Ministry of Employment and the Economy, Ministry for Foreign Affairs, Tekes and Finpro). Despite the proof-of-concept, and the success of FINNCHI in China, this key element of the Team Finland model was short-lived in India for reasons not altogether clear. Keith Bonnici who designed FinNode India and was expected to lead it was replaced at the last minute by someone else who led FinNode in New Delhi for a few years before moving to Vietnam after which FinNode was not heard of again in India. This damaged Finnish credibility in a society where institutional longevity breeds reliability, confidence and respect and short-lived tactical manoeuvres that promise a lot but deliver little are treated with suspicion.

The Finns are much better organised (although less prepared) for engaging with India, whereas Indians (government, businesses and academia) are inadequately organised and less prepared to engage with Finland. Some of the reasons are structural, others systemic. In the Indian structure, the Joint Secretary, Central Europe deals with several countries and Finland has not been a priority country. The threshold of trade engagement between Finland and India did not cross 1 billion euros until recently. Commerce and trade are structurally delinked from the Ministry of External Affairs (MEA) in India. There persist serious problems of awareness about Finland in India (inadequate availability of basic business information about Finland in English since the Finnish side says 'Come to our parastatal institutions' and few Indian businesses would ever take a first step without independently evaluating feasibility themselves, for which they have capacity, but not adequate information about Finland). There is also a lack of awareness about India in Finland. Finnish businesses have access to information about India in English, but many of them do not know what to get and where to get it. There is also the need to develop management acumen for organising internationalisation of nascent technologies in situations where risk-taking cannot be offset by the Host or Home Country Government.

The urgency of this from the Finnish side concerns fundamental economic loss of vitality from an ageing population, slow commercialisation of technology investments, mixed experience with trade-substituting investments. From the Indian side, the international utilisation of a young-skilled workforce, the existence of buoyant capital market for raising funds, slow diversification of the traditional basket of trade with Finland, and trade-substituting private foreign commercial presence that can enable dependant services, elimination of market barriers to trade in services, and of investments are some priorities inadequately reflected in the current set of special purpose vehicles and bridges.

The short-term time horizons of project modalities in business, academia and government are incapable of being sustained beyond their budgeted timelines. This is especially so when focus is on limited aims of large actors capable of doing things on their own who seek support mainly to subsidise their costs and acquire more commercial advantages. These can crowd out significant synergies for small- and medium-sized enterprises that exist and which do not enable Finnish high-tech products that require services to link commercially for innovations to be seeded.

Finnish Plans

Funding for Finnfund is to be increased for strengthening its special risk-financing activities. This is expected to improve the prospects of Finnish companies for participating in investment projects with greater risks, particularly in developing countries. But funding of Finnish firms is not a huge constraint for investments in India because of the buoyancy of the capital market, the size of public outlays available for infrastructure projects and the abundance of available private partners for greenfield joint venture initiatives and acquisitions.

The promotion of inwards foreign direct investment to Finland has so far depended on the activities of the foundation, 'Invest in Finland'. These operations would now be part of Team Finland so that the global network can identify new investment ideas. Finland Promotion Board is responsible for country branding within Team Finland. Funding services are to be developed for providing single-window funding alternatives with better attention to client needs, without being hampered by dispersed responsibility for granting funding among various agencies. This will take time to achieve. The funding application processing is to be piloted by Team Finland 'LetsGrow' service. This may enable the new model to be extended to all governmental initiatives and subventions designed to support internationalisation.

The development group for overseas travel subsidies for export promotion is jointly chaired by the Ministry for Foreign Affairs and the Ministry of Employment and the Economy. The purpose is to have collaborative road shows organised by Team Finland. It remains to be seen if relevant recommendations made in the investment strategy report "Investointeja Suomeen" by Jorma Eloranta are implemented. Holmström et al. (2014) believe that nimbler implementation of value-adding projects can be more valuable than breakthroughs that are slow to be commercialised. The government-financed internationalisation services within 'Team Finland' are now grouped into service areas with roles and responsibilities as depicted by the Government of Finland's model that is reproduced in Fig. 9.1 from the Government's own website:

Fig. 9.1 Team Finland internationalisation services

The thematic priorities identified by Finland are shown in Table 9.1 reproduced below from the Government of Finland website in order to examine and discuss this thematic initiative.

Table 9.1 Thematic priorities

Themes	Examples
Cleantech	• Energy and material efficiency • Renewable energy • Intelligent systems and services in urban environments • Industrial water treatment and purification • Sustainable mineral extraction industry • Intelligent energy systems, green ICT • Waste management and waste-to-energy • Air quality
Bioeconomy	• Chemical forest industry • Mechanical forest industry and wood construction • Biorefining, including bioenergy, biomaterials, biochemicals and biofuels • Bioeconomy equipment • Bioeconomy services, including ecosystem services
ICT and digitalization	• Games and gamification • Cybersecurity • Mobile/Wireless solutions and enabling technologies • Online trading • The Internet of Things, including the industrial Internet and the reinvention of traditional industry, intelligent transport
Life sciences, health care and foods	• Medical technology, including ICT for health and diagnostics • Healthcare and care service concepts • Healthy food, functional food, high-quality foods and raw materials • Food technology and food safety
Arctic competence	• Marine industry and logistics • Building, infrastructure and ICT • Energy and environmental technology • Mining and minerals
Creative industries and design	• Industrial design • Audiovisual production • Creative digital concepts • Design brands and fashion • Architecture
Education and learning	• Digital learning solutions, serious games • Vocational education • Teacher training • Consultation related to educational systems

The foresight model associated with the thematic priorities is depicted in Fig. 9.2, also reproduced below from the Finnish government website for comments and for the reader to view the model, for thinking about its scope and its limitations.

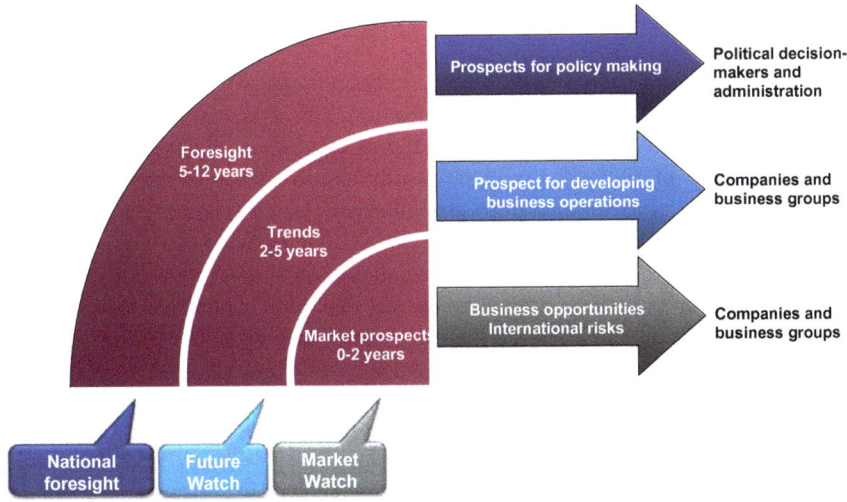

Fig. 9.2 Segments of market data and foresight. *Source* "Cooperative and continuous foresight: A proposal for a national foresight model". Prime Minister's Office Report 1/2014

According to the official announcement in the Team Finland: Strategy Update 2015 published from the Prime Minister's Office in July 2014, beyond the EU, "*Finland has three priority areas in trade policy during the current strategy period: The United States, Russia and China*". India is not yet a priority area. The Report cited explains that the resource allocation across geographies for Finnish business development overseas is determined on the basis of the following criteria: "(1) financial significance of the target country as measured by exports and investments; (2) market potential of the target country measured in terms of the economic outlook of the target country and the trade outlook with Finland in comparison with key peer countries but factor markets also need to be included, not merely product markets (3) demand for services measured through market research and consumer surveys; (4) the special added value of the government as a service provider measured by the government's role in the target country's economy, and the number of barriers to trade and business and (5) limitations arising from the location of the current Team Finland offices (including the location of embassies)".

Here, India features among the countries and regions included in Category 1: Russia, China (Beijing and Shanghai), the USA (East and West coast), India, Brazil and (in Europe) Germany, Sweden and Turkey (a non-EU European country that is in the EU customs union). It is noted that strong teams are needed in Japan, Korea, Southeast Asia and Africa. A balance is being sought between developing markets and neighbouring markets. The only fly in the ointment is that the Government of Finland wants to review priority countries annually as part of Team Finland (TF) steering. This time horizon militates against strategic initiatives and longer term actions that would be required when dealing with a huge country like India. It is noteworthy that due to the special governance characteristics of Finland, the country's cultural and science institutions, would have autonomy in functioning and could set their own time frames.

There are new initiatives in the offing. There are opportunities worldwide that people who have ties with Finland can introduce. The knowledge and contacts of international students, expatriates and foreigners living in Finland or who have previously lived in Finland would be worth mobilising. A web-based service (Finland Alumni), something akin to the Fulbright alumni that the USA uses, can serve as a shared forum for these groups.

International business information, especially about Finnish investments abroad and foreign trade in services, can serve as an input for evaluations of potential. Tilastokeskus (Finland's Official Statistical Agency) needs to reorganise statistics compilation methods and outputs. This work involves development of internationally harmonised definitions and methods, besides partnerships with other statistical agencies such as the Central Statistical Organisation (CSO) of India.

Policy Gaps

A better international business policy environment would not be achieved merely by increasing the outlays for Business Finland or its constituents such as Finpro and TEKES or SITRA in Finland. There are many challenges. One of them is to know whether the outcomes of R&D expenditures provide acceptable returns. The study by Eija Koski (2008) evaluated commercial adaption of outcomes from TEKES funded projects and published a dismal picture. The problem is that mandates need modifying or reinterpreting to systematically address all the factors that influence innovation processes, systems, structures including management of foreign direct investments inwards and outwards. An innovation policy must be holistic and innovation issues need to be connected with other enabling levers.

The innovation councils in Finland and South Korea operate quite differently. In Finland, the Council Secretariat has two employees, in Korea 160. This enabled Korean enterprises to identify management development as an important intervention alongside technology development already in the mid-90s. Finland remained in the hope that technology would bring about management adaptations through market adjustments. Market actors are not infallible, and public action is sometimes necessary to solve problems of missing markets.

Future of India

The brightest aspect of India is the growth story and the spread of development that fuels people's aspirations even further. India has always been an active participant in world affairs and is an influence on international regimes. More people have been lifted out of poverty here than anywhere else on the planet. India has produced leaders in every field of endeavour. In business, the alumni of Indian Institutes of Management occupy board positions in Fortune 500 companies such as Pepsi, Mastercard and Unilever. The CEOs of Microsoft, Google and Nokia are of Indian origin. As the world's most populous democracy, India has succeeded in remaining so with robust institutions.

The tension in relations with Pakistan over continued terrorist infiltration and with China over differences in perception about the northern border have different trajectories. With China, there is constructive dialogue and continued commitment to demilitarization of the border, whereas with Pakistan, it could remain a dialogue of the deaf for some more time due to sticky polarities. And India is likely to continue being the world's biggest purchaser of defence equipment. Within India, the disturbed areas in Chhattisgarh, Andhra Pradesh and the North-Eastern states of Manipur and Nagaland have shrunk and economic growth is changing the landscape with better infrastructure, more education and health facilities, and availability of renewable energy at grid parity. India is playing a bigger role in international fora but the size of its Foreign Service remains small and there is often more show than substance when diplomats are reduced to becoming event managers than messengers of hope for the many Indias of the future. India's challenges are on many dimensions, but the horizons of hope are not lacking.

The choice for both Finland and India is to engage with each other or to let inertia prevail. It is always possible to be tempted by Joxter, a literary character in Tove Jansson's 'Exploits of Moominpappa' who remarked, "Lets steer straight ahead and just roll and sleep and never arrive anywhere". But an awakening could take us into a new dawn.

References

Aggarwal A (2010) Examining impact of strategic leadership on effectiveness of business organisations, Ph.D. Dissertation, IIT Bombay 30th June 2010

Government of Finland (2013) Report of the Government appointed expert working group chaired by the Matti Alahuhta tasked with examining the Finnish system of promoting exports and internationalization, Helsinki

Government of Finland (2018) Government report on the future, Prime Minister's Office, Helsinki. URL: https://vnk.fi/en/government-report-on-the-future. Accessed 3 Feb 2019. Part 2 available at http://urn.fi/URN:ISBN:978-952-287-677-5

Harrison S (1960) India: the most dangerous decades. Oxford University Press, New Delhi

Holmström B, Korkman S, Pohjola M (2014) Suomen talouskriisin luonne ja kasvun edellytykset (The nature of Finland's economic crisis and conditions for growth). Memorandum to the Economic Council, 21 February 2014

Jönsson S, Bromwich M, Liukkonen P, Virolainen VM (2006) Research programme on finnish companies and the challenges of globalisation. Academy of Finland, Helsinki

Koski H (2008) Public R & D subsidies and employment growth-microeconomic evidence from Finnish firms. Research Institute of the Finnish Economy, ETLA, Helsinki

Koski H, Tuuli J (2010) Business subsidies in Finland: the dynamics of application and acceptance stages. Research Institute of the Finnish Economy, TLA, Helsinki

Koski H, Pajarinen M (2011a) The Role of business subsidies in job creation of start-ups, gazelles and incumbents. Research Institute of the Finnish Economy, ETLA, Helsinki

Koski H, Pajarinen M (2011b) Do business subsidies facilitate employment growth?. Research Institute of the Finnish Economy, ETLA, Helsinki

Liu YA (1996) Will the Scandinavian model collapse? Futures 28(5):471–490

Mathur A, Ryynänen M, and Nystedt A (2003) Communities at Risk, University of Tampere, Tampere

Nelimarkka S (2015) Marimekko hame nilkoissa": Marimekon plagiointikriisi mainekriisin ja median näkökulmasta (in Finnish), University of Helsinki

OECD (2018) Economic survey of Finland. OECD, Paris

Oksanen K (2017) Government report on the future, 13c/2017, Prime Minister's Office, Helsinki. URL: http://julkaisut.valtioneuvosto.fi/handle/10024/80120

UNCTAD (2018) World investment report 2018: investment and new industrial policies. United Nations, Geneva

World Economic Forum (2019) Future of consumption in fast-growth consumer markets: India. World Economic Forum, Geneva

Chapter 10
Conclusions: After the End and with New Beginnings

> *Isn't life exciting? Everything can change all of a sudden. for no reason at all.*
> Moomintroll in 'Moominpappa at Sea' by Tove Jansson

> *You want proof that the Sun exists, so you stay up all night talking about it. Finally you sleep as the Sun comes up.*
> Rumi

> *Wisdom is an inner fortress which enemies cannot destroy.*
> Thirukkural 200 B.C.

Abstract Anticipations and preparedness for surprises in a dynamic environment require access to timely and relevant information as well as ready bridges where people from both sides can connect and provide support to emerging initiatives, test new ideas, share knowledge and experiences and mobilise responses in an effective cost-efficient way. This concluding chapter proposes a new institutionality for Finland–India business to provide a platform for bringing together businesses, governments and academia in the two countries: Finland and India.

Introduction

Organisations can be information rich and knowledge poor. Information is an objectified discrete representation fixed in time. Nothing depreciates faster than information. Knowledge is always dependent on the context and to be used would always need to be infused with purpose. So how business intelligence is produced and consumed has far-reaching implications. There would always be events and outcomes which are difficult to evaluate from a distance. For example, when India demonetised 86% of its currency, the growth rate remained 7–7.5% per annum which astounded economists. And Finland's growth rate during 2016–18 has remained unaffected despite trade imbalances something that is equally incredible. Norway recently made a $12 billion investment from its pension funds in India. To quote the Norwegian Prime Minister Erna Solberg, "Norway has recently developed a new strategy for engaging with India" (Indian Express 9th January 2019, p.18). The implications of such shifts can be tectonic and remain unnoticed without antennas tuned into all that presents opportunities or competition. Throughout this book, there has been a discussion on how arbitrage between costs and prices of two locations is only one modality for locating trade potential or trade-substituting investments. Adaptation, aggregation and assimilation are three other levers that businesses in Finland and India can use by changing the assumptions over what can be combined and where collaborations can replace or supplement exchanges, transactions and cooperations.

No choices are free of constraints, risks and responsibilities. Patterns of influence and disruption need recognising with attention to early warning signals for market risks, political risk and country risk. Business contexts require alertness and sensitivity to quite different competitive circumstances, factor markets, policy environments, regulatory authorities, media organs and change-inducing forces and factors. Responses in a dynamic environment require access to timely and relevant information and an understanding of which signals need attention in what time frame, distinguishing the important from the insignificant, determining how to make interventions, and when and where to mobilise responses and support. In this context, let me share an idea for new beginnings.

Need for a New Finland–India Institutional Bridge

On their own, businesses can only do what their short-term horizons entail and they would seldom nourish potential spaces or nurture capabilities to learn from each other or to inform and learn from research inquiries of interest and relevance to them that business schools are capable of. There is a lot of scholarly research in international business in management institutes or business schools that is directed at publishing but how much of it is inquiring into questions and coming up with answers that inform policy-makers or practitioners and can be tested? Business and Academia, even if brought together to collaborate could miss out on important institutional and policy gateways just as business and government even when conferring with each other miss out on trends and find themselves entrenched when it comes to removal of policy barriers. This is especially the case when the intervention requires shoehorning in two national spaces with informed decision-making by all actors.

The Finnish employers' Federation EK made 64 proposals to the Finnish government in 2010 and most of them are still languishing. Had these been made on a platform co-owned by business, government and academia of two countries, a lot could have been implemented by now. A forum that enables academia, business and government from two countries to be equal stakeholders can enable dialogues, inquiries, sharing in ways that no project can deliver. This cannot be achieved if it were organised only by one country (as Finland has so far done) or in one country because it would then seem to be unequally focusing on the interests of only one side to the actors in the other country.

Deeper engagement than what FinNode could promote can be fostered by designing an institutional bridge that makes connections between enterprises, governments and academia in both countries, Finland and India. A new type of tripartite or tripolar institution with representation from government, business and academia from two countries together for promoting bilateral economic relations is possible to visualise between any pair of countries. A pioneering attempt could be to do this for Finland and India. The main features of such institutionalisation can be:

1. Access to sustainable low-cost (and in the long run, self-supporting) permanent platform with tripartite representation of business, academia and government with physical nodes hosted in collaborating academic institutions in two countries (for example, IIM Ahmedabad and Aalto University/Turku School of Economics).
2. Capacity to function as a clearing house of ideas, a consultative forum for reflections, action research and engagement that would inform (rather than serve) policy-makers about problems to be solved and barriers to be removed for making business easier through policy reforms in both countries.
3. Ability to signal and facilitate practitioners into investing in missing markets through capacity building initiatives (for new foreign commercial presence, new cross-border entrepreneurship and internationalising of SMEs).
4. Capacity to identify research worthy inquiries to be undertaken as short-term and long-term projects by academia, businesses and governments in collaboration through public–private partnerships and through researchers and students of international business in the collaborating institutions.
5. Commitment to enhancing cultural awareness of Indian culture in Finland and Finnish culture in India to raise awareness can increase mutual interest and dissolve biases.
6. Network development meetings of Indian and Finnish scientists, engineers and entrepreneurs could be systematically organised by such a forum instead of being left to the vagaries of annual or biannual G2G contact or lobby groups.
7. Practical initiatives for funding and facilitating specific collaborations would be easy to facilitate.
8. A consultative window (with empanelled expertise including domain experts from both countries) could co-exist alongside business information databases.

This idea has been discussed by me in Finland with Turku Chamber of Commerce (Jari Lähteenmäki), with the Finnish government (including with previous Ministers Mauri Pekkarinen, Paavo Väyrynen, and three former Prime Ministers Esko Aho, Anneli Jäätteenmäki and Matti Vanhanen) and Finnish Academia (Hannu Seristö and Tomi Laamanen at Aalto University and Esa Stenberg and Niina Nummela of Turku School of Economics) and with Ambassadors Nina Vaskunlahti and Ashok Kumar Sharma and can be developed and modified further.

There is no conflict involved with any existing initiatives on the Finnish side such as by Business Finland, Team Finland or any of its constituents Tekes, Finpro, FINNODE, SITRA, VTT, since none of the initiatives by them go this far and they could themselves be participants in this. There is also no conflict with the work of the Indo-Finnish Joint Commission which is only a G2G initiative or with bilateral

Indo-Finnish trade, scientific (mainly biotech and cleantech), economic or civil parliamentary initiatives. In fact, such an institutionality would cement and buttress some of these initiatives which have not yet yielded their full potential. On the Indian side, while CII and FICCI can always be involved as industry representatives, and IIM Ahmedabad (with its new school of public policy inside IIMA on campus) could well be an anchor on the Indian side, there is a need to clarify whether Niti Aayog, Indian Trade Promotion Organisation (ITPO), Export Promotion Councils, National Productivity Council, Ministry of Trade and Commerce and Ministry of Industry could also be involved in such an institution.

The unrealised potential value that can be created through trade, investment and strategic business and academia linkages spanning India and Finland is vast as documented in previously published Finland–India studies and now updated and expanded in this book with specific scoping of synergies. The Finland–India Economic Relations (FIER) Project initiated in 2005 (supported by Liikesivistysrahasto and Indian Institute of Management Ahmedabad) analysed and disseminated the experience of businesses, academia and government in each of this pair of countries in engaging with the other country from the perspective of untapped potential in product-service linkages and also identified barriers and gateways. This database, if institutionalised as a platform into a tripartite stakeholding partnership with business, academia and government in India and Finland with six collaborating partners (business, academia and government from the two countries), can be an important clearing house for business ideas, innovations, product-service linkages and a resource centre for continuously tracking and sharing experiences (positive and negative), knowledge and capabilities building that would be invaluable to those structuring collaborations and business start-ups of all kinds between Finland and India.

Workshops and listening posts have been convened in India (in Ahmedabad, Mumbai, Delhi, Pune) and in Finland (Helsinki, Tampere, Oulu, Lahti, Turku) by me in collaboration with Finnish researchers Niina Nummela, Esa Stenberg, Satu Teerikangas and Sari Mattila. In Finland, the Finnish Parliament constituted a group to engage with India for the first time, SITRA conducted an awareness campaign and TEKES and the Academy of Finland have launched projects in biotechnology, life sciences and healthcare together with Indian counterparts. But without the kind of institution proposed, the situation characterised by paucity of new investments by Indian firms in Finland and Finnish firms in India may not change as rapidly as is possible.

Only an institution can effectively interface with other institutions. The absence of such an institution (as proposed here) produces fragmentation on the Indian side in dealing with well-coordinated institutional initiatives from the Finnish side. This adversely impacts India from finding the kinds of synergies that Finland is able to find in India. Even though opportunities found by Finland in India are very few compared to the potential, the fact that an overwhelming majority of Indo-Finnish enterprise linkages are Finnish and that the trade balance until recently was in favour of the much smaller country, speaks for itself.

In India, the academia node could be any of the older IIMs but an obvious choice would be India's top-ranked management institution, the Indian Institute of Management Ahmedabad which has recently launched a school of public policy within itself. In Finland, the academic nodes identified are Turku School of Economics, University of Turku and/or Aalto University. IIMA Faculty and Faculty from these two Finnish institutions have collaborated in many ways over a long time and this idea has developed from these interactions. In India, the government could be represented by the Council for Scientific and Industrial Research, the Niti Aayog, ITPO, National Productivity Council or a Ministry (such as MEA or Trade and Commerce). In Finland, the government representation has not been identified, but it could be Team Finland or some other body. Business interests in India would be represented by the Chambers of Commerce FICCI and CII and large industrial houses who evince interest in services, research, workshops and programmes organised by the FIER Center could become subscribing partners too. Once the stakeholders have been constituted, they would develop common aims and activities to support the aims and evolve governance and review mechanisms to guide the centre. The centre would need to have offices in both countries for example at IIM Ahmedabad (http://www.iima.ac.in/) and/or some other institution in India and Turku School of Economics in Finland (http://www.tse.fi) and/or Aalto University (http://www.aalto.fi). There would also be resources linked to these websites and downloadable by membership of the FIER centre which can admit institutional members providing seed capital and individual members from enterprises. The centre would finance itself through corporate subscriptions and affordable charges for services (including services to SMEs at a notional subsidised rate) when seeded and only initially require some seed money from the six identified stakeholding groups to constitute the initial capital.

It may be noted that Israel has also placed a lot of emphasis on developing business in India and have set up an IIMB Israel Centre (http://www.iimb.ac.in/israel-centre-at-iimb) at the Indian Institute of Management Bangalore.

Why Development Cooperation Would Not Work as a Bridge

While development cooperation can also be used as an instrument facilitating the establishment of Finnish companies in markets that are yet to be developed, this is ruled out in the case of India which does not accept development aid from countries smaller than itself as a policy. The systematic foresight project organised by the Ministry for Foreign Affairs and Tekes for observing change signals and mapping new business opportunities could be brought into the Finland–India institution envisaged above. If it were attempted as a purely Finnish initiative, it would fail in India for two reasons. First, given the complexity of India, properly assessing country risk, political risk and investment risk without ongoing engagement with

Indian counterparts will render the foresight incomplete and unreliable. Second, the pace of change, the scope of change and the dimensions of change would be impossible to scope for any pair of countries without being grounded in both countries to understand not only motives underlying changes but also shifts in powerbases. Thirdly, a purely Indian initiative only for Finland sans a Nordic dimension may not find support and would struggle to organise for keeping informed about Finnish economy, business and its institutions.

Let me end with one quote from the Bhagavad Gita and another quote from Goethe:

Vimrashya etad asheshan yatha ichhasi tatha kuru.

(Contemplate on this in totality and do as you wish).

Krishna to Arjuna at the end of the Bhagavad Gita

Whatever you can do or dream you can, begin it. Boldness has genius, power and magic in it.

Goethe

This work ends here.

Annexure I
Finnish RCA-Led Exports to the World Importable by India

Code	Item
2710	Oils obtained from tar and bituminous minerals, other than crude; preparations not elsewhere specified or included, containing by weight 70% or more of petroleum oils
2905	Acyclic alcohols and their halogenated, sulphonated, nitrated or nitrosated derivatives
2907	Phenols; phenol-alcohols
3004	Medicaments excluding serum preparations, vaccines and microorganism cultures; coated impregnated dressings for therapeutic or prophylactic uses
3105	Mineral or chemical fertilisers containing two or three of the fertilizing elements nitrogen, phosphorus and potassium; other fertilisers; goods of this classification in packaged forms
3206	Dyes and colouring matter; excluding dyes of vegetable or animal origin, synthetic organic preparations, inorganic products of a kind used as luminophores
3901	Polymers of ethylene, in primary forms
3902	Polymers of propylene or of other olefins, in primary forms
3920	Other plates, sheets, film, foil and strip, of plastics, non-cellular and not reinforced, laminated, supported or similarly combined with other materials
3926	Polymers of ethylene, propylene, styrene, halogenated olefins, amino resins, phenolic resins, silicon(s), cellulose derivations and petroleum resins
4403	Wood in the rough, whether or not stripped of bark or sapwood, or roughly squared
4703	Chemical wood pulp, soda or sulphate, other than dissolving grades
4801	Newsprint, in rolls or sheets
4810	Paper and paperboard, coated on one or both sides with kaolin (China clay) or other inorganic substances, with or without a binder, and with no other coating, whether or not surface-coloured
4901	Printed books, brochures, leaflets and similar printed matter, whether or not in single sheets
4911	Other printed matter, including printed pictures and photographs
7108	Gold (including gold plated with platinum) unwrought or in semi-manufactured forms, or in powder form
7204	Ferrous waste and scrap; remelting scrap ingots of iron or steel

(continued)

© Springer Nature Singapore Pte Ltd. 2019
A. N. Mathur, *Finland–India Business Opportunities*,
https://doi.org/10.1007/978-981-10-8019-7

(continued)

Code	Item
7208	Flat-rolled products of iron or non-alloy steel, of a width of 600 mm or more, hot-rolled, not clad, plated or coated
7210	Flat-rolled products of iron or non-alloy steel, of a width of 600 mm or more, clad, plated or coated
7219	Flat-rolled products of stainless steel, of a width of 600 mm or more
7225	Flat-rolled products of other alloy steel, of a width of 600 mm or more
7326	Other articles of iron or steel
7403	Refined copper and copper alloys, unwrought
7502	Unwrought nickel
7901	Unwrought zinc
8408	Compression-ignition internal combustion piston engines (diesel or semi-diesel engines)
8409	Parts suitable for use solely or principally with spark-ignition reciprocating or rotary internal combustion piston engines
8413	Pumps for liquids, whether or not fitted with a measuring device; liquid elevators
8414	Air or vacuum pumps, air or other gas compressors and fans, ventilating or recycling hoods incorporating a fan, whether or not fitted with filters
8418	Refrigerators, freezers and other refrigerating or freezing equipment, electric or other; heat pumps other than air conditioning machines (compressor based and vapour absorption cooling)
8419	Machinery, plant or laboratory equipment, whether or not electrically heated, for the treatment of materials by a process involving a change of temperature such as heating, cooking, roasting
8421	Centrifuges, including centrifugal dryers; filtering or purifying machinery and apparatus, for liquids or gases
8426	Ships derricks; cranes, including cable cranes; mobile lifting frames, straddle carriers and work trucks fitted with a crane
8429	Self-propelled bulldozers, angle dozers, graders, levelers, scrapers, mechanical shovels, excavators, shovel loaders, tamping machines and road rollers
8430	Other moving, grading, levelling, scraping, excavating, tamping, compacting, extracting or ores; piledrivers and pile-extravators; snow ploughs and snow blowers
8431	Parts suitable for use solely or principally with pulley tackle, hoist and jacks, etc.
8462	Machine tools (including presses) for working metal by forging, hammering or die-stamping; machine tools (including presses) for working metal by bending, folding, straightening, flattering, shearing
8471	Automatic data processing machines and units thereof; magnetic or optical readers, machines for transcribing data onto data media in coded form and machines for processing such data
8473	Parts and accessories (other than covers, carrying cases and the like) suitable for use solely or principally with typewriters, word processing machines, calculating machines, accounting machines, postage-franking machines, ticket issuing machines, cash registers, magnetic or optical readers, transcription machines, bank note dispensers, coin sorting machines, wrapping machines

(continued)

(continued)

Code	Item
8474	Machinery for sorting, screening, separating, washing, crushing, grinding, mixing or kneading earth, stone, ores or other mineral substances, in solid (including powder or paste) form
8479	Machines and mechanical appliances having specific functions for consumers, individual and B2B
8481	Taps, cocks, valves and similar appliances for pipes, boiler shells, tanks, vats or the like, including pressure-reducing valves and thermostatically controlled valves
8483	Transmission shafts (including crankshafts) and cranks; bearing housings and plain shaft bearings; gears and gearing; ball screws; gear boxes and other speed changers, including torque converters
8501	Electric motors and generators (excluding generating sets)
8502	Electric generating sets and rotary converters
8503	Parts suitable for use solely or principally with electric motors and gensets
8504	Electrical transformers, static converters (e.g. rectifiers) and inductors
8517	Electrical apparatus for line telephony or line telegraphy, including such apparatus for carrier-current line systems or for digital line systems, videophones
8525	Transmission apparatus for radio-telephony, radio-telegraphy, radio-broadcasting or television, whether or not incorporating reception apparatus or sound recording or reproducing apparatus; televisions
8528	Reception apparatus for television, whether or not incorporating radio-broadcast receivers or sound or video recording or reproducing apparatus, video monitors and video projectors
8529	Parts suitable for use solely or principally with communication devices in 8525 and 8528 above
8536	Electrical apparatus for switching or protecting electrical circuits, or for making connections to or in electrical circuits (e.g. switches, relays, fuses, surge suppressors, plugs and sockets)
8537	Boards, panels (including numerical control panels), consoles, desks, cabinets and other bases, equipped with two or more apparatus, for electric control or the distribution unit
8538	Parts suitable for use solely or principally with electrical circuits
8542	Electronic integrated circuits and microassemblies
8544	Insulated (including enamelled or anodized) wire, cable (including co-axial cable) and other insulated electric conductors, whether or not fitted with connectors; optical fibre cables
8703	Motor cars and other motor vehicles principally designed for the transport of persons (excluding tractors), including station wagons and racing cars
8708	Parts and accessories of buses, coaches, cars, special purpose motor vehicles
8802	Other aircraft (e.g. helicopters, aeroplanes); spacecraft (including satellites) and spacecraft launch vehicles
8901	Cruise ships, excursion boats, ferry boats, cargo ships, barges and similar vessels for the transport of persons or goods

(continued)

(continued)

Code	Item
9018	Instrument and appliances used in medical, surgical, dental or veterinary sciences, including scientific apparatus, other electro-medical apparatus and sight-testing instruments
9022	Apparatus based on the use of X-rays or of alpha, beta or gamma radiations, whether or not for medical, surgical, dental or veterinary uses, including radiography or radiotherapy apparatus, X-ray tubes
9027	Instrument and apparatus for physical or chemical analysis (e.g. polarimeters, refractometers, spectrometers, gas or smoke analysis apparatus); instruments and apparatus for measuring or checking
9030	Oscilloscopes, spectrum analyzers and other instruments and apparatus for measuring or checking electrical quantities (excluding gas liquid and electricity supply or production meters) instruments and apparatus for measuring
9031	Measuring or checking instruments, appliances and machines, profile projectors
9032	Automatic regulating or controlling instruments and apparatus
9403	Furniture and furniture parts

Annexure II
High-Value Items Exportable from Finland to India

[The **bolded rows** indicate current exports over €10 million]

Code	Item
3206	Dyes and colouring matter; excluding dyes of vegetable or animal origin, synthetic organic preparations, inorganic products of a kind used as luminophores
4703	**Chemical wood pulp soda or sulphate other than dissolving grades**
4801	**Newsprint in rolls or sheets**
4804	**Uncoated Kraft Paper and Paperboard**
4810	**Paper/paper board coated on one/both sides with potassium alkaline/other inorganic substances and no other coating w/n surface coloured/decorated/printed in rolls/sheets**
7219	Flat-rolled products of stainless steel, of a width of 600 mm or more
7404	**Copper waste and scrap**
7502	**Unwrought nickel**
8408	Compression-ignition, internal combustion piston engines (diesel/semi-diesel)
8409	Parts suitable for use solely or principally with spark-ignition reciprocating or rotary internal combustion piston engines
8413	Pumps for liquids; w/n fitted with a measuring device; liquid elevators
8419	**Machinery, Plant and Laboratory Equipment**
8421	Centrifugals, including centrifugal dryers; filtering or purifying machinery and apparatus, for liquids/gases
8430	**Other moving, grinding, levelling, scrapping, excavating, tampering, compacting, extracting/boring machinery, from earth, minerals/ores; piledriver; snow-plough, etc.**
8431	Parts suitable for use solely or principally with pulley tackle, hoist and jacks, etc.
8471	Automatic data processing machines and units; magnetic/optical readers, machines for transcribing data onto data media in coded form
8474	Machinery for sorting, screening, separating, washing, crushing, etc. of mineral substances, in solid form machines for shaping mineral fuel and forming moulds of

(continued)

(continued)

Code	Item
8479	**Machines and mechanical appliances having individual functions**
8481	**Taps, cocks, valves and similar appliances for pipes, boiler shells, tanks, vats/the like, including pressure-reducing valves and thermostatically controlled valves**
8483	Transmission shafts and cranks; gears; ball screws; bearing housing and other plain shaft bearings speed changers including torque converters of flywheels;
8501	Electric motors and generators (excluding generating sets)
8502	Electric generating sets and rotary converters
8503	Parts suitable for use solely or principally with electric motors and gensets
8504	**Electrical transformers, static converters (e.g. rectifiers) and inductors**
8517	**Electrical apparatus for line telephony/telegraphy, including telephone sets with cordless handset carrier-current line system; videophone**
8523	**Unrecorded Media for Sound Recording**
8525	Transmission apparatus for radio-telephony, etc. incorporating reception apparatus/sound recording/reproducing apparatus; TV cameras, etc.
8529	Parts suitable for use solely or principally with communication devices in 8525 and 8528
8536	Electrical apparatus for switching/protecting electrical circuits, etc. (e.g. switches relays) for a voltage not excluding 1000 V
8542	**Electronic Integrated Circuits and Microassemblies**
8544	Insulated (including enamelled/anodized) wire, etc. optical fibre cables w/n fitted with connectors/assembled with electric conductors
9018	Instruments and appliances used in medical, surgical, dental/veterinary sciences, including scant graphic apparatus electro-medical apparatus and sight-testing instruments
9031	Measuring/checking instruments, appliances and machines, n.e.s. profile projectors
9032	Automatic regulating/controlling instruments and apparatus

Annexure III
Indian Imports from EU that Finland Exports Worldwide

Code	Item
2905	Acyclic alcohols and their halogenated, sulphonated, nitrated or nitrosated derivatives
2907	Phenols; phenol-alcohols
3004	Medicaments excluding serum preparations, vaccines and microorganism cultures coated impregnated dressings for therapeutic or prophylactic uses
3901	Polymers of ethylene, in primary forms
3926	Polymers of ethylene, propylene, styrene, halogenated olefins, amino resins, phenolic resins, silicon(s), cellulose derivations and petroleum resins
4801	Newsprint, in rolls or sheets
4802	Uncoated paper and paperboard, of a kind used for writing, printing or other graphic purposes, and punchcard stock and punch tape paper, in rolls or sheets, other than newsprint
4810	Paper and paperboard, coated on one or both sides with kaolin (China clay) or other inorganic substances, with or without a binder, and with no other coating, whether or not surface-coloured
4901	Printed books, brochures, leaflets and similar printed matter, whether or not in single sheets
7108	Gold (including gold plated with platinum) unwrought or in semi-manufactured forms, or in powder form
7204	Ferrous waste and scrap; remelting scrap ingots of iron or steel
7208	Flat-rolled products of iron or non-alloy steel, of a width of 600 mm or more, hot-rolled, not clad, plated or coated
7210	Flat-rolled products of iron or non-alloy steel, of a width of 600 mm or more, clad, plated or coated
7219	Flat-rolled products of stainless steel, of a width of 600 mm or more
7225	Flat-rolled products of other alloy steel, of a width of 600 mm or more
7326	Other articles of iron or steel
8408	Compression-ignition internal combustion piston engines (diesel or semi-diesel engines)

(continued)

(continued)

Code	Item
8409	Parts suitable for use solely or principally with spark-ignition reciprocating or rotary internal combustion piston engines
8412	Other engines and motors
8413	Pumps for liquids, whether or not fitted with a measuring device; liquid elevators
8414	Air or vacuum pumps, air or other gas compressors and fans, ventilating or recycling hoods incorporating a fan, whether or not fitted with filters
8419	Machinery, plant or laboratory equipment, whether or not electrically heated, for the treatment of materials by a process involving a change of temperature such as heating, cooking, roasting
8421	Centrifuges, including centrifugal dryers; filtering or purifying machinery and apparatus, for liquids or gases
8426	Ships derricks; cranes, including cable cranes; mobile lifting frames, straddle carriers and work trucks fitted with a crane
8430	Other moving, grading, levelling, scraping, excavating, tamping, compacting, extracting or ores; piledrivers and pile-extravators; snow ploughs and snow blowers
8431	Parts suitable for use solely or principally with pulley tackles, heists, winches and capstans, jacks, ships' derricks, cranes, cable cranes, mobile lifting frames, straddle and works' trucks, forklift trucks, escalators, conveyers, teleferics, bulldozers, angle dozers, graders, levelers, scrapples, mechanical shovels, excavators, road rollers, piledrivers, snow ploughs and snow blowers
8462	Machine tools (including presses) for working metal by forging, hammering or die-stamping; machine tools (including presses) for working metal by bending, folding, straightening, flattering, shearing
8471	Automatic data processing machines and units thereof; magnetic or optical readers, machines for transcribing data onto data media in coded form and machines for processing such data
8473	Parts and accessories (other than covers, carrying cases and the like) suitable for use solely or principally with typewriters, word processing machines, calculating machines, accounting machines, postage-franking machines, ticket issuing machines, cash registers, magnetic or optical readers, transcription machines, bank note dispensers, coin sorting machines, wrapping machines
8474	Machinery for sorting, screening, separating, washing, crushing, grinding, mixing or kneading earth, stone, ores or other mineral substances, in solid (including powder or paste) form
8479	Machines and mechanical appliances having specific functions for consumers, individual and B2B
8481	Taps, cocks, valves and similar appliances for pipes, boiler shells, tanks, vats or the like, including pressure-reducing valves and thermostatically controlled valves
8483	Transmission shafts (including crankshafts) and cranks; bearing housings and plain shaft bearings; gears and gearing; ball screws; gear boxes and other speed changers, including torque converters
8501	Electric motors and generators (excluding generating sets)
8502	Electric generating sets and rotary converters
8503	Electric motors, generators, rotary converters
8504	Electrical transformers, static converters (e.g. rectifiers) and inductors

(continued)

(continued)

Code	Item
8517	Electrical apparatus for line telephony or line telegraphy, including such apparatus for carrier-current line systems or for digital line systems, videophones
8525	Transmission apparatus for radio-telephony, radio-telegraphy, radio-broadcasting or television, whether or not incorporating reception apparatus or sound recording or reproducing apparatus; televisions
8529	Parts suitable for use solely or principally with radar apparatus, radio-telephony, navigational aids sound and image recording devices, remote control devices, television sets, video monitors and video projections
8536	Electrical apparatus for switching or protecting electrical circuits, or for making connections to or in electrical circuits (e.g. switches, relays, fuses, surge suppressors, plugs and sockets)
8538	Parts suitable for use solely or principally with electrical switching, electrical circuits, relays, fuses, consolers, desks, cabinets
8542	Electronic integrated circuits and microassemblies
8544	Insulated (including enamelled or anodized) wire, cable (including co-axial cable) and other insulated electric conductors, whether or not fitted with connectors; optical fibre cables made up of individual units
8708	Parts and accessories of the special purpose motor vehicles, cars, tractors
8802	Other aircraft (e.g. helicopters, aeroplanes); spacecraft (including satellites) and spacecraft launch vehicles
9018	Instrument and appliances used in medical, surgical, dental or veterinary sciences, including scientific and graphic apparatus, other electro-medical apparatus and sight-testing instruments
9022	Apparatus based on the use of X-rays or of alpha, beta or gamma radiations, whether or not for medical, surgical, dental or veterinary uses, including radiography or radiotherapy apparatus, X-ray tubes
9027	Instrument and apparatus for physical or chemical analysis (e.g. polarimeters, refractometers, spectrometers, gas or smoke analysis apparatus); instruments and apparatus for measuring or checking
9030	Oscilloscopes, spectrum analyzers and other instruments and apparatus for measuring or checking electrical quantities, excluding calibrating meters and meter for checking gas, liquid or electric supply
9031	Measuring or checking instruments, appliances and machines, not specified or included elsewhere in this chapter; profile projectors
9032	Automatic regulating or controlling instruments and apparatus

Annexure IV
High-Value Indian Imports from EU that Finland Exports to India

Code	Item
4801	Newsprint, in rolls or sheets
4810	Paper and paperboard, coated on one or both sides with kaolin (China clay) or other inorganic substances, with or without a binder, and with no other coating, whether or not surface-coloured, surfaces
7219	Flat-rolled products of stainless steel, of a width of 600 mm or more
8408	Compression-ignition internal combustion piston engines (diesel or semi-diesel engines)
8409	Parts suitable for use solely or principally with compression-ignition internal combustion piston engines (diesel or semi-diesel engines)
8413	Pumps for liquids, whether or not fitted with a measuring device; liquid elevators
8421	Centrifuges, including centrifugal dryers; filtering or purifying machinery and apparatus, for liquids or gases
8430	Other moving, grading, levelling, scraping, excavating, tamping, compacting, extracting or ores; piledrivers and pile-extravators; snow ploughs and snow blowers
8431	Parts suitable for use solely or principally with pulley tackles, heists, winches and capstans, jacks, ships' derricks, cranes, cable cranes, mobile lifting frames, straddle and works' trucks, forklift trucks, escalators, conveyers, teleferics, bulldozers, angle dozers, graders, levelers, scrapples, mechanical shovels, excavators, road rollers, piledrivers, snow ploughs and snow blowers
8471	Automatic data processing machines and units thereof; magnetic or optical readers, machines for transcribing data onto data media in coded form and machines for processing such data
8474	Machinery for sorting, screening, separating, washing, crushing, grinding, mixing or kneading earth, stone, ores or other mineral substances, in solid (including powder or paste) form
8479	Machines and mechanical appliances having specific functions for consumers and B2B
8481	Taps, cocks, valves and similar appliances for pipes, boiler shells, tanks, vats or the like, including pressure-reducing valves and thermostatically controlled valves

(continued)

(continued)

Code	Item
8483	Transmission shafts (including crankshafts) and cranks; bearing housings and plain shaft bearings; gears and gearing; ball screws; gear boxes and other speed changers, including torque converters
8501	Electric motors and generators (excluding generating sets)
8502	Electric generating sets and rotary converters
8503	Electric motors, generators, rotary converters
8504	Electrical transformers, static converters (e.g. rectifiers) and inductors
8517	Electrical apparatus for line telephony or line telegraphy, including such apparatus for carrier-current line systems or for digital line systems, and videophones
8525	Transmission apparatus for radio-telephony, radio-telegraphy, radio-broadcasting or television; TVs
8529	Parts suitable for use solely or principally with radar apparatus, radio-telephony, navigational aids sound and image recording devices, remote control devices, television sets, video monitors and video projections
8536	Electrical apparatus for switching or protecting electrical circuits, or for making connections to or in electrical circuits (e.g. switches, relays, fuses, surge suppressors, plugs and sockets)
8544	Insulated (including enamelled or anodized) wire, cable (including co-axial cable) and other insulated electric conductors, whether or not fitted with connectors; optical fibre cables
9018	Instrument and appliances used in medical, surgical, dental or veterinary sciences, including scientific/graphic apparatus, other electro-medical apparatus and sight-testing instruments
9031	Measuring or checking instruments, appliances and machines not categorised above; profile projectors

Annexure V
High-Value RCA-Led Indian Exports to the World Importable by Finland

Code	Item
901	Coffee, whether or not roasted or decaffeinated; coffee husks and skins; coffee substitutes containing coffee in any proportion
2601	Iron ores and concentrates, including roasted iron pyrites
2710	Petroleum oils and oils obtained from bituminous minerals, other than crude; preparations not elsewhere specified or included, containing by weight 70% or more of petroleum oils
2902	Cyclic hydrocarbons
2905	Acyclic alcohols and their halogenated, sulphonated, nitrated or nitrosated derivatives
3004	Pharmaceutical products for therapeutic or prophylactic uses put up in measured doses or in forms or packing
3204	Synthetic organic colouring matter, whether or not chemically defined; preparations based on synthetic organic colouring matter; synthetic organic products
3808	Insecticides, fungicides, herbicides, anti-sprouting products and plant growth regulators, disinfectants and similar products, put up in forms or packings for retail sale
3901	Polymers of ethylene, in primary forms
3902	Polymers of propylene or of other olefins, in primary forms
3907	Polyacetals, other polyethers and epoxide resins, in primary forms; polycarbonates, alkyd resins, polyallyl esters and other polyesters, in primary forms
3920	Other plates, sheets, film, foil and strip, of plastics, non-cellular and not reinforced, laminated, supported or similarly combined with other materials
3923	Articles for the conveyance or packing of goods, of plastics; stoppers, lids, caps and other closures, of plastics
3926	Natural polymers (e.g. alginic acid) and modified natural polymers (e.g. hardened materials, chemical derivatives of natured rubber) ion-exchange resins
4011	New pneumatic tyres of rubber
4901	Printed books, broachers, leaflets and similar printed matter, whether or not in single sheets
6109	T-shirts, singlets and other vests, knitted or crocheted

(continued)

(continued)

Code	Item
6110	Jerseys, pullovers, cardigans, waistcoats and similar articles, knitted or crocheted
6203	Men's or boys' suits, ensembles, jackets, blazers, trousers, bib and brace overalls, breeches and shorts (other than swimwear)
6204	Women's or girls' suits, ensembles, jackets, blazers, dresses, skirts, divided skirts, trousers, bib and brace overalls, breeches and shorts (other than swimwear)
6302	Bed linen, table linen, toilet linen and kitchen linen
6403	Footwear with outer soles of rubber, plastics, leather or composition leather and uppers of leather
7202	Ferro-alloys
7210	Flat-rolled products of iron or non-alloy steel, of a width of 600 mm or more, clad, plated or coated
7219	Flat-rolled products of stainless steel, of a width of 600 mm or more
7225	Flat-rolled products of other alloy steel, of a width of 600 mm or more
7304	Tubes, pipes and hollow profiles, seamless, of iron (other than cast iron) or steel
7306	Other tubes, pipes and hollow profiles (e.g. open seam or welded, riveted or similarly closed), of iron or steel
7307	Tube or pipe fittings (e.g. couplings, elbows, sleeves), of iron or steel
7308	Structures (excluding prefabricated buildings) and parts of structures (e.g. bridges and bridge-sections, lock gates, towers, lattice masts, roofs, roofing frameworks, doors)
7318	Screws, bolts, nuts coach screws, screw hooks, rivets, cotters, cotter pins, washers (including spring washers) and similar articles, or iron or steel
7326	Other articles of iron or steel
7408	Copper wire
7601	Unwrought aluminium
8302	Base metal mountings, fittings and similar articles suitable for furniture, doors, staircases, windows, blinds, coachwork, saddlery, trunks, chests, caskets or the like; base metal hat racks, hat peg
8409	Parts suitable for use solely or principally with compression-ignition internal combustion piston engines (diesel or semi-diesel engines)
8413	Pumps for liquids, whether or not fitted with a measuring device; liquid elevators
8414	Air or vacuum pumps, air or other gas compressors and fans, ventilating or recycling hoods incorporating a fan, whether or not fitted with filters
8419	Machinery, plant or laboratory equipment, whether or not electrically heated, for the treatment of materials by a process involving a change of temperature such as heating, cooking, roasting
8421	Centrifuges, including centrifugal dryers; filtering or purifying machinery and apparatus, for liquids or gases
8471	Automatic data processing machines and units thereof; magnetic or optical readers, machines for transcribing data onto data media in coded form and machines for processing such data
8473	Parts and accessories (other than covers, carrying cases and the like) suitable for use solely or principally with typewriters, word processing machines, calculating machines, accounting machines, postage-franking machines, ticket issuing machines, cash registers, magnetic or optical readers, transcription machines, bank note dispensers, coin sorting machines, wrapping machines

(continued)

(continued)

Code	Item
8479	Machines and mechanical appliances having specific functions for consumers, individual and B2B
8481	Taps, cocks, valves and similar appliances for pipes, boiler shells, tanks, vats or the like, including pressure-reducing valves and thermostatically controlled valves
8482	Ball or roller bearings
8483	Transmission shafts (including crankshafts) and cranks; bearing housings and plain shaft bearings; gears and gearing; ball screws; gear boxes and other speed changers, including torque converters
8501	Electric motors and generators (excluding generating sets)
8504	Electrical transformers, static converters (e.g. rectifiers) and inductors
8524	Records, tapes and other recorded media for sound or other similarly recorded phenomena, including matrices and masters for the production of records, but excluding photographic equipment, paper, film rolls, cinematographic film and chemical preparations for photographic uses
8528	Reception apparatus for television, whether or not incorporating radio-broadcast receivers or sound or video recording or reproducing apparatus, video monitors and video projectors
8536	Electrical apparatus for switching or protecting electrical circuits, or for making connections to or in electrical circuits (e.g. switches, relays, fuses, surge suppressors, plugs and sockets)
8541	Diodes, transistors and similar semiconductor devices; photosensitive semiconductor devices, including photovoltaic cells whether or not assembled in modules or made up into panels; light-emitting units
8544	Insulated (including enamelled or anodized) wire, cable (including co-axial cable) and other insulated electric conductors, whether or not fitted with connectors; optical fibre cables
8701	Tractors excluding forklift trucks
8703	Motor cars and other motor vehicles principally designed for the transport of persons (but not buses), including station wagons and racing cars
8704	Motor vehicles for the transport of goods
8708	Parts and accessories of the special purpose motor vehicles, cars, tractors
8711	Motorcycles (including mopeds) and cycles fitted with an auxiliary motor, with or without side-cars; side-cars
8901	Cruise ships, excursion boats, ferry boats, cargo ships, barges and similar vessels for the transport of persons or goods
9018	Instrument and appliances used in medical, surgical, dental or veterinary sciences, including scintigraphic apparatus, other electro-medical apparatus and sight-testing instruments
9403	Furniture and furniture parts
9506	Articles and equipment for general physical exercise gymnastics, athletics, other sports (including table tennis) or outdoor games, not specified or included elsewhere, swimming pools, paddle pools, etc.

Annexure VI
High-Value RCA-Led Indian Exports to EU importable by Finland

Code	Item
901	Coffee, whether or not roasted or decaffeinated; coffee husks and skins; coffee substitutes containing coffee in any proportion
2601	Iron ores and concentrates including roasted iron pyrites
2710	Petroleum oils and oils obtained from bituminous mineral other than crude preparations n.e.s.; containing 70% or more by weight of these oils
3004	Medicaments excluding serum preparations, vaccines and microorganism cultures coated impregnated dressings for therapeutic or prophylactic uses
3808	Insecticides, fungicides, herbicides, anti-sprouting products and plant growth regulators, disinfectants and similar products
3901	Polymers of ethylene in primary forms
3920	Other plates, sheets, film, foil and strip, of plastics, non-cellular and not reinforced laminated supported/similarly combined with other materials
3923	Articles for the conveyance or packing of goods, of plastics; stoppers, lids, caps and other closures, of plastics
4011	New pneumatic tyres of rubber
6109	T-shirts, singlets and other vests, knitted or crocheted
6110	Jerseys, pullovers, cardigans, waistcoats and similar articles, knitted/crocheted
6203	Men's or boys' suits, ensembles, jackets, blazers, trousers, bib and brace overalls breeches and shorts (other than swimwear)
6204	Women's/girls' suits, ensembles, jackets, dresses, skirts, trousers, bib and brace overalls, breeches and shorts, etc. (except swimwear)
6302	Bed linen, table linen, toilet linen and kitchen linen
6403	Footwear with outer soles of rubber, plastics, leather/composition leather and uppers of leather
7202	Ferro-alloys
7210	Flat-rolled products of iron/non-alloy steel of width >=600 mm, clad, plated/coated
7225	Flat-rolled products of other alloy steel of width 600 mm or more
7307	Tube or pipe fittings (e.g. couplings, elbows, sleeves), of iron or steel

(continued)

(continued)

Code	Item
7318	Screws, bolts, nuts, coach screws, screw hooks rivets, cotters, cotter pins, washers (including spring washers) and similar articles of iron/steel
7326	Other articles of iron or steel
8302	Base metal mountings, fittings and similar articles for furniture, doors, etc.; base metal hatracks, brackets, etc., castors automatic door closers of base metal
8409	Parts suitable for use solely or principally with compression-ignition internal combustion piston engines (diesel or semi-diesel engines)
8413	Pumps for liquids; w/n fitted with a measuring device; liquid elevators
8473	Parts and accessories (other than covers, carrying cases and the like) suitable for use solely or principally with typewriters, word processing machines, calculating machines, accounting machines, postage-franking machines, ticket issuing machines, cash registers, magnetic or optical readers, transcription machines, bank note dispensers, coin sorting machines, wrapping machines
8479	Machines and mechanical appliances having individual functions
8481	Taps, cocks, valves and similar appliances for pipes, boiler shells, tanks, vats/the like, including pressure-reducing valves and thermostatically controlled valves
8482	Ball or roller bearings of certain types
8483	Transmission shafts and cranks; gears; ball screws; bearing housing and other plain shaft bearings' speed changers including torque converters of flywheels
8504	Electrical transformers, static converters (e.g. rectifiers) and inductors
8536	Electrical apparatus for switching/protecting electrical circuits, etc. (e.g switches relays) for a voltage not excluding 1000 V
8541	Diodes, transistors and similar semiconductor devices, etc. w/n assembled in modules/made up into panels, etc. mounted piezo-electric crystals
8703	Motor cars and other motor vehicles principally designed for the transport of persons (but not buses), including station wagons and racing cars
8708	Parts and accessories of the special purpose motor vehicles, cars, tractors
9403	Furniture and furniture parts
9506	Articles and equipment for gymnastics, athletics, other sports (including table tennis)/outdoor games, n.e.s.; swimming pools and paddling pools

Annexure VII
Top Ten Indian High-Value Exports to Finland According to CMIE Data

Code	Item
3004	Pharmaceutical products (generics) and ayurvedic medicines
3808	Insecticides, fungicides, herbicides, anti-sprouting products and plant growth regulators, disinfectants and similar products
6109	T-shirts, singlets and other vests, knitted or crocheted
6110	Jerseys, pullovers, cardigans, waistcoats and similar articles, knitted/crocheted
6204	Women's/girls' suits, ensembles, jackets, dresses, skirts, trousers, bib and brace overalls, breeches and shorts, etc. (except swimwear)
6403	Footwear with outer soles of rubber, plastics, leather/composition leather and uppers of leather
8481	Taps, cocks, valves and similar appliances for pipes, boiler shells, tanks, vats/the like, including pressure-reducing valves and thermostatically controlled valves
8517	Electrical apparatus for line telephony/telegraphy, including telephone sets with cordless handset carrier- current line system; videophone
8528	Reception apparatus, with/not incorporating radio-broadcast receivers/sound/video recording/reproducing apparatus, video monitors, etc.
8803	Gliders, hang gliders, balloons and dirigibles and other non-powered aircraft; parts of aeroplanes, helicopters, satellites, spacecrafts and spacecraft launch vehicles

Annexure VIII
High-Value Indian Exports to European Union importable from India by Finland

Code	Commodity name
2933	Heterocyclic compounds with nitrogen hetero atoms(s) only; nucleic acids and their salts
2942	Other organic compounds
3003	Medicaments consisting of two/more constituents mixed together for bulk pharmaceutical supplies to hospitals and wholesales
3004	Pharmaceutical products for retail sales
3808	Insecticides, fungicides, herbicides, anti-sprouting products and plant growth regulators, disinfectants and similar products
4202	Trunks, suitcases and other case holster and travelling bags, handbags and other similar containers, bags, wallets, boxes, purses
4203	Articles of apparel and clothing accessories of leather or of composition leather
5702	Carpets and other textile floor coverings, woven, not tufted or flocked, whether or not made up, including 'Kelem', 'Schumacks', 'Karamanie' and similar hand-woven rugs
5705	Carpets and other textile floor coverings, w/n made up
6104	Women's/girls' suits, ensembles, jackets, dresses, skirts and divided skirts, trousers, bib, brace overalls, etc., knitted/crocheted
6105	Men's/boys' shirts, knitted/crocheted
6109	T-shirts, singlet and other vests, knitted or crocheted
6110	Jerseys, pullovers, cardigans, waistcoats and similar articles, knitted/crocheted
6204	Women's/girls' suits, ensembles, jackets, dresses, skirts, trousers, bib and brace overalls, breeches and shorts, etc. (except swimwear)
6205	Men's or boy's shirts
6304	Furnishing articles excluding mattresses, quilts, eiderdowns, cushions, pillows
6307	Other made up articles including dress patterns
6403	Footwear with outer soles of rubber, plastics, leather/composed leather and uppers of leather
7102	Diamonds, whether or not worked, but not mounted or set

(continued)

© Springer Nature Singapore Pte Ltd. 2019
A. N. Mathur, *Finland–India Business Opportunities*,
https://doi.org/10.1007/978-981-10-8019-7

(continued)

Code	Commodity name
7113	Articles of jewellery and parts thereof, of precious metal or of metal clad with precious metal
7325	Other cast articles of iron or steel
8481	Taps, cocks, valves and similar appliances for pipes, boiler shells, tanks, vats/the like, including pressure-reducing valves and thermostatically controlled valves

Annexure IX: Finland's 500 Biggest Companies (The Talouselämä 500)

Rank 2016	Rank 2017	Company	Sectors (SITC 2-digit codes)	RCA	Sub-sectors (SITC 4-digit codes)
1	1	Nokia	Hardware-telecommunications (85)	Yes	Telephone sets and equipments (8517, 8518, 8522), services (S)
2	2	Nestle	Foods and beverages (11), cereals (04) and dairy products (02)	NO	Cereal for breakfast (1104), ice cream (210500), non-alcoholic beverages (2201, 2202)
3	3	Kesko	Retail-trade	NA	S
5	4	UPM-Kymmene	Paper (48) and forest products (44)	Yes	Plywood (4412), paper for printing (4802), paper for packaging and office (4819, 4821)
4	5	Stora Enso	Paper (48) and forest products (44)	Yes	Paper for printing (4802), paper for packaging (4819, 4821), wood for construction (4407, 4409), plain wood (4403)
6	6	Kone	Mechanical/industrial engineering (84)	Yes	Escalators and elevators (8428)
8	7	SOK	Retail (Trade)	NA	S
7	8	Varma	Insurance	NA	S
10	9	OP Ryhma	Financial services	NA	S
12	10	Sampo	Financial services	NA	S

(continued)

© Springer Nature Singapore Pte Ltd. 2019
A. N. Mathur, *Finland–India Business Opportunities*,
https://doi.org/10.1007/978-981-10-8019-7

(continued)

Rank 2016	Rank 2017	Company	Sectors (SITC 2-digit codes)	RCA	Sub-sectors (SITC 4-digit codes)
16	11	Outokumpu	Steel (72)	Yes	Stainless steel both hot rolled and cold rolled (7229, 7220), Bars, rods and coils of steel (7277), semi-finished products (6728), wires of steel (7224)
9	12	Ilmarinen	Insurance	NA	S
11	13	Wartsila	Mechanical/industrial engineering [power-generating machinery (85), general industrial machinery (84)]	Yes	Generating sets (8501), engines for marine propulsion (8408, 8412), valves (8481), fuel pumps (8413), compressors (8414), ball bearings (8482)
17	14	Metsa Group	Paper (48) and forest products (44)	Yes	Paper for printing (4802), paper for packaging (4819, 4821), wood for construction (4407, 4409), plain wood (4403)
14	15	North European Oil Trade	Oil and energy [petroleum products (27)]	NO	Liquid fuel (2710)
15	16	St1 Nordic	Oil and energy [fuel (27), instruments and apparatus (87)]	NO	Gaseous hydrocarbons (2711), petroleum oils and products (2710, 2712, 2713), electricity supply (271600)
13	17	Elo	Insurance	NA	S
18	18	Fortum	Utilities, electricity, natural gas (27, 44)	NA	Electricity supply (271600), natural gas supply (2711, 270500), biofuel/wood fuel (44)
43	19	Cargotec	Logistics and transportation [general industry machinery (86) road vehicles (87)]	Yes	Container and equipments for handling (860900), trucks for warehouses (8709), tractors (8701)
19	20	Nordea Pankki Suomi	Banking	NA	S
21	21	Veikkaus	Gambling and casinos	NA	S

(continued)

Annexure IX: Finland's 500 Biggest Companies (The Talouselämä 500)

(continued)

Rank 2016	Rank 2017	Company	Sectors (SITC 2-digit codes)	RCA	Sub-sectors (SITC 4-digit codes)
20	22	Valmet	General industry machinery (84)	Yes	Laundry equipments (8450, 8466), machinery for textile industry (8444, 8445, 8446, 8447), machinery for pulp, paper and paperboard (8439, 8441)
22	23	Huhtamaki	Packaging and containers (48, 63)	Yes	Packing materials (4819) and other fibre packing (6305)
32	24	Amer Sports	Sporting goods [footwear (64, 94), apparels and accessories (61)]	Yes	Sports footwear (6405), sports goods (9406), sports apparels and accessories (6112)
23	25	Metso	General industry machinery (74), machinery for specialised industries (72)	Yes	Mining machinery (7233, 7234, 7283, 7284), machinery for pulp, paper (7251, 7252), machinery for gaseous (7417, 7436)
25	26	Caverion	Industrial services-designing, installation, advisory, etc.	NA	S
24	27	Kemira	Chemicals (28, 47, 39, 38, 26)	Yes	Chlorides (2827), chemical pulp (470500), polymers (3901, 3902, 3913), municipal waste and sewage sludge (2621), chemical products (3825)
29	28	Nordea Henkivakuutus	Financial services	NA	S
27	29	Finnair	Airways	NA	S
26	30	ABB	Electrical equipments (73, 74, 76), power-generating machinery and equipments (85), electricity (27)	Yes	Generators and motors (8501, 8502, 8412), transformers (8504), electricity-producing equipments (7312, 741300, 7614), electricity (271600)
30	31	Ahlstrom-Munksjo	Paper (48) and forest products (44)	Yes	Paper for printing (4802), paper for packaging (4819, 4821), wood for construction (4407, 4409), plain wood (4403)

(continued)

(continued)

Rank 2016	Rank 2017	Company	Sectors (SITC 2-digit codes)	RCA	Sub-sectors (SITC 4-digit codes)
31	32	Konecranes	Electrical equipments (84)	Yes	Crane, hoists, straddle carriers, grabbers (8426, 8425, 8426, 7448)
41	33	Supercell	Gaming	NA	S
34	34	Lahitapiola-ryhma	Insurance	NA	S
28	35	Microsoft Mobile	Telecommunication equipments (85)	Yes	Mobile and equipments (8517, 8518, 8529)
37	36	St1 Group	Oil and energy (27), electricity (27)	NO	Petroleum products (2710, 2712, 2713), gases (2711), electricity (271600)
40	37	HOK-Elanto	Gaming, lodging and restaurant	NA	S
39	38	HKScan	Food industry	NA	
38	39	Wihuri International	Retail-trade, packaging	Yes	Packaging for food and medical supplies (3923, 4819, 6305)
33	40	Teboil	Oil and energy (27), electricity (27)	NO	Petroleum products (2710, 2712, 2713), gases (2711), electricity (271600)
—	41	SSAB Suomi	Steel (72, 73)	Yes	Steel and iron products (7225, 7226, 7210, 7211), steel sheets (7301), bars and rods (7227)
47	42	Lemminkainen	Construction and mineral manufactures (25, 84)	Yes	Construction materials (2521, 2522, 2523, 381600), construction machinery (8464)
46	43	YIT	Construction and building	NA	S
48	44	Oriola	Pharmaceutical-distributors	NA	S
49	45	Valio	Beverages (20)	NO	Juices (2009)
54	46	Sanoma	Media and publishing (S)	NA	S
50	47	Elisa	Telecommunications (voice and data)	NA	S
44	48	Posti	Logistics and postal services	NA	S
52	49	Fazer	Food production (17 and 19)	NO	Confectionery items (1704), bakery products (1905)
53	50	Tieto	IT services, professional services	NA	S

(continued)

(continued)

Rank 2016	Rank 2017	Company	Sectors (SITC 2-digit codes)	RCA	Sub-sectors (SITC 4-digit codes)
56	51	Luvata	Electrical equipments, power-generating machinery and equipments (85, 84)	Yes	Heat transfer solution like A/C, heaters, coolers (8516, 8415), motors (8501, 8412), generators (8502)
45	52	Tamro	Pharmaceutical-distributors	NA	S
55	53	Lidl Suomi	Retail-groceries	NA	S
60	54	Nokian Renkaat	Automotive-tyre manufacturing (62)	Yes	Automotive tyres (4011, 4012, 4013)
58	55	Telia Suomi	Telecommunications	NA	S
59	56	Atria	Food industry [meat and meat preparations (01)]	NA	NA
61	57	Stockmann	Retailing-departmental stores	NA	S
62	58	Veho	Retail-automotive	NA	S
64	59	Fiskars	Consumer products	Yes	Tableware (4419), cookware products (7321), glasses (702000), cutlery products (8214, 8215, 8209), lamps and lightings (7011, 702000)
72	60	VR-Yhtyma	Transportation and logistics	NA	S
63	61	Alko	Alcoholic beverages (11)	Yes	Non-alcoholic beverage (220300, 2204, 2205, 220600)
57	62	Uponor	Building materials service solutions	NA	S
66	63	Orion	Pharmaceutical products (54)	Yes	Pharmaceutical goods (3006, 3003, 3004)
69	64	Outotec	Metals and mining-industrial solutions	NA	S
74	65	Onvest	Investment management	NA	S
93	66	Ahlstrom Capital	Investment	NA	S
70	67	Etera	Insurance	NA	S
75	68	Skanska	Construction-management and construction services	NA	S
71	69	Rettig	Industrial equipments (74, 85, 25)	Yes	Valves (7478), air conditioning machines (8481), solar panels (8537), limestone products (2521, 2522)

(continued)

(continued)

Rank 2016	Rank 2017	Company	Sectors (SITC 2-digit codes)	RCA	Sub-sectors (SITC 4-digit codes)
68	70	Paulig	Food and beverages (11, 18, 21, 22, 20)	NO, 22 (Yes)	Coffee roasted (180100), coffee products (2101), non-alcoholic beverage (220300, 2204, 2205, 220600) food products (2001, 2104, 1104)
76	71	Osuuskauppa Hameenmaa	Retailing-departmental stores	NA	S
73	72	SRV Yhtiot	Construction-building services	NA	S
77	73	DNA	Telecommunications-data and voice	NA	S
78	74	PKC Group	Electrical machinery and parts (84, 85, 87)	Yes	Electrical equipments for vehicles (8706, 8409), equipments for power distribution (8537, 8535, 8536)
79	75	Gasum	Oil and energy—gas (27)	NO	Natural gas (2711)
80	76	Bayer	Pharmaceuticals (54), chemicals (38), food (12)	NO, 20 and 38 (Yes)	Fungicides, insecticides and herbicides (3808), seeds for agricultural products (120300, 120400, 1205, 1206, 1207), pharma goods (3003, 3004, 3006)
81	77	Pirkanmaan Osuuskauppa	Retailing-trade	NA	S
100	78	Meyer Turku	Ship building-transport equipments (84, 89)	Yes	Ships, ferries (8426, 8901), yachts and other vessels (8903)
97	79	Helen	Oil and energy-electricity (27, 84, 85, 90)	No, 84, 85, 90 (Yes)	Electricity (271600), electricity supply (9028), heating and cooling (8404, 8516)
87	80	Tokmanni Group	Retail-departmental stores	NA	S
90	81	Osuuskauppa Arina	Retail-distribution	NA	S
91	82	Fennia	Insurance	NA	S
85	83	Consolis	Industrial solutions	NA	S
92	84	Planmeca	Medical equipment and devices (92, 94, 70, 84)	Yes	Medical instruments (9402), medical furniture (9403), medical apparatus (7017, 8419, 9022), implants (9021)

(continued)

Annexure IX: Finland's 500 Biggest Companies (The Talouselämä 500)

(continued)

Rank 2016	Rank 2017	Company	Sectors (SITC 2-digit codes)	RCA	Sub-sectors (SITC 4-digit codes)
82	85	Hankkija	Agricultural products (12, 31, 29) and machinery	NO, 39 (yes)	Seeds (120300, 120400, 1205, 1206, 1207), fertilisers (3102, 3103, 3104), vitamins (2936), agricultural machinery (8432, 8433)
84	86	Danske Bank	Banking	NA	S
94	87	Cramo	Construction-equipment rental service	NA	S
122	88	NCC Suomi	Construction-services	NA	S
86	89	Kauppahuone Laakkonen	Retail-automotive	Yes	Vehicles (8703), spare parts (8708)
102	90	Ramirent	Construction-machinery (84, 68)	Yes	Machinery for sorting, grinding, crushing (6804, 8461, 8462, 8463, 8464, 8429), machinery for lifting, loading, unloading (8427, 8428), pumps (8413, 8414)
95	91	Norilsk Nickel Harjavalta	Metals and mining (26, 71, 75)	NO, 71 and 75 (Yes)	Nickel ores and metals (260400, 7501, 7502), platinum and other metals of platinum (7110), copper products (260300), cobalt (260500), silver products (7106), gold (7108)
89	92	Lassila and Tikanoja	Waste and environ services and equipments	NA	S
96	93	Sandvik Mining and Construction	Construction and mining-machinery (84, 72)	Yes	Machines for drilling (8461), boring machinery (7233), excavators (8429), hammers for demolition and breaking of materials (8462)
115	94	Yara Suomi	Chemicals (31, 84, 38)	NO, 38 and 84 Yes	Fertilisers (3102, 3103, 3104), farming equipments (8432, 8433), other chemical products (3825)
200	95	Osuuskauppa KPO	Retail-departmental stores	NA	S

(continued)

(continued)

Rank 2016	Rank 2017	Company	Sectors (SITC 2-digit codes)	RCA	Sub-sectors (SITC 4-digit codes)
108	96	Veikko Laine	Retail-departmental stores	NA	S
98	97	Veritas Elakevakuutus	Insurance	NA	S
153	98	Osuuskauppa Keskimaa	Retail-trade	NA	S
51	99	DT Finland	Construction materials (25, 44, 68)	Yes	Construction materials (2521, 2522, 2524, 6811), articles of wood (4416)
99	100	Mehilainen	Healthcare facilities and services (S)	NA	S
103	101	Tuko Logistics	Transportation and logistic (S)	NA	S
104	102	Fingrid	Oil and energy-electricity (27)	NA	Electricity (271600)
111	103	Tikkurila	Chemicals (32, 34)	Yes	Paints and varnishes (3208, 3209, 3210), detergents (3402)
117	104	TOK-Yhtyma	Retail-trade (S)	NA	S
88	105	Osuuskauppa Peeassa	Retail-trade in foods and services (S)	NA	S
105	106	Delta Motor Group	Dealer-automotive (87)	Yes	Passenger cars (8703) and parts (8708)
124	107	Andritz	Machinery for industries (84, 26)	NO, 84 (Yes)	Machinery for pulp and paper (8439, 8441), municipal waste and sludge (2621)
120	108	3 Step IT Group	Commercial services-asset management, IT lease (S)	NA	S
116	109	Poyry	Engineering and management consulting (S)	NA	S
188	110	Viking Line	Gaming, lodging and restaurant (S)	NA	S
121	111	Ponsse	Machinery for industries (84)	Yes	Agricultural, horticulture or forestry machines (8432), harvesting machinery (8433), cranes (8426), lifting, handling, loading, unloading machinery (8428), hardware (8301)
113	112	Schenker East	Transportation and logistics (S)	NA	S
118	113	Scanfil	Hardware-telecommunications and electrical machinery (85)	Yes	Telecommunication equipments (8517, 8518), cabinets and casings (8537), other electrical equipments (8543)

(continued)

Annexure IX: Finland's 500 Biggest Companies (The Talouselämä 500)

(continued)

Rank 2016	Rank 2017	Company	Sectors (SITC 2-digit codes)	RCA	Sub-sectors (SITC 4-digit codes)
110	114	PVO Yhtiot	Construction-repairing work (S)	NA	S
109	115	Salcomp	Telecommunication equipments (85), electric machinery and parts (77)	Yes	Telecom equipments (8517), telecom spare parts (8518), set-top boxes, gateways, routers (8525, 8526, 8527)
129	116	Lujatalo	Construction-building services (S)	NA	S
126	117	Kuusakoski Group	Waste and environ services and equipments and metallic products (72, 76)	Yes	Aluminium products (7610), stainless steel (7219, 7220)
107	118	Gigantti	Retail-distribution	NA	S
106	119	Patria	Aerospace and defence (87, 88, 91)	Yes	Armoured wheels (871000), aeroplanes and spacecraft (8802, 910400, 8803, 8804)
125	120	Tradeka-Yhtyma	Retail-departmental stores	NA	S
–	121	Finnlines	Transportation and logistics services	NA	S
134	122	Terveystalo	Healthcare facilities and services	NA	S
65	123	Yleisradio	Media entertainment and services	NA	S
123	124	Toyota Auto Finland	Dealer-automotive (87)	Yes	Passenger cars (8703) and parts (8708)
119	125	SLO	Distributors-wholesaler	NA	S
141	126	Aspo	Wholesale-industrial services (19, 17)	NO	Bakery products and confectionery items (1904, 1905, 1704)
138	127	Finnfrost	Logistics and supply chain	NA	S
114	128	Suur-Seudun Osuuskauppa	Consumer finance	NA	S
128	129	Attendo Finland	Healthcare facilities and services	NA	S
130	130	Etela-Pohjanmaan Osuuskauppa	Retail-trade	NA	S
112	131	Raisio	Foods (19, 16, 17)	NO	Confectionery items (1704), bakery products (1902, 1904, 1905), cereals products (1904), fish processed (1604, 1605), meat products (1602, 1603)

(continued)

(continued)

Rank 2016	Rank 2017	Company	Sectors (SITC 2-digit codes)	RCA	Sub-sectors (SITC 4-digit codes)
127	132	ISS Palvelut	Construction-real estate	NA	S
133	133	Kymen Seudun Osuuskauppa	Retail-consumer goods	NA	S
148	134	ALSO Finland	Distributors-IT and consumer electronics	NA	S
144	135	Suominen	Textiles (56) and personal hygiene (33, 34)	NO, 33 (Yes)	Soap products (3401), personal hygiene products (3303, 3304, 3305, 3307), non-woven fabrics (5603)
135	136	Sappi Finland Operations	Distributors-wholesaler (33, 38, 62, 70, 84, 90, 95)	NO, 38, 64, 70, 84, 90, 95 (Yes)	Personal hygiene products (3303, 3304, 3305, 3307), insecticides (3808), babies garments and accessories (6209), footwear (6405, 6406), medical and laboratory equipments (7017, 9022, 9402), forklift trucks (8427), sports equipments (9506)
140	137	Fujitsu Finland	Hardware-IT services	NA	S
137	138	Kamux	Retail-automotive	NA	S
147	139	CGI Suomi	IT and professional services	NA	S
152	140	Pihlajalinna	Healthcare facilities and services	NA	S
132	141	KWH-yhtyma	Manufacturing and logistics (73, 68)	Yes	Net fabrics (7314), foam (6806), abrasives and polishing (6805)
–	142	Vapo	Oil and energy (44, 27, 85)	NO, 44 and 85 (Yes)	Fuel wood (4401), peat products (2703), heating networks (8516)
157	143	Apeti	Food (10, 12, 22, 16)	NO	Grain products (10200, 1104), oilseeds (1207), frozen fishes (1604), seafood (1605), frozen vegetables (2204), fruits (2208)
214	144	Caruna Networks	Utilities (27)	NO	Electricity (271600)
142	145	Kokkolan Halpa-Halli	Retail-departmental stores	NA	S

(continued)

Annexure IX: Finland's 500 Biggest Companies (The Talouselämä 500)

(continued)

Rank 2016	Rank 2017	Company	Sectors (SITC 2-digit codes)	RCA	Sub-sectors (SITC 4-digit codes)
186	146	Finavia	Transportation and logistics-operation and maintenance services	NA	S
149	147	Paroc Group	Construction-building services	NA	S
187	148	Verkkokauppa.com	Retailer-consumer electronics	NA	S
146	149	Tallink Silja	Transportation and logistics services	NA	S
171	150	Volvo Car Finland	Automotive (87)	Yes	Passenger cars (8703) and parts (8708)
136	151	Vattenfall	Oil and energy (27)	NO	Petroleum products (2710, 2712, 2713), gases (2711), electricity (2716000)
177	152	John Deere	Machinery (84)	Yes	Harvest machineries (8433), forestry machinery (8432)
156	153	Lehto Group	Construction-building services	NA	S
155	154	Altia	Beverages (22)	Yes	Alcoholic beverages (2203, 2204, 2205, 2206)
180	155	Satakunnan Osuuskauppa	Retail-departmental stores	NA	S
151	156	Alma Media	Media	NA	S
169	157	Powerflute	Home and office products (44)	Yes	Wood for paper and forest products (4407, 4412, 4421), fuel wood (4401)
154	158	Kojamo	Real estate-services	NA	S
166	159	Rudus	Construction materials (69) (68)	Yes	Concrete materials (6810, 381600), tubes and pipes (690600), structures (6911), facades (3214)
172	160	Osuuskauppa Suur-Savo	Media-Internet services	NA	S
164	161	Wiklof Holding	Asset management	NA	S
160	162	Empower	Construction and maintenance services	NA	S
170	163	Aktia	Banking	NA	S
139	164	IKEA	Retail-furniture products (94), (44)	NO, 44 and 94 (Yes)	Furniture (8302, 4419, 9404, 9403)
163	165	Arla	Consumer products-dairy products	NA	NA
194	166	Kayttoauto	Automotive-distributors	NA	S

(continued)

(continued)

Rank 2016	Rank 2017	Company	Sectors (SITC 2-digit codes)	RCA	Sub-sectors (SITC 4-digit codes)
175	167	Citycon	Construction-building Services	NA	S
161	168	Osuuskauppa Varuboden-Osla	Retail-cooperative stores	NA	S
168	169	Etola	Industrial goods, baby toys and clothes, transmission equipments (39, 44, 6284, 85)	Yes, 62 (NO)	Rubbers, plastics, tapes, etc. (4402, 3925, 3926, 3919, 3920, 3921), hydraulics (8410), ball bearing (8482), grinding (6804), transmission equipment (8535, 8536, 8537, 8542), toys (9501, 9503), babies clothing and accessories (6209)
101	170	Versowood Group	Construction materials (44) (85)	Yes	Plywood (4412), wood (4407), wooden boxes (4415), wood decoratives (4421), poles for electricity (8535)
165	171	LVI-Dahl	Industrial equipment (81, 84, 39) and energy (27)	Yes	Heating equipments (8402), air conditioning (8145), industrial pipes (3917), electricity (271600)
183	172	Lindstrom	Textiles (58, 62) and personal hygiene (33)	No, 63 (Yes)	Textile materials (5811, 6302, 6304), apparels (6210), personal hygienes (3303, 3304, 3305, 3307)
240	173	Yliopiston Apteekki	Pharmaceuticals products (30)	Yes	Pharmaceutical items (3003, 3004, 3005, 3006)
174	174	Hartela	Construction and engineering services	NA	S
167	175	Olvi	Beverages (22)	Yes	Non-alcoholic beverages (2203, 2204, 2205, 2206), juices (2209)
158	176	Rolls-Royce	Mechanical equipments (89, 84)	Yes	Vessels (8901, 8902), marine equipments (8407, 8408)
159	177	Prysmian Finland	Electrical equipments (90)	Yes	Telecom cables and equipments (9001, 9006, 9007)

(continued)

Annexure IX: Finland's 500 Biggest Companies (The Talouselämä 500)

(continued)

Rank 2016	Rank 2017	Company	Sectors (SITC 2-digit codes)	RCA	Sub-sectors (SITC 4-digit codes)
179	178	Vaisala	Electrical equipments-weather forecasting (90)	Yes	Weather instruments (9030, 9031, 9032, 9033)
190	179	Pohjois-Karjalan Osuuskauppa	Retail-food, beverages and tobacco (21, 22, 24)	NO, 22 (Yes)	Food products (2106), non-alcoholic beverages (2203, 2204, 2205, 2206), tobacco products (2403)
178	180	Aro-Yhtyma	Distributors-automotive (87)	Yes	Vehicles (8702), accessories and spare parts (8708)
191	181	Sato	Real estate-investment	NA	S
216	182	Hartwall	Beverages (22)	Yes	Non-alcoholic beverages (2203, 2204, 2205, 2206), juices (2209)
173	183	Elenia	Oil and energy (27, 84)	NO, 84 (Yes)	Gases (270500, 2711), electricity (271600), heating (8402, 8404)
182	184	Axus Finland	Fleet management-rental services	NA	S
192	185	Berner	Distributors-wholesaler (33, 62, 64, 70, 90, 94, 84)	Yes, 33, 62 (NO)	Personal hygiene products (3303, 3304, 3305, 3307), insecticides (3808), babies' garments and accessories (6209), footwear (6405, 6406), medical and laboratory equipments (7017, 9022, 9402), forklift trucks (8427), sports equipments (9506)
150	186	Harjavalta	Home and office products (83, 44, 94)	Yes	Furniture (8302, 4419, 9404, 9403)
193	187	Teknos Group	Chemicals (32, 44, 88, 94, 34)	Yes	Paints and varnishes (3208, 3209, 3405), furniture products (8302, 4419, 9404, 9403)
185	188	Valmet Automotive	Automotive-manufacturing (78)	Yes	Vehicles (7812, 7821, 7831, 7842), accessories and spare parts (7843, 7783), electric vehicles (7868)

(continued)

(continued)

Rank 2016	Rank 2017	Company	Sectors (SITC 2-digit codes)	RCA	Sub-sectors (SITC 4-digit codes)
189	189	Ahlsell	Retail-IT products	NA	Services
143	190	Broman Group	Retail-automotive (87, 89)	Yes	Accessories and spare parts for automotives (8708), boats for pleasure/fishing (8903)
206	191	Saastopankki-ryhma	Banking	NA	S
203	192	Accenture	Commercial services-consultancy	NA	S
209	193	Walki	Paper (48) and forest products (48), mining and metals, i.e. steel and iron (72)	Yes	Plywood (4412), paper for printing (4802), paper for packaging and office (4819), stainless steel both hot rolled (7219, 7220), bars, rods and coils of steel (7227.7228), semi-finished products (7218), wires of steel (7229)
195	194	Vestas Finland	Construction services	NA	S
131	195	Etela-Karjalan Osuuskauppa	Retail-consumer goods, autorepairs, tourism	NA	S
211	196	Snellman	Distributors-meat products (16)	NO	Processed meat products (1602), sausages (160100)
238	197	GE Healthcare	Medical equipment and devices (94, 90)	Yes	Diagnostic machines and parts (9022, 9402, 9033)
184	198	Otava	Media-retailing (48, 49)	Yes	Books and other educational material (4820, 4902, 4901)
219	199	Sinebrychoff	Beverages (22)	Yes	Non-alcoholic beverages (2203, 2204, 2205, 220600)
279	200	Freeport Cobalt	Chemicals and metals (28)	Yes	Various cobalt oxides, metals (2820, 2822, 260500), inorganic salts and oxides (2842, 2881)
145	201	Oulun Energia	Energy-electricity (27, 90)	NO, 84 and 90 (Yes)	Electricity (271600), heating equipments (8402), electricity supply (9028)
196	202	Osuuskunta KPY	Real estate and financial investment services	NA	S
263	203	Solemo	Commercial services-industrial	NA	S

(continued)

Annexure IX: Finland's 500 Biggest Companies (The Talouselämä 500)

(continued)

Rank 2016	Rank 2017	Company	Sectors (SITC 2-digit codes)	RCA	Sub-sectors (SITC 4-digit codes)
199	204	EM Group	Asset management	NA	S
217	205	Vantaan Energia	Oil and energy (27, 90, 84)	NO, 84 and 90 (Yes)	Gases (270500, 2711), electricity (2711600, heating (8403, 8404), electricity supply (9028)
234	206	Wurth	Machinery (73, 96, 84, 68)	Yes	Tools like screw, fasteners, handpowers (7318, 9606, 9607, 8467) abrasives (6805)
212	207	Finnvera	Financial services	NA	S
198	208	Eltel Networks	IT and services	NA	S
215	209	Lansiauto	Distributor-automotive (87)	Yes	Vehicles (8703), accessories and spare parts (8708)
254	210	Tampereen Sahkolaitos	Energy-electricity (27, 90)	No, 90 (Yes)	Electricity (271600), electricity supply (9028)
202	211	AGCO Power	Machinery (85, 84, 87)	Yes	Generators (8501, 8502), agro-equipments and machinery (8432, 8433), tractors (8701), pumps (8413, 8414)
205	212	Rinta-Joupin Autoliike	Retail-automotive (87)	Yes	Vehicles for passengers (8702), light vehicles (8703)
226	213	EPV Energia	Energy-electricity (27, 90, 84)	YES, 27 (NO)	Electricity (271600), heating equipments (8403, 8404), electricity supply (9028)
230	214	Barona Group	Commercial services-RPO	NA	S
201	215	Tuike Finland	Engineering and construction services	NA	S
208	216	F9 Distribution	Distributors-IT products (85)	Yes	Computer equipments (8542, 8543)
181	217	BRP Finland	Machinery-automotive (84)	Yes	Engines for water crafts and boats (8412) engines for four wheelers (8407, 8408), parts and accessories of motor vehicles (8708), recreational vehicles (8903)

(continued)

Rank 2016	Rank 2017	Company	Sectors (SITC 2-digit codes)	RCA	Sub-sectors (SITC 4-digit codes)
218	218	Koskitukki	Forest and paper products (44)	Yes	Wood for paper and forest products (4407, 4412, 4421), fuel wood (4401)
210	219	Consti Yhtiot	Construction-renovation and tech services	NA	S
252	220	Scania Suomi	Retail-automotive (87)	Yes	Trucks (8709), buses (8702), passenger cars (8703)
220	221	Rapala VMC	Distributors-fishing equipments and sports goods	Yes	Sports goods (9506), fishing equipment recreational goods (9507)
197	222	Osuuskunta ItaMaito	Distributors-dairy products (02)	NA	NA
246	223	Hewlett-Packard	Distributor-IT products and services (85, 84)	Yes	Computer and PC equipments (8542, 8543), printers (8469)
239	224	Teleste	IT products and services (85)	Yes	Optical fibres for cable networks (9001), broadcasting and transmission equipments (8526, 8527, 8519) broadband transmission equipments (8517)
213	225	Sponda	Real estate-leasing offices, building, etc.	NA	S
207	226	Ingman Group	Asset management	NA	S
281	227	Finn-Power	Industrial machinery (75, 74, 82)	Yes	Metal sheets (7409, 7506), machinery for punching, shearing and bending (8201, 8202), laser processing (8515)
225	228	Turku Energia	Energy-electricity (27)	NO	Electricity (271600)
231	229	Saarioinen	Food production (04 and 09)	NO	Bakery products (1905), meat product (160100, 1602, 1603), vegetable food (2001, 2004), sauces (2103), ice creams (210500), jams (2007), soups (2104)
222	230	Tech Data Finland	IT services	NA	S

(continued)

Annexure IX: Finland's 500 Biggest Companies (The Talouselämä 500)

(continued)

Rank 2016	Rank 2017	Company	Sectors (SITC 2-digit codes)	RCA	Sub-sectors (SITC 4-digit codes)
204	231	Tukkuheino	Distributors-groceries (19, 16, 20)	NO	Bakery products (1905), meat product (160100, 1602, 1603), vegetable food (2001, 2004), sauces (2103), ice creams (210500), jams (2007), soups (2104)
251	232	Boliden Harjavalta	Metals and mining (74)	Yes	copper products (7407, 7419), silver (7106), gold (7108)
262	233	Huntsman P&A Finland	Chemicals (28)	Yes	Titanium oxides, dioxides (2823)
356	234	Aurubis Finland	Metals and mining (74)	Yes	Copper products including bars, rods and wires (7407, 7408, 741300)
232	235	L-Fashion Group	Distributors-discretionary (62, 61, 65)	NO, 63, 95 (Yes)	Apparels and accessories (6210, 6217, 6114, 6117), socks, knitwears (6115), jackets (6201, 6202, 6203, 6204), swimwears (6211), headgear (650300, 6506), T-shirts (6109), blankets (6301), bed linens (6302), sportswears (9506)
228	236	Oras Invest	Asset management-industrial holding	NA	S
229	237	Ford	Retail-automotive (87)	Yes	Vehicles/passenger cars (8702, 8703), parts and accessories of vehicles (8708, 8714)
265	238	Power Finland			
221	239	Wetteri	Distributors-automotive (87)	Yes	Vehicles/passenger cars (8702, 8703), trucks (8709), trailers (8716)
176	240	Unity Technologies Finland	Gaming-game developers	NA	S
332	241	Vacon	Machinery (85)	Yes	AC drive and convertors (8504, 8537)

(continued)

(continued)

Rank 2016	Rank 2017	Company	Sectors (SITC 2-digit codes)	RCA	Sub-sectors (SITC 4-digit codes)
236	242	IBM	Hardware and software (85)	Yes	Hardware equipment and accessories (8542, 8471), semiconductors (8541)
241	243	Eckero Rederi	Transportation and logistics-services	NA	S
256	244	Boliden Kokkola	Metals and mining (71, 26, 78, 28)	Yes, 26 and 79 (NO)	Copper products (260300), silver (7106), gold (7108), zinc and zinc alloys (7901.260800) aluminium and it alloys (2606, 7601), lead and its alloys (7801, 260700), sulphuric acids (2807)
250	245	Polar Electro	Medical equipment and devices (90, 91, 84)	Yes	Sports watches with GPS (9101, 9102), heart rate monitors (9031) and other specialised machinery (8438)
162	246	Makita	Home and office products (44, 82, 84, 85, 73, 69)	Yes	Tools for drilling and boring (8459, 8460), batteries and other equipments (8507), tools of wood and metals (8201, 7317, 7318, 8214, 7418, 6978, 4421)
235	247	MetroAuto	Retail-automotive (87)	Yes	Vehicles/passenger cars (8703), spare parts (8714)
244	248	Agnico Eagle Finland	Metals and mining (26, 71, 78, 79, 25)	71, 79 (Yes), No	Copper products (260300), silver (7106), gold (7108), zinc and zinc alloys (7901.260800) aluminium and it alloys (2606, 7601), lead and its alloys (7801, 260700), minerals (2530)
249	249	R-kioski	Retail-departmental stores	NA	S
237	250	Helkama-Auto	Automotive (87)	Yes	Vehicles/passenger cars (8702, 8703), parts and accessories of vehicles (8708, 8714)

(continued)

(continued)

Rank 2016	Rank 2017	Company	Sectors (SITC 2-digit codes)	RCA	Sub-sectors (SITC 4-digit codes)
266	251	Atea Finland	Technology services	NA	S
273	252	Borealis Polymers	Manufactured goods-rubbers and plastics (39)	Yes	Polymers of propylene (3902)
224	253	Accountor Holding	Commercial services-human resources and financial services	NA	S
243	254	Kotkamills	Construction materials-forest and paper (44, 48)	Yes	Laminated paper (4821), wood and paper for packing (4415, 4817), swan wood (4407)
303	255	Rinta-Jouppi Jarmo	Retail-automotive (87)	Yes	Vehicles/passenger cars (8703, 8708)
267	256	Siemens	Home and office products-services	NA	S
246	257	Saint-Gobain Rakennustuotteet	Energy-services	NA	S
242	258	Pohjolan Maito	Food production (15)-dairy products (NA)	NO	Edible oils (1517)
274	259	Suomen Nestle	Food-(21) dairy and baby food (NA)	NO	Ice cream (210500)
253	260	E. Hartikainen	Commercial services-non-classifiable established	NA	S
285	261	Umo Capital	Asset management	NA	S
340	262	Normet Group	Manufacturing-construction materials and vehicles (68, 84)	Yes, 93 (No)	Construction materials (6810, 6811, 6902), explosives chargers (9303), lifting equipments (8428, 8426), machinery for drilling (8430, 8459), special-purpose vehicles (8705)
485	263	Peab	Construction-building services	NA	S
248	264	S-Pankki	Finance	NA	S
318	265	Jatke	Construction-building services	NA	S
258	266	Keitele Forest	Construction materials (44)	Yes	Wood products (4403, 4408, 4412, 4421, 4412)
255	267	Catamount	Distributors-automotive (87)	Yes	Vehicles/passenger cars (8703, 8708), trucks and trailers (8709, 8716)
259	268	MTV	Media-broadcasting services	NA	S
257	269	Ramboll Finland	Engineering and construction services	NA	S
343	270	Huawei Technologies	IT-related services	NA	S

(continued)

(continued)

Rank 2016	Rank 2017	Company	Sectors (SITC 2-digit codes)	RCA	Sub-sectors (SITC 4-digit codes)
283	271	Halton Group	Consumer durables (85)	Yes	Vacuum cleaners (8508)
278	272	Unilever Finland	Consumer products (17, 21)	NA	Tea (2101), chocolates and confectionery (1704, 1806), soups (2104), jams (2007), sauces (2103), ice creams (210500)
275	273	Polttimo	Food and beverages (11, 20, 12, 19)	NO	Malt (1107), flour (1208, 1901), cereals (1108, 1102, 1103, 1104), Fruit (22009)
294	274	Containerships	Transportation and logistics-cargo services	NA	S
311	275	Volvo Finland	Retail-automotive (87)	Yes	Vehicles (8702, 8703), accessories and spare parts (8708, 8714)
269	276	SCA Hygiene Products	Household products (33, 62, 44)	Yes, 62, 33 (NO)	Diapers (6209), personal care products (3303, 3304, 3305, 3307, 3308), forest and paper products for packings (4415, 4817, 4819)
260	277	Jyvaskylan Energia	Energy-electricity (27, 90)	Yes, 27 (NO)	Electricity (271600), electricity supply (9028), heating (8402, 8516)
271	278	Rani Plast	Containers and packaging (63, 39)	Yes	Plastic bags (6305, 3926), films (3919, 3920, 3921)
289	279	Rovio Entertainment	Software-game developers	NA	S
291	280	Hennes and Mauritz	Apparel and textile products (61, 64, 89, 62)	NO	Socks, knitwears (6115), jackets (6103, 6104), swimwears (6211), undergarments (6115), headgear (640400, 6405) shirts and T-shirts (6105, 6106, 6109, 6110), sportswears (8947), underpants and trousers (6107, 6108), suits and jackets (6203, 6204), other apparel items (6217, 6215, 6216)

(continued)

Annexure IX: Finland's 500 Biggest Companies (The Talouselämä 500)

(continued)

Rank 2016	Rank 2017	Company	Sectors (SITC 2-digit codes)	RCA	Sub-sectors (SITC 4-digit codes)
264	281	Pohjola Rakennus	Engineering and construction-service	NA	S
272	282	Rexel Finland	Distributors-electrical wholesalers (63, 74, 73, 85)	Yes	Cables (6310, 7312, 741300, 7614), lamps (8513, 7011, 8539, 9405), telecommunication equipments (8517, 8518, 8529)
282	283	Indutrade			
270	284	TUI Finland	Recreation facilities and services-travel and tourism	NA	S
342	285	AGA	Oil–gas (27, 90)	NO	Industrial gas (270500, 2711)
317	286	BMW Suomi	Retail-automotive (87)	Yes	Vehicles/passenger cars (8702, 8708)
284	287	Kaleva Henkivakuutus	Insurance	NA	S
297	288	AGCO Suomi	Distributors-agricultural equipments (84, 87)	Yes	Agricultural equipments and machinery (8432, 8433), tractors (8701)
299	289	Wallac	Medical equipment and devices (90)	Yes	Medical equipments (9021, 9022, 9018)
286	290	Savon Voima	Energy-electricity (27, 90)	NO	Electricity (271600), electricity supply (9028)
276	291	Kuntarahoitus	Financial services	NA	S
308	292	Componenta	Machinery (84)	Yes	Trucks (8426, 8427), drilling machinery (8430, 8460), machinery and mechanical appliances for specialised industries (8438)
334	293	Billerudkorsnas Finland	Forest and paper products (48, 44)	Yes	Paper for printing (4802), paper for packaging (4817), wood for construction (4407, 4409), plywood (4403)
298	294	Fortaco Group	Commercial services (84, 83)	Yes	welding equipments (8468), frames, booms and lifting equipments (8426, 8308, 8428), excavators and loaders (8429), parts for nuclear reactors and windmill (8409, 8410, 8411, 8412)

(continued)

(continued)

Rank 2016	Rank 2017	Company	Sectors (SITC 2-digit codes)	RCA	Sub-sectors (SITC 4-digit codes)
–	295	Inspecta Group	Institutional financial services	NA	S
277	296	Kreate	Engineering and construction-contractor services	NA	S
288	297	Scandic Hotels	Hospitality	NA	S
352	298	Abloy	Electrical equipments-commercial and restaurant building equipments and services (85)	Yes	Locking system and architectural hardware (8517, 8518, **8529**)
–	299	Helsingin Kaukokiito	Transportation and logistics-services	NA	S
307	300	LM Ericsson	Hardware-communication equipments (76)	Yes	Communication equipments (7642, 7643, 7648)
280	301	Energia Myynti Suomi	Energy-electricity (27, 90)	NO	Electricity (271600), electricity supply (9028)
–	302	Salomaa Yhtiot	Commercial services-consultancy	NA	S
392	303	Transmeri Group	Retail discretionary (33, 34, 38, 96)	NO, 34 and 38 (Yes)	Personal care products (3303, 3304, 3305, 3307, 3401), pesticides (3808), detergents (3402), cleaners (9605)
316	304	Lahti Energia	Energy and gas-electricity (27, 90)	NO	Electricity (271600), electricity supply (9028), natural gas (2711)
323	305	Delete Group	Waste and environ services-recycling and waste management services	NA	S
325	306	Eriksson Capital	Commercial services-health care, cellulose/fibre packing, leasing aircrafts, stock trading (39, 85, 63, 48)	Yes	Packing materials (3923, 4819, 6305), healthcare tubing solutions (8540) and films (3919, 3920, 3921)
290	307	Peikko Group	Construction materials (69, 25, 84, 82, 68, 85)	Yes	Construction material (6902, 6905, 2524, 6811), lifting equipments (8428), punchers (8207), sockets (8537)
295	308	Panostaja	Investment	NA	S

(continued)

Annexure IX: Finland's 500 Biggest Companies (The Talouselämä 500)

(continued)

Rank 2016	Rank 2017	Company	Sectors (SITC 2-digit codes)	RCA	Sub-sectors (SITC 4-digit codes)
268	309	Metos	Home and office products (39, 82, 84, 63, 70, 73)	Yes	Kitchen products (3924, 8215, 8211, 6302, 7013), freezing equipment (8418), cooking and heating equipment (7321), other dishwashing machines (8422)
375	310	Technopolis	Commercial services-construction	NA	S
302	311	J. Karkkainen	Retail-consumer durables (33, 95, 84, 69, 96, 48)	Yes, 33, 96 (NO)	Beauty products (3303, 3304, 3305, 3307, 3401), books and stationery (4820, 490300, 9609, 9608), toys (9501, 9503), household appliances (8421), other household goods (6911)
310	312	Koiviston Auto	Retail-automotive (87, 84)	Yes	Vehicles (8703), accessories and spare parts (8708), trucks (8709, 8427)
301	313	RAO Nordic	Energy-trading	NA	S
328	314	Airbus Defence and Space	Defence and space (87, 88)	Yes	Aircraft and spacecraft (8802, 8803, 8805), armed vehicles (870100)
363	315	Suomen Transval	Transportation and logistics-services	NA	S
305	316	C.J. Hartman	Retail-building materials (69, 63, 94, 25, 83)	Yes	Construction materials (6902, 6905, 2524, 6811), furnishing materials (9404, 6304, 6303, 8302, 9403)
306	317	Santen	Biotech and pharma (30)	Yes	Ophthalmologic drugs (3003, 3004, 3006)
327	318	Fira	Construction-design and development services	NA	S
314	319	Algol	Distributor-wholesale (70, 40, 30, 39)	Yes	Laboratory equipments (7017, 8419), industrial rubber (4001, 4002), articles of plastics (3926), pharma products (3003, 3004, 3006)

(continued)

(continued)

Rank 2016	Rank 2017	Company	Sectors (SITC 2-digit codes)	RCA	Sub-sectors (SITC 4-digit codes)
424	320	Virala	Engineering and consulting company	NA	S
304	321	Golden Heights	Retail-jewellery (71, 91)	Yes	Jewellery of gold/silver (7113, 7114), watches (9101)
347	322	Osuuskauppa Maakunta	Retail-non-classifiable established	NA	S
355	323	HP Finland	IT-related services	NA	S
341	324	Maitosuomi	Distributors-dairy products	NA	NA
287	325	BE Group	Distributors-steel, aluminium and stainless steel (72, 76)	Yes	Stainless steel products (7219, 7220), bars, wires and coils (7227, 7228, 7229), aluminium products (7601, 7604, 7605, 7606, 7616)
329	326	Lenovo Technology	Distributors—electrical machinery (85)	Yes	Computer and PC equipments (8517, 8518)
293	327	Sulzer Pumps Finland	Machinery-pumps (84)	Yes	Pumps (8413, 8414)
83	328	Porhon Autoliike	Retail-automotive (87)	Yes	Vehicles (8703), accessories and spare parts (8708)
326	329	Helvar Merca	Machinery (84, 78, 85)	Yes	Ballasts (8417), containers (8422, 7863, 7311), construction and building machinery (8457), sound recording equipments (8519, 8520, 8523), video recording equipments (8521)
331	330	TS-Yhtyma	Media services	NA	S
361	331	F-Secure	Software-cyber security services	NA	S
313	332	Boliden Kevitsa Mining	Metals and mining (75, 26, 71)	Yes, 26 (NO)	Nickel products (7502, 750, 7506, 7507, 7508, 260400), copper ore (260300), platinum metals (7110)
443	333	Dustin Finland	Retail-IT products (85)	Yes	Telecommunication equipments (8517, 8518)
312	334	Ovako Imatra	Iron and steel (72)	Yes	Steel bars (7227, 7228)

(continued)

(continued)

Rank 2016	Rank 2017	Company	Sectors (SITC 2-digit codes)	RCA	Sub-sectors (SITC 4-digit codes)
348	335	Securitas	Commercial-security services	NA	S
425	336	Vaasan	Retail-bakery (17)	NO	Bakery products and confectionery items (1704)
309	337	Maintpartner	Industrial-construction and installation services	NA	S
322	338	Holiday Club Resorts	Hospitality	NA	S
382	339	Asuntosaation Asumisoikeus	Real estate-services	NA	S
337	340	Ferratum	Asset management	NA	S
223	341	Thermo Fisher Scientific	Medical equipment and devices-research (84, 38, 30, 70, 98)	Yes	Freezers (8418), vaccines (3002), laboratory equipments (7017, 8417, 8419, 980200, 3822)
333	342	Afarak Group	Metals and mining (72, 28, 26)	Yes, 26 (NO)	Ferro and chromium alloys (7202, 7203, 7204, 2610, 2819)
321	343	Esperi Care	Healthcare facilities and services	NA	S
319	344	Kiilto Family	Chemicals (35, 39, 34, 33)	Yes, 35 and 33 (NO)	Adhesives (3506), floor or ceiling coverings (3918), cleaners (3402), personal care (3303, 3304, 3305, 3307, 3401)
366	345	Omya	Metals and mining (48, 35, 30, 68, 32, 69)	Yes, 35 and 30 (NO)	Paper for printing (4802), paper for packaging (4819), paints (3207, 3208), adhesives (3506), plaster (6809), articles of plastics (8939), ceramic (6902), cement products (2521, 2523), pharma goods (3003, 3004, 3006)
324	346	Koivunen	Distributors-automotive (85, 87, 73)	Yes	Vehicles (8703), accessories and spare parts (8708), batteries (8506), screws (7318)
362	347	Keskisuomalainen	Media-publishing and broadcasting	NA	S

(continued)

(continued)

Rank 2016	Rank 2017	Company	Sectors (SITC 2-digit codes)	RCA	Sub-sectors (SITC 4-digit codes)
406	348	SGN Group	Sporting goods (87, 95, 61)	Yes, 61 (NO)	sporting good and recreational equipments (9506, 6112) and, motor bikes (8711)
354	349	Coriant	IT services	NA	S
339	350	Nammo Lapua	Defence (93)	NO	Bullets, calibre cartridges and components (9306, 930400)
351	351	Palodex Group	Medical equipment and devices (90)	Yes	X-ray equipments and devices (9021, 9022, 9018)
371	352	DSV Road	Transportation and logistics-services	NA	S
359	353	Basware	Software-financial solutions	NA	S
365	354	Polkky	Forest and paper products (44)	Yes	Wood products (4407, 3805, 4409, 4402, 4403)
335	355	Graniittirakennus Kallio	Engineering and construction (69)	Yes	Construction materials (6902, 6905, 6903, 6904)
338	356	Bassadone Automotive	Retailer-automotive (87)	Yes	Vehicles (8703), parts and accessories (8708)
386	357	Pori Energia	Energy-electricity (27, 85, 84)	Yes, 27 (NO)	Electricity (271600), electricity supply (9028), heating (8516, 8403)
383	358	Omnicom Media Group	Media-publishing and broadcasting	NA	S
344	359	Steveco	Transportation and logistics-services	NA	S
367	360	Suur-Savon Sahko	Construction-ship building	NA	S
247	361	Musti Group	Retail-pet products (70, 42)	NO, 70 (Yes)	Pet products and accessories (420100), aquariums (7013)
300	362	Isku-Yhtyma	Telecom-voice and data services	NA	S
374	363	Sucros	Sugar (17)	NO	Sugar beet and products (1701, 1702)
346	364	Loiste	Media-advertising services	NA	S
345	365	Alandsbanken	Asset management	NA	S

(continued)

Annexure IX: Finland's 500 Biggest Companies (The Talouselämä 500)

(continued)

Rank 2016	Rank 2017	Company	Sectors (SITC 2-digit codes)	RCA	Sub-sectors (SITC 4-digit codes)
350	366	Adven Group	Energy-electricity (27, 90) and other products (84, 85)	Yes, 27 (NO)	Electricity (271600), electricity supply (9028), heating (8516, 8403), refrigeration (8418), industrial steams (8402, 843, 8404), gas (270500, 2711)
296	367	Kuehne + Nagel	Transportation and logistics-services	NA	S
353	368	SL Yhtiot	Real estate-renting, buying and selling	NA	S
436	369	Contineo	Commercial services-non-classifiable established	NA	S
370	370	Keula	Retail-departmental stores	NA	S
315	371	Santander	Consumer finance	NA	S
–	372	Katterno	Energy-electricity (27, 90)	NO	Electricity (271600), electricity supply (9028)
330	373	Vaasan Sahko	Energy-electricity (27, 90)	NO	Electricity (271600), electricity supply (9028)
380	374	Turun Seudun Energiantuotanto	Energy-electricity (27, 90), wood fuels (24)	Yes, 27 (NO)	Electricity (271600), electricity supply (9028), heating (8516, wood fuel (2450)
412	375	Secto Automotive	Retail-rental passenger cars (87)	Yes	Vehicles/passenger cars (8703), spare parts (8714)
417	376	Shell Aviation Finland	Oil–petroleum products (27)	NO	Petroleum products (2710, 2712, 2713, 2714, 2715)
378	377	SAP Finland	Software-application and software development	NA	S
376	378	Bauhaus & Co.	Consumer services-retail stores	NA	S
372	379	NCC Industry	Engineering and construction-services	NA	S
410	380	RTV-Yhtyma	Transportation and logistics-services	NA	S
390	381	General Motors Finland	Distributors-automotive (87)	Yes	Vehicles (8702, 8703, 8704, 8705), trucks, vans (8603, 8709), trailers (8716) and parts (8708, 8715)
379	382	Inwido Finland	Home and office products (73, 83)	Yes	Doors and windows (7308, 8302), aluminium structures (7610)

(continued)

(continued)

Rank 2016	Rank 2017	Company	Sectors (SITC 2-digit codes)	RCA	Sub-sectors (SITC 4-digit codes)
381	383	Autosalpa	Retail-automotive (87)	Yes	Vehicles/passenger cars (8703), spare parts (8714)
336	384	Andament Group	Construction and building-services	NA	S
377	385	Finnfeeds	Chemicals-non-classifiable established		
391	386	Nets	Industrial-financial services	NA	S
463	387	Janssen - Cilag	Biotech and pharma (30)	Yes	Pharmaceutical goods (3003, 3004, 3006)
358	388	Huurre Group	Transportation and logistics-services	NA	S
360	389	Tjareborg	Hospitality and tourism	NA	S
429	390	Inchcape Motors	Distributors-automotive (87)	Yes	Vehicles/passenger cars (8703), spare parts (8714)
409	391	Dentsu Aegis Network	Media-advertising and marketing services	NA	S
399	392	Restamax	Hospitality-restaurants	NA	S
369	393	Fonecta	Communication-Internet based services	NA	S
357	394	Tervakoski	Forest and paper products (48)	Yes	Cigarette paper (4813) and paper packaging (4817, 4819)
227	395	Lampopuisto	Oil–petroleum products (27)	NO	Petroleum products (2710, 2712, 2713, 2714, 2715)
401	396	Espoon Asunnot	Real estate-services	NA	S
407	397	Staffpoint Holding	Commercial services-consultancy	NA	S
385	398	Martela	Home and office products (94, 70, 83)	Yes, 83 (NO)	Furniture products (8302, 9403, 9404, 7013)
414	399	TA-Yhtyma	Real estate-services	NA	S
–	400	Kymppivoima Hankinta	Energy-electricity (27, 90)	NO	Electricity (271600), electricity supply (9028)
388	401	Molnlycke Health Care	Medical equipment and devices (90, 30)	Yes	Surgical instruments (9021), pharma goods (3003, 3004, 3006)
416	402	Schneider Electric	Energy-electricity (27, 90)	NO	Electricity (271600), electricity supply (9028)
387	403	DHK Freight	Transportation and logistics-services	NA	S
389	404	Energiameklarit	Energy-electricity (27, 90)	NO	Electricity (271600), electricity supply (9028)

(continued)

Annexure IX: Finland's 500 Biggest Companies (The Talouselämä 500)

(continued)

Rank 2016	Rank 2017	Company	Sectors (SITC 2-digit codes)	RCA	Sub-sectors (SITC 4-digit codes)
403	405	Sodexo	Commercial-outsourcing and managemant services	NA	S
449	406	XXL Sports and Outdoor	Retail-sports (61, 64, 95, 89, 87, 40, 91)	Yes, 61, 95 (NO)	Sports footwear (6405), sporting goods (9506), swimwears (6112), binoculars (9005), rowing machines (8903), camping goods (6306), watches (9102), equipment for horses and dogs (402100), bags (6305), motorbikes (8711), parts and accessories of motorbikes (8713), headphones and loudspeakers (8518)
396	407	PricewaterhouseCoopers	Commercial services-consultancy	NA	S
427	408	Lappeenrannan Energia	Energy and gas (27, 90)	NO	Electricity (271600, electricity supply (9028), gas (270500, 2711)
458	409	Finnsementti	Construction materials (25)	Yes	Cement products (2521, 2522, 2523)
430	410	PRT-Forest	Housing and construction (94, 63, 44)	Yes	Prefabricated buildings (9406), windows and doors (8302), furnishing products (9404, 9406, 6304, 6303, 6302, 6301), laminated wood (4408, 4412)
373	411	Harvestia	Forest and paper products (44)	Yes	Wood products (4403, 4404, 4407, 4409, 4415, 4416)
420	412	Moventas Gears	Electrical equipments (84, 98)	Yes, 98 (NO)	Gear and gearing products for transmission (8483, 9801), turbine (8406, 8410, 8411), parts and accessories of turbines (8431)
500	413	SEO	Distributors-equipments (84, 90)	Yes	Laboratory equipments (8419, 9021), scientific instruments (9025, 9026, 9027, 9030), drafting instruments (9031)

(continued)

(continued)

Rank 2016	Rank 2017	Company	Sectors (SITC 2-digit codes)	RCA	Sub-sectors (SITC 4-digit codes)
413	414	Murata Electronics	Electrical equipments (85, 90)	Yes	Oscillators (9030), capacitors (8532)
394	415	Rocia	Dairy products	NA	NA
451	416	Reka	Electrical equipments (85)	Yes	Voltage (8535, 8536), communication equipments (8517, 8518), power machinery and equipments (8454, 8466, 7711)
418	417	Hong Kong Group	Retail-departmental stores	NA	S
428	418	KPMG	Commercials services-consultancy	NA	S
397	419	Lumon Invest	Home builders	NA	S
439	420	Pyhasalmi Mine	Metals and mining-non-classifiable established	NA	S
404	421	CRF Box	Commercial services-clinical online	NA	S
402	422	Veljekset Keskinen	Retail-departmental stores	NA	S
438	423	Tuottajain Maito	Distributors-dairy products	NA	NA
440	424	SSR Group	Construction-services	NA	S
233	425	Cor Group	Commercial services-healthcare services	NA	S
421	426	Lindorff Finland	Commercial services-finance	NA	S
405	427	Bang and Bonsomer	Chemicals (39, 84, 32, 35)	Yes, 35 (NO)	Adhesives (3506), polymers (3901, 3902, 3903), printing ink (8443), paints and varnish (3208, 3209)
292	428	Danisco Sweeteners	Healthcare facilities and services	NA	S
408	429	Realia Holding	Real estate-services	NA	S
461	430	Jysk	Retail-home products (44, 83, 94, 70)	Yes, 83 (NO)	Decoratives (4421), furniture goods (8302, 9403, 9404, 7013)
364	431	Turva	Commercial services-securities	NA	S
–	432	PAF	Gambling and casinos-hospitality	NA	S
434	433	PlusTerveys	Hospital and health care	NA	S
483	434	Ernst and Young	Commercial services-consultancy	NA	S
419	435	Atoy	Distributors-automotive (87)	Yes	Vehicles (8703), spare parts (8708)

(continued)

(continued)

Rank 2016	Rank 2017	Company	Sectors (SITC 2-digit codes)	RCA	Sub-sectors (SITC 4-digit codes)
445	436	Raute	Machinery-for wood products (72)	Yes	Machinery for producing wood products (8465)
456	437	ALMACO Group	Construction-shipbuilding services	NA	S
423	438	Hes-Pro Finland	Distributors-supermarkets	NA	S
460	439	Affecto	Commercial services-IT	NA	S
433	440	Bewi Styrochem	Chemicals (39)	Yes	Polystyrene (3903)
464	441	Lival	Electrical/electronic manufacturing (94, 85)	Yes	Lighting products (9405, 8539)
455	442	Roche	Pharmaceuticals (33)	Yes	Pharmaceutical goods (3303.3304, 3306)
432	443	Microsoft	Software and IT services	NA	S
–	444	Whirlpool Nordic	Consumer electronics (84, 85)	Yes	Dishwashing, refrigerators, AC (8418, 8422), vacuum cleaners (8508), laundry equipments (8450), electrothermic and mechanic devices (8509, 8540)
–	445	Kemppi	Welding solutions	NA	S
415	446	KSS Energia	Energy-electricity (27)	NO	Electricity (271600, electricity supply (9028)
459	447	Pohjantahti	Insurance	NA	S
435	448	Brown-Forman Finland	Beverages (22)	Yes	Non-alcoholic beverages (220300, 2204, 2205, 220600)
450	449	A-Katsastus	Automotive-inspection services	NA	S
393	450	Minimani Yhtiot	Real estate-services	NA	S
467	451	Forchem	Chemicals (27, 13, 39)	Yes, 13, 27 (NO)	Oil products (2710), resins (1301, 3909, 3911)
486	452	Anvia	Telecommunications-services	NA	S
–	453	Insta Group	Defence, automation and IT services	NA	S
442	454	Novartis Finland	Pharmaceuticals (30)	Yes	Pharmaceutical goods (3003, 3004, 3006)
431	455	Ahola	Transportation and logistics-services	NA	S
446	456	OSTP Finland	Mining and metals (72)	Yes	Steel bars (7228, 7229), steel products (7224, 6732, 7306)

(continued)

(continued)

Rank 2016	Rank 2017	Company	Sectors (SITC 2-digit codes)	RCA	Sub-sectors (SITC 4-digit codes)
422	457	Nordic Regional Airlines	Airline aviation services	NA	S
462	458	Unisport-Saltex Group	Sporting goods (95)	Yes, 61 (NO)	Sporting wears and goods (9506, 6112, 6405)
477	459	Instru Optiikka	Retail-optics (90)	Yes	Eyeglasses, sunglasses, lenses (9003, 9004, 9005)
471	460	Future Group	Software and IT services	NA	S
454	461	Westas	Forest and paper products (44, 48)	Yes	Plywood (4412), paper for printing (4802), paper for packaging and office (4817, 4819)
–	462	Glaston	Commercial services-events	NA	S
484	463	LM Tietopalvelut	Information services	NA	S
444	464	Transtech	Manufacturing-railroad (86)	Yes	Railway vehicles (860400, 860500, 8606, 8607, 8608)
–	465	SKS Group	Industrial automation	NA	S
398	466	Panasonic Marketing	Consumer electronics (85)	Yes	Electrical equipments (8517, 8518, 7811)
480	467	Cp Kelco	Chemicals (13, 38, 40)	Yes, 13 (NO)	Cellulose and products (1301, 3805, 3806, 4001)
–	468	Viessmann Refrigeration Systems	Mechanical/industrial engineering (84)	Yes	Refrigeration products for Industry (8418)
261	469	Visma Ohjelmistoyhtiot	Software solutions and services	NA	S
447	470	Ebookers Finland	Insurance	NA	S
496	471	Flakt Woods	Mechanical/industrial engineering (84)	Yes	Air and heating equipments (8418, 8415, 8516)
453	472	Pohjois-Karjalan Sahko	Energy-electricity (27, 90)	NO	Electricity (271600), electricity supply (9028)
441	473	Cupori	Construction materials (69)	Yes	Construction materials (6902, 6903, 6904, 6905)
476	474	International Paper Nordic Sales Company	Paper and forest products (48)	Yes	Paper for printing (4802), paper for packaging and office (4817, 4819), paperboard (4804, 4805, 4808, 4811)
–	475	Nordic Morning	Marketing and advertising	NA	S

(continued)

Annexure IX: Finland's 500 Biggest Companies (The Talouselämä 500)

(continued)

Rank 2016	Rank 2017	Company	Sectors (SITC 2-digit codes)	RCA	Sub-sectors (SITC 4-digit codes)
495	476	Jujo Thermal	Paper and forest products (48)	Yes	Paper for printing (4802), paper for packaging and office (4817, 4819), paperboard (4804, 4805, 4808, 4811)
437	477	Isojoen Konehalli	Wholesale-industrial services (84, 87)	Yes	Agricultural equipments and machinery (8432, 8433), tractors (8701), parts (8708)
472	478	Mobility Finland			
–	479	Orkla Confectionery and Snacks Finland	Distributor-confectionery and snacks (17)	NO	Confectionery items and snacks (1704)
–	480	Burger-In	Restaurants	NA	S
481	481	Bronto Skylift	Mechanical/industrial engineering (84)		Rescue and firefighting platforms for construction works (8424, 8426)
490	482	Silmaasema Fennica	Retail-optics (90)	Yes	Eyeglasses, sunglasses, lenses (9003, 9004, 9005)
–	483	Nobina Finland	Passenger transportation-services	NA	S
426	484	Terrafame Group	Metals and mining (26, 75, 79)	Yes	Nickel ores and metals (260400, 7502, 7505, 7506), zinc and zinc alloys (7901, 7905, 7906)
–	485	Volvo Construction Equipment Finland	Machinery-construction (69, 87, 86)	Yes	Construction materials (6902, 6903, 6904, 6905), trucks (8709, 8603), trailers (8716)
457	486	Dow Suomi	Chemicals (26, 28, 39, 47)	Yes, 26 (NO)	Articles of plastics (3926), chlorides (2827), chemical pulp (470200, 470300), polymers (3901, 3902), municipal waste and sewage sludge (2621)
–	487	A-Lehdet	Media-publishing	NA	S
–	488	Mi-Hoiva	Asset management	NA	S
–	489	Evac Group	Maritime services	NA	S
487	490	Forcit	Chemicals (36, 93)	NO	Civil and military explosives (3602, 9306)

(continued)

(continued)

Rank 2016	Rank 2017	Company	Sectors (SITC 2-digit codes)	RCA	Sub-sectors (SITC 4-digit codes)
–	491	Kuopion Energia	Energy-electricity (27, 87, 24, 85)	Yes, 27 (NO)	Electricity (271600), electricity supply (8731), heating (8516), wood fuel (2450)
488	492	Comptel	IT and services	NA	S
–	493	Eaton Power Quality	Electrical equipments (85)	Yes	Uninterrupted power supply equipments (8537, 8538)
–	494	PostNord	Logistics and supply chain-services	NA	S
–	495	Parker Hannifin	Mechanical/industrial engineering (84)	Yes	Hydraulic filters (8421)
498	496	GlaxoSmithKline	Distributors-pharmaceutical (30)	Yes	Pharmaceutical goods (3002, 3003, 3004, 3006)
499	497	Nizhex Scandinavia	Chemicals (39, 24)	Yes	Propylene (3902), other polymers (3901, 3904, 2907)
478	498	Samlink	IT and services	NA	S
384	499	Quattro Mikenti	Building services	NA	S
448	500	Capgemini Finland	Commercial services-consultancy	NA	S

1. NA: Not Applicable means the company is into services (S) or its products/services were not analysed beyond single-digit category of SITC HS classification
2. NO: Means that the Company was not found to be in an RCA (revealed comparative advantage) sector or sub-sector, or that RCA is zero or indeterminate
3. Yes: Means the company is in an RCA sector or sub-sector
Source: The list of Companies included above is from the Finnish Journal Talouelämä that annually publishes lists of Finland's biggest companies. The analysis of these companies from the perspective of Finland-India business potential and the RCA attribution is part of this Study to locate correspondences between the 500 biggest companies of Finland and India.
4. Note: The above list and the RCAs have uses that are not limited to the 500 biggest companies. SMEs in the RCA sectors are also part of clusters that can benefit when matches are found for potential trade and trade-substituting investments based on Chaps. 2 and 3 and Annexures 1 to VIII

Annexure X: India's 500 Biggest Companies (The ET-500)

Rank	Company name	Sector (SITC 2-digit codes)	RCA	Sub-sector (SITC 4-digit codes)
1	Indian Oil Corporation Ltd.	Petrochemicals and gaseous (27)	Yes	Bitumen (2714), cooking gas (2711), paraffin wax (2712), industrial and aviation fuel (270900, 2710)
2	Reliance Industries Ltd.	Petrochemicals and gaseous (27)	Yes	Bitumen (2714), cooking gas (2711), paraffin wax (2712), industrial and aviation fuel (270900, 2710)
3	Tata Motors Ltd.	Automotive (87)	Yes	Cars and buses (8703, 8704), spare parts and accessories (8708) and trucks (8709)
4	State Bank of India	Banking (S)	NA	S
5	Bharat Petroleum Corporation Ltd.	Petrochemicals and gaseous (27, 28)	Yes	Bitumen (2714), cooking gas (2711), paraffin wax (2712), industrial and aviation fuel (270900, 2710)
6	Hindustan Petroleum Corporation Ltd.	Petrochemicals and gaseous (27, 28)	Yes	Bitumen (2714), cooking gas (2711), paraffin wax (2712), industrial and aviation fuel (270900, 2710)
7	Rajesh Exports Ltd.	Manufacturing unassembled jewellery (71)	Yes	Gold manufacturing (7113, 7114, 7108), diamonds (7102)

(continued)

© Springer Nature Singapore Pte Ltd. 2019
A. N. Mathur, *Finland–India Business Opportunities*,
https://doi.org/10.1007/978-981-10-8019-7

Annexure X: India's 500 Biggest Companies (The ET-500)

(continued)

Rank	Company name	Sector (SITC 2-digit codes)	RCA	Sub-sector (SITC 4-digit codes)
8	Oil and Natural Gas Corporation Ltd.	Petrochemicals and gaseous (27, 28)	Yes	Bitumen (2714), cooking gas (2711), paraffin wax (2712), industrial and aviation fuel (270900, 2710)
9	Tata Steel Ltd.	Steel manufacturing and construction materials (72, 73 and 84)	Yes	Stainless steel (7218, 7219, 7220), bar, rods and wires (7221, 7222, 7223, 7229, 7312), plates, bearings and tubes (7305, 7306), balls and bearings (8482)
10	Tata Consultancy Services Ltd.	Software services (S)	NA	S
11	Bharti Airtel Ltd.	Telecommunications (S)	NA	S
12	Larsen & Toubro Ltd.	Construction services	NA	S
13	ICICI Bank Ltd.	Banking (S)	NA	S
14	Hindalco Industries Ltd.	Alloys of copper and aluminium (74, 76, 71, 26)	Yes, 26 (NO)	Hard and special aluminium alloys (7601, 2606), wires, rods, ingots and billets of aluminium (7604, 7605, 7608, 7616), copper rods and cathodes (7407, 7402), silver, gold, platinum (7108, 7106, 7110)
15	Coal India Ltd.	Coal and its products (27)	Yes	Coke (2704, 2705), tar (2706) and other oil products (2707)
16	NTPC Ltd.	Energy (27)	Yes	Electrical energy/electricity (271600)
17	Mahindra & Mahindra Ltd.	Automotive (87)	Yes	Cars and buses (8703, 8704), spare parts and accessories (8708), trucks (8709) and tractors (8701)
18	HDFC Bank Ltd.	Banking (S)	NA	S
19	Vedanta Ltd.	Metals mining (72, 74, 76, 78, 79) and gaseous (28)	Yes, 78 and 79 (NO)	Zinc (7901), aluminium (7601), lead (7801), copper (7403), silver (7106), iron (7202)

(continued)

(continued)

Rank	Company name	Sector (SITC 2-digit codes)	RCA	Sub-sector (SITC 4-digit codes)
20	Infosys Ltd.	Software services (S)	NA	S
21	Maruti Suzuki India Ltd.	Automotive (87)	Yes	Cars (8703), spare parts and accessories (8708)
22	Punjab National Bank	Banking (S)	NA	S
23	GAIL (India) Ltd.	Banking (S)	NA	S
24	Wipro Ltd.	Banking (S)	NA	S
25	Housing Development Finance Corporation Ltd.	Banking (S)	NA	S
26	Bank of Baroda	Banking (S)	NA	S
27	Axis Bank Ltd.	Banking (S)	NA	S
28	Canara Bank	Banking (S)	NA	S
29	Bank of India	Banking (S)	NA	S
30	Adani Enterprises Ltd.	Energy (27), gases (28), fuel (27), edible oils (15)	Yes	Coal and its products (2701, 2704), natural gas (2711), edible oils (1517)
31	HCL Technologies Ltd.	Software services (S)	NA	S
32	JSW Steel Ltd.	Steel manufacturing (72)	Yes	Stainless steel (7218, 7219, 7220), bar, rods and wires (7221, 7222, 7223, 7229, 7312), plates, bearings and tubes (7305, 7306), balls and bearings (8482)
33	ITC Ltd.	Tobacco products (24), FMCG (33, 34), apparel and clothing accessories (61), paper products (48)	Yes, 24 (NO)	Cigarettes (2402), breads, cakes and biscuits (1905), paper boards and papers (4802, 4813, 4821, 4823, 4820), trousers (6103), shirts (6105, 6109), other apparel products (6109, 61300), juices and beverages (2009), other food products (1806, 1902, 2104, 2016), personal care (3401, 3303, 3304, 3305)

(continued)

(continued)

Rank	Company name	Sector (SITC 2-digit codes)	RCA	Sub-sector (SITC 4-digit codes)
34	Mangalore Refinery And Petrochemicals Ltd.	Petrochemicals (27)	Yes	Petroleum products (2709, 2710, 2711, 2712)
35	Steel Authority of India (SAIL) Ltd.	Steel manufacturing (72)	Yes	Stainless steel (7218, 7219, 7220), bar, rods and wires (7221, 7222, 7223, 7229, 7312), plates, bearings and tubes (7305, 7306), balls and bearings (8482)
36	Tata Power Company Ltd.	Energy (27)	Yes	Electrical energy/electricity (271600)
37	Motherson Sumi Systems Ltd.	Automotive (87) and industrial machinery (84)	Yes	Spare parts and accessories (8708), air compressor (8414), metal mining machinery (8459, 8461, 8464)
38	Grasim Industries Ltd.	Textile and fibres (55, 59), cement (25), chemicals and fertilisers (29)	Yes, 55 and 59 (NO)	Viscose fibre (5902), cement products (2521, 2523), caustic soda (2815), synthetic yarn (5509, 5510, 5511)
39	Union Bank of India	Banking (S)	NA	S
40	Idea Cellular Ltd.	Telecommunications (S)	NA	S
41	Redington (India) Ltd.	Software services (S)	NA	S
42	Hindustan Unilever Ltd.	Personal care and hygiene (33, 34), food (16, 18, 19, 20)	NO, 33 and 34 (Yes)	Juices and beverages (2009), other food products (1806, 1902, 2104, 2016), personal care (3401, 3303, 3304, 3305)
43	IDBI Bank Ltd.	Banking (S)	NA	S
44	Ruchi Soya Industries Ltd.	Edible oils (12, 15)	Yes	Oilseeds (1207), edible oils (1517)
45	Hero MotoCorp Ltd.	Automotive (87)	Yes	Motorcycles (8711), bicycle (8712), parts and accessories (8714)
46	Sun Pharmaceutical Industries Ltd.	Pharmaceutical products (30)	Yes	Pharmaceutical goods (3003, 3004, 3005, 3006)

(continued)

Annexure X: India's 500 Biggest Companies (The ET-500)

(continued)

Rank	Company name	Sector (SITC 2-digit codes)	RCA	Sub-sector (SITC 4-digit codes)
47	Bharat Heavy Electricals Ltd.	Construction machinery (84 and 85)	Yes	Boilers (8401, 8402), compressors and fans (8414), turbines (8406), valves (8481), generators (8405), semiconductors, batteries and cells (8486, 8506, 8540)
48	Kotak Mahindra Bank Ltd.	Banking (S)	NA	S
49	Central Bank of India	Banking (S)	NA	S
50	Power Finance Corporation Ltd.	Financial services (S)	NA	S
51	Petronet LNG Ltd.	Natural gas (27)	Yes	Liquified gases (2711)
52	Tech Mahindra Ltd.	Consultancy (S)	NA	S
53	Chennai Petroleum Corporation Ltd.	Petroleum products (27)	Yes	Petroleum products (2710, 2711, 2712, 2713, 2714)
54	Indian Overseas Bank	Banking (S)	NA	S
55	UltraTech Cement Ltd.	Construction and building materials (25, 68, 39)	Yes	Tiles and adhesives (3918, 3919), cements (2521, 2522, 2523), plasters (6809)
56	Syndicate Bank	Banking (S)	NA	S
57	Adani Power Ltd.	Energy (27)	Yes	Electrical energy/electricity (271600)
58	Rural Electrification Corporation Ltd.	Financial services(S)	NA	S
59	Aditya Birla Nuvo Ltd.	Financial services (S), telecommunications (S), apparels (61)	Yes	Garments (6103, 6105, 6107, 6109, 6114)
60	Bajaj Auto Ltd.	Automotive (87)	Yes	Motorcycles (8711), parts and accessories (8714)
61	Jet Airways (India) Ltd.	Air transportation (S)	NA	S
62	Reliance Communications Ltd.	Telecommunications (S)	NA	S

(continued)

(continued)

Rank	Company name	Sector (SITC 2-digit codes)	RCA	Sub-sector (SITC 4-digit codes)
63	Power Grid Corporation of India Ltd.	Energy (27)	Yes	Electrical energy/electricity (271600)
64	Oriental Bank of Commerce	Banking (S)	NA	S
65	Ashok Leyland Ltd.	Automotive (87)	Yes	Buses (8702), trucks (8709, parts and accessories (8714, 8708), tractors (8701)
66	Corporation Bank	Banking (S)	NA	S
67	Allahabad Bank	Banking (S)	NA	S
68	Tata Communications Ltd.	Telecommunications (S)	NA	S
69	UCO Bank	Banking (S)	NA	S
70	Andhra Bank	Banking (S)	NA	S
71	Reliance Infrastructure Ltd.	Energy (27)	Yes	Electrical energy/electricity (271600)
72	MMTC Ltd.	Retail metal (76, 72, 79, 26)	Yes, 26 and 79 (NO)	Alloys (7202, 7601, 7901), ores (2601, 2602, 2603, 2604, 2605, 2606, 2607)
73	Jindal Steel and Power Ltd.	Construction material (84, 86, 72, 73)	Yes, 86 (NO)	Railway wagons (8606), boilers (8402), railway or tramway tracks (8608), angles and channels (7216), wire, cables, ropes (7313), articles of iron (7325)
74	Indian Bank	Banking (S)	NA	S
75	Tata Chemicals Ltd.	Chemicals and fertilisers (25, 28, 31)	Yes, 31 (NO)	Carbonates (2836), cement (2521, 2522, 2523), urea (284700), fertilisers (3101, 3102, 3103)
76	Jaiprakash Associates Ltd.	Hospitality (S), construction services	NA	S
77	Hindustan Zinc Ltd.	Metals manufacturing (79, 28, 71, 81)	Yes, 28 and 71 (NO)	Lead (7801), silver (7106), zinc (7901), cadmium (8107), sulphuric acid (2807)

(continued)

Annexure X: India's 500 Biggest Companies (The ET-500)

(continued)

Rank	Company name	Sector (SITC 2-digit codes)	RCA	Sub-sector (SITC 4-digit codes)
78	Asian Paints Ltd.	Paints and coatings (32, 35, 96)	NO, 35 (Yes)	Paints and varnishes (3208, 3209, 3210), adhesives (3506), brushers and rollers (9603)
79	InterGlobe Aviation Ltd.	Air transportation (S)	NA	S
80	YES Bank Ltd.	Banking (S)	NA	S
81	Dr. Reddy's Laboratories Ltd.	Services	NA	S
82	EID Parry (India) Ltd.	Sugar manufacturing (17), energy (271600)	NO, 27 (Yes)	Sugar (1701, 1702), molasses (1703), electrical energy/electricity (271600)
83	IndusInd Bank Ltd.	Banking (S)	NA	S
84	Lupin Ltd.	Pharmaceutical products (30)	Yes	Pharmaceutical goods (3003, 3004, 3005, 3006)
85	Videocon Industries Ltd.	Consumer electronics (84), telecommunications (S)	Yes	Home appliances (8479), washing machines (8445)
86	Amtek Auto Ltd.	Automotive (87)	Yes	Parts and accessories (8708, 8711)
87	Gitanjali Gems Ltd.	Retail jewellery (71)	Yes	Jewellery (7113, 7114, 7115, 7116)
88	Bank of Maharashtra	Banking (S)	NA	S
89	Aurobindo Pharma Ltd.	Pharmaceutical products (30)	Yes	Pharmaceutical goods (3003, 3004, 3005, 3006)
90	PTC India Ltd.	Energy (27)	Yes	Electrical energy/electricity (271600)
91	Cipla Ltd.	Pharmaceutical products (30)	Yes	Pharmaceutical goods (3003, 3004, 3005, 3006)
92	GMR Infrastructure Ltd.	Energy (27) and construction services	Yes	Electrical energy/electricity (271600)
93	MRF Ltd.	Rubber tyres (40)	NO	Rubber tyres and inner tubes (4011, 4012, 4013)
94	Bajaj Finserv Ltd.	Financial services (S)	NA	S

(continued)

(continued)

Rank	Company name	Sector (SITC 2-digit codes)	RCA	Sub-sector (SITC 4-digit codes)
95	UPL Ltd.	Chemicals and fertilisers (28, 31)	Yes, 28 (NO)	Carbonates (2836), urea (284700), fertilisers (3101, 3102, 3103)
96	Alok Industries Ltd.	Textile (52, 58, 60, 61.63)	Yes, 58 and 61 (NO)	Garments (6114, 6111), sportwear (6112), clothing accessories (6117), bed linen (6302), handkerchiefs (6213), handbags (6305), cotton yarn (5207), terry towel (5802)
97	Bharti Infratel Ltd.	Telecommunications (S)	NA	S
98	Vijaya Bank	Banking (S)	NA	S
99	Sundaram Clayton Ltd.	Automotive (87)	Yes	Parts and accessories (8708, 8711)
100	Eicher Motors Ltd.	Automotive (87)	Yes	Buses (8702), trucks (8709, parts and accessories (8714, 8708), tractors (8701)
101	LIC Housing Finance Ltd.	Financial services (S)	NA	S
102	CESC Ltd.	Energy (27)	Yes	Electrical energy/electricity (271600)
103	Torrent Power Ltd.	Energy (27)	Yes	Electrical energy/electricity (271600)
104	ACC Ltd.	Construction materials (25)	Yes	Cement products (2521, 2522, 2523)
105	Apollo Tyres Ltd.	Automotive (40)	NO	Tyres for passenger and heavy vehicles (4011, 4012, 4013)
106	Bhushan Steel Ltd.	Steel (72)	Yes	Rolled products of steel (7219, 72220), sheets and coils (7229, 7301)
107	Max Financial Services Ltd.	Financial services (S)	NA	S
108	Coromandel International Ltd.	Fertilisers (31, 38)	Yes, 38 (NO)	Fertilisers, insecticides and pesticides (3103, 3104, 3808)
109	TVS Motor Company Ltd.	Automotive (87)	Yes	Two-wheeler vehicles (8711), parts and accessories (8714)

(continued)

(continued)

Rank	Company name	Sector (SITC 2-digit codes)	RCA	Sub-sector (SITC 4-digit codes)
110	Siemens Ltd.	Industrial machinery (85)	Yes	Electric motors and generators (8501, 8502), transformers (8504), rail vehicles and traffic signalling (8512, 8530)
111	United Bank of India	Banking (S)	NA	S
112	Dena Bank	Banking (S)	NA	S
113	Titan Company Ltd.	Jewellery and accessories (91)	Yes, 91 (NO)	Watches (9101), eyewear (9004, 9005), jewellery (7113) and other accessories (7115)
114	Godrej Industries Ltd.	Personal care and hygiene (33, 34), food (15), organic chemicals (29)	Yes	Soaps and perfumes (3401, 3303, 3304, 3305, 3307), edible oils (1517, 1513), alcohols (2905, 2907, 2908, 2909)
115	Oil India Ltd.	Oil and gas (27)	Yes	Crude oil (2710), natural gas (2710, 2705)
116	Reliance Power Ltd.	Energy (27)	Yes	Electrical energy/electricity (271600)
117	Bosch Ltd.	Automotive (87) and industrial machinery (84, 85)	Yes	Spare parts and accessories (8708, 8714), chassis and bodies (8706, 8707), motors and generators (8501, 8502), semiconductors and senors (8541), hammers and drillers (8462, 8460, 8461)
118	Suzlon Energy Ltd.	Industrial machinery (84)	Yes	Turbines and engines (8406, 8410, 8411)
119	State Trading Corporation Of India Ltd.	Trading	NA	S
120	United Spirits Ltd.	Alcoholic beverages (22)	NO	Spirits and beverages (2201, 220300, 220600)
121	State Bank of Travancore	Banking (S)	NA	S

(continued)

(continued)

Rank	Company name	Sector (SITC 2-digit codes)	RCA	Sub-sector (SITC 4-digit codes)
122	Chambal Fertilisers and Chemicals Ltd.	Chemicals and fertilisers (28, 31)	NO	Fertilisers, insecticides and pesticides (3103, 3104, 3808)
123	State Bank of Bikaner and Jaipur	Banking (S)	NA	S
124	Cairn India Ltd.	Oil and gas (27)	Yes	Crude oil (2710), natural gas (2710, 2705)
125	Rain Industries Ltd.	Petrochemicals and chemicals (27, 29, 39)	Yes	Petroleum coke (2713), coal tar (2707, 2708), phenolics (2907), resins (3911)
126	JSW Energy Ltd.	Energy (27)	Yes	Electrical energy/electricity (271600)
127	Shriram Transport Finance Company Ltd.	Financial services(S)	NA	S
128	NHPC Ltd.	Energy (27)	Yes	Electrical energy/electricity (271600)
129	Zuari Agro Chemicals Ltd.	Chemicals and fertilisers (28, 31)	Yes, 38 (NO)	Fertilisers, insecticides and pesticides (3103, 3104, 3808)
130	Reliance Capital Ltd.	Financial services (S)	NA	S
131	Cadila Healthcare Ltd.	Pharmaceutical products (30)	Yes	Pharmaceutical goods (3003, 3004, 3005, 3006)
132	Shree Renuka Sugars Ltd.	Sugar manufacturing (17), energy (27)	NO, 27 (Yes)	Sugar (1701, 1702), molasses (1703), electrical energy/electricity (271600), ethyl alcohol (2207, 2208)
133	Future Enterprises Ltd.	Retail trade (S)	NA	S
134	Ambuja Cements Ltd.	Construction materials (25)	Yes	Cement products (2521, 2522, 2523)
135	DLF Ltd.	Real estate (S)	NA	S
136	NCC Ltd.	Construction services (S)	NA	S
137	Exide Industries Ltd.	Electronic machinery (85)	Yes	Batteries (8506)

(continued)

Annexure X: India's 500 Biggest Companies (The ET-500)

(continued)

Rank	Company name	Sector (SITC 2-digit codes)	RCA	Sub-sector (SITC 4-digit codes)
138	Indiabulls Housing Finance Ltd.	Financial services (S)	NA	S
139	Punjab & Sind Bank	Banking (S)	NA	S
140	Bombay Burmah Trading Corporation Ltd.	Automotive (87)	Yes	Parts and accessories (8708)
141	Hindustan Construction Company Ltd.	Construction services (S)	NA	S
142	IDFC Ltd.	Financial services (S)	NA	S
143	Godrej Consumer Products Ltd.	Consumer goods (33, 34, 38, 48)	Yes	Soaps, talcum and perfumes (3401, 3303, 3304, 3305, 3307), insecticides (3808), wipes and tissues (480300)
144	Havells India Ltd.	Electrical equipments (84, 74, 73, 84, 85)	Yes	Home appliances (8479, 7418), boards and switches (8535, 8536, 8537), pumps (8413, 8414), fans and coolers (8414), capacitors (8532), batteries and cells (8506), wires and cables (7312, 741300)
145	JBF Industries Ltd.	Industrial products (51, 52, 59)	NO, 52 (Yes)	Polyester (5902) sewing thread (5204, 5207), yarn (5109)
146	Britannia Industries Ltd.	Food (19)	NO	Bakery products (1904, 1905)
147	Tube Investments of India Ltd.	Automotive (87), construction material (73) and fitness equipments (95)	Yes, 95 (NO)	Steel tubes and strips (7304), bicycle, parts and accessories (8712, 8714, 8705), fitness equipments (9506)
148	Rashtriya Chemicals & Fertilizers Ltd.	Chemicals and fertilisers (28, 31, 25)	Yes, 31 (NO)	Fertilisers (3103, 3104, 3808), urea (284700), nitric acid (2808), sulphuric acid (2807), ammonium nitrate and biocarbonates (2836, 2834), gypsum (2520)

(continued)

(continued)

Rank	Company name	Sector (SITC 2-digit codes)	RCA	Sub-sector (SITC 4-digit codes)
149	IL&FS Transportation Networks Ltd.	Construction services (S)	NA	S
150	Dabur India Ltd.	Consumer goods (20, 33, 38)	Yes	Fruit juices (2009), personal care (3305, 3304), herb products (3808)
151	Federal Bank Ltd.	Banking (S)	NA	S
152	Arvind Ltd.	Textiles and apparels (55, 39), industrial machinery (84, 73)	Yes, 55 and 59 (NO)	Fabric (5515, 5516), polyester viscose (5902), polymers (3901), centrifuges (8421), containers and vessels for gas (7311)
153	Lanco Infratech Ltd.	Mining, energy (27) and construction services (S)	Yes	Electrical energy/electricity (271600), coal (2701)
154	KEC International Ltd.	Construction services (S), electrical equipments (74, 93)	Yes	Power cables (741300), optical fibres (9001)
155	Tata Global Beverages Ltd.	Beverages (21, 22)	NO	Beverages (2101, 2201, 2202)
156	NLC India Ltd.	Energy (27)	Yes	Electrical energy/electricity (271600)
157	Welspun Corp Ltd.	Construction services (S), textile (48, 58)	Yes, 58 (NO)	Towel (480300, 5802)
158	Uttam Galva Steels Ltd.	Steel (72, 73)	Yes	Hot and rolled steel (7225, 7226), steel sheets (7301)
159	NMDC Ltd.	Mining and exploration (26, 71)	Yes, 26 (NO)	Iron (2601), copper (260300), manganese (2602), diamonds (7102), tungsten (261100), platinum (7110), gold (7108)
160	Nestle India Ltd.	Consumer eatables (17, 18, 19, 21)	NO	Chocolate (1704, 1806), prepared food (1904, 1905, 1902), ice creams and beverages (210500, 2101)
161	ABB India Ltd.	Electrical equipments (85)	Yes	Electric motors and generators (8501, 8502), transformers (8504), circuits (8535, 8536)

(continued)

Annexure X: India's 500 Biggest Companies (The ET-500)

(continued)

Rank	Company name	Sector (SITC 2-digit codes)	RCA	Sub-sector (SITC 4-digit codes)
162	Bharat Electronics Ltd.	Electrical equipments (85)	Yes	Radars (8526, 8527), batteries (8506), transformers (8504)
163	Century Textiles and Industries Ltd.	Textiles and apparels (61, 62, 63, 54), construction material (25), pulp and paper (48)	Yes, 63 (NO)	Cement products (2521, 2522, 2523), bed linen (6302), shirts (6109), suits (6203), sulphuric acid and chlorides (2807, 2806), caustic soda (2815), chlorine (2801), tissue papers (480300), packaging paperboards (4819), yarn filament (5401)
164	Adani Ports and Special Economic Zone Ltd.	Construction services (S)	NA	S
165	State Bank of Mysore	Banking (S)	NA	S
166	Sintex Industries Ltd.	Textile and fabrics (50, 59, 52)	NO, 52 (Yes)	Silk yarn (5004), viscose rayon and nylon (5902), cotton yarn (5205)
167	Dewan Housing Finance Corporation Ltd.	Financial services (S)	NA	S
168	Jindal Saw Ltd.	Iron and steel (74, 72)	Yes	Carbon alloys (7403), stainless steel products (7218)
169	National Fertilizers Ltd.	Chemicals and fertilisers (28, 31, 38)	Yes, 28 (NO)	Fertilisers (3102, 3103, 3104), insecticides, herbicides (3808), urea (284700), nitric acids (2808), nitrates (2834)
170	Bharat Forge Ltd.	Automotive parts, 87, 86), construction equipments (84)	Yes	Valves (8481), turbines (8410), shafts (8483), rail parts (8607), piston (8407, 8408), chassis (8706)
171	Glenmark Pharmaceuticals Ltd.	Pharmaceutical products (30)	Yes	Pharmaceutical goods (3003, 3004, 3005, 3006)
172	Shree Cements Ltd.	Construction materials (25)	Yes	Cement (2521, 2522, 2523)

(continued)

(continued)

Rank	Company name	Sector (SITC 2-digit codes)	RCA	Sub-sector (SITC 4-digit codes)
173	Jindal Stainless Ltd.	Iron and steel (74, 72)	Yes	Ferro-alloys (7202), hot and roll steel (7221), wires and sheets (7223, 7221, 7301)
174	L&T Finance Holdings Ltd.	Financial services (S)	NA	S
175	National Aluminium Company Ltd.	Metal and chemicals (28, 76)	Yes	Aluminium products (7604, 7605, 7606, 7616), caustic soda (2815)
176	Kalpataru Power Transmissions Ltd.	Construction services (S)	NA	S
177	Bajaj Finance Ltd.	Financial services (S)	NA	S
178	PC Jeweller Ltd.	Jewellery and accessories (91)	Yes	Jewellery (7113, 7114, 7115, 7116)
179	Jammu & Kashmir Bank Ltd.	Banking (S)	NA	S
180	Jindal Stainless (Hisar) Ltd.	Steel (72)	Yes	Products of stainless steel (7219, 7221, 7222, 7223)
181	Gujarat Fluorochemicals Ltd.	Chemicals (39)	Yes	Synthetic resins (3907, 3909, 3911), articles of plastics (3921, 3923, 3926)
182	Jindal Poly Films Ltd.	Chemicals (39)	Yes	Films (3919, 3920, 3921)
183	JK Tyre & Industries Ltd.	Automotive (40)	NO	Tyres for passenger and heavy vehicles (4011, 4012, 4013)
184	Jain Irrigation Systems Ltd.	Agricultural solutions (S)	NA	S
185	Piramal Enterprises Ltd.	Pharmaceutical products (30)	Yes	Pharmaceutical goods (3003, 3004, 3005, 3006)
186	Torrent Pharmaceuticals Ltd.	Pharmaceutical products (30)	Yes	Pharmaceutical goods (3003, 3004, 3005, 3006)
187	Kothari Products Ltd.	Trading (S)	NA	S
188	Vardhman Textiles Ltd.	Textile and fibre (52, 55, 59)	Yes, 59 (NO)	Yarn (5205, 5511, 5504, 5506, 5206, 5207), viscose (5902)
189	Container Corporation of India Ltd.	Logistics (S)	NA	S

(continued)

Annexure X: India's 500 Biggest Companies (The ET-500)

(continued)

Rank	Company name	Sector (SITC 2-digit codes)	RCA	Sub-sector (SITC 4-digit codes)
190	Dalmia Bharat Ltd.	Construction materials (25)	Yes	Cement (2521, 2522, 2523)
191	Mahindra & Mahindra Financial Services Ltd.	Financial services (S)	NA	S
192	Kwality Ltd.	Edibles (21)	NO	Ice creams (210500)
193	Mphasis Ltd.	Software services (S)	NA	S
194	Gujarat State Fertilizer and Chemicals Ltd.	Chemicals and fertilisers	Yes, 31 (NO)	Fertilisers (3102, 3103, 3104), ammonium (2813), sulphuric acid (2806, 2807)
195	Marico Ltd.	Consumer goods	Yes	Personal care (3303, 3304, 3305, 3307)
196	Gujarat Gas Ltd.	Gases (27)	Yes	Gases (2711)
197	Karur Vysya Bank Ltd.	Banking (S)	NA	S
198	Uflex Ltd.	Plastics (35, 37, 39, 69)	Yes, 37 and 63 (NO)	Films (3919, 3920, 3921), bags (6305), adhesives (3506, 3707)
199	Apollo Hospitals Enterprise Ltd.	Hospitality (S)	NA	S
200	South Indian Bank Ltd.	Banking (S)	NA	S
201	Aditya Birla Fashion and Retail Ltd.	Textile, apparels and accessories (91, 90, 71, 64, 61, 62)	Yes, 64 and 91 (NO)	Watches (9101), eyewear (9004, 9005), jewellery (7113) and other accessories (7115), Footwear (6403, 6404, 6405), suits, shirts and trousers (6103, 6104, 6105, 6106, 6204, 6205), babies garments (6111)
202	Welspun India Ltd.	Construction services (S), textile (48, 58)	Yes, 58 (NO)	Towel (480300, 5802)
203	Zee Entertainment Enterprises Ltd.	Media (S)	NA	S
204	CG Power and Industrial Solutions Ltd.	Electrical equipments (84, 85)	Yes	Transformers (8504), circuits (8535, 8536, 8542), motors and generators (8501, 8502), shafts (8483)

(continued)

(continued)

Rank	Company name	Sector (SITC 2-digit codes)	RCA	Sub-sector (SITC 4-digit codes)
205	Voltas Ltd.	Electrical equipment and industrial machinery	Yes	Dumpers and loaders (8429), conveyor (8428), pumps and fans (8414, 8415)
206	Simplex Infrastructures Ltd.	Construction services (S)	NA	S
207	NBCC (India) Ltd.	Construction services (S)	NA	S
208	DCM Shriram Ltd.	Sugars and chemicals (17, 28, 25) and fertilisers (31)	Yes, 17 and 31 (NO)	Sugar (1701, 1702), urea (284700), caustic soda (2815), chlorines (2801), hydrochloric acid (2806), cement (2521), fertilisers (3102, 3103, 3104)
209	Jubilant Life Sciences Ltd.	Pharmaceutical products (30)	Yes	Pharmaceutical goods (3003, 3004, 3005, 3006)
210	CEAT Ltd.	Automotive	NO	Tyres for passenger and heavy vehicles (4011, 4012, 4013)
211	Raymond Ltd.	Textile, apparels and (51, 59, 50, 61) industrial equipments (82, 84)	NO, 61 and 84 (Yes)	Wool (5101), viscose (5902), suits (6101), shirts (6105), silk (5002), shawls and scarves (6214), metal cutters (8203), pulleys (8425), hammer and other tools (8462)
212	Allcargo Logistics Ltd.	Logistics (S)	NA	S
213	Religare Enterprises Ltd.	Financial services (S)	NA	S
214	Prism Cement Ltd.	Construction material (25)	Yes	Cement (2521, 2522, 2523)
215	Thermax Ltd.	Industrial equipments (84, 85)	Yes	Boilers (8401, 8402), transformers (8504), heaters (8516), pumps and valves (8413, 8414), cooling equipments (8418)
216	Karnataka Bank Ltd.	Banking (S)	NA	S
217	Gammon India Ltd.	Construction services (S)	NA	S

(continued)

Annexure X: India's 500 Biggest Companies (The ET-500)

(continued)

Rank	Company name	Sector (SITC 2-digit codes)	RCA	Sub-sector (SITC 4-digit codes)
218	Pidilite Industries Ltd.	Paints and coatings (32, 37, 39)	NO, 39 (Yes)	Adhesives (3707), paints and varnishes (3208, 3209, 3210), printing ink (3215), synthetic resins (3907, 3909)
219	Cummins India Ltd.	Energy, oil and gas (27)	Yes	Oil and gas (2710, 2711), electrical energy (271600)
220	Centrum Capital Ltd.	Financial services (S)	NA	S
221	SpiceJet Ltd.	Airline services (S)	NA	S
222	Edelweiss Financial Services Ltd.	Financial services (S)	NA	S
223	IRB Infrastructure Developers Ltd.	Construction services (S)	NA	S
224	Mahindra CIE Automotive Ltd.	Automotive (87)	Yes	Spare parts and accessories (8708, 8714), chassis and bodies (8706, 8707)
225	Alkem Laboratories Ltd.	Pharmaceutical products (30)	Yes	Pharmaceutical goods (3003, 3004, 3005, 3006)
226	Apar Industries Ltd.	Industrial equipments (84, 85, 27, 33)	Yes	Engines (8408), compressor (8414), paraffin (2712), personal care (3305, 3304), Transformers (8504), conductors (8541)
227	United Breweries Ltd.	Alcoholic beverages (22)	NO	Spirits and beverages (2201, 220300, 220600)
228	Sundaram Finance Ltd.	Financial services (S)	NA	S
229	HCL Infosystems Ltd.	Technological solutions (S)	NA	S
230	Kesoram Industries Ltd.	Automotive (40)	NO	Tyres for passenger and heavy vehicles (4011, 4012, 4013)
231	Muthoot Finance Ltd.	Financial services (S)	NA	S

(continued)

(continued)

Rank	Company name	Sector (SITC 2-digit codes)	RCA	Sub-sector (SITC 4-digit codes)
232	BASF India Ltd.	Pharmaceutical (30), agrochemicals (38), petrochemicals (27)	Yes	Pharmaceutical goods (3003, 3004, 3005, 3006), insecticides (3808), detergents (3401), petrochemicals (2710, 2712, 2713)
233	India Cements Ltd.	Construction materials (25)	Yes	Cement (2521, 2522, 2523)
234	Weizmann Forex Ltd.	Financial services (S)	NA	S
235	Bajaj Hindusthan Sugar Ltd.	Sugar and industrial alcohol (17, 22)	NO	Sugar (1701, 1702), alcohol (2207, 2208)
236	Mindtree Ltd.	Software services (S)	NA	S
237	Indian Hotels Company Ltd.	Hospitality (S)	NA	S
238	Shoppers Stop Ltd.	Retail trade (S)	NA	S
239	Amara Raja Batteries Ltd.	Electrical equipment (85)	Yes	Batteries (8506)
240	Prestige Estates Projects Ltd.	Real estate (S)	NA	S
241	Kansai Nerolac Paints Ltd.	Paints and Varnishes (32)	NO	Paints and varnishes (3208, 3209, 3210), brushers and rollers (9603)
242	Berger Paints (India) Ltd.	Paints and varnishes (32)	NO	Paints and varnishes (32)
243	Kama Holdings Ltd.	Chemicals and polymers (39, 59) and pharmaceuticals (30)	Yes, 59 (NO)	Packaging films (3919, 3920, 3921), nylon cord and polyester (5902), pharmaceuticals (3006)
244	Gujarat Narmada Valley Fertilizers & Chemicals Ltd.	Chemicals and fertilisers (28, 31)	Yes	Urea (284700), fertilisers (3102, 3103, 3104), nitric acid (2808), acetic acid (2001), ammonium carbonate (2836)
245	Bajaj Electricals Ltd.	Electrical and industrial equipments (69, 84.73.82, 85)	NO, 73 and 85 (Yes)	Chimneys (6905), home appliances (8451, 8452), rice cookers, grinders, stoves (7321, 7322, 7323), choppers (8214), refrigerators (8418), vacuum cleaners (8508)
246	IFCI Ltd.	Financial services (S)	NA	S

(continued)

Annexure X: India's 500 Biggest Companies (The ET-500)　　　　　　　　　　297

(continued)

Rank	Company name	Sector (SITC 2-digit codes)	RCA	Sub-sector (SITC 4-digit codes)
247	SRF Ltd.	Chemicals (39), electrical equipments (84), fabrics (59, 95)	Yes, 59 and 95 (NO)	Fishnets (9507), nylon fabrics (5902), refrigerators (8418), air conditioner (8414), polyester films (3920, 3921)
248	Fortis Healthcare Ltd.	Healthcare services (S)	NA	S
249	GlaxoSmithKline Consumer Healthcare Ltd.	Pharmaceuticals (30)	Yes	Pharmaceutical goods (3003, 3004, 3005, 3006)
250	ISGEC Heavy Engineering Ltd.	Industrial equipments (84, 85)	Yes	Boilers (8401, 8402), transformers (8504), heaters (8516), pumps and valves (8413, 8414), cooling equipments (8418), Bagasse (2303)
251	Wockhardt Ltd.	Pharmaceutical products (30)	Yes	Pharmaceutical goods (3003, 3004, 3005, 3006)
252	Inox Wind Ltd.	Industrial equipments (84, 85)	Yes	Turbines and engines (8406, 8410), generators (8501)
253	Deepak Fertilisers & Petrochemicals Corporation Ltd.	Chemicals (28) and fertilisers (31)	Yes	Nitric acids (2808), ammonia (2814), fertilisers (3102, 3103)
254	KSK Energy Ventures Ltd.	Energy (27)	Yes	Electricity (271600)
255	Punj Lloyd Ltd.	Construction services (S)	NA	S
256	Pratibha Industries Ltd.	Construction services (S)	NA	S
257	Oracle Financial Services Software Ltd.	IT solutions (S)	NA	S
258	Ballarpur Industries Ltd.	Pulp and paper (48)	Yes	Printing paper (4802), pulp products (481200, 4822, 4823)
259	Bombay Rayon Fashions Ltd.	Textile and fabrics (52, 54, 61, 55)	Yes, 55 (NO)	Yarn (5205, 5511, 5504, 5506, 5206, 5207), apparels (6105, 6107, 6109, 6205), fabrics (5208, 5212, 5407)

(continued)

(continued)

Rank	Company name	Sector (SITC 2-digit codes)	RCA	Sub-sector (SITC 4-digit codes)
260	PDS Multinational Fashions Ltd.	Garments and personal care (61, 62, 33)	Yes	Babies garments (6111), apparels for men and women (6105, 6107, 6109, 6205, 6104, 6106, 6202, 6115, 6204, 6206, 6208), beauty products (3304)
261	BS Ltd.	Construction services (S)	NA	S
262	GVK Power & Infrastructure Ltd.	Construction services (S)	NA	S
263	Jaiprakash Power Ventures Ltd.	Energy (27)	Yes	Electrical energy/electricity (271600)
264	Thomas Cook (India) Ltd.	Financial services (S)	NA	S
265	Shipping Corporation of India Ltd.	Transportation (S)	NA	S
266	Biocon Ltd.	Pharmaceuticals (30)	Yes	Pharmaceutical goods (3006, 3303, 3304)
267	APL Apollo Tubes Ltd.	Steel and iron (73, 83)	Yes, 83 (NO)	Steel tubes and pipes (7304), iron pipes (7303, 7306), door frames (8301, 8308
268	Whirlpool of India Ltd.	Electronic machinery (84)	Yes	Refrigerators (8418), air conditioner (8414), washing machines (8450), other electrical machines (8453)
269	Cholamandalam Investment and Finance Company Ltd.	Financial services (S)	NA	S
270	Colgate-Palmolive (India) Ltd.	Personal care (99)	Yes	Toothpaste, toothbrush, mouthwash and other oral care products (9999)
271	Usha Martin Ltd.	Steel (72, 73)	Yes	Wires and ropes (7312), steel bars (7221, 7222, 7227)
272	SRS Ltd.	Asset management (S)	NA	S
273	Binani Industries Ltd.	Construction materials (25) and energy (27)	Yes	Electricity (271600), cement (2521, 2522, 2523)

(continued)

(continued)

Rank	Company name	Sector (SITC 2-digit codes)	RCA	Sub-sector (SITC 4-digit codes)
274	Great Eastern Shipping Company Ltd.	Logistics (S)	NA	S
275	IDFC Bank Ltd.	Financial services (S)	NA	S
276	Shriram City Union Finance Ltd.	Financial services (S)	NA	S
277	IIFL Holdings Ltd.	Financial services (S)	NA	S
278	Sadbhav Engineering Ltd.	Construction services (S)	NA	S
279	Supreme Industries Ltd.	Consumer durables (39, 34, 83, 94)	Yes, 83 (NO)	Furniture (8302, 9403), crates and boxes (4819), films (3919, 3920), petrochemical products (3403)
280	Shirpur Gold Refinery Ltd.	Metal mining	Yes	Gold (7108, 710900)
281	Shilpi Cable Technologies Ltd.	Technical equipments (74, 73)	Yes	Copper wires, bars, rods (7407, 7408), cables (7312)
282	Forbes & Company Ltd.	Hospitality (S)	NA	S
283	Divi's Laboratories Ltd.	Pharmaceutical products (30)	Yes	Pharmaceutical goods (3003, 3004, 3006)
284	Blue Star Ltd.	Furniture and office products (70, 83, 84, 94)	Yes	Furniture and office products (7013, 8305, 8302, 9403), air conditioning machines (8415), refrigerators (8418)
285	JK Cement Ltd.	Construction materials (25, 39)	Yes	Cement (2521, 2522, 2523), floor covering adhesives (3918, 3919)
286	Rolta India Ltd.	IT solutions (S)	NA	S
287	Bayer CropScience Ltd.	Agro-products (38, 52, 10, 12)	Yes, 12 and 15 (NO)	Insecticides, pesticides (3808), rice (1006), cotton (5201), oilseeds (1207)
288	Uttam Value Steels Ltd.	Steel	Yes	Flat-rolled and hot-rolled products of steel (7225, 7226)
289	Trident Ltd.	Home products (48, 63, 94), batteries and sulphuric acid (28, 85)	Yes, 63 (NO)	Towel (480300, 5802), blankets and bed linen (6301, 6302, 6303), cushions (9404), batteries (8506), sulphuric acid (2807)

(continued)

(continued)

Rank	Company name	Sector (SITC 2-digit codes)	RCA	Sub-sector (SITC 4-digit codes)
290	Indraprastha Gas Ltd.	Gases (27)	Yes	Gases (2711)
291	The Ramco Cements Ltd.	Construction materials (25, 38, 68)	Yes	Cement (2521, 2522, 2523), concretes (381600, 6810)
292	Nagarjuna Fertilizers and Chemicals Ltd.	Chemicals and fertilisers (28, 31)	Yes, 31 (NO)	Fertilisers (3102, 3103, 3104), ammonium (2813), sulphuric acid (2806, 2807), zinc sulphate (2832), urea (284700)
293	Gokul Agro Resources Ltd.	Food (10, 11, 15)	Yes, 11 (NO)	Cereals (1108), edible oil (1507, 1508, 1509, 151000, 1511, 1512, 1514)
294	Mahanagar Telephone Nigam Ltd.	Services (S)	NA	S
295	Escorts Ltd.	Construction equipments (84)	Yes	Forklift trucks (8427), crane (8426), roller (8482), graders and loaders (8429)
296	Balkrishna Industries Ltd.	Automotive (40)	NO	Tyres for heavy vehicles (4011, 4012, 4013)
297	Future Lifestyle Fashions Ltd.	Apparels (61)	Yes	Men's and Women's wear (6101, 6102, 6103, 6104, 6105, 6106, 6107, 6108, 6109, 6110)
298	Network 18 Media & Investments Ltd.	Media (S)	NA	S
299	Birla Corporation Ltd.	Construction materials (25), jute (53) and other products (63, 57)	NO, 25 (Yes)	Cement (2521, 2522, 2523), jute products (5303, 5307, 5310), bags (6305), carpets (5701, 5703, 5704)
300	GE T&D India Ltd.	Electrical machinery and equipment (85)	Yes	Electrical transformers, static converters (e.g. rectifiers) and inductors (8504)
301	Hatsun Agro Products Ltd.	Dairy (19)	NO	Dairy powders (1105)

(continued)

Annexure X: India's 500 Biggest Companies (The ET-500) 301

(continued)

Rank	Company name	Sector (SITC 2-digit codes)	RCA	Sub-sector (SITC 4-digit codes)
302	KRBL Ltd.	Cereals (10)	Yes	Rice (1006)
303	Gokul Refoils & Solvent Ltd.	Edible oil (12)	Yes	Groundnut oil and its fractions (1508)
304	Castrol India Ltd.	Energy (27)	Yes	Petroleum oils (2710)
305	City Union Bank Ltd.	Banking (S)	NA	S
306	Aban Offshore Ltd.	Energy (27)	Yes	Petroleum and oil (2710, 2713)
307	Hinduja Global Solutions Ltd.	Banking (S), energy (27)	Yes	S, petroleum and oil (2710, 2713)
308	Sundram Fasteners Ltd.	Industrial equipments (84, 96, 72)	Yes, 96 (NO)	Pumps (8413, 8414), fasteners (9606, 9607), shafts (8483), rods (7227)
309	Balmer Lawrie & Company Ltd.	Cereals (10)	Yes	Buckwheat, millet and canary seed; other cereals (1008)
310	Strides Shasun Ltd.	Pharmaceutical products (30)	Yes	Pharmaceutical goods (3003, 3004, 3005, 3006)
311	SREI Infrastructure Finance Ltd.	Banking (S)	NA	S
312	KPIT Technologies Ltd.	Software services (S)	NA	S
313	Firstsource Solutions Ltd.	Software services (S)	NA	S
314	Polyplex Corporation Ltd.	Chemicals (59)	NO	Tyre cord fabric of high tenacity yarn of nylon or other polyamides, polyesters or viscose rayon (5902)
315	BGR Energy Systems Ltd.	Energy (27)	Yes	Electricity/electrical energy (271600)
316	Cyient Ltd.	Software services (S)	NA	S
317	Vakrangee Ltd.	Financial services (S)	NA	S
318	Coffee Day Enterprises Ltd.	Coffee (9)	NO	Malt, whether or not roasted (1107)
319	Alembic Pharmaceuticals Ltd.	Pharmaceutical products (30)	Yes	Pharmaceutical goods (3003, 3004, 3005, 3006)
320	Hexaware Technologies Ltd.	Software services (S)	NA	S

(continued)

(continued)

Rank	Company name	Sector (SITC 2-digit codes)	RCA	Sub-sector (SITC 4-digit codes)
321	Force Motors Ltd.	Automotive (87)	Yes	Cars and buses (8703, 8704), spare parts and accessories (8708) and trucks (8709)
322	Dish TV India Ltd.	Television image and sound recorders and reproducers (85)	Yes	Electrical lighting or signalling equipment (8512)
323	Compuage Infocom Ltd.	Software services (S)	NA	S
324	IVRCL Ltd.	Beverages (22)	NO	Waters, including natural or artificial mineral waters and aerated waters, not containing added sugar or other sweetening (2201)
325	ITD Cementation India Ltd.	Construction material (25)	Yes	Cement (2521, 2522, 2523)
326	Surya Roshni Ltd.	Electronic goods (	Yes	Bulbs and lamps (8539, 7011, 8513), fans (7322), water heaters (8516)
327	SJVN Ltd.	Energy (27)	Yes	Electricity (271600)
328	Tata Teleservices (Maharashtra) Ltd.	Communication (s)	NA	S
329	Zensar Technologies Ltd.	Software services (S)	NA	S
330	BEML Ltd.	Industrial equipments (84)	Yes	Mining equipments, excavators and loaders (8429, 8460, 8461, 8462), pumps (8413, 8414), engines and motors (8407, 8408)
331	Mangalore Chemicals & Fertilizers Ltd.	Chemicals and fertilisers (29, 31)	Yes, 31 (NO)	Caustic soda (2815), fertilisers (3102, 3103, 3104), urea (284700)
332	Jyoti Structures Ltd.	Energy (27)	Yes	Electrical energy/electricity (271600)
333	LT Foods Ltd.	Cereals (10)	Yes	Rice (1006)
334	RSWM Ltd.	Textile (52, 55)	Yes, 55 (NO)	Cotton (5201), fabrics (5208, 5209, 5212), yarn (5509, 5510, 5511)

(continued)

(continued)

Rank	Company name	Sector (SITC 2-digit codes)	RCA	Sub-sector (SITC 4-digit codes)
335	Mukand Ltd.	Steel and industrial machinery (72, 84)	Yes	Bars, rods, wire and other products of alloy steel (7225, 7226, 7227, 7228, 7229), crane, rollers, loaders and excavators (8426, 8429, 8482)
336	Dhunseri Petrochem Ltd.	Energy (27)	Yes	Petroleum oils and oils obtained from bituminous minerals other than crude preparations n.e.s.; containing 70% or more by weight of these oils (2710)
337	Sun TV Network Ltd.	Media (S)	NA	S
338	RattanIndia Power Ltd.	Energy (27)	Yes	Electricity (271600)
339	GlaxoSmithKline Pharmaceuticals Ltd.	Pharmaceutical products (30)	Yes	Pharmaceutical goods (3003, 3004, 3005, 3006)
340	Ipca Laboratories Ltd.	Pharmaceutical products (30)	Yes	Pharmaceutical goods (3003, 3004, 3005, 3006)
341	Jaypee Infratech Ltd.	Construction services (S)	NA	S
342	Electrosteel Steels Ltd.	Steel (72)	Yes	Bars, rods, wire and other products of alloy steel (7225, 7226, 7227, 7228, 7229)
343	Lakshmi Vilas Bank Ltd.	Banking (S)	NA	S
344	Patel Engineering Ltd.	Construction services (S)	NA	S
345	Cox & Kings Ltd.	Travel and services (S)	NA	S
346	JK Paper Ltd.	Paper (48)	Yes	Plain paper (4802), colour paper (4811), cards (4817), boxes of paper (4819), other paper products (4821)
347	Balrampur Chini Mills Ltd.	Sugars (17)	NO	Sugar products (1701, 1702, 1703)

(continued)

(continued)

Rank	Company name	Sector (SITC 2-digit codes)	RCA	Sub-sector (SITC 4-digit codes)
348	OCL India Ltd.	Construction materials (25&69)	Yes, 69 (NO)	Cement (2521, 2522, 2523), refractory products (6902, 6903, 6904)
349	Akzo Nobel India Ltd.	Paints, coatings (32, 35, 39)	Yes, 32 (NO)	Paints and varnishes (3208, 3209, 3210), adhesives (3506), polymers (3901, 3902)
350	Ramky Infrastructure Ltd.	Construction services (S)	NA	S
351	Indiabulls Real Estate Ltd.	Real estate (S)	NA	S
352	Aarti Industries Ltd.	Pharmaceutical products (30)	Yes	Pharmaceutical goods (3003, 3004, 3005, 3006)
353	Supreme Petrochem Ltd.	Chemicals (39)	Yes	Polystyrene (3903)
354	Gujarat Ambuja Exports Ltd.	Food (15, 17)	Yes, 17 (NO)	Palm oil (1511), cotton oilseeds (1512), vegetable fats and oils (1515, 1516, 1517), glucose/glycogen (1702)
355	Lakshmi Machine Works Ltd.	Textile machinery (84)	Yes	Turning, milling and turnmill (8445), weaving machinery (8446), knitting (8447)
356	Godrej Properties Ltd.	Real estate (S)	NA	S
357	Mercator Ltd.	Industrial equipments (89), oil and gas (27)	Yes	Dredgers (8905), oil and gas (2711, 2712), coal (2701)
358	Leel Electricals Ltd.	Industrial machinery and equipment (85, 84, 73)	Yes	Heat exchangers (8516), air conditioning (8415), radiators (7322)
359	Tamil Nadu Newsprint and Papers Ltd.	Paper (48), cement (25), energy (27)	Yes	Printing and writing paper (4802), paperboard (4808, 4811, 4817), cement (2522, 2523), electricity (271600)
360	Sanwaria Consumer Ltd.	Food (12, 10, 25, 17, 11)	Yes, 17 and 11 (NO)	Oilseeds (1207, 1208, 1209), rice (1006), salt (2501), sugar (1702), soyabeans (120100), wheat flour (110100)

(continued)

(continued)

Rank	Company name	Sector (SITC 2-digit codes)	RCA	Sub-sector (SITC 4-digit codes)
361	NIIT Technologies Ltd.	IT solutions (S)	NA	S
362	JK Lakshmi Cement Ltd.	Construction materials	Yes	Cement products (2520, 2521, 2522)
363	Himachal Futuristic Communications Ltd.	Communication (90)	Yes	Optical fibres (9001)
364	Magma Fincorp Ltd.	Financial services (S)	NA	S
365	Ashoka Buildcon Ltd.	Construction services (S)	NA	S
366	Abbott India Ltd.	Pharmaceutical products (30)	Yes	Pharmaceutical goods (3004, 3005, 3006)
367	Jayaswal Neco Industries Ltd.	Steel products (72), industrial equipments (87, 73, 84)	Yes, 83 (NO)	Pig irons (7224, 7225), other steel products (7227, 7228, 7229), automotive spare parts (8706, 8708, 8714), pipes and fittings (7303, 7304, 7305), valves and pumps (8481, 8413, 8414), gears (8483)
368	McNally Bharat Engineering Company Ltd.	Construction services (S)	NA	S
369	Emami Ltd.	Personal care (33)	Yes	Oil, face cream and other personal care products (3304, 3305, 3307, 3308)
370	HT Media Ltd.	Media and entertainment services (S)	NA	S
371	JMC Projects (India) Ltd.	Construction services (S)	NA	S
372	Atul Ltd.	Industrial chemicals	Yes	Sulphites (2832), sulphates (2833), nitrites (2834), polymers (3913)
373	Kirloskar Brothers Ltd.	Industrial equipments	Yes	Pumps (8413, 8414), valves (8481), turbines (8406, 8410, 8411)
374	KPR Mill Ltd.	Textile (52, 58, 60, 61)		Cotton yarn (5205, 5206, 5207), knitted or crocheted fabric (6002, 6003, 6004, 6006), embroidery (5810), garments (6111, 6114)

(continued)

(continued)

Rank	Company name	Sector (SITC 2-digit codes)	RCA	Sub-sector (SITC 4-digit codes)
375	SEL Manufacturing Company Ltd.	Textile (51, 52, 60)	NO, 52 (Yes)	Cotton yarn (5205, 5206, 5207), knitted or crocheted fabric (6002, 6003, 6004, 6006), combed yarn (5107)
376	Bilcare Ltd.	Technological solutions (S)	NA	S
377	Blue Dart Express Ltd.	Logistics (S)	NA	S
378	Procter & Gamble Hygiene & Healthcare Ltd.	Pharmaceutical (30), personal care (33)	Yes	Pharmaceutical goods (3003, 3004), skin care (3304)
379	Trent Ltd.	Retail trade (S)	NA	S
380	Indo Rama Synthetics (India) Ltd.	Textile (59, 51) and energy (27)	NO, 27 (Yes)	Polyester (5902), yarn (5109), electricity (271600)
381	GHCL Ltd.	Chemicals and polymers (34, 28, 59)	Yes, 59 (NO)	Soaps, detergents and cleaning compounds (3401, 3402), sodium products (2815), carbonates (2836), viscose (5902)
382	Bata India Ltd.	Footwear (64)	NO	Footwear (6401, 6402, 6405, 6406)
383	Va Tech Wabag Ltd.	Construction services (S)	NA	S
384	Minda Industries Ltd.	Automotive (87, 84)	Yes	Auto parts and accessories (8708, 8714), castings (8454)
385	Transport Corporation of India Ltd.	Transportation (S)	NA	S
386	Kirloskar Oil Engines Ltd.	Industrial machinery (84)	Yes	Generators (8501, 8502), engines (8408, 8418), pumps (8413, 8414)
387	Finolex Cables Ltd.	Cables and rods (73, 74), electronic equipments (85), industrial machinery (84)	Yes	Cables (7312, 741300), copper rods (7407), batteries (8506), elevators (8428), water heaters (8516)
388	TeamLease Services Ltd.	Consultancy (S)	NA	S
389	Finolex Industries Ltd.	Chemicals (39), tubes and pipes (40)	Yes, 40 (NO)	PVCs (3904), tubes and pipes (3917, 4009)

(continued)

Annexure X: India's 500 Biggest Companies (The ET-500)   307

(continued)

Rank	Company name	Sector (SITC 2-digit codes)	RCA	Sub-sector (SITC 4-digit codes)
390	SKF India Ltd.	Industrial machinery (84)	Yes	Ball and bearing (8482), roller (8432)
391	Minda Corporation Ltd.	Electrical equipments and consumer durables (83 and 84)	Yes, 83 (NO)	Padlocks and locks (8301), motors (8501), connector (8485, 8487)
392	Time Technoplast Ltd.	Financial services (S)	NA	S
393	Paul Merchants Ltd.			
394	Rane Holdings Ltd.	Automotive parts (87)	Yes	Parts and accessories (8708, 8714), chassis (8706)
395	Godfrey Phillips India Ltd.	Cigarettes and tobacco	NO	Cigarettes (2402), tobacco (2403)
396	Jubilant FoodWorks Ltd.	Restaurant (S)	NA	S
397	Madhucon Projects Ltd.	Construction services (S)	NA	S
398	Kajaria Ceramics Ltd.	Ceramics (39)	Yes	Tiles and adhesives (3918, 3919)
399	PNC Infratech Ltd.	Construction services (S)	NA	S
400	Garden Silk Mills Ltd.	Textile, dress materials, fabrics (59)	NO	Polyester yarn (5902), textile fabrics (5903)
401	Persistent Systems Ltd.	Software services (S)	NA	(S)
402	Heritage Foods Ltd.	Dairy product (4)	NA	4
403	Manappuram Finance Ltd.	Non-banking financial company (S)	NA	(S)
404	TVS Srichakra Ltd.			
405	KEI Industries Ltd.	Electrical equipments (85)	Yes	Electrical wire (8544)
406	MBL Infrastructures Ltd.	Construction services (S)	NA	(S)
407	India Glycols Ltd.	Chemical products (38)	Yes	Fatty acids (3823)
408	Hindusthan National Glass & Industries Ltd.	Glass packages (70)	Yes	Glass wear (7010)
409	Sanofi India Ltd.	Pharmaceutical products (30)	Yes	Pharmaceutical goods (3003, 3004, 3005, 3006)
410	PI Industries Ltd.	Chemical products (38)	Yes	Insecticides, fungicides and herbicides (3808)

(continued)

(continued)

Rank	Company name	Sector (SITC 2-digit codes)	RCA	Sub-sector (SITC 4-digit codes)
411	Sutlej Textiles & Industries Ltd.	Apparel and textile (59)	NO	Polyester yarn (5902), textile fabric (5903)
412	Responsive Industries Ltd.			
413	Dhampur Sugar Mills Ltd.	Sugar (17)	NO	Sugar (1701, 1702, 1703)
414	Adani Transmission Ltd.	Transmission services (S)	NA	(S)
415	IL&FS Engineering & Construction Company Ltd.	Non-banking financial company (S)	NA	(S)
416	Jagran Prakashan Ltd.	Printing industries (49)	Yes	Magazines (4901), newspapers (4902)
417	Lycos Internet Ltd.	Software development, digital marketing solutions (S)	NA	(S)
418	Diamond Power Infrastructure Ltd.	Power transmission equipment (85)	Yes	Conductors (8544)
419	Aegis Logistics Ltd.	Logistics (S)	NA	(S)
420	Asahi India Glass Ltd.	Glass products (70)	Yes	Tempered glasses (7007)
421	Essel Propack Ltd.	Plastics products (39)	Yes	Plastic tubes (3917), bathing caps (3922)
422	Indo Count Industries Ltd.	Textile, dress materials, fabrics (59)	NO	Textile fabric (5903), fabrics coats (5901)
423	Honeywell Automation India Ltd.	Automation, distribution service (S)	NA	(S)
424	Electrosteel Castings Ltd.	Iron and steel manufacturing (72)	Yes	Bars and rods (7213)
425	Sterlite Technologies Ltd.	Telecommunications products (90)	Yes	Optical fibres (9001)
426	Venky's (India) Ltd.	Poultry businesses services (S)	NA	(S)
427	AIA Engineering Ltd.	Consultancy (S)	NA	(S)
428	Infinite Computer Solutions (India) Ltd.	IT services (S)	NA	(S)
429	Mahanagar Gas Ltd.	Natural gas distribution (S)	NA	(S)

(continued)

Annexure X: India's 500 Biggest Companies (The ET-500)

(continued)

Rank	Company name	Sector (SITC 2-digit codes)	RCA	Sub-sector (SITC 4-digit codes)
430	3M India Ltd.	Technological solutions (S)	NA	S
431	Carborundum Universal Ltd.	Ceramic products (69)	NO	Ceramic bricks (6904)
432	Pfizer Ltd.	Pharmaceutical products (30)	Yes	Pharmaceutical goods (3003, 3004, 3005, 3006)
433	Electrotherm (India) Ltd.	Steel and iron (72), electrical equipment (85)	Yes	Stainless steel (7218, 7219, 7220), bar, rods and wires (7221, 7222, 7223), plates, bearings and tubes (7305, 7306)
434	Hathway Cable & Datacom Ltd.	Telenetwork services (S)	NA	(S)
435	Siyaram Silk Mills Ltd.	Textile, dress materials, fabrics (59)	NO	Textile fabric (5903)
436	SPML Infra Ltd.	Construction services (S)	NA	(S)
437	Gillette India Ltd.	Personal care and hygiene (82)	NO	Razor blades (8212)
438	DB Corp Ltd.	Printing industries (49)	Yes	Magazines (4901), newspapers (4902)
439	Unitech Ltd.	Construction services (S)	NA	(S)
440	Prakash Industries Ltd.	Power transmission equipment (85)	Yes	Cable (8544)
441	HSIL Ltd.	Plastics products (39)	Yes	Kitchenware (3924), washbasin (3922)
442	Nahar Spinning Mills Ltd.	Textile, dress materials, fabrics (59)	NO	Polyester yarn (5902), textile fabrics (5903)
443	Polaris Consulting & Services Ltd.	Financial company (S)	NO	Polyester yarn (5902), textile fabrics (5903)
444	Huhtamaki PPL Ltd.	Packaging and labelling (48)	Yes	Cartons (4819)
445	Castex Technologies Ltd.	Vehicle (89)	Yes	Parts and accessories (8708)
446	MEP Infrastructure Developers Ltd.	Construction services (S)	NA	(S)
447	Avanti Feeds Ltd.	Animal feed (23)	Yes	Preparation of animal feed (2309)
448	Sunil Hitech Engineers Ltd.	Construction services (S)	NA	(S)

(continued)

(continued)

Rank	Company name	Sector (SITC 2-digit codes)	RCA	Sub-sector (SITC 4-digit codes)
449	Wheels India Ltd.	Electrical machinery (84)	Yes	Machinery equipment (8419)
450	McLeod Russel (India) Ltd.	Tea (9)	NA	9
451	Gujarat Alkalies and Chemicals Ltd.	Pharmaceutical products (30)	Yes	Pharmaceutical goods (3003, 3004, 3005, 3006)
452	Nilkamal Ltd.	Furniture (94)	Yes	Furniture parts (9403)
453	Southern Petrochemicals Industries Corporation Ltd.	Chemicals and fertilisers	Yes, 31 (NO)	Urea (284700), fertilisers (3102, 3103, 3104), nitric acid (2808), ammonium carbonate (2836)
454	Sonata Software Ltd.	IT services (S)	NA	(S)
455	Essar Shipping Ltd.	Logistics (S)	NA	(S)
456	Triveni Engineering & Industries Ltd.	Machinery (84)	Yes	Machinery (8419)
457	Optiemus Infracom Ltd.	Trading services (S)	NA	(S)
458	VLS Finance Ltd.	Consultancy (S)	NA	(S)
459	DCB Bank Ltd.	Banking and financial services (S)	NA	(S)
460	Phillips Carbon Black Ltd.	Carbon black (28)	Yes	Electrical energy/electricity (271600), carbon (2803)
461	Himatsingka Seide Ltd.	Textile, dress materials, fabrics (59)	NA	Polyester yarn (5902), textile fabrics (5903)
462	Monnet Ispat & Energy Ltd.	Iron and steel manufacturing (72)	Yes	Iron or steel alloy (7207)
463	Prime Focus Ltd.	Media and entertainment services	NA	(S)
464	PVR Ltd.	Entertainment services	NA	(S)
465	Bombay Dyeing & Manufacturing Company Ltd.	Textile, dress materials, fabrics (59)	NO	Textile fabric (5903)
466	Capital First Ltd.	Financial services (S)	NA	(S)
467	Orient Paper & Industries Ltd.	Paper (48)	Yes	Tissue (480300)

(continued)

(continued)

Rank	Company name	Sector (SITC 2-digit codes)	RCA	Sub-sector (SITC 4-digit codes)
468	Sobha Ltd.	Real estate	NA	S
469	Kkalpana lndustries (India) Ltd.			
470	WABCO India Ltd.	Vehicle (89)	Yes	Vehicles for transport (8704)
471	V-Guard Industries Ltd.	Electrical equipments (84, 85)	Yes	Batteries (8506), water heaters (8516), motors (8412, 8501), pumps (8413, 8414), boards (8537), stoves (7321), cables (741300), fans (8414)
472	IFB Industries Ltd.	Electrical equipments (84)	Yes	Dishwashing machines (8422), washing machines (8450), air conditioners (8415), parts and accessories (8431), automotive parts (8702)
473	EIH Ltd.	Investment (S)	NA	S
474	GE Power India Ltd.	Industrial equipments (84, 85), energy (27)	Yes, 27 (NO)	Boilers (8402, 8403), generators (8501), steam turbines (8406), electricity (271600
475	Godawari Power & Ispat Ltd.	Energy (27)	Yes	Electricity (271600)
476	Crompton Greaves Consumer Electricals Ltd.	Electrical appliances (84, 85, 93)	Yes, 93 (NO)	Lamps (8513, 9305), water heaters (8516), fans (8414), domestic appliances (8509)
477	Tara Jewels Ltd.	Jewellery and accessories (71)	Yes	Articles of jewellery (7102, 7103, 7104, 7106, 7108, 7113, 7114)
478	Phoenix Mills Ltd.	Real estate (S)	NA	S
479	Fertilisers and Chemicals Travancore Ltd.	Chemicals and fertilisers (25, 28, 31)	NO, 25 (Yes)	Fertilisers (3102, 3103, 3104), urea (284700), gypsum (2520)
480	Spice Mobility Ltd.	Telecommunications (S)	NA	S
481	Ashapura Minechem Ltd.	Construction materials (98, 69)	NO	Refractory materials (6902, 381600)

(continued)

(continued)

Rank	Company name	Sector (SITC 2-digit codes)	RCA	Sub-sector (SITC 4-digit codes)
482	Tata Coffee Ltd.	Coffee (18, 21)	Yes, 18 (NO)	Coffee (180100, 2101)
483	Page Industries Ltd.	Apparels (61, 62)	Yes	Undergarments (6115, 6207, 6208)
484	ITI Ltd.	Telecommunications (S)	NA	S
485	Schaeffler India Ltd.	Industrial machinery (84, 40, 59)	Yes	Roller and bearings (8482), conveyor (4010, 5910), textile machinery (8444, 8445.8446), gears (8483)
486	Future Consumer Ltd.	Retail trade (S)	NA	S
487	Nahar Industrial Enterprises Ltd.	Textile and energy (52, 53, 27)	NO, 52 (Yes)	Cotton (5201, 5203), spun (5302), polyester (5902), electricity (271600)
488	Engineers India Ltd.	Construction services (S)	NA	S
489	Metalyst Forgings Ltd.	Automotive and engineering components (84, 87, 96)	Yes, 96 (NO)	Vehicles (8709, 8701, 8702, 8711, 8712, 8793), crankshafts (8483), fasteners (9607)
490	TIL Ltd.	Industrial equipments (84, 87)	Yes	Cranes (8426), crusher (8435), trucks (8709), forklift trucks (8427)
491	Ajanta Pharma Ltd.	Pharmaceutical products (30)	Yes	Pharmaceutical products (3303, 3304, 3306)
492	Ratnamani Metals & Tubes Ltd.	Steel (73)	Yes	Steel tubes and pipes (7304)
493	VRL Logistics Ltd.	Logistics (S)	NA	S
494	Somany Ceramics Ltd.	Ceramics (39, 69)	NO, 39 (Yes)	Sanitary (3922), tiles (6902, 6904, 6905)
495	GTL Ltd.	Telecommunications (S)	NA	S
496	Astral Poly Technik Ltd.	Tubes and pipes (37, 39, 40)	NO, 39 (Yes)	Adhesives (3707), pipes (4009, 3917)
497	Relaxo Footwears Ltd.	Footwear (64)	NO	Footwear (6401, 6402, 6405, 6406)

(continued)

(continued)

Rank	Company name	Sector (SITC 2-digit codes)	RCA	Sub-sector (SITC 4-digit codes)
498	Star Ferro and Cement Ltd.	Construction materials	Yes	Cement (2521, 2522, 2523)
499	West Coast Paper Mills Ltd.	Paper (48)	Yes	Printing paper (4802), writing paper (4821)
500	Brigade Enterprises Ltd.	Real estate (S)	NA	S

1. NA: Not applicable means the company is into services (S) or its products/services were not analysed beyond single-digit category of SITC HS classification
2. NO: Means company was not found to be in an RCA (revealed comparative advantage) sector or sub-sector or that the value for RCA is zero or indeterminate
3. Yes: Means the company is in a RCA sector or sub-sector

Note: The Economic Times 500 (The ET-500) list and the analysis of RCAs has uses not limited to the biggest 500 companies. SMEs in the RCA sectors are also part of clusters that can benefit when matches are found for potential trade and trade-substituting investments based on Chaps. 2 and 3 and Annexures I to VIII.

Glossaries

Glossary of Important Finnish Words and Expressions

aika **Time**. Finnish winter time is 2 h ahead of GMT and 3.5 h behind Indian time; Summer Time is 2.5 h behind Indian time. Finns generally think in terms of a 24 h clock instead of a.m. or p.m. Summer Time begins from the last Sunday in March and ends on the last Sunday in October.

aikataulu **Timetable, Schedule**. Finns like to plan ahead. It is important to know what kind of schedule is being thought about for visits, meetings, skypecalls, etc. Finnish workplaces usually work from 8 to 16 Finnish time, with minor variations.

aineeton omaisuus **Intangible property**. Includes all forms of non-material Intellectual Property Rights. Since knowledge-intensive business services are Finland's mainstay, this can be a deal maker or deal breaker.

alioikeus **Court of First Instance**. The equivalent of a civil court or *munsif* court in India.

ALKO **Liquor Sales Outlet**. The alcohol distribution monopoly organised by the government in Finland to regulate, on public health grounds, the control of sale and prices of all alcohol products equivalent to SYSTEM BOLAGET in Sweden. Finland had alcohol prohibition in the past with referenda over prohibition as a civic and political question.

Amanuenssi **Bursar cum Registrar of a University Department**.

ammatti **Profession, vocation, trade or calling**. This is an important part of individual personal identity in Finland and is often prefixed or suffixed to names when referring to people. This is despite titles not being used in Finland generally.

ammattiyhdistys **Professional or vocational association or trade union.** Union density is high in Finland because traditionally most workers (even academics, doctors, scientific workers, etc.) are represented in negotiations for work arrangements through trade unions and associations. Remuneration revisions are negotiated annually in multi-tier structures with associations and unions being part of syndicated federations at the national level. Unions have power because they have traditionally controlled wage earner funds that finance unemployment insurance.

antaa **To give.** According to the Finnish frequency dictionary [Frequency dictionary of Finnish by Pauli Saukkonen, Söderström, Helsinki, 1979], the antonym, '*saada*', meaning 'to get' is used three times more frequently than '*antaa*'.

arvo **Value.** An important word frequently used in business discussions and political discourse as a reference point for justifying a point of view.

arvonlisävero (ALV) **VAT.** The equivalent of General Sales Tax (GST) in India.

Arvopaperi **Commercial Paper, Bond or Security Paper.**

asianajaja **Advocate.**

asunto **Living abode, house, apartment.**

aurinko **Sun.** Equivalent of 'arun' in Hindi/Sanskrit. Highly valued by Finns as there is so little of it except in summer when daylight hours are long. In the Arctic Circle, the Sun doesn't rise or set at all for parts of the year. Hence, the epithet, 'Land of the Midnight Sun'.

auto **Car.** Owning a particular model of car can be associated with status. In India, 'auto' means 'autorickshaw', a motorised three-wheeled vehicle used as privately hired means of public transport.

Ay (Avoin yhtiö) **General partnership.**

äidinkieli **Mother tongue.** Officially refers to Finnish or Swedish.

Bruttokansantuote **Gross National Income.**

dl (desilitra) **Decilitre.** The unit of measure commonly used for liquids in Finland unlike cubic centilitre (cc) in India.

Eduskunta **The Unicameral National Finnish Parliament.**

Elinkeino **Means of livelihood through trade, business, occupation, profession, vocation.**

emoyhtiö **Parent company or holding company.**

eräpäivä **Set date for completing an act such as payment due on an invoice or a dateline that marks expiry of a period of consideration.**

EU European Union.

EVL Business Income Tax Act, Finland (Laki elinkeinotulon verottamisesta laki 24.6.1968/360) commonly referred as EVL.

evvk Full form, 'ei voisi vähempää kiinnostaa' commonly used expression to signify that **one is not even the least bit interested** in something or that one couldn't care less!

haastemies Bailiff.

hakemus Petition, application.

hallinto Administration.

hallinto-oikeus **Court of justice dealing with cases concerning public law and those arising from appeals against decisions of administrative tribunals.**

henkilö Person, official.

Helsingin Sanomat **Finland's leading newspaper colloquially referred as 'Hesari'.**

Hallitus Governance, board of directors.

Hei! Hello!

hei hei! The equivalent of a friendly '**Bye bye**'; the formal goodbye is '*näkemiin*'.

hengeltä Per person.

Hesari **Colloquial name for newspaper Helsingin Sanomat.**

Hiihtoloma Skiing vacation. In February for a week in schools, and also some organizations.

Hinta Price.

hovioikeus Court of Appeal.

huutokauppa Auction.

ihmisoikeudet **Human rights.** Finland withdrew its reservations against human rights and fully adopted the European Convention on Human Rights in 1998.

ilmainen Free.

ilmoittaa Inform or notify.

investointi Investment.

isännöitsijä **Guardian of a residential complex.** Uniquely Finnish notion of instituting a Coordinator representing owner-residents and responsible for governing residential facilities, environmental interfaces and administrative arrangements for residents in a building complex.

itsepalvelu **Self-service.**

johtokunta Board of Management.

joulu Christmas.

joulupukki Santaclaus.

juomaraha Tip or literally extra money for drinks. Not a Finnish custom.

järvi Lake.

kaari Code of law; or reference to code in law.

Kahvi Coffee.

Kala Fish.

Kalenteri Diary containing calendar of dates for planning.

Kantelu Complaint.

Kassa Cash counter.

Katsotaan Lets see. A non-committal response indicating consideration.

Käräjäoikeus Trial Court, Circuit Court.

käteinen Cash

Kauppa Shop, trade, business.

Kauppakamari Chamber of Commerce.

Kaupunki Town.

Kaveri Buddy.

Kollega Colleague.

Kehoitus Request.

KELA Social Insurance Institution (full form kansaneläkelaitos).

Kello Time, Bell.

Kesä Summer.

Kielto Prohibition or injunction or restraint.

KHO Supreme Administrative Court of Finland (*korkein hallinto-oikeus*).

KKO Korkein oikeus (Supreme Court of Finland).

Kieli Language, tongue.

Kiitos! Thank You!

Kiitos viimeisestä! **Thanks for the previous time!** Finns customarily express thanks at the next contact for a previous favour or grace or kindness or gift received.

kippis! **Cheers!** As when raising a glass for a toast.

kirjasto **Library**.

kiky **Abbreviation for kilpailukyky** meaning competitive rationalization at the workplace usually entailing giving up some customary or contractual right or privilege to remain competitive in the market.

kilpailu **Competition**.

KKO **Supreme Court of Justice of Finland (for private law cases)**.

Konkurssi **Bankruptcy**.

Korko **Interest**.

Kokoaikainen **Full time**.

Kokonaistyöaika **Total working time**.

Kokous **Meeting**.

Koti **Home** (similar to 'kothi' in Hindi).

Kotimainen **Domestic, within the country**.

Korkeakoulu **Higher Educational Institution**.

Koulu **School**.

Koulutus **Education**.

Kuitti **Receipt**. Typically proof of payment that one is quits.

Kunta **Community, municipality**.

Kustannukset **Expenses, costs**.

Kutsu **Invitation**.

Kuu **Moon**.

Ky **Limited Partnership** (*kommandiittiyhtiö*).

Kyy **Viper snake**. The one and only poisonous snake in Finland.

Laki **Law or Act**.

laktoosi-intoleranssi **Lactose intolerance**. A common condition in Finland that comes in the way of consuming milk products and milk-based confectionaries.

lähdevero **Withholding tax**.

lämpötila **Temperature**.

lasku, eritelty lasku **Invoice**.

lausunto **Opinion**.

liitto **Association**.

loma Vacation or holiday.

lomake Form.

lopettamisilmoitus Notice of closure.

lumi, lunta Snow. There are also many other words for snow in Finnish to distinguish softly falling snow, sleet, wet snow, hard snow, hail, ice, etc.

luonnonoikeus Natural justice.

luonto Nature.

luottokortti Credit Card

maahanmuuttaja Migrant (incoming to Finland). Millions of Finns have migrated and settled abroad over two centuries. However, this term is used only for incoming migrants who may be confused with refugees (*pakolaisia*).

mainos Advertisement.

maksu Payment.

marja Berry.

markkinointi Marketing.

matka Travel.

mekaanikkosääntö 183-day rule for determining fiscal domicile.

meri Sea.

metsä Forest.

mökki Cottage.

munakauppa Barter trade. A colloquial reference to erstwhile *vaihtokauppa*, barter trade with Russia.

myynti Sale.

myyjä Seller.

nimenomaan Precisely. Indicating agreement.

nimipäivä Name-day.

nimikirja Name-roll. An official document that contains the certified record of a person's qualifications, roles and experience in service.

oikeudenkäymiskaari Code of judicial procedure.

oikeus Justice.

oikeusturva Right of judicial safety.

oma Own.

opisto Educational institution.

osasto Department.

OSK Finnish cooperative society (*osuuskunta*).

Osto Purchase.

Oy Private company limited by shares (*osakeyhtiö*).

Oyj Public company limited by shares (*julkinen osakeyhtiö*).

Pakolainen Refugee.

Palkka Salary.

Palvelu Service.

Pankki Bank.

Pesänjakaja **Nest-divider**. Court-appointed adjudicator for the division of family assets following death or divorce under inheritance laws of Finland.

Pörssi Bourse, stock exchange.

pöytäkirja Minutes of the meeting.

PRH **Abbreviation for patentti-ja rekisterihallitus**. The organization that governs recording of intellectual property rights and functions as Registrar of Companies.

Protestilista **List published in newspaper of defaulters who have not settled bills, invoices, payments due**. Not merely a name and shame feature to bring defaulters to the attention of the public—it is a statutory requirement to notify intention to sue for recovering dues.

/pv (päivältä) **Per day**.

Raha **Money, means of payment**. As in Hindi *raha* (means) or *saadhan*. Culturally, there have been historically various means of payment other than bank notes or coins. Legal tender has included squirrel skins in the past.

Revontulet **Aurora Borealis**. Literally means 'fox fires' based on a legend that a red fox runs across the sky and initiates the magnificent play of fires in the sky.

Ruokaa Food.

Saada **To get**. According to the Finnish Frequency Dictionary, the antonym, '*antaa*', meaning 'to give' occurs three times less frequently than '*saada*'. This can be due to the culture of entitlements brokered by the state as a way of receiving rather than social reciprocity.

Satama Harbour.

Sauna **Sauna**. A uniquely Finnish institution that has functions way beyond being merely a place for taking a steam bath.

Selvitysmies **Fact-finder appointed to construct and present the salient features of a situation.**

Seteli **Currency note.**

Sieni **Mushroom.** Every person has the right to pick mushrooms and berries from the forests.

Siirtotyöläiset **Migrant workers.**

Sijoitus **Investment.**

Sisu Guts, daring, grit, courage, bravery. An important distinctive Finnish value that is culturally and socially symbolic of capacity for resilience and 'never say die' spirit. With 'sisu', the Finns fought several wars with Russians and although they lost some of them, they fought bravely.

SITRA Full form, Suomen itsenäisyyden juhlarahasto. **The Finnish Innovation Fund** under supervision of the National Parliament. Sitra invests in companies and start-ups to create new profitable business.

Sopimus **Agreement, contract.**

STAKES Finnish acronym for **National Research and Development Center for Welfare and Health.** STAKES was renamed National Institute for Health and Welfare in 2009 after being merged with the National Public Health Institute.

Suomi The real name for Finland. The word also refers to the Finnish language.

Suunitelma **Plan, scheme.**

Sää **Weather.** Weather changes rapidly in Finland; hence, considerable attention is paid to weather forecasts in order to plan activities and movements.

Sähköposti **E-mail.**

Talkoot **Community voluntary unpaid labour** for tasks engaged with collectively for everyone's benefit. For example, repairing a pathway or road, painting a building, emptying and cleaning communal dry toilets.

Talo **Building.**

Talousarvio **Budget Estimate.**

talonmies **Building Caretaker.**

tervehdys **Greeting.**

tehdas **Factory.**

TE-palvelut **Acronym for the Regional Centre for work, livelihood life and entrepreneurship.**

TEKES Acronym for the **Finnish Funding Agency for Technology and Innovation**, a part of Finnish Ministry of Employment and the Economy. The most important parastatal agency for R&D funding in Finland. Fused with Finpro in 2018 as 'Business Finland' to provide seamless support from R&D stages to exports.

Tekijänoikeus **Intellectual property right of a creator/author**.

Terva **Tar**. Tar is an important substance in Finland and the source of numerous useful derivatives for medicines, nutraceuticals, chemicals, soaps, shampoos, energy, adhesion, road-building, etc.

Tieto **Information, knowledge**. There is no separate word for knowledge which is also tieto. The expression '*hiljainen tieto*' (which literally means, quietly held information) has been coined to refer to tacit knowledge.

Tilinpäätos **Statement of Accounts**.

Tilintarkastaja **Auditor**.

Todistus **Certificate, testimonial**.

toiminimi **Trade name, business name**.

toimisto **Office**.

tuki **Support**. As in scholarship or subsidy or subvention.

Tulo **Income**.

Tulli **Customs at the border**.

Tunnilta **Per hour**.

Turva **Security, safety**.

TVL (tuloverolaki) **Income Tax Act**.

Työ **Work**.

Työnantaja **Employer**.

Työsuhde **Work relations, employment**.

Työntekijä **Worker, employee**.

Ulkomainen **Foreign**.

Ulkomaalainen **Foreigner**

Ulosottonmies **Liquidator**.

urheilu **Sports**.

uusi **New**. According to the Finnish Frequency dictionary, this is one of the 20 most frequently used words in the language indicative that new is valued greatly, not what is old.

Vaatimus Claim.

Vahingonkorvauslaki Damages Act for Compensations.

Vahtimestari General Utility Official coordinating entry and exit of artefacts, post, and attending to maintenance and security of a building from an office at the entrance.

vakuutus Insurance.

valitus Complaint, appeal.

valtakirja Authorization of proxy, power of attorney.

vapaa Not reserved or restricted.

vapaa-aika Free time.

varaus Reservation.

velka Debt.

verkko Network.

vero Tax.

verotus Taxation.

vienti Exports.

viikko Week.

virastomestari Estate Manager.

virka Position or role or office.

viimeinen käyttöpäivä Use before/Expiry Date.

viini Wine.

VTT Acronym for **Technical Research Centre of Finland Ltd**, a state-owned and controlled non-profit limited liability company. VTT provides research and innovation funding.

Yhteiskunta **Community, society**. In Finland, this can refer to the aggregate national community rather than local community.

yhtymä Partnership.

yle Acronym for **The public radio and television company**.

yliopisto University.

yrittäjä Entrepreneur.

Yritys Corporate entity, corporation, enterprise.

Glossary of Important Indian Words and Expressions

Aadhaar Card The Unique Identification Card introduced by the Government of India for all residents in India with biometric check as a requirement for availing government subsidies and filing income tax returns by residents.

Achchhaa Okay, I see, lets see, right, really? Good.

Acharya Educator eg: Professor or other teacher or other learned person.

Agni Fire. Worshipped in the culture as a sacred element Symbolically important for prayers, marriages, cremations. India's long-range missile system is also named Agni. The Rig Veda begins with an invocation to fire.

Ahimsa Non-violence. Despite this normative value that was intrinsic to Gandhian ideas about protest, the taboo against aggression and violence is not yet established in the country.

Artha Money, commerce. Also connotes 'meaning'.

baisakhi Harvest festival celebrated in the Punjab and parts of North India.

bandh General strike. A form of civic and political protest that stops all work, transport, trade, commerce and business in a particular area.

bhoomi puja A ceremonial ritual before new land is dug for plantation or construction.

Bindi The coloured dot (usually red) that women wear on their foreheads as an adornment.

Baksheesh Tip or monetary reward paid in appreciation of favour or respect received. Often regarded by recipients as a customary right.

Bhagavad Geeta The divine song in which Krishna dissolves fears and anxieties of the Mahabharat protagonist Arjuna and reminds him of his duties and of the transitory nature of the world.

Bharat India. The real name of India in Hindi.

Brahma The Creator in the divine trinity whose consort is Saraswati, the Goddess of Learning. There is only one Brahma temple in the world located by the Pushkar Lake in Rajasthan, India.

Chaat Snack usually consisting of cut fruits and potatoes in a spicy tangy sauce traditionally served in a cup made of leaves and which can occasionally be made from fermented milk products.

Chaprasi Office worker whose work is to convey messages, carry files and documents and regulate flow of visitors.

Chouth Fourth day after a funeral when the mourning period is brought to an end with a prayer meeting for the departed. 'Terhvi' (13th day after death) is observed as the end of a longer mourning period by some families.

Chowkidar Security guard.

Churidar A trouser like lower garment worn by men and women. Gets its name from churi, the bangles worn by women because this is the way the garment falls around the legs.

Coolie Porter. Identifiable by their red shirt uniforms and uniquely numbered brass token arm bands at railway stations.

Daftari Roleholder who maintains office files, records and basic office services including punching, filing and binding of loose documents.

Dahsanskara Funeral rites associated with cremation.

Dhanyavad Thanks! Literally, a blessing spoken out of gratitude.

Dharma That which ought to be done; duty. Not quite religion although frequently treated as a synonym in expressions such as 'dharma nirapekshata' implying equal treatment for all faiths-the Indian version of secularism contrastable from the western notion of secularism as non-religious. Root meaning of dharma is 'that which holds'.

Dussehra The tenth day of war in the Ramayana when the mythical hero Rama slayed the demon king Ravana. Effigies of Ravana are burnt on this day to signify the victory of good over evil.

Diwali The moonless autumn night when the festival of lights is celebrated to commemorate the return home of Rama after the war.

Durga puja The shakti worship tradition in Eastern India of worshipping the Goddess Durga who slayed demons.

Firangi Foreign. Firang = the long dress worn by early Europeans seen in India.

Ganesha The son of Shiva and Parvati who has the head of an elephant and is considered auspicious to be worshipped at the beginning of any important activity to seek blessings that the activity may proceed and succeed unhindered. 'Ganesha Puja' was begun in Maharashtra by political leaders as part of national revival and is one of the most important festivals of Mumbai.

Gherao A form of protest that started from Bengal in which those being protested against are surrounded, confined and prevented from leaving.

Ghodadeem A Bengali expression, literally 'the egg of a horse' signifying disbelief of 'bullshit' (Rubbish!). A Tamil equivalent would be '*parkalam*'.

Gotra Hypothetical claimed line of descent traced from human communities/clans as flocks shepherded/spiritually guided by Rishis of ancient India.

Glossaries

Guru The word guru consists of two syllables: gu meaning darkness, ignorance; and ru annihilation of darkness by insight or illumination. Originally limited to refer to a spiritual leader who helps dispel darkness or ignorance among acolytes, the term has been grossly abused and misused to signify any kind of leadership arising from authority of skill or domain.

Gurudwara Sikh temple which is always open and where anyone may worship or visit to receive food. Literally, the gateway to reach the Guru.

Halal A way of cutting meat favoured by Muslims (=kosher) that lets out blood from the animal's body.

Hanuman A character from the Ramayana; the monkey god that served as Rama's envoy and who carried out numerous superhuman tasks to support Rama; worshipped as a deity for protecting from dangers; many Indians would not eat non-vegetarian food or have haircuts on Tuesdays out of respect for Hanuman.

Harijan Meaning 'God's own' a term coined by Gandhiji for the fourth caste of untouchables in his fight against untouchability.

Holi Festival of colours where people spray/rub colours on each other. The festival is significant in four ways: it celebrate the harvest, there is spring cleaning with bonfires, and it commemorates the victory of Prahalad when Holika gets burnt despite a boon that she would never burn; and it is the only time when people who would otherwise not touch each other due to taboos of incest or inequality may touch others with colours. So, it provides social levelling for a day.

Horn A source of considerable noise pollution on roads because everybody honks a lot as a way of trying to create space to move in congested circumstances and to announce and caution others in traffic to get out of the way. Treated as a complement to the accelerator.

Jati Caste, clan, tribe or community of kinship.

Ji Suffix for respect added after names, greetings, words for relatives.

Jugaad Improvisation, cunning, ingenuity, resourcefulness, creativity, connections, trick, manipulation, stretch, out-of-box solution.

Kal Yesterday, tomorrow. It can mean either! Derived from kaal which refers to time.

Kama Lust, Sex, Eros.

Kanyadaan Father giving away the bride. A Hindu marriage involves the bride moving from her family of origin to her new family by marriage and ritually involves the bride's father into gifting his daughter and entrusting her to the care and traditions of the new family by marriage.

Karma Act, duty. Also signifies the fruit of one's actions as residuals to be transacted in this or next birth.

Khalsa The martial order created by the Sikh Guru Gobind Singh mandating five distinguishing emblems to be carried at all times as icons of purity: kesa (long uncut hair), kangha (comb), kara (bracelet), kachha (underwear), kirpan (dagger).

kumkum Vermillion powder applied as cosmetic or religious adornment.

Lakshmi Goddess of wealth. Worshipped at Diwali which businesses regard as the beginning of their new year.

Langur Indian Macaque. Found in many urban locations, besides forests. Monkeys are afraid of macaques and in localities where there are hordes of monkeys, macaques are intentionally introduced to scare away the monkeys.

Lingam Phallic symbol signifying the God Shiva (the destroyer of the Trinity) and worshipped in temples and also in open places.

Mahabharata India's second epic said to be authored by Vyasa who is also one of the characters in the epic about a great war between two warring clans that is believed to have ended in 3102 B.C.—the epic is eight times as long as Iliad and Odyssey put together.

Mandala Representational universe.

Mantra Syllables of sound combinations that evoke bodily resonances for enhancing awareness and consciousness.

Masjid Mosque, a place of worship where Muslims assemble and pray.

Maya Transitory illusion. Maya is the abbreviated form of the expression 'Mati Iti ma, Yati iti ya' to describe the measurable reality that is passing away or disappearing even as it is measured, because it is transitory.

Muhoortam Auspicious time.

Mukhwas Mixture of betel nut and aniseed eaten as a mouth freshener and digestive after a meal.

Muni Monk.

Nakki Sealing a deal.

Namaskar! Greetings!

Namaste! The Indian greeting that is complete only when both hands are joined with fingers towards the person(s) being greeted. Literally signifies that I am now turning all my five senses towards you.

Nowruz Nowruz is the first day of Farvardin, the first month of the Iranian solar calendar. In the Fasli/Bastani variant of the Zoroastrian calendar, and Navroz is always the day of the vernal equinox (nominally falling on March 21).

navjot The parsee ceremony of initiating youth into the Zoroastrian religion. Rite of passage, comparable to the Hindu upanayan or the Jewish Bar Mitzvah.

Onam A religious and cultural harvest festival that originated in Kerala.

PAN Permanent Account Number. Everyone with taxable income is required to obtain a permanent account number (PAN) that is required to be mentioned also for all high-value financial transactions.

Paan Betel leaf. Symbolically signifies accepting responsibility in the context of undertaking commitments or making contracts when ceremonially offered. Else, merely a post-prandial digestive after a meal.

Padyatra A journey by foot usually signifies a purposeful pedestrian journey to signify or commemorate a happening, sanctify an intention or register empathy, sacrifice or protest.

Pagadi Headgear worn that is distinctive of local cultural and ethnic community identities. A symbol of respect, identity.

Pugdee Lumpsum advance required for renting a premises particularly for the landlord/landlady to have a security deposit to offset likelihood of tenancy abuse in the form of refusal to vacate or when market rent is in excess of regulated rent under statutory rent control.

Peon Messenger, carrier of papers/files, attendant. From the early days of the British Raj, armed attendants.

Perkele! Rubbish! Nonsense!

poi varukiren I am going and shall return.

poi varungal Go and return.

pongal Harvest festival in Tamil Nadu and some other parts of South India.

purdah Veil. The custom of keeping covered a woman's body wholly or partly as a way of concealing and segregating from contact with men from outside the family. Ghoonghat is the name for a veil covering only the head and face and burkha the name for the head-to-toe veil. As an institution, 'purdah' signifies a way of life in which women keep to themselves and regulate interfaces with others, especially men from outside the family.

rahukalam Inauspicious time when people would be reluctant to do anything. Observed widely in South India.

rakhi, rakshabandhan Tradition of the full moon day in August observed as sisters' and brothers' day when sisters tie a ceremonial piece of string on the wrists of brothers as a gesture of filial affinity signifying obligation on the part of brothers to protect their sisters from harm and brothers reciprocate with gifts. Not limited to real sisters and brothers and women may tie rakhis also on those who they regard as brothers.

Ramayana Hindu epic (originally said to be composed by Valmiki) about the dutiful prince Rama, his exile in the forest, the abduction of his wife Sita and the war with the demon king of Sri Lanka signifying the victory of good over evil.

Rasa The essence of aesthetic quality in an emotional state.

rishi Seer, spiritually developed person with special insights.

roza Ritual fasting by muslims during Ramadan.

sadhu Hermit.

sannyasi Mendicant, renunciate.

Sarkar Government.

sari The draped garment worn by women in India in different styles.

Sat sri akal Sikh greeting and response meaning 'truth is eternal'.

Satyagraha Non-violent peaceful protest for a noble cause or for truth to be upheld.

shakti Power, force.

Shamshan Funeral place, cremation grounds.

Shiva The deity associated with destruction in the trinity of Brahma (creator), Vishnu (maintainer/sustainer) and Mahesh (destroyer).

Shukriya! Thanks!

swachha bharat abhiyan Clean India Campaign.

swadeshi Made in India, indigenous manufacture.

talak Divorce.

thanedar Officer in charge of a police station.

theek hai Okay, fine, its alright.

Upanishads Dialogues and commentaries written to explain the Vedas, literally at the end of the Vedas (Vedanta).

Upvaas Fasting.

Vanakkam Greetings! (in Tamil).

Varna Caste, literally colour marker of caste.

Vascut Waistcoat. Indian version of waistcoat that is commonly seen as part of the national 'uniform' of academics, politicians and others in public life.

Veda Circumscribing the knowledge that cannot be bound.

Vidya Knowledge or skill.

Vishnu The deity associated with preservation in the trinity of Brahma (Creator), Vishnu (maintainer/sustainer) and Mahesh (destroyer).

Worker Legal concept of a role in a factory, mine, shop or establishment that carries rights to pay, freetime, leave, safety, health, environment and obligation for regulated hours of work.

workman Statutory concept of employee whose employment, work, changes in conditions of work and termination for misconduct or as part of layoff, retrenchment or closure of establishment are regulated and protected under the Industrial Disputes Act, 1947.

Yama God of death.

Index

A

Aalto University, 10, 219, 221
Abloy, 148
Abuse of dominant position, 138
Academy of Finland, 204
Accident insurance premia, 127
Accounting for deferred income taxes, 125
Acquisitions, 126
Act on assessment procedure, 129
Acyclovir, 80
Adaptation, 192
Advance ruling, 130
Aerial reflectors, 56
Agency commissions, 138
Aggregation, 193
Ahlstrom, 148, 175
Air Pollution, 68
A&J Intelli Systems, 149
Aldehydes, 80
Aluminium foils, 84
Aluminium sheets and strips, 84
Amer, 169
Amlodipine, 81
Amoxycillines, 81
Ampicillins, 81
Analgin, 81
Angles, 83, 84
Angry Birds, xi, 3, 92
Anika, 148
Anilines, 80
Anoraks, 83
Antiamoebic, 81
Antibiotics, 80
Antifungal, 81
Antihelminitic and antiprotozoal drugs, 81
Anti-vibration technologies, 57
Apparel and clothing, 82
Arbitrage, 192, 193
Arbitration, 172
Articles of Iron or Steel, 48
Arvind Mills, 145
Asian Paints, 144
Aspectum, 149
Assessment adjustment boards, 130
Asset revaluation, 125
Assimilation, 193
Athletics equipment, 85
Auditors, 126
Aurinko matka, 108
Automatic route, 173
Avocados, 85
Avoin yhtiö, 124
Ayurvedic medicines exported as neutraceuticals, 81

B

Babies garments, 82
Bacibact, 80
Bags of leather including travel bags, 87
Bajaj Auto, 144
Ballasts for fluorescent lamps, 85
Bananas, 85, 86
Bandage gauzes, 81
Bank of Finland, 14
Barrels, 61
Bars, 84
Bathrobes, 82, 83
Bedlinen, 82

© Springer Nature Singapore Pte Ltd. 2019
A. N. Mathur, *Finland–India Business Opportunities*,
https://doi.org/10.1007/978-981-10-8019-7

Bedspreads, 82
Belladona extracts used in medicated dressings, 86
Belts and bandoliers, 87
Bentonite clays, 80
Benzyl alcohol, 80
Betonimestarit, 148
Beverages, spirits and vinegar, 50
Bharat, 175
Bharatiya Janata Party, 38
Bharat net, 36
Bibs, 83
Bicycle inner tubes, 87
Bicycles, 85
Bilateral investment treaty, 162
Biocity Turku, 7
Biotech and biopharma investments made by Indian investors, 126
Blankets, boatsails, raincoats and swimwear, 82
Blazers, 83
Blue Star Infotech, 91
Blouses, 82, 83
Boilers, 84
Bollywood, 64
Bombay Stock Exchange (BSE), 178
Bonus, 132
Bouquets, 85
Bovine hides and skins, 61
Bras, 82
Breeches and shorts, 82
Bridges from Finland to India, 147
Bridges from India to Finland, 145
Brexit, xii
Builder's hardware, 84
Building stones, 80
Bulldozers, 55
Business communities, 180
Business ecosystem in Finland, 183, 187
Business Finland, 143, 163, 200
Business income tax act, 129
Business practices and commercial laws, 137

C
Cadmatic, 149
Calcined coke, 80
Calendar, 106
Camphor oil, 86
Candles, 86
Cannulae, 85
Capacitors and semi-conductor devices, 85
Capitalisation of production overhead, 125
Capital markets in India, 177
Caps, 83

Capsicum, 86
Captopril, 81
Cardigans, 83
Cargo containers, 56
Cargotec, 148
Carpets of silk, 83
Cartels, 179
Cashew nuts, 85
Casks, 61
Cassette tapes and floppy disks (blank and music), 87
Caste, 105
Caste and class in India, 105
Casual labour, 132
Catheters, 85
Cefadroxil, 81
Cefoxitin, 81
Celery, 86
Central authority for advance rulings, 130
Central bank, 173
Central Bank of Finland, 143
Central heating boilers, 55
Centre lathes, 84
Centrifuges, 55, 84
Cephalexin, 81
Cephalosporins, 81
Cereals, 85
Changes at the workplace, 132
Charminar, 175
Chemical plant machinery, 87
Chemicals, 62
Chempolis, 148
Child labour, 132
China, 22, 29, 145
Chloramphenicol, 81
Chromium, 84
Chromium bars and rods, 84
CII, 165
Cimetidines, 81
Cinefilm, 86
CITEC, 149
Clamps, 84
Classifying faiths, 104
Cleantech water and waste management, 157
Climate Change, 34–35
Cloaks, 83
Closures, 133
Clothes hangers, 87
Clothing, 61
Clove, 86
Clove oil, 86
Club resorts, 126
Coats, 82
Coconuts, 85

Cod, 86
Code law, 123
Code law justice system, 135
Code on industrial relations, 132
Code on safety & working conditions, 132
Code on social security & welfare, 132
Code on wages, 132
Coir mattresses, 82
Cold war politics, 16
Collaborative joint ventures, 175
Collective bargaining, 110, 132
Commission agents, 124
Common law, 123, 171
Communities at risk, 143, 200
Company tax rates, 127
Compensation and notice periods, 133
Competition act, the 2002, 179
Competition appellate tribunal, 179
Competition Commission of India (CCI), 179
Competition policy in India, 179
Competition Law of Finland, 137–138
Computer accesories, 87
Concurrent list, 170
Confederation of Finnish Industries (EK), 24
Congress Party, 38
Connectors, 87
Constitution of Finland, 134
Constitution of India, 170
Construction machinery, 55
Consumer durables, 59
Consumer protection laws, 138, 180
Consumption Abroad (CA), 63
Contact lenses, 85
Continuation war, 16
Contract act, 138
Contract labour, 132
Contract labour (regulation and abolition) act, 1970, 132
Contract negotiations, 137
Conveyer belting, 81
Copper and articles of copper, 54
Copper and articles thereof, 48
Corrugated paper, 88
Corsets, 82
Corticosteroid hormones, 81
Cost of Living, 26, 187–188
Cotton, 81
Cotton corduroy pieces, 83
Cotton ensembles, 82
Cotton fabrics, 82
Cotton twine, 83
Cotton Yarn, 82
Council of Scientific and Industrial Research (CSIR), 159

Couplings, 84
Court of first instance, 136
Creams, 87
Cross Border Supply (CBS), 63
Curtain fabrics, 83
Cushion covers, 83
Customs duties, 128
Cut flowers, 85
Cutlery, 84
Cutting knives, 84
Cyclic hydrocarbons, 80

D

Dairy machinery, 55
Dairy products, 85
Datamatics, 175
Dates, 85
Decent work, 132
Definition of industry in India, 132
Definitions of residence, 130
Demographic dividend, 201
Demographic transition, 200
Demography, history and governance trajectory of Finland, 14
Denim, 82
Dental cements and filings, 81
Dentrifices, 81
Department of Industrial Policy and Promotion (DIPP), 173, 174
Depreciation for accounting and tax purposes, 125
Diapek, 175
Digital India, 36
Diloxanide furoates, 81
Dinex Ecocat, 148
Diodes and transistors, 87
Direct taxes on incomes, 179
Discontinued operations, 125
Diwali, 108
Door and window frames, 84
Double taxation avoidance treaties, 32, 130–131
Double taxation, 130
Downsizing trends in Finland, 204
Drawing instruments, 85
Dresses, 83
Dried onion powder, 85
Dried vegetables, 85
Druggets, 83
Durga puja, 108
Dussehra-diwali, 108
Duvets, 83
Dyed parachute fabrics, 83
Dyed woven cotton fabrics, 82

E

Ease of doing business, 156
Ease of Living, 26, 187–188
East India Company, 24
EC interest-royalty directive, 129
EC merger directive, 129
Economic policy, 20
Economic times-500, 151
Economic times list, 46
Ecopower, 148
Ecosible, 148
Eco-S Oy, 150
Eco technology, 175
EC parent-subsidiary directive, 129
EC savings directive, 130
Edible preparations from fruits and nuts, 86
Education and skill development, 159
Eesters, 80
E.I.D. Parry, 175
EK, 10
Elbows, 84
Elcoteq, 65
Electrical machinery, 51, 55, 85
Electrical machinery and equipments, 48
Electrical transformers, 56
Electrode quality stainless steel wires, 84
Electro-magnets, 87
Elematic, 148
Elomatic, 149
Emmas, 175
Employment contracts, 131
Employment security, 132
Enalapril, 81
Enforcement of foreign judgements, 172
Engagement of contract labour, 132
Engine parts and piston rings, 55
Ensembles, jackets, blazers, trousers, 82
Ensembles, 83
Enso, 15, 169
Ensto, 148
Enterprise formation, 124
Entry costs, 136
Entry costs for India, 135
Entry criteria and preferred forms, 175
Environmental clearance, 179
Environment impact assessment, 179
Environment protection law, 179
Equal pay for equal work, 132
Erythromycins, 81
Escalator parts, 84
Escalators, elevators, work trucks, 55
Establishing a business in India, 172
ETLA, vii, 4

Ethylene, 86
European Central Bank, 24
European company, 124
European company form (SE), 125
European Economic Interest Groupings (EEIG), 124
European Integration, 16
European patent convention, 138
European Union, 8, 61
Exim Bank, 10
Exit policies, 139
Exit procedures, 172
Expatriates, 177
External Commercial Borrowing (ECB), 177
Extraordinary items in Finnish GAAP, 125
Extruding dies, 84
Eyedrops, 81

F

Facebook, Apple, Amazon, Netflix and Google (FAANG), 203
Factories act, Shops and Establishments acts, Mines act, 132
Failure rate of foreign enterprises, 184
Famotidines, 81
Fazer, 15
Foreign Direct Investment (FDI), 137, 173
FDI equity inflows, 36
FDI policy, 173
Federation of Indian Chambers of Commerce & Industry (FICCI), 10, 165–166
Fencing wires, 84
Fenugreek, 86
Fibre cellulose pulp machinery, 55
Figs, 85
Finance bill, 180
Finance commissions, 129
Financing a business in India, 177
Finland
  nature and climate, 13
Finlandia Vodka, 92
Finland-India Double Taxation Avoidance Agreement (FIDTAA), 131
Finland-India double-taxation treaty, 127
Finland-India joint commission, 31, 156
Finland-India trade, 58
Finland-India trade agreement, 31
Finland-India value chains, 152
Finland's exports to world and India, 46
Finland's political system, 17
Finland's welfare state model, 124
Finlayson, 15
Finnair, xi, 7, 32

Finncrisp, 12
Finnfund, 133, 210
Finnish academy, 156
Finnish branded consumer products, 59
Finnish calendar, 106
Finnish code law, 124
Finnish companies act, 124, 138
Finnish competition law, 137
Finnish distributed enterprising model, 193
Finnish factor markets, 126
Finnish Generally Accepted Accounting Principles (GAAP), 125
Finnish India trade association, 163
Finnish industrial structure, 90
Finnish internationalization, 41
Finnish law, 135
Finnish Meteorological Institute (FMI), 158
Finnish national identity, 100, 101
Finnish paper industry, 191
Finnish Plans, 210
Finnish priorities, 64
Finnish stock market, 138
Finnish summer Time, 106
Finnish winter time, 106
FinNode, 209
Finnpartnership, 133
Finpro, 133, 134, 206, 209, 214
Finnvera, 133, 134, 209
First wave of finnish investments, 147
Fish hooks, 87
Fishing rods, 85
Fiskars, 60, 92, 175
Floor coverings, 61
Floorings, adhesives and structural bondings, 57
Flower buds, 85
Fluid couplings, 55
Foliage, 85
Folic acid, 80
Footballs, 85, 87
Footwear, 81
Foreign Business Investments by Indian firms, 144
Foreign Commercial Presence (FCP), 63
Foreign copyright holders, 138
Foreign Direct Investment (FDI), 177
Foreign directors of Indian companies, 127
Foreign exchange control act, 137
Foreign Exchange Management Act (FEMA), 137
Foreign Exchange Management Act, 1999 (FEMA), 173

Foreign Investment Promotion Board (FIPB), 173
Foreign judgements, 172
Forest industry, 191
Forest machinery, 55
Fortum, 148, 157
Forward markets commission, 178
Foxconn, 151
Freedom of association, 132
Fruit juices, 86
Fruit preparations, 86
Fruit pulp, 85
Fruits, 85
Fundamental Rights in India, 170
Fungicides, 86
Furnishing fabrics, 82
Furniture, 51, 57, 61
Future of India, the, 214

G
5G digital network business, 56
Galvanised iron and stainless steel flanges, 84
Gardening, 87
Garlic oil, 86
Gas cylinders for liquefied gases, 84
Gats enabled services trade, 5, 63, 95, 96, 142, 143
Gender equity, 110
General Sales Tax (GST), 129
Gifts, 113
Glass and glassware, 54
Gloves and mittens of different types and for various uses ranging from housecleaning, 87
GNVC, 175
Godrej, 175
Golf balls, 85, 87
Golf clubs, 85
Gonadotrophins, 81
Goods and Services Tax (GST), 11
Governance system in India, 171
Government route, 173
Government to Government Business (G2G), 153
Gramex, 138
Gratuity, 132
Green court, 179
Green Party, 19
Greeting cards, 88
Grinding, 85
GST structure, 180
Guavas, 85

Gutzeit, 15
Gymnasium, 85
Gymnastic and athletic equipment, 87

H
Hackman, 15
Hair dyes, 86
Handicrafts, 87
Handkerchiefs, 83
Handloom fabrics, 82
Handmade paper, 88
Handtools, 61
Hanseatic league, 190
Harley, 149
Harmonised System (HS), 46
Harness and saddlery for horses and dog-coats, 87
Havells, 3, 126
Health insurance, 132
Helsinki Graduate School of Economics, 149
Heroes, 118–119
High growth sectors, 26, 152
Hindustan Copper, 175
Hinges, 84
Hoists, 84
Holidays, 106–109
Holi, the festival of colours, 108
Home and host government intervention, 31
Honey, 86
Hooks, 85
Horizontal agreements, 179
Hosiery, 82, 83
Hot and cold taps, 61
Housing market, 126
Huhtamäki, 65, 147, 169, 175
Hydrographic instruments, 85

I
Ibuprofen, 81
Ibuprufen, 80
Iittala, 15, 59
Immo, 149
Implementation of court judgements, 139
Incap, 149
Income tax act, 129
Incrementalism, 41
India and climate change, 34
India-Finland collaborations, 7
India-Finland Joint Commission, 31
Indian acquisitions, 126
Indian Almanac, 106
Indian capital market, 37, 178
Indian companies act, 124, 137

Indian economy's trajectory, the, 35
Indian export potential to Finland, 77
Indian government budget, 107
Indian Insolvency and Bankruptcy Code, 11
Indian Institute of Management Ahmedabad, 6, 218–221
Indian IT industry, 193
Indian jurisprudence, 135
Indian linguistic diversity, 101
Indian politics, 37
Indian priorities, 91
Indian secularism, 103
Indian Space Research Organisation, 6
Indian Standard Time (IST), 105
Indian tax year, 179
India's chemical imports, 53
India's companies act, 2013, 170
India's Department of Science and Technology, 156
India's education policy, 102
India's governance frame, 170
Indirect taxes, 179
Indo-Finnish business forum, 163
Indo-Finnish joint commission, 153
Indo-Finnish Joint working group, 155
Indo-Gulf fertilisers & chemicals, 175
Industrial, 84
Industrial boilers, 84
Industrial Disputes (ID) act, 1947, 132
Industrial employment standing orders act, 1946, 132
Industrial establishments, 132
Industrial goods, 60
Industrial licensing system, 26, 32
Industrial scissors and blades, 61
Industrial tribunals, 132
Industrial uses to surgery in hospitals, 87
Industrial valves, 85, 87
Information Technology Agreement (ITA), 162
Information Technology and telecommunications, 160
Infrastructure, 180
Infringements of foreign IPR, 208
Initial Public Offerings (IPO), 178
Injection moulding equipment, 55
Innerwear, 83
Insolvency and bankruptcy code, 139
Institutional differences, 123
Instruments, 61
Insulated cables, 87
Insulation fittings, 85
Insurances, 127
Integrated circuits, 85

Intellectual Property Rights (IPR), 178
Intellectual property rights protection, 138
Interlocutory orders, 136
International Financial Reporting Standards (IFRS), 125
Internationalisation of small and medium-sized enterprises (SMEs), 205
International orientation of Finnish firms, 22
International orientation of Indian firms, 28
International taxation in Finland and India, 129
Investment incentives and disincentives, 139
Invest in Finland, 133, 211
Investment property accounting, 125
Invisibles in India's balance of payments, 29, 30
Iron, 84
Iron and steel, 48, 61, 83
Iron and steel products, 54
ITC, 3
Ivo power, 175

J
Jackets, 83
James Finlay, 15
Jams, 86
Jelly, 86
Jerseys, 83
Jewellery boxes, 87
Joint development projects, 157
Joint Working Groups (JWG), 154
Jotwire, 148
Jurisdiction of a dispute, 138
Justified terminations, 131
Jute bags, 87
JVV, 175

K
Kalevala collection, 83
Kemira, 23, 175
Kemppi, 149
Keskusta, 15
Ketones, 80
Kiilto, 23
Kitchenware, 61
Knitted fabrics, 82
Knowledge Intensive Business Services (KIBS), 62, 203
Kokoomus, 18
Kommandiittiyhtiö, 124
Kone, 23, 65, 147, 175
Konecranes, 149
Kurtas, 83

Kurtis, 83
KWH Pipe, 175
Kymen, 175

L
Laboratory diagnostic reagents, 86
Labour courts, 132
Labour standards, 132
Lacidipine, 81
Lacto protein, 175
Lamb, 87
Laminated fabrics, 83
Lamps, 85
Language, 100
Lansoprazole, 81
Lapland War, 16
Largest 500 companies of Finland, 151
Largest 500 Companies of India, 151
Latex sponges, 81
Law of injunctions, 136
Layoffs, retrenchments, 133
Leaf springs, 84
Leather, 81
Leather and leather goods, 81
Leather and skins of goat, 87
Leather cases and bags, jackets, gloves, 81
LetsGrow, 211
Liability of foreign-ness, 184
Liability of outsidership, 136, 169, 184
Lifting and hoisting chains, 84
Lightning arrestors, 84
Limited liability partnerships, 174
Lindstrom, 148
Linoxyn floor coverings, 86
Lisinopril, 81
Liver extracts, 81
Lobsters, 86
Local-global dialectic, 92
Local talent, 177
Loudspeakers, 87
Lundia, 59
Luteinising hormones, 81

M
Machinery, 84
Machine tools, 55
Mackerels, 86
Macrolides, 81
Made by Finland, 39
Made by Finland and India, 69
Made by India, 39
Made in Finland, 39

Made in India, 39
Mahindra Group, 126
Maillefer Extrusion, 148
Make in India, 69, 156
Management prerogatives, 110
Management style and practices, 133
Managing cultural differences, 99
Manganese sulphate, 80
Mangoes, 85
Marble, 80
Marimekko, 208
Marine propulsion turbines, 84
Marmalades, 86
McNeilly, 175
Mechanical appliances, 84
Mechanical appliances, reactors and boilers, 55
Mechano paper, 175
Media markets, 194
Medical, measuring, optical and other instruments, 57
Medicaments, 80
Meloxicam, 81
Men's suits, 82
Menthol, 80
Menthol crystals, 81
Mergers and acquisitions, 138
Metalastic products, 57
Metco, 175
Metsäliitto yhtymä, 16
Metso, 147
Metso Minerals, 65
Mica flakes, 80
Micro-organism cultures, 81
Microwave ovens, 85
Mineral fuel and oils, 47, 80
Minerals, 80
Minimum capital requirement, 125
Minimum capital subscription, 125
Minimum share capital, 125
Minimum wages, 132
Ministry for foreign affairs, 133
Ministry of commerce, 173
Ministry of employment and the economy, 133
Ministry of industry and trade, 134
Mirasys, 149
Misconduct, 133
Missing markets, 4
Molluscs, 86
Mosquito nets, 83, 87
Mosquito repellants, 86
Motorcycles, 85
MOU on textiles, 32
Movement of Natural Persons (MNP), 63
M-Real, 23

Mufflers, 82
Musical instruments, 85, 87
Mussels, 86
Mustard oil, 86

N
Namaste, 112
Napkins, 83
Nasscom, 6
National Stock Exchange (NSE), 178
Natural justice, 135
Need for a new Finland-India institutional bridge, 218
Needles, 83, 84
Neem and sandalwood based herbal toothpastes, 87
Neste, 23
Network of finnish vocational institutions, 159
Neutraceuticals, 87
New airports, 70
New economic policies of 1991, 31
New opportunities for Finland–India trade, 94
New Year's days, 107
Nickel, 84
Nifedipine, 81
Nirafon, 149, 175
Nirma, 144
Niti Aayog, 11
Nitrogenated hydrocarbons, 80
NK Cables, 175
Nokia, 3, 91, 92, 126, 148, 151, 169, 192, 193
Nokia in Sriperumbudur, 151
Nokia Phenomenon, the, 191
Nokia Siemens Networks, 193
Nokia's tax dispute, 131
Non-electric braille typewriters, 85
Non-malleable cast-iron articles, 84
Non-residents, 128, 131
Non-tariff barriers, 137, 162
Nordic business model, 183
Nordic Council, 17
Nordic model, 188
Normet, 148
Nowo development, 175
Nuclear reactors, 84
Nuclear reactors and boilers, 48
Nutmeg, 86
Nuts, 85
Nuts and fruits, 61

O
OECD Model Income Tax Convention, 130
Office furniture, 85
Ofloxacins, 81

Index 341

Oil and gas projects, 72
Oilon, 148
Oil refining equipment, 55
Ojala, 148
Olegnus fruits and oil seeds, 86
Omeprazole, 81
Opportunities financed by Government Outlays and Multilateral Assistance, 66
Optical fibre cables, 85
Optical, photographic, cinematographic instruments, 49
Oranges, 85
Oras, 59
Organic Chemicals, 47
Orientation of finnish firms, 169
Orion, 149
Ornamental fish, 85
Osakeyhtiö, 125
Osuuspankki, 16
Other articles of jute and coir, 87
Outokumpu, 23, 148, 175
Outotec, 148
Ovako, 23
Overalls, 82
Overcoats, 83
Oysters, 86

P

Padlocks, 61
Paid news, 180
Paint solvents and thinners, 86
Panties, 82
Pantographs, 85
Papayas, 85
Paper and paperboard, 48, 60
Paper machinery, 55
Paper stationery, 88
Paracetamol, 81
Parliament of India, 170–172
Partek, 23
Parts for earth-moving equipment, 84
Parts of mechanical appliances, 85
Pasta, 86
Past precedents, 135
Patent Office and Registry (PRH), 125
Payment of wages, 132
Payroll issues, 127
Peak customs tariff rate, 128
Peak marginal tax rate, 128
Pearls, gems and jewellery, 83
Penicillins, 81
Pension insurance premia, 127
Pensions, 128

Pepper, 85
Perennial nature of jobs, 132
Perindopril, 81
Perlos, 151
Permanency, 132
Permanent establishments, 175
Personal space, 115
Perussuomalaiset, 15
Pharmaceuticals and neutraceuticals, 62
Pharmaceuticals products, 50, 53, 80
Pharmalab, 149
Pigments, 80
Pillowcases, 83
Pincers, 84
Pineapples, 85
Pinewood, 61
Pins, 84
Pipes and hoses, 86
Pipes used in oil and gas pipelines, 84
Plantation labour acts, 132
Plantations, 174
Plant extracts used in perfumes and cosmetics, 86
Plastics, 47, 81
Plastic tableware and kitchenware, 87
Pliers, 84
Pneumatic tools, 85
Policy gaps, 214
Polishing machines, 85
Political spectrum, the, 18
Polyester and mixed fabrics, 83
Polymers, 81
Polyplex, 145
Pomfret fish, 86
Positioning talent, 177
Post-War Finland, 16
Potential finnish exports To India, 59
Potential unconventional Indian exports to Finland, 86
Poultry products, 85
Power grid, 175
Prepared culture media for microorganisms, 86
Preserved vegetables, 85
Pressure containers for compressed gases, glass chimneys, and steel structurals for the construction industry, 61
Pressure valves, 55
Primary products, 85
Principle of subsidiarity in the EU treaties, 190
Printed circuits, 56
Private limited company, 124, 125, 172
Product liability, 138
Product-services linkages, 75

Professional liabilities, 127
Profitably exportable products, 4
Propylene and styrene polymers, 86
Provident fund and pensions, 132
Provincial administrative courts, 131
Psychic distance, 111
Public interest litigation, 135, 171
Public issues, 177
Public limited company, 124, 125, 172
Public-Private-Partnerships (PPP), 173
Pullovers, 83
Pulp, 48, 53
Purchasing Power Parity, 2, 40
Purses, 87

Q
Qualified Institutional Buyers (QIBs), 178
Quilted wadding, 83

R
Radial summer tyres for cars, 87
Raincoats, 83
Ramipril, 81
Ranbaxy, 145
Rannikon koneteknikka, 149
Rare earth metals, 60
Rautaruukki, 23
RCAF Values, 50
Readymade garments, 83
Reciprocating territories, 139
Recypa, 148
Registrar of Companies and Patents (PRH), 124
Regulatory authorities, 180
Religion, 102
Religion in business life, 104
Representative agents, 124
Reserve Bank of India (RBI), 174
Restricted holidays, 107
Restructuring frequency of domestic enterprises, 183
Revealed Comparative Advantage Index, 49, 50–52, 77–79, 87–88
Revealed Comparative Advantage (RCA) methodology, 49
Right to Information Act (RTI), 171
Rigidity of factor markets, 183
R-Kioski's, 7
Roads infrastructure, 70
Road vehicles and parts, 56
Rockdrills, 61
Rods, 84
Roller chains, 84

Royalties, 130
Royalty income, 131
Rubber, 50, 81
Rubber and plastic tubes, 86
Rubber contraceptives, 87
Rudders for boats and ships, 61
Rugs (of kelem, schmks, karamanie and smlr varieties), 83

S
Sagar Mala Programme, 36
Salaries from employment Abroad of Finnish residents, 130
Salpaus Consortium, 160
Sanako, 149
Sasken, 91
Sauces and condiments, 86
Saw blades, 84
Scarves, 82, 83
Scooters and bicycles, 87
Screws, 84
SEBI guidelines, 178
Securities and Exchange Board of India (SEBI), 177
Seeds and spices, 86
Sensor technologies, 57
Seppo Ralli, 175
Services trade, 57
Sewerage and waste treatment, particularly solid waste, 57
Sewing thread, 82
Shawls, 82, 83
Sheep, 87
Sheets and strips, 84
Ship, boat and floating structures, 56
Shipping, 71
Shirts, 82
Shiva, 175
Shock absorbers, 85
Shorts, 83
Shrimps, 86
Sickness insurance, 128
Sign plates, 84
Silicons, 86
Silk, 82
Silk embroidery, 82
Sinebrychoff, 15
SITRA, 32, 134, 146, 181, 187, 209, 214
Ski-jackets, 83
Skirts, 83
Ski suits, 82
Sleeves, 84
SLUSH, 69

Smart cities, 166
Soaps, 87
Social and cultural barriers, 120
Social Democratic Party, 18
Software, 87
Sonata, 3
Sound amplifiers, 85
Spanners, 84
Special Economic Zones (SEZs), 9, 180
Special features of the Indian market, 180
Special purpose tyres, 61
Spectacle lenses, 85
Spices like cardamom, cinnamon, nutmeg, 85
Spices oil, 86
Sports nets, 85
Spun yarn, 83
SSAB, 23
Stainless steel articles, 84
Stainless steel utensils, 84
Standard International Trade Classification (SITC), 46
Startup India, 156
State list, 170
Static convertors, 85
Steam turbines, 84
Steel plates, 84
Steel wires hand tools, 84
Steering and rudder equipment for ships and boats, 84
Stock exchanges, 138
Stockings, 82
Stora, 15
Streptomycins, 81
Stuffed toys, 87
Subsidiarity, 209
Suits, 83
Sukka, 175
Supreme administrative court, 131
Supreme court of Finland, 136
Surgical drapes, 87
Surgical dressings, 81
Surgical knives, 85
Swadeshi, 137
Sweaters, 83
Swil, 175
Swimwear, 83
Synthetic rubber, 81
Syringes, 85

T
Table linen, 82
Tableware, 61
Talouselämä list of 500, 46
Talouseläma-500, 151
Tata, 3
Tata Tea, 15
Tax appeals, 130
Taxation, 179
Tax authorities in Finland, 128
Tax-free zones, 128
Tax holidays, 128
Tax treatment of inter-corporate dividends, 129
TCS, 91
Tea, gems and jewellery, 61
Team Finland, 162, 206–211
Teamwork, 133
Technical collaborations, 175
Tekes, 133, 134, 156, 187, 209, 214
Telecom, 72
Tennis and badminton rackets, 85
Tenoxicam, 81
Teosto, 138
Textile reagents, 86
Textiles, 61, 82
Textiles sector, 161
Textured polyester yarns, 82
The Energy and Resources Institute (TERI), 158
Thermax, 148
Threaded bolts and nuts, 84
Threaded nuts, 84
Threaded nuts and washers, 61
Ties and cravats, 82, 83
Tieto, 149
Tietoenator, 151
Time, 105
Time limit to appeal in tax cases, 131
Titanium, 80
Toilet articles, 61
Toiminimi, 124
Tooltech, 91
Total FDI inflows, 36
Toulene, 80
Tourism cooperation, 161
Towels, 82
Toys, 86
Track suits, 82, 83
Trade barriers, taxation, and customs tariffs, 162
Trade diversion, 4, 152
Trade Facilitation Agreement (TFA), 161
Trade promotion measures, 162
Trade register, 124
Trade-substituting investments, 62, 75, 165

Trade-substituting potential, 89
Trade union power, 191
Trivitron, 3
Transfer pricing, 130
Transfer pricing adjustments, 130
Transmission bearings, 55
Transmission belting, 84
Transparency of investment regimes, 136
Transparency of trading regimes, 136
Transportation—road, railway, aviation & shipping, 160
Travel bags and packaging materials and travelgear, 61
TRIPS, 178
Trousers, 83
Trousers and shorts, 82
T-shirts, 82, 83
Tubes, pipes, 83
Tubs, 61
Tungsten carbide tips, 84
Turmeric, 86
Tweezers, 84
Twinning Finland and India, 1

U
Umbrellas, 83
Underpants, 82
Uniform civil code, 136
Union budget, 180
Union density, 110
Union list, 170
Union power, 111
UN Model Tax Convention, 130
Unprocessed ilmenite, 80
UPM, 148
Urea resins, 86

V
Valio, 169
Valio engineering, 175
Valkeakosken Betoni, 149
Valmet, 149, 169, 175, 177
Value Added Tax (VAT), 127, 179
Value Added Tax (VAT) rates, 127
Vanity cases and satchels, 87
Vappu, 107
Vats, 61
Vegetables, 85
Vehicles other than railway or tramways, 48
Velvet fabrics, 83

Verapamil, 81
Vertical agreements, 179
Vibrant Gujarat, 9
Vices, 84
Vienna convention on the law of treaties, 130
Vikas, 175
Vinyl chloride bags, 87
VME Group, 149
VTT, 134, 209

W
Wärtsilä, 65, 147, 175
Wärtsilä Diesel, 12, 56
Wallets, 87
Walnuts, 85, 86
Warehousing, 180
War reparations, 16
Washers, 84
Watches, 85
Water boilers, 55
Water pollution, 68
Wealth tax, 128
Where FDI is prohibited, 174
Windpower, 57
Winter war, 16
WinWinD, 126
WIPRO, 3, 91
Wire meshes, 84
WMI Konecranes, 148
Women's suits, 82
Wood, 48
Wood and wood articles, 53
Wool, 82, 83
Working hours act, 131
Workmen, 132
Woven fabrics, 82
Wrenches, 84
Writ jurisdiction, 134, 171
Writ jurisdiction under Article 226, 170
WTO, 6

X
Xanthium gums and oleoresins, 86
X-ray (Roentgen) machines, 85

Z
Zensar, 91
Zips, 84

GPSR Compliance

The European Union's (EU) General Product Safety Regulation (GPSR) is a set of rules that requires consumer products to be safe and our obligations to ensure this.

If you have any concerns about our products, you can contact us on

ProductSafety@springernature.com

In case Publisher is established outside the EU, the EU authorized representative is:

Springer Nature Customer Service Center GmbH
Europaplatz 3
69115 Heidelberg, Germany

www.ingramcontent.com/pod-product-compliance
Lightning Source LLC
LaVergne TN
LVHW050013270326
834688LV00068B/26